Edwin M. Borchard – *Convicting The Innocent* and *State Indemnity For Errors Of Criminal Justice*

Compiled and Introduction by Hans Sherrer

Edward M. Borchard — Convicting The Innocent, and State Indemnity For Errors Of Criminal Justice

Compiled and Introduction by Hans Sherrer

Published by:
The Justice Institute
PO Box 68911
Seattle, WA 98168
www.justicedenied.org
info@justicedenied.org

First edition, August 2013

Trade Paperback ISBN: 0-9855033-1-9
Trade Paperback ISBN-13: 978-0-9855033-1-4
LCCN: 2013912921

Back cover photograph courtesy of Yale University Library

Printed in the U.S.A.
This book is printed on acid free paper

Table Of Contents

Table Of Contents

Introduction

Edwin Montefiore Borchard was honored in 2007 by *Justice Denied—the magazine for the wrongly convicted*, as an inaugural member of its Wrongful Conviction Hall of Honor that publicly recognizes the extraordinary contribution deserving people in the United States and other countries have made to rectifying, alleviating, or publicizing wrongful convictions. *Justice Denied's* 2007 article about Borchard is included herein as Chapter 1.

Borchard's interest in wrongful convictions and compensation for persons exonerated of their convicted crimes resulted in him authoring in 1913, *European Systems Of State Indemnity For Errors of Criminal Justice*, included herein as Chapter 3, and in 1932, *Convicting The Innocent: Sixty-Five Actual Errors of Criminal Justice*, included herein as Chapter 4.

Convicting the Innocent has not lost its luster as one of the most insightful books published on the topic of wrongful convictions. Seventy-one years after its publication the multitude of causes underlying the cases of injustice it details not only continue to plague the legal system in the United States, but they are arguably more prevalent today than when the book was published, with the exception of confessions extracted by physical violence.

One hundred years after Borchard's article about indemnifying wrongly convicted persons, one can surmise he would be pleased the federal government and the majority of states have enacted legislation financially compensating persons deemed to meet the applicable statute's definition of a wronged person. However, it seems likely Borchard would be dismayed that only one state – Texas, which provides a lump sum payment of $80,000 per year of wrongful imprisonment and a generous lifetime annuity – has a system that fairly determines an exonerated person's eligibility *and* then adequately compensates that person. As Borchard explains in his 1913 article (Chapter 3), many European countries were more advanced in providing indemnification 100 years and more ago, than is the norm in the United States in 2013. That is still true, except it doesn't just apply to European countries, because in the "U.S. policy and legislation to ensure the right to compensation for wrongful conviction is among the poorest in the world."[1] A significant portion of Borchard's article concerns the history of indemnifying wrongful convictions, which puts the current concerns about state and federal indemnification in the perspective that it is an issue that has been debated for centuries.

Of topical importance in a post-9/11 world is that during World War II, Borchard used his position and legal skills to oppose the federal government's policies that disregarded individual rights in the name of promoting national security. Some of his efforts defending the rights of people victimized by those policies are explained in Chapter 1.

Borchard was a professor at the Yale Law School for 33 years (1917-1950).[2] Although he had a deep interest in issues related to wrongful convictions and individual rights, during his lifetime he was most well-known as one of the United States' leading international law experts.

Edwin Borchard's national notoriety was such that when he died on July 22, 1951 at the age of 66, the *New York Times* published an 18 paragraph, 740 word Obituary. Borchard's *New York Times* Obituary is included herein as Chapter 2.

Borchard was the first consistent voice in this country for innocent people enmeshed in the legal system. So it is important that it be remembered his works laid the foundation for today's advocates for wrongly convicted persons, and the encouragement of public policies that may prevent wrongful convictions and ensure adequate indemnification when they occur.

Given the legal system's inertia and resistance to meaningful reforms, it may well be that Borchard's analysis of the causes of wrongful convictions and the general inadequacy of indemnification for exonerated persons will be as relevant many decades from now as it is today.

Hans Sherrer
July 25, 2013

---

[1] Jason Costa; "Alone In The World: The United States' Failure To Observe The International Human Right To Compensation For Wrongful Conviction"; 19 Emory International Law Review 1615 (2005), 1618.

[2] Edwin M. Borchard's personal papers were donated to Yale University's Sterling Memorial Library in New Haven, Connecticut.

Edwin Montefiore Borchard
(Yale University Library)

Chapter 1

Edwin M. Borchard: Pioneer In Analyzing Wrongful Convictions And Advocate For Compensation

By Hans Sherrer
Justice Denied—the magazine for the wrongly convicted,
Issue 35, Winter 2007, pgs. 24-5

Two years after becoming law librarian of Congress, 28-year-old Edwin Montefiore Borchard wrote *European Systems Of State Indemnity For Errors of Criminal Justice* in 1913.[1] The 35-page document advocated providing compensation to a person victimized by a miscarriage of justice.

During his tenure from 1911 to 1916 as the Law Librarian of Congress Borchard also wrote *Diplomatic Protection of Citizens Abroad* (1915), which is considered a classic text in its area.[2]

After Borchard's appointment in 1917 as a professor at Yale University Law School, his specialized knowledge of international law resulted in contacts with the country's leading political and legal figures. He also traveled widely around the world as a result of his involvement in resolving international disputes and participation in international law conferences. His legal stature internationally was such that he was the first American professor invited to lecture at the University of Berlin after WWI.

Knowing of Borchard's keen interest in legal reform, Harvard law professor and future Supreme Court Justice Felix Frankfurter suggested he write a book about the persistent problem of wrongful convictions. This was shortly after Frankfurter's valiant failed effort to stave off the 1927 execution of Sacco and Venzetti, whose innocence he passionately wrote about.[3] Borchard acted on Frankfurter's suggestion and several years later *Convicting the Innocent: Sixty-Five Actual Errors of Criminal Justice*, was published by Yale University Press (1932).

---

[1] Edwin M. Borchard, "European Systems Of State Indemnity For Errors of Criminal Justice," 3 *J. Am. Inst. Crim. L. & Criminology* 685 (May 1912 to March 1913). Available on JD's website, www.justicedenied.org/borchard_1913.pdf

[2] During a period from 1913-1914 Borchard served as Assistant Solicitor for the Department of State.

[3] Felix Frankfurter, "The Case of Sacco and Vanzetti," *Atlantic Magazine*, 1927.

Convicting the Innocent was widely read, and along with Borchard's behind the scenes advocacy, contributed to the enactment in 1938 of a federal law compensating persons erroneously convicted in federal court. *The New York Times* wrote, President Roosevelt "presented to Mr. Borchard the pen used in enacting the bill into law in recognition of the role the Yale jurist played in the legislation."[4] The compensation amounts specified in that 1938 bill remained unchanged for 66 years, until they were increased by The Justice For All Act of 2004.

A less well-known aspect of Borchard's career is that as one of the world's leading experts on international law, he was a life-long advocate of U.S. neutrality.[5] He was a vocal critic of the United States' entry into WWI – arguing that there was no national interest to do so. He was also the country's leading legal professional opposed to 1936's so-called "Neutrality Bill." In his January 1936 testimony before the House Foreign Affairs Committee, Borchard described the bill as misnamed because it altered established rules of international law that ensured the United States' neutrality in disputes between other countries. Borchard prophetically told the Congressional committee that the bill "would be likely to draw this country into the wars it is intended to avoid."[6]

In 1937 Borchard co-authored the seminal work advocating U.S. neutrality, *Neutrality for the United States* (rev. ed. 1940).[7] After his worst fears about what would result from the failure of the U.S. to follow neutral policies were realized and the country became embroiled in WWII, Borchard opposed the federal government's disregard for the rights of Americans in the name of national security. Borchard wrote briefs in two of the most important cases to reach the Supreme Court involving challenges to the U.S. military's summary imprisonment of 120,000 innocent Japanese-Americans in concentration camps. The two cases were *Hirabayashi v U.S.*, 320 U.S. 81 (1943), and *Korematsu v. U.S.*, 323 U.S. 214 (1944).[8]

In June 1950 Borchard retired after 33 years as a member of Yale Law School's faculty. Borchard was born in New York City on October 17, 1884, and he was 66 when he died in Hamden, Connecticut on July 22, 1951.

---

4 "Edwin Borchard, Law Expert Dead, Obituary," *The New York Times*, July 23, 1951, 17.

5 For background information about Mr. Borchard's advocacy a non-interventionist foreign policy see, "The Anti-interventionist Tradition: Leadership and Perceptions," by Justus D. Doenecke, *Literature of Liberty: A Review of Contemporary Liberal Thought*, Vol. IV, No 2, Summer 1981, 31-2

6 "Neutrality Bill Is Called Peril," *The New York Times*, January 10, 1936.

7 Edwin M. Borchard and William Potter Lage, *Neutrality for the United States* (New Haven: Yale University Press, 1937; rev. 1940).

8 For background information about *Korematsu v. United States*, see, "In Memoriam, Fred Korematsu (1919-2005)," *Justice:Denied*, Issue 28, Spring 2005, p.5.

Chapter 2

Edwin Borchard, Law Expert, Dead

The New York Times, July 23, 1951, pg 17

Retired Yale Professor Was Adviser to Federal Bodies—Exponent of Neutrality

Special to *The New York Times*,
NEW HAVEN, Conn., July 22—

Prof. Edwin M. Borchard, an authority on law and international relations, who was a member of the Yale Law School faculty for more than thirty years before his retirement in June, last year, died today at his home in suburban Hamden. His age was 66.

A life-long exponent of American neutrality, Mr. Borchard opposed the entry of the United States into both World Wars. His book, "Neutrality for the United States," published in 1938, was widely quoted in Congress during the debate on the neutrality legislation before the second conflict.

Born in New York, Mr. Borchard attended City College there, received a Bachelor of Laws degree, cum laude, from New York Law School in 1905 and B. A. and Ph. D. degrees from Columbia in 1908 and 1913. Degrees were awarded to him by the Universities of Berlin and Budapest.

Mr. Borchard was elected to Phi Beta Kappa scholastic society while attending Columbia. In 1942 he was made a founding member of Phi Beta Kappa Associates. After serving as Law Librarian of Congress, assistant solicitor for the Department of State, chief counsel for the Peru, Tacna-Arica arbitration, and attorney for the National City Bank of New York, Mr. Borchard joined the Yale Law School faculty in 1917.

Appointed by Coolidge

In conjunction with his teaching duties, he was a special legal adviser to the Treasury Department, and in 1925 was appointed by President Coolidge to serve on the Central American Arbitration tribunals. Mr. Borchard also continued to serve in an advisory capacity to many other government departments.

The jurist, who lectured widely in the United States and Europe, was the first American professor to lecture at the University of Berlin after the first World War, presenting a seminar in American jurisprudence and speaking on American constitutional law in 1925.

He had been one of the prominent lecturers at the International Academy of Law at the Carnegie Peace Palace in The Hague, the Netherlands, two years earlier.

In commenting on Mr. Borchard's death, President A. Whitney Griswold of Yale University said:

> "Professor Borchard's death is .a profound loss to the world of scholarship, to the New Haven community, and to Yale. He was one of the most eminent and versatile scholars in the university; renowned in the field of international and constitutional law, and a public spirited citizen who contributed unstintingly to the cultural life of New Haven."

Much of Mr. Borchard's law career was devoted to legal reforms. Two of his books, "Declaratory Judgments" and "Convicting the Innocent," were concerned with this phase of his work.

The latter, published in 1932, was devoted to an intensive study of miscarriages of justice, in which innocent persons had been wrongly convicted of crimes.

President Roosevelt in 1938, as a direct result of this volume, approved an act granting relief to individuals erroneously convicted in United States courts, The President presented to Mr. Borchard the pen used in enacting the bill into law in recognition of the role the Yale jurist played in the legislation.

Served at The Hague

Mr. Borchard was a member of the commission of experts for the modification of laws in Lima, Peru, during 1938, and the International Academy on Comparative Law at The Hague. He had advised the State Department, the Patents and Judiciary Committees, the Office of Civilian Defense and the Maritime Commission.

Mr. Borchard was named to a three-man committee to select a new dean of the Yale Law School in 1927 when the then dean, Thomas W. Swan, was appointed United States Circuit Court judge of the second district. That same year he was made Justus S. Hotchkiss Professor of Law, a chair he held until his retirement. He was also an associate fellow of Timothy Dwight College.

In addition to the writings already mentioned, Mr. Borchard wrote "The Diplomatic Protection of Citizens Abroad," and, with William H. Wynne, a Washington economist, he published last April a two-volume work, "State Insolvency and Foreign Bondholders."

He was also active for many years in New Haven community projects. He had played violin in the New Haven Symphony Orchestra and from 1935 to 1944 was president of the New Haven Orchestra Association.

Surviving are his widow, Mrs. Corinne Brackett Borchard; two daughters, Mrs. R. Gregory Durham of Winnetka, Ill., and Mrs. William M. Couch Jr. of New Canaan, Comm.; two sisters, Mrs. Samuel Greene of Montclair, N. J., and Miss Gertrude Borchard of New York, and five grandchildren.

Chapter 3

EUROPEAN SYSTEMS OF STATE INDEMNITY FOR ERRORS OF CRIMINAL JUSTICE

By Edwin M. Borchard

3 *J. Am. Inst. Crim. L. & Criminology* 684 (1913)

A reprint of the original 35-page article begins on the next page. This article was also published as United States Senate Document 974, sixty-second Congress, third session (1913).[1]

[1] See, Alice S. Borchard, "Those Wrongly Convicted: No Redress for Them Under Our System of Laws," *The New York Times*, August 22, 1916, 8.

EUROPEAN SYSTEMS OF STATE INDEMNITY FOR ERRORS OF CRIMINAL JUSTICE.

EDWIN M. BORCHARD,
Law Librarian of Congress.

In an age when social justice is the watchword of legislative reform, it is strange that society, at least in this country, utterly disregards the plight of the innocent victim of unjust conviction or detention in criminal cases. No attempt whatever seems to have been made in the United States to indemnify these unfortunate victims of mistakes in the administration of the criminal law, although cases of shocking injustice are of not infrequent occurrence. The case of Andrew Toth, who was convicted of murder in Pennsylvania, sentenced to life imprisonment, and after having served twenty years was found to have been absolutely innocent, is still fresh in the public mind. There was no provision of law for relieving his terrible condition, the state legislature declined to make compensation, and only through the generosity of Andrew Carnegie, who pensioned him at forty dollars a month, was the man able to return to Hungary, his native land.[1] In England, the flagrant injustice meted out to Adolf Beck, who through the most lax administration of the criminal law was convicted for the crime of another man and was imprisoned for seven years, resulted at least in the establishment of the court of criminal appeal (7 Edw. VII, c. 23), though it left the unfortunate Beck without the slightest legal redress.[1a]

Up to the present moment Anglo-American public law is wholly opposed to granting an indemnity to such victims of the errors of criminal justice. The safeguarding of society by the prosecution of crimes against it is, to be sure, an attribute inherent in all governments, one of the *jura majestatis*. For mistakes in exercising this sovereign right, says our law, there can be no liability of the state. We go even further. Whether the injury to the individual is accidental or intentional, on the part of the state or on the part of the *judge* (except one of most inferior jurisdiction), the injured person is left without redress.

---

[1]Virginia Law Register, v. 17, p. 405.

[1a]For a full report of this remarkable case of mistaken identity see Parliamentary Papers, 1905, v. 62, Cd. 2315, Committee of Inquiry into the case of Mr. Adolf Beck. Report from the Committee, London, 1904; Sims, George. The martyrdom of Adolf Beck. London, Daily Mail Office, 1904; Lowell, Government of England, New York, 1908, v. 2, p. 463. Parliament to some extent subsequently vindicated English justice by granting Beck a gratuity of five thousand pounds. The Epps case, reported in the Chicago *Tribune* of Sept. 23, 1912, and the Hartzell case in Chicago, reported in the press October 25, 1912, are typical of such injustice.

Yet, within certain spheres of governmental action involving similarly a public interference with private rights, we admit freely that the state owes compensation to those individuals upon whom special damage is inflicted. When property is taken from individuals for the public use, our fundamental law prescribes that just compensation must be paid. Publicists as far back as Grotius, Puffendorf and Bynkershoek recognize that compensation is a necessary incident to the exercise of the right of eminent domain.[2] On the other hand, when in the administration of the criminal law, an equally sovereign right, society takes from the individual his personal liberty, a private right at least equally as sacred as the right of property, it dismisses him from consideration—regardless of the gross injustice inflicted upon an innocent man—without even an apology, much less compensation for the injury. Jurists, who uphold the right of the state to prosecute and convict innocent persons without making compensation, have been driven to draw fine distinctions between the taking of property and the taking of liberty for the public use. We shall discuss these distinctions below.

The ultimate end and object of government is to protect those rights which, as Blackstone denominates them, are the absolute rights of all mankind—the right to personal security, to liberty and to property. The unquestioned manner with which in Anglo-American law the liberty of innocent persons is sometimes taken is all the more startling in view of the history of individual rights since *Magna Charta.*

The object of this article is to show the methods by which the legislatures of Europe have solved the problem of indemnifying those innocent individuals who, in the exercise of a sovereign right beneficial to society and to the state in its function as the preserver of the public peace, have been unjustly arrested, detained, or convicted and punished. First of all, it may be well briefly to review the law in this country and on the continent in order to show the wide difference in the civil remedies granted to persons who are erroneously arrested or convicted.

In the United States, we, of course, recognize the right of an individual wrongfully prosecuted on private information or complaint to sue the complaining witness for false imprisonment or malicious prosecution without probable cause. Likewise if his unfortunate predicament is due to the malfeasance, misfeasance or nonfeasance of an officer exercising ministerial powers, or even of certain judicial officers of inferior jurisdiction, the law gives redress to the injured person by an

[2]Citations in article of Henry Wade Rogers, Compensation as an incident of the Right of Eminent Domain, Southern Law Review, v. 5, N. S., 1879-80, p. 5.

action for damages against the officer.[3] Where, however, the unjust detention or conviction results from the error, or even from the malice, fraud or corruption of a judge of general jurisdiction or where it results from an unfortunate concurrence of circumstances, the individual is without a civil remedy.[3a] The rule in this country may be expressed as follows:

"No action lies in any case for misconduct or delinquency, however gross, in the performance of judicial duties. * * * If corrupt he [the judge] may be impeached or indicted, but the law will not tolerate an action to redress the individual wrong which may be done."[4]

"As a general rule no person is liable civilly for what he may do as judge while acting within the limits of his jurisdiction, nor is he liable for neglect or refusal to act. The rule is especially true where the judge is one having general jurisdiction, and in such case there is no liability even though he exceeds his authority. The overwhelming weight of authority is to the effect that where a judge has full jurisdiction of the subject-matter and of the parties, whether his jurisdiction be a general or limited one, he is not civilly liable where he acts erroneously, illegally, or irregularly. * * * Nor is he liable for a failure to exercise due and ordinary care, or where he acts from malicious or corrupt motives."[5]

The reason for the rule is thus stated by Mechem:

"Courts are created on public grounds; they are to do justice as between suitors, to the end that peace and order may prevail in the political society, and that rights may be protected and preserved. The duty is public, and the end to be accomplished is public; the individual advantage or loss results from the proper and thorough or improper and imperfect performance of a duty for which his controversy is only the occasion. The judge performs his duty to the public by doing justice between individuals, or, if he fails to do justice as between individuals, he may be called to account by the state in such form and before such tribunal as the law may have provided. But as the duty neglected is not a duty to the individual, civil redress, as for an individual injury, is not admissible."[6]

The general rule of the immunity from civil suit of a judge having jurisdiction for injuries resulting to private individuals from his acts, however malicious or corrupt, is therefore, well established in our law. In the absence of statute any liability of the state is of course absolutely excluded and up to the present time no such statutory liability has been assumed either in England or in the United States.

---

[3]Throop, Public Officers, New York, 1892, § 724.

[3a]Excess of jurisdiction must be distinguished from entire *absence* of jurisdiction. For wrongful acts in cases where he has no jurisdiction at all the judge is civilly liable. See Mechem, Public Offices and Officers, § 628, and § 629; *Bradley v. Fisher,* 13 Wall., 335, 351; *Hughes v. McCoy,* 11 Colo. 591.

[4]Throop, Public Officers, New York, 1892, § 713.

[5]23 Cyc., pp. 568-9 and authorities there cited.

[6]Mechem, Public Offices and Officers, Chicago, 1890, § 619, citing Cooley.

In most of the European countries, on the other hand, the innocent individual unjustly arrested, prosecuted or convicted has the civil remedies recognized by us—*first,* a right of action against the complaining witness or other person who has wrongfully accused him or otherwise aided in his prosecution,[7] and *secondly,* a right of action against the officer through whose act he has been injured, where there has been an excess or abuse of the officer's legal powers.

But at this point the similarity ceases. The extensive immunities of a judge from private suit in this country are only recognized by the civil law within the narrowest limits. On principle the continental judge is liable for his tortious acts in excess or abuse of his authority like any other officer, the only qualification being that in matters within his judicial discretion he is allowed considerable leeway. But corrupt or malicious exercise of judicial powers in all cases involves the personal liability of the judge.[8] Besides the right of action against ministerial officer or judge, however, the individual has certain remedies unknown to Anglo-American law. He has *thirdly* a right of action *against the state* for the illegal acts of its officers, including its judges. This is a subsidiary liability of the state fixed by statute which renders

[7]See, for example, art. 373 of the French penal code.

[8]See, for example, *Austria,* Art. 9 of the Organic Law of Dec. 21, 1867, and the Law of July 12, 1872, on the Judicial Power and the right of action for torts by judicial officers in the exercise of their functions. Also, *Spain,* Ley de Enjuiciamiento Civil, 1881, art. 903, et seq. Sec. 505 of the *French* Code of Civil Procedure provides that judges are liable to civil suit in the following cases: First, if there has been malice or deceit (*dol*), fraud (*fraude*), or extortion, committed either in the proceedings or in the judgment; * * * Fourthly, for a denial of justice. In France, the procedural difficulties of bringing an action against a public officer are somewhat greater than in Germany, although the substantive rights against a wrong doing officer are now practically the same in both countries. Up to the last decade the French officer enjoyed greater immunity for his official acts than the German. The *German* Civil Code, §839, paragraph 1, provides: "If an officer wilfully or negligently commits a breach of official duty incumbent upon him as towards a third party, he shall compensate the third party for any damage arising therefrom." Paragraph 2 provides that "if an officer commits a breach of his official duty in giving judgment in an action, he is not responsible for any damage arising therefrom, unless the breach of duty is punished with a public penalty to be enforced by criminal proceedings." This last clause applies to cases of wilful perversion of justice under § 336 of the penal code and includes malicious or corrupt exercise of the judicial power. The commentaries of Planck and Staudinger explain the narrow limitations of paragraph 2 just quoted. It applies first to a *final judgment only* and does not excuse gross negligence, malice or corruption. For all intermediate and interlocutory orders and decrees—as in negligently ordering an arrest or attachment, declining to receive evidence, failure to call a witness demanded by a defendant, a disregard of undisputed testimony—the judge is civilly liable and is not protected by the immunity granted in paragraph 2 of § 839. See Nöldeke, *Die civilrechtliche Haftung des Richters nach dem B. G. B.,* in Gruchot's *Beiträge zur Erläuterung des deutchen Rechts,* volume 42, 1898, p. 795, at pp. 808, 821-822; Delius, *Haftpflicht der Beamten,* Berlin, Guttentag, 1899, pp. 206, et seq.

the state and the officer liable *in solido* for the injury to the individual.[9] It will be noted that under this head state liability apart from judicial and personal culpability, is not recognized. *Fourthly,* certain constitutions, such as those of several of the cantons of Switzerland, under the head of personal liberty, allow a direct claim against the state for illegal arrest. These cover cases of arrest in disregard of the forms of law or of its substantial provisions. While *habeas corpus,* with the possibility of action against some inferior officer, would probably be the remedy in this country, a *direct* action against the state is permitted in these Swiss cantons. The claim here does not arise from the admitted innocence of the accused, but from the illegal infringement or interference with his personal liberty. *Fifthly,* and lastly, we have in Europe the case of an indemnity awarded by the state to those erroneously arrested, detained and imprisoned individuals whose innocence is subsequently established.

Most of the countries of Europe, after years of struggle on the part of reformers, have now by statute recognized the liability of the state for injustice thus inflicted. The discussion of this subject will occupy the remainder of this article.

HISTORY.[10]

In Greece and Rome the procedural distinctions between civil and criminal law were not clearly marked. Prosecution was by the individual who suffered the consequences of the specific act. Nevertheless, it was even then admitted that the private complainant, *calumniator,* was liable to the defendant in damages for a wrongful accusation or prosecution. The recognition of this liability of the complaining witness continues throughout the middle ages. In the *Constitutio Criminalis Carolina* of Charles V of 1532, it is provided, (article 12) that the complainant must furnish bail for the damages suffered by the accused should the complaint not be sustained. When the prosecution of crime became the function of the state alone and purely a matter of public law, the question of compensation to an unjustly accused or convicted

[9]Ziegler, E. Die direkte oder subsidiäre Haftung des Staates und der Gemeinden für Versehen und Vergehen ihrer Beamten und Angestellten, in Zeitschrift für Schweizerisches Recht. n. F. v. 7, (1888), pp. 481-562. See also, Stengel, Karl, v. Die Haftung des Staates für den durch seine Organe und Beamten Dritten zugefügten Schaden, in Hirth's Annalen des deutschen Reichs, 1901, pp. 481-508, 561-592.

[10]The history of the movement, both in legislation and in literature, for the indemnification of unjustly arrested, detained and convicted persons, may be found in Geyer, Die Entschädigung freigesprochener Angeklagten. Nord und Süd, v. 18, 1881, pp. 167-184; Pascaud, H. Erreurs judiciaires in Nouvelle Revue, Jan. 1, 1891, v. 68, pp. 144-162, and in Revue critique de législation, 1888, pp. 597-637; Riecker, W. Die Entschädigung unschuldig Verhafteter und Bestrafter, Tübingen, 1911; Bernard, M. P. De la réparation des erreurs judiciares, Revue critique de législation, v. 37, 1870, pp. 360-415, 481-523.

person, where the state was the complainant, was left out of considera-tion.

The movement for the indemnification by the state of erroneously convicted persons was begun toward the end of the eighteenth century in France, the land of "liberty, equality and fraternity," and of the "social contract." One of its most earnest champions was Voltaire, the friend of the oppressed. He had taken a prominent part in securing the acquittal and restoration of the rights of Calas, of the Sirven family, of De La Barre and others.[11] It was probably due to the intimate correspondence between Voltaire and Frederick the Great that we find in Prussia in 1766 the first legislative expression of the obligation of the state to indemnify unjustly arrested and detained persons.[12] This decree provided:

> "If a person suspected of crime has been detained for trial, and where, for lack of proof, he has been released from custody, and in the course of time his complete innocence is established, he shall have not only complete costs restored to him, but also a sum of money as just indemnity, according to all the circumstances of the case, payable from the funds of the trial court, so that the innocent person may be compensated for the injuries he has suffered."

This equitable provision was probably short-lived. At all events, it is not found in the Prussian Code of Criminal Procedure of December 11, 1805.

In 1781 the Academy of Sciences and Fine Arts at Chalons-sur-Marne again agitated the question, prompted undoubtedly by the severe cases of injustice by erroneous conviction which had then lately occurred in France. The Academy awarded two prizes for the best essays on the following question:

> "When the civil society, having accused one of its members, by the agency of its public authorities, fails in its accusation, what would be the most practicable and least expensive means to secure to the citizen, recognized as innocent, the indemnity which is due him by natural law?"

Prizes were awarded to the authors of two monographs, which have since become classics in the literature of the subject.

The author of the first work, *Le sang innocent vengé ou Discours sur les réparations dues aux accusés innocents,* is Jean Pierre Brissot de Warville; the second, by the Intendent of Finances, Louis Philipon de la Madelaine is entitled *Des moyens d' indemniser l'innocence injuste-*

---

[11]Hertz, Voltaire und die französische Strafrechtspflege, Stuttgart, 1887, p. 1 ff., p. 83 ff.

[12]Neue Verordnung um die Prozesse zu kürzen, § 9, cited from Berolzheimer's Die Entschädigung unschuldig Verurteilter und Verhafteter, 1891, p. 7. Berolzheimer obtained a copy of the decree of Jan. 15, 1766, from the Prussian Staarsarchiv.

ment accusée et punie.[13] Their thesis briefly was that while it is an injury to the public interest if we hesitate to prosecute a suspected guilty person for fear of striking an innocent person, still, public prosecution being a compulsory act, it would be wrong to punish the public prosecutor who has prosecuted an accused person subsequently declared innocent by the courts. The accused citizen, however, ought to receive compensation from the state. Brissot calls attention to the indifference of society to the fate of the innocently accused person and advances the argument that the withholding of an indemnity is inconsistent with the social contract.

Since that time many of the foremost publicists of Europe have given serious study to the question and it may not be out of place in the course of this paper briefly to direct attention to their labors.

Between 1786 and 1792 the question under consideration was constantly agitated in the French Parliament and by French jurists.[14] In 1788 Louis XVI presented to the States General an ordinance accompanied by a declaration that he was surprised that nothing had been done in France to indemnify persons erroneously convicted, and that the king considered such indemnification as a debt of justice. In 1790 Pastoret in his *Théories des Lois Pénales* devoted a chapter to this subject (v. 4, p. 116 et seq.). He compared the misfortune of being innocently convicted to being struck by lightning and declared that the conviction of innocent persons was "as unavoidable a misfortune in our social order for the *moral* existence of the citizen, as hail or lightning is for his *physical* existence." In the same year Duport in his draft of a code of criminal procedure, which he submitted to the French Assembly, inserted an article which provided for indemnification by the state for those declared innocent of an indicted crime, leaving its amount to be determined by the jury. The French revolution put an end to the further consideration of this reform, with many other projected reforms, and not until one hundred years later (1895) did France by legislation undertake to solve the problem.

In 1783 the great Italian, Filangieri[15] suggested the establishment of an indemnity fund to compensate those unjustly arrested through false complaints. In 1786 the suggestion was incorporated into the

[13]Both monographs are printed in the Bibliothèque philosophique du legislateur, du politique et du jurisconsulte, Berlin, 1782, v. 4, pp. 275-329; v. 6, pp. 169-243.

[14]Pascaud, Op. Cit. Revue Critique, 1888, pp. 617-618. See also Berlet, De la réparation des erreurs judiciaires. Paris, 1896. Also, Bernard, op. cit.

[15]Filangieri. La Scienza della Legislazione, 1783, Book III, chap. 22, Milano. 1855 ed., v. 1, pp. 610 et seq.

renowned code of Leopold of Tuscany, later Leopold the Second, in which it was provided (Sec. 46) that

"A fund shall be established out of the fines collected by the courts to indemnify those who have suffered from a crime, when the criminal can not make reparation,[16] as well as those who without intention or negligence, but through an unfortunate concurrence of circumstances, have been arrested and subsequently acquitted, provided in both cases that the judge declare an indemnity as due under the circumstances and fix the amount."

The penal code of the Two Sicilies, chapter 6, article 5, contained a similar provision.[17] Since then many Italian criminologists and jurists have supported the principle, among others, Carrara and Lucchini.[18] Lucchini, the draftsman of the proposed code of criminal procedure of Italy has incorporated in his draft a provision covering state indemnity for unjustly convicted persons, but in spite of the vigorous campaign waged in its behalf, the principle still awaits legislative recognition in Italy.[19]

In England, Jeremy Bentham was the first champion of the doctrine of state indemnification for errors of criminal justice.[20] He considered the obligation of the state so obvious that any attempt to demonstrate it could only obscure it. On May 18, 1808 Samuel Romilly,[21] an apostle of criminal law reform in England, introduced a bill in Parliament leaving it to the trial court to determine whether any and how much indemnity is due to an innocent individual acquitted after an unjust conviction. Solicitor-General Plumer opposed the bill on the ground that it created a distinction between those acquitted with and without the approval of the judge, and declared this a task equally dangerous and unconstitutional. The bill was withdrawn and no attempt has since been made in England to regulate the question, although Parliament has on several occasions granted lump sum indemnities as a

---

16 It is interesting in this connection to examine Bentham's proposals in his Traité de Législation civile et penale, Paris, 1802, v. II, p. 370, et seq.

17 Geyer, Op. cit. Nord und Süd, p. 174.

18 Carrara, Programa del corso di diritto criminali, § 858, 5th ed., 1877. Lucchini, L. Il carcere preventivo, 1872, 2nd ed., Venezia, 1873, Appendix, p. 258, et seq; also in his Elementi di procedura penale, 2nd ed., Firenze, 1899, p. 403.

19 Rocco, arturo La riparazione alle vittimi degli errori giudiziare, in Rivista penale, v. 56, 1902, pp. 249-274; 395-435.

20 Bentham, Jeremy. Op. Cit. v. II, p. 378. See also Nicolas, R. Des réparations aux victimes d'errours judiciaires. Revue critique de législation, 1888, N. S. 17, pp. 348-356.

21 Memoirs of the Life of Sir Samuel Romilly. 3rd ed., London, J. Murray, 1841, v. 2, pp. 84-86.

matter of grace to various innocent individuals released after having suffered imprisonment upon erroneous conviction.[22]

In Spain, the principle, expressed in an unusually liberal form, had a brief existence of fifteen months in the ill-fated penal code of 1822.[23]

While the question of indemnity was again agitated vigorously in France during the middle of the nineteenth century, finding among its supporters some of the leading jurists of the time,[24] yet the principle was first accepted in modern legislation in the cantons of Switzerland, where so many modern political reforms have received their first legislative expression.[25]

The provisions of the codes of these various cantons are by no means uniform, some recognizing the right of indemnity only for imprisonment by reason of a conviction subsequently reversed on appeal, others for arrest and detention preliminary to acquittal only, (*Untersuchungshaft, détention preventive*), and still others for both. To some extent we shall discuss the provisions of these codes in connection with the laws of the other countries of Europe (*infra*).

Brief code provisions authorizing the award of an equitable compensation to an erroneously convicted person are found in the codes of criminal procedure of Baden, March 18, 1864, (art. 184) and of Wirttemberg, April 17, 1868 (art. 484), and in the penal codes of Mexico,[26] Dec. 7, 1871 (art. 344) and of Portugal,[27] June 14, 1884 (art. 126, sec. 6 and 7).

It is only, however, within the last twenty-five years that the countries of Europe have shown by their legislation, a determined and fully

---

[22]The Law Times, Feb. 3, 1912, pp. 325-326; the Law Journal, London, Oct. 19, 1912, p. 623.

[23]Spain, Penal Code of 1822, arts. 179-181, Appendix, p. 705.

[24]Merlin, Répertoire, Bruxelles, 1826. *V. Denonciateur* and *Réparation civile.* Legraverend. *Traité de législation criminelle,* Paris, 1830, introduction, p. XXV. Dupin, *Observations sur plusieurs points importants de législation criminelle,* Paris, 1821. Faustin-Hélie. *Théorie du Code pénal,* Paris, 1843, t. I, p. 234. Bonneville de Marsangy. *De l'amélioration de la loi criminelle,* Paris, Cotillon, 1864, v. 2, ch. 18.

[25]Tobler, Hans. Die Entschädigungspflicht des Staates gegenüber schuldlos Verfolgten, Angeklagten und Verurteilten, mit Berücksichtigung des schweizerischen Rechts. Zurich, 1905. The most specific provisions on the subject are found in the codes of criminal procedure of Vaud, articles 254, 267 and 539; Berne, articles 235, 243, 343, 367; Tessin, articles 52, 135; Aargau, articles 278, 364; Balle-Ville (Baselstadt), articles 63, 101, 107 and the law of Dec. 9, 1889, Appendix, p. 707; Fribourg, articles 220, 230, 350, 378, 388, 380; Neuchâtel, articles 245, 249, 303, 347, 431, 508. The constitution of Geneva of 1794 had provided for the award of an indemnity based on the number of days detention. The principle, extended, is preserved in the code of criminal procedure of Jan. 1, 1885.

[26]Mexico, Appendix, p. 708.

[27]Portugal, Appendix, p. 708.

considered intention to fulfil the obligation of society toward the innocent victims of the errors of criminal justice. The Scandinavian countries, Sweden, Norway and Denmark, in the order named, enacted, in 1886, 1887 and 1888 respectively, extensive and elaborate laws on the subject. In considerable detail they worked out the conditions under which the right to indemnity shall be exercised, its various limitations, and the procedure for giving it effect as a remedy to the injured individual.[28] Indemnity is accorded both to erroneously convicted persons and to those erroneously arrested and detained. Of the three the law of Sweden is the most conservative, the law of Denmark the most liberal—in fact, the most liberal of all the countries of Europe. In 1892, Austria (Act of March 16, 1892)[29] enacted a law providing for compensation only to convicted persons acquitted on appeal and rehearing. The draft of a new law extending the indemnity to cases of detention pending trial has been under debate since 1905. A similar restriction of the class indemnified—erroneously convicted persons only—is found in the French law of June 8, 1895.[30] Hungary,[31] the following year, in §§576-589 of its code of criminal procedure of December 4, 1896, provided compensation under certain conditions for both erroneously convicted and erroneously arrested and detained persons.

The leading country of continental Europe, Germany, waited until almost all the other important countries had by statute dealt with the matter before itself enacting legislation on the subject. It was not until 1898, in the law of May 20,[32] that Germany enacted a law which, under very stringent limitations, awarded an indemnity to persons erroneously convicted, who on the rehearing of their case and reversal of the judgment

[28]Sweden, Norway and Denmark, Appendix, pp. 709, 710, 711.

[29]Austria, Appendix, p. 712. One of the best discussions of the Austrian law, including the legislative debates and "motives" is found in Hœgel, Das gesetz betreffend die Entschädigung für ungerechtfertigte erfolgte Verurteilung. Wien, 1901. See also Klewitz, A., in Archiv für öffentliches Recht, v. 7, pp. 311-329; Löffler, A. Die Entschädigung unschuldig Verhafteter, Wien, 1906; Krzymuski, Ed., in Revue Penitentiaire, v. 18, 1894, pp. 806-815.

[30]France, Appendix, p. 713. A useful study of the law of June 8, 1895, with the legislative history of the question, is found in Berlet, A. De la réparation des erreurs judiciaires. Paris, 1896. See also, Pascaud, Bernard and Nicolas, op. cit.

[31]Hungary, Appendix, p. 714. Doleshall's article in Gerichtssaal, v. 53, 1895-97, pp. 253-285, is by all means the best article on the Hungarian statute.

[32]Germany, Appendix, pp. 716, 717. There is a prolific literature in Germany. The debates of publicists are found in the Verhandlung des deutschen Juristentags (German Bar Association) 11, 12, 13, 16 and 22 session. The legislative history is best brought out in Berichte der XI Kommission des Reichstages vom 20 April, 1896. IV Session 1895-97. Drucksachen 294, and Entwurf nebst Begründung (Motives), Same Session, 9 Leg. Per. v. I, No. 73. The best commentaries on the Acts are those of Burlage, Berlin, 1905; Krause, Hannover, 1906; and Kähler, Halle, 1904.

were declared innocent. Six years later (Act of July 14, 1904) Germany extended the principle of indemnification to those under detention pending trial (*Untersuchungshaft*). Italy and Holland are debating the question and will probably soon join their neighbors in similar legislation.

THE THEORY.

It may seem strange that this principle of compensation, involving such an obvious act of justice on the part of the state, which had, moreover, received the general recognition and support of jurists, publicists and legislators should have had to wait so many decades before acceptance in the actual legislation of modern states. The reason for the delay was in part the unwillingness to open already cramped treasuries to unlimited inroads and the inability of lower and upper houses of legislatures to agree upon the proper limitations of the right, while not by any means the least obstacle was the bitter disagreement between jurists as to whether the indemnity was to be considered an act of grace and equity on the part of the state, or a legal duty and obligation. Before enacting legislation, the European legislator demands the support of sound legal as well as economic theory. For years lawyers debated this question back and forth. The statement in Merkel's *Juristische Enzyklopädie,* (1st ed., 1885, § 63), explains much:

> "That such an indemnity would represent the real feelings of justice of the German people of the present time there can be no doubt. The reason why we at the same time hesitate to give this feeling legislative expression is partly (although by no means only) because we can not base it on a dogmatic legal ground."

Arguing from legal principle a large group of jurists, whose authority carried weight among legislatures and the people, advanced three arguments which seriously hampered the enactment of legislation on the subject.

The first argument is that the state in administering justice acts in its sovereign capacity and can not be held accountable in law for the burdens which particular individuals may have to suffer, when its sovereign right has been legally exercised. To err is not illegal. If an innocent individual is by mistake convicted, this is a burden which as a citizen of the state he must bear. This is the "act of state" theory, and a frank avowal of the "assumption of risk" doctrine. If, said these jurists, there has been an intentional wrong or illegality anywhere in the case, either on the part of the complaining witness, ministerial officer, court official or judge, the law gives the injured individual ample redress.[33]

[33]Anschütz, Gerhard. Der Ersatzanspruch aus Vermögensbeschädigungen durch rechtmässige Handlhabung der Staatsgewalt, in Verwaltungsarchiv. v. 5, (1896-97), p. 1 ff.

To this the answer has been made that, while the individual in modern public law must bear the burdens of citizenship without compensation, this applies only to the general burdens borne by all the citizens as a whole, and not to special sacrifices asked from the individual in the interests of the entire community.[34] When we ask a citizen to become a juryman or a witness,[34a] when his diseased animal is killed for fear of contagion,[35] when his house is destroyed to prevent the spread of conflagration, when his property is taken by eminent domain for public use, compensation is made for the special sacrifices he makes for the general benefit of society.

An ingenious replication is made to the contention that the taking of property and the taking of liberty for public use are analogous. By the taking of property, say the proponents of the "act of state" theory, the community is enriched, for which reason compensation is paid on the civil law doctrine of unjust enrichment. In the case of unjust conviction the state receives no equivalent. The deprivation of the liberty of the individual is no gain to the state.

If the compensation in eminent domain represented the public gain, this specious argument might carry weight. But it does not. The advantage to society generally exceeds by far the monetary value of the property to the individual from whom it is taken. The price paid represents not the gain of the state, but the loss of the individual. It is a special sacrifice that is asked of the individual, for which society compensates him.

Two other arguments against which the champions of the obligation of state indemnity had to contend were drawn from the civil law. The first was *Qui jure suo utitur, neminem laedit;* in other words, the state acting legally can legally injure no one. But in private law, from which this analogy is drawn, there has been a gradual change from this view of the legality of an act. The principle that he who legally uses his own incurs no legal liability has been restricted in application to the narrowest limits. Even a slight invasion of the rights of third persons (under an otherwise prima facie lawful use of one's own) has given rise to the application of the principle *sic utere tuo ut alienum non laedas.* The transition in point of view took place definitely in England

[34]Mayer, Otto. Deutsches Verwaltungsrecht, Leipzig, 1896, v. 2, pp. 345 ff; Bluntschli, Allgemeines Staatsrecht, Book X, ch. 5, München, 1868 ed., p. 409 ff.

[34a]These illustrations show that at least in some of its applications the principle of compensation by the state for a deprivation of liberty is not unknown.

[35]Löffler. Die Entschädigung unschuldig Verhafteter. Wien, 1906, p. 8.

in 1862, in the case of Bamford v. Turnley.[36] The general rule of both public and private law now is that a private act is considered lawful and is permitted by the state, there being admittedly no negligence or fault, only to the extent that it does not infringe the legal rights of others.[37]

The other objection drawn from the civil law was: "without fault no liability," and for many years it proved one of the most serious. This principle of "no liability without fault" has been incorporated into the civil or private law of all civilized countries, and although American statutory and non-statutory law reveals many cases of liability without fault, the principle has been one of the great obstacles which the workmen's compensation laws have had to overcome.[38] Modern social and economic conditions, however, have brought about an important modification in the rigidity of the doctrine, so that for large classes of cases liability is predicated on the mere causal relation between the act and the injury, whether inflicted with or without fault. The workmen's compensation acts are perhaps the clearest illustration of this change in legal principle, at least as applied to cases in which a large social group is subjected to the danger of recurring accident and a more equitable distribution of the loss is mandatory.

The state, says Löffler, has escaped this obvious duty up to the present time because our feelings of law and equity are directed more toward property than toward liberty. Theft is a more reprehensible act than intentional personal injury and false imprisonment. The taking of private property, the killing of a man's diseased animal—these were recognized as subjects for compensation long before the taking of his liberty. Löffler ascribes this largely to the fact that the owners of property are a powerful social group and have induced an early social and legislative recognition of their rights, whereas those affected by wrongful arrest or conviction are a weak social group, whose voice is almost unheard, and whose rights are only at this late day securing slight recognition because of a general altruistic feeling of social justice.

It requires no further demonstration therefore to show that society rather than the individual should bear the risk of accident in the admin-

---

[36] *Bamford v. Turnley,* Law Times Rep., v. 6, N. S. 721 at p. 723. The principle *qui jure suo utitur neminen laedit* may be directly traced to Justinian's Digest 50. 17. 151—*nemo damnum facit, nisi qui id fecit quod facere jus non habet.* It has, however, always been narrowly limited. See Blackstone III, 217, citing *Morley v. Pragnel,* Cro. Car. 510.

[37] Löffler, Op. cit., p. 10. For examples of such action, see Unger, Joseph. Handeln auf eigene Gefahr, 3rd ed., Wien, 1904.

[38] *Ives v. South Buffalo Street Railway Company,* 201 New York, 271, at pp. 285, 293-4, 298. See 46 American Law Review (1912), pp. 99-100, citing article by James Parker Hall in Journal of Political Economy, October, 1911.

istration of criminal justice. Legislation having this end in view is supported by the same theory as compulsory social insurance, and general average in admiralty law. Where the common interest is joined for a common end, each individual member being subject to the same danger, the loss, when it occurs, should be borne by the community and not alone by the injured individual.

THE STATUTES.

An analysis of the European statutes may be useful to show particularly the limitations which European countries have placed on the granting of the indemnity. It will be seen that they have endeavored to restrict the indemnity to those only who are clearly shown to deserve it. Therefore, first, the class that has the right to receive the indemnity is strictly defined; secondly, to exclude the undeserving, specific and general limitations on the right are established from various points of view, such as censurable conduct of the claimant; thirdly, the injury indemnified is in general confined to the pecuniary loss only; fourthly, a very brief statute of limitations is provided; and lastly, the indemnity is in other respects restricted so that the burden on the State Treasury will not be oppressive. The debates preceding the enactment of many of the statutes show clearly that the fear of inroads on the State Treasury prevented the extension of the right and the removal of limitations in cases where an award was otherwise recognized as just. We shall discuss the statutes under the four heads: (a) who may be indemnified; (b) the limitations on the right; (c) the extent of the indemnity; and (d) the procedure for making the right effective.

WHO IS INDEMNIFIED.

As we have seen, Austria, France, Portugal and Geneva (code of criminal procedure, January 1, 1885), grant an indemnity for the injury suffered by reason of conviction and imprisonment where on retrial an acquittal takes place. Indemnification both for acquittal on appeal after a conviction, and for detention pending trial followed by acquittal or discharge is provided for in Sweden, Norway, Denmark, Germany, Hungary, Berne, Fribourg, Neuchatel, Basle and Tessin. The award of an indemnity is *compulsory* in case of acquittal on appeal after a conviction—that is, a right of action is given to the individual—in Germany, Norway, Denmark, Hungary, Portugal, Mexico, Neuchatel and Basle. It is also compulsory in case of detention followed by a discharge from custody or acquittal on first trial in Germany, Denmark and Norway. In Germany, however, before the action lies, the court acquitting the accused on retrial, must, simultaneously with the judgment of acquittal, issue a decree to the effect that an indemnity in the case is warranted by the facts, which decree is a condition precedent to the right of action. The relief is *discretionary* in both cases—acquittal after conviction and detention pending trial—in Sweden and Fribourg. It is discretionary in case of acquittal after conviction only in Austria and France, and discretionary in cases of discharge from custody in Hungary, Vaud, Neuchatel and Basle. In Norway and Vaud, it is also discretionary in case of a *nolle prosequi;* in general, however, a *nolle prosequi* does not open the right to the indemnity at all, a valid judgment or order of the court being required. It is explained by the committee report on the French law that the indemnity was left discretionary with the judge for the reason that it was considered best, instead of making the relief compulsory and specifying the conditions which limited the right, to prescribe no conditions, leaving the judge to determine in each case the effect to be given to the concrete circumstances in limiting the propriety of an award.

Innocence must be shown affirmatively on the part of the claimant in France, Germany, Norway, Hungary, Sweden, Mexico and Neuchatel. In Germany the claimant may show in the alternative that there is no longer a well-founded suspicion against him. In Hungary and in Sweden in case of unjust detention pending trial he must show any one of three things: First, in both countries, that the act for which he is held has not been committed. Second, in Hungary, that the accuser has not committed it; in Sweden, that its author was another than the accused. Third, in Sweden, that from all the circumstances it could not have been committed by him; in Hungary, that while committed by him it was not in a legal sense a punishable act.

Hungary makes an interesting distinction between cases of unjust conviction and cases merely of unjust detention pending trial. In the first case, where the sentence has been served, damages are due *ipso facto,* even though there is a *non liquet* acquittal. The *not guilty* are indemnified. In the second case, where as we have seen the award of an indemnity is discretionary, innocence must, nevertheless, be proved. The *innocent* only are indemnified. While this is not clear from the statute itself, the committee reports leave no doubt on the subject.[39] In this respect, the Hungarian law occupies an intermediate position between the two extremes. In cases of unjust conviction, Hungary has followed the Danish law; in cases of unjust detention, where proof of innocence is required, the Norwegian law has been accepted as a prototype.

[39]Dolcshall, Op. cit., p. 271.

Bonneville de Marsangy, an ardent proponent of state indemnity, advocated that innocence be proved affirmatively by the claimant, as this was a new action, and on the plaintiff should fall the burden of proof. This theory was strenuously opposed by Heinze,[40] who in 1865 brought the subject prominently before the public in Germany, and by Zucker and Geyer, who claimed that our criminal law recognizes only one form of guilt or innocence—the state must prove a man guilty or else he is innocent. It would make an odious distinction between those acquitted with and without indemnity, between those proven innocent and those acquitted for lack of sufficient proof of guilt. As we have seen, however, a number of states have adopted the principle that innocence must be affirmatively proved by the claimant.

Other states do not require proof of innocence, but base the indemnity upon the mere fact of acquittal or discharge from custody, as for example, Austria, Denmark, Baselstadt and Tessin. In case of erroneous conviction, Denmark requires that it be "regularly proved that the penalty was not justified." Some of the Swiss cantons show peculiar conditions in this respect. Berne in its penal code of 1854 permits in the alternative the establishment of innocence, acquittal because of doubtful guilt, and *nolle prosequi* for insufficiency of evidence, which is a most liberal if not a hazardous extension of the right. Fribourg in its code of criminal procedure of 1873 indemnifies acquitted, *nolle prossed* and not guilty "convicted persons." Vaud strangely enough in its code of criminal procedure of 1850, indemnified persons *nolle prossed* but not those acquitted by valid judgment. Luzerne in § 313 of its code of criminal procedure requires that the accused should have been prosecuted without basis *(auf ganz grundloser Weise)*. By this is meant the absence of suspicious conduct, lying, attempt to run away, to conceal evidence, etc.,—what the Germans call *prozessuales Verschulden*.

It is curious to note that in Schwyz and Zurich where the legislator has not provided for indemnity the courts have at times allowed it.[41] They have limited it to such cases as show an entire absence of guilt and denied it where the evidence indicates a well-founded suspicion. This tendency to base the indemnity on the probability of guilt finds strong opponents among those authorities and courts in whose opinion mere acquittal justifies the indemnity.

The chief objections raised against the German law are that it fails to indemnify accused innocent persons who are *nolle prossed*, per-

[40]Heinze, Rudolf. Das recht der Untersuchungshaft. Leipzig, 1865.
[41]Tobler, Op. cit., p. 35.

sons whose property has been attached in criminal proceedings and those who, by giving bail, have escaped detention pending trial.

There is considerable difference in the legislation of these various countries as to the right of third persons injured by the conviction or detention of another to sue for the indemnity. In Germany, those who have a legal right to support from the unjustly accused person, have an independent action, limited, however, to the amount of the support of which they have been deprived. In Hungary, these same persons have a right of action for their lost support only where the accused has declined to bring the action himself. It is, moreover, limited to cases of unjust conviction, and not merely unjust detention pending trial. In Austria, a claim for lost support can be brought only by the surviving husband or wife, children or parents, where the accused began but dropped the action or where he is deceased. In most countries, Germany being practically the only exception, death of the erroneously accused (or desertion of family, as in Sweden), is a condition precedent to the bringing of the action by third persons, either heirs or dependents. In France, Austria and Hungary the right passes to his surviving spouse, ascendants and descendants in a direct line. In Denmark, ascendants are excluded. In Hungary, in case the erroneously accused person has already paid the death penalty, those who have the legal right to support may bring the action, provided they can show *that they are dependent* on the support of which they have been unjustly deprived.

Earnest objections have been raised against this limitation of the heritability of the claim. It is said[42] that the moral integrity of the person is the common property of his family, and that damage to property rights is the basic element of the individual rights of each. Claims of both categories, therefore, must be heritable. Legislation having in mind only a right to support disregards these considerations. In spite of Jellinek's assertion that this right to indemnity is a public subjective right, and therefore personal only,[43] most of the states of Europe have recognized the heritability of the right so far as pecuniary damage is concerned. Binding even recommends, and we believe properly so, that both the moral satisfaction and the claim to pecuniary indemnity should be transferable *ab intestato*. This point of view is followed by the Danish and the French law, but is rejected by the Swedish, Austrian, German and Hungarian law. In France it is provided that relatives of a

[42]Doleshall. Op. cit., p. 274, et seq.

[43]Jellinek, G. Staatsrechtliche Erörterungen über die Entschädigung unschuldig Verurtheilter, Zeitschrift f. d. privat— u öffentliche Recht der Gegenwart, v. 20, 1892, pp. 455-467.

degree further removed than would involve a material injury to them have no right to the claim.

(B). LIMITATIONS.

A limitation almost uniformly expressed in the statutes is that the claimant shall not have intentionally or by gross negligence caused his detention. The statutes of some of the countries such as Germany, Hungary, Norway, and Sweden, specifically mention certain limitations in cases where the detention or conviction may be said to have been due to the act of the claimant himself—thus, for example, where there has been an attempt to flee, a false confession, the removal of evidence, or an attempt to induce a witness or an expert to give false testimony or opinion, or an analogous attempt to suppress such testimony or opinion. The statute of Denmark recognizes the possibility of extenuating circumstances. It is there provided, that where, for example, the attempt to flee or the making of false statements, etc., is considered by the judge as having been due to fear, annoyance or excusable error, he need not refuse the indemnity. He may award an indemnity reduced in proportion to the offense.

Germany has gone furthest of all in defining the conditions and limitations under which the claim shall be excluded. In the act of 1904, the claim may be rejected if it appears that the act charged involved an infamous or immoral transaction, or was committed during a state of drunkenness which excluded the exercise of free will, or when it appears from the circumstances that the accused had prepared to commit a felony or lesser crime. These may be called conditions of exclusion bearing on the *substantial* justice of the claim. Similar restrictions are found in the Hungarian statute. But Germany has gone even further and has provided expressly that certain other delinquencies of the claimant, having no connection whatever with the act charged, shall likewise deprive him of his right to relief. Thus, article 2 of the German Act of 1904 provides that the claim may also be denied where the accused at the time of his release is not in possession of his civic rights, or was under police surveillance, or where he has been punished or sentenced to the penitentiary and three years have not elapsed since the termination of the sentence. In most countries these extraneous delinquencies and their effect on the right are left to the discretion of the authorities passing on the claim, whether judge or administrative board.

As we have shown above, France expressly declined to specify any limitations on the right, leaving it to the judge to determine what acts or facts shall constitute a sufficient objection to the payment of an indemnity. A slight differnce between the Hungarian and German statute may here be mentioned, in that Hungary considers the failure to note an objection or appeal against the verdict as sufficient to warrant a denial of the indemnity, whereas Germany expressly provides that such failure to note an appeal shall not be construed as negligence. The draft of the proposed law of Austria governing unjust detention provides that

"Where the accused through inexcusable negligence has failed to object to the imposition or prolongation of the detention when he had good ground so to do, he shall be denied the award of an indemnity."

Several of the statutes exclude the remedy where the act has been committed under duress, necessity, or self-defense, but this appears to us as an unjust limitation.

A very brief statute of limitations is generally provided—from three months to six months is the usual time limit for making the claim. Denmark makes an exception in permitting the action to be brought within a year from the day on which the accused had knowledge of the circumstances on which he bases his demand. This provision is rather elastic, and we have been unable to ascertain how it has been interpreted by the courts.

(c). EXTENT OF THE INDEMNITY.

As a general rule, with but few exceptions, only the pecuniary damage is compensated. In this respect, more than in any other, the statutes have fallen short of the wishes of their advocates, because in case of an unjust detention or conviction the moral damage is by far the more serious element of injury. Even the Carolina Code of 1532 recognized that *"Schmach und Schande"* (suffering and shame) were proper elements of compensation.

Germany, Austria, Sweden and Norway indemnify for the pecuniary injuries suffered. Germany considers that these include not merely physical injuries and lost profits, but also the losses to *future* income, but they do not of course extend to moral injuries. In the statutes indemnifying for erroneous conviction, it is the injury suffered from the execution of the sentence, the actual wrongful imprisonment, which is compensated. Sweden provides expressly that the indemnity is to cover the "suspension or restriction of his means of existence resulting from the deprivation of his liberty." The French, Danish and some of the Swiss statutes are the most liberal. France provides indemnity for the damages (*dommages-interêts*) suffered. In practice, however, so the authorities say, account is taken of the moral injury resulting from an unjust conviction, which is, indeed, hard to separate from the pecuniary. The Danish statute extends the indemnity to "the wrong, injury, and pecuniary losses which he has suffered." Whereas most of the Swiss codes of criminal procedure provide for indemnity without specifying what injuries are to be indemnified, the code of criminal procedure of Neuchatel in article 508 provides that

"In case the new decision declares the condemned person innocent, there shall be awarded to him by the court damages proportioned to the material and moral injury he has suffered by the erroneous conviction."

The Hungarian statute requires first, a return of all money penalties; secondly, the return of the costs of proceedings and the value of confiscated property; thirdly, compensation for income lost during the imprisonment; and fourthly, money damages may generally be granted. How these are to be estimated and what they are to cover is not stated. Whether they cover the loss of position, diminution and falling off in business, and loss of credit, or whether they are simply confined to the definite actual fixed property losses can not be established. The committee reports (motives) lead to the inference that more than the property loss was intended to be covered, for the Swedish and Austrian statutes are characterized as unsatisfactory in this regard. It may be stated in addition that it is the general rule in Europe to provide in the codes of criminal procedure for a return of costs to an accused person declared to be innocent.

The French law notes an express difference between material and moral injuries in the matter of heritability. Both pecuniary and moral losses are the subject of indemnity on the part of those who are sufficiently near in relationship to the accused for the presumption to be drawn that they have suffered by the conviction of their relative. But, as we have shown, the right is not extended to relatives of a degree further removed than would involve a material injury resulting to them from the unjust conviction.

It is curious to note that the draft of the proposed Austrian law according indemnity for unjust detention, denies any indemnity for a detention of less than eight days. The debates show that this is based on financial considerations. The German statute of 1904 similarly excludes from indemnity the mere arrest and detention preliminary to commitment for trial, except when followed by detention pending trial, in which latter event the preliminary detention is calculated as a part of the whole. This limitation is unjust, and is so recognized by the commission redrafting the Code of Criminal Procedure,[44] who recommend indemnification even for a brief preliminary detention. Only

[44] Protokolle der Kommission zur Reform des Strafprozesses, II, p. 284, ff.

where the arrest is followed by almost immediate release, where there is practically no real detention, is an indemnity, says the commission, unnecessary. A provable injury is in such cases, in the opinion of the commissioners, generally impossible. To us, this proposition seems open to debate, at least.

In general the statutes recognize the obligation to accord satisfaction for the moral injury by providing for the publication of the decree of acquittal at the domicil of the accused,[45] at the jurisdiction of the appellate court, and at various other places, which presumably will aid the accused to obviate and allay any prejudice from which he may have suffered by the publication of the fact of his detention or conviction. France goes the furthest in this direction, providing that

"The decree or judgment on appeal whence results the innocence of a convicted person shall be posted in the city where the conviction was first pronounced; in the place where the judgment was reversed; in the community or place where the crime or misdemeanor shall have been committed; at the domicil of those who demanded the appeal; and at the last domicil of the victim of the judicial error, if he is deceased, and shall be officially published in the *Journal Officiel,* and its publication in five newspapers, at the choice of the appellant, shall be ordered besides, if he requests it."

(D). PROCEDURE.

As will be seen from the statutes quoted in the Appendix, the procedure is generally very complicated; in fact so complicated that it is hard to understand how the poor acquitted individual thrown out on the world can ever find the means to prosecute his claim. The statutes vary greatly from one another, only one country, Denmark, making it a right justiciable before the ordinary courts in first instance. In general, it is regarded as an administrative proceeding, which perhaps more than anything else shows that the indemnity is considered an act of grace and not a matter of legal right. Sweden requires that the claim shall be addressed to the King and shall be examined by the Minister of Justice, who is to pass upon the justice of the claim and the amount of the indemnity. In Austria the trial court pronouncing the acquittal makes an official inquiry into the facts on which the claim for indemnity is based, and the sealed documents with an opinion of the court are then laid before the Minister of Justice, who in turn fixes the amount of the award. An appeal from his finding lies to the Supreme Court. In Hungary the trial court makes the investigation, places its findings before the highest court, which in turn, should it decide that the indem-

[45]The codes of criminal procedure often provide for the publication of the judgment of acquittal in the Official Gazette (Reichsanzeiger); see, for example, the German Strafprozessordnung, sec. 411, paragraph 4.

nity is justified, sends the papers to the Minister of Justice. On the basis of the findings of the highest court, the Minister of Justice fixes the amount of the indemnity.

In Germany, whose statute is the latest, it is provided that the second trial court, besides its decree of acquittal, shall hand down a decree as to whether an indemnity in the case is warranted by the facts disclosed.[46] This decree can not be appealed from. If it decides in favor of the claimant, he must make a formal application for indemnification to the district attorney in the jurisdiction where the trial court sat. The district attorney as a ministerial act sends the papers to the highest administrative board of the state *(Landesjustizverwaltung)*. This board fixes the amount of indemnity, from which an appeal through the regular legal channels is granted to the claimant. Germany, therefore, has at least made this concession to those who have always contended that the right to indemnity is a strictly legal right and should be justiciable in the law courts.

Practically all the statutes provide that the state shall have a subrogated right against those individuals, officers or judges who by their negligence, corruption, or malicious conduct shall have caused or contributed to the detention or to its undue prolongation, or to the conviction of the innocent accused person.

CONCLUSION.

Such are the salient features of the more important European statutes on indemnification by the state of those whom, in the administration of its criminal justice, it has erroneously and unjustly arrested, detained or convicted. The principle has been clearly recognized, but as the examination of the statutes discloses the remedy in practice is granted only within the narrowest of limits. Nevertheless, a step has been taken in the right direction and one which we in this country would do well to follow. How we shall apply the principle, whether the relief shall be compulsory or discretionary, whether court or jury shall estimate the extent of the injury, within what limits and under what conditions the indemnity shall be awarded, are matters which legislatures can work out with little difficulty. While it is true that our lax methods of administering the criminal law, the possibility of acquittal on technical grounds[47] and the requirement of unanimity on the part of twelve jurymen, bring about nine cases of unjust *acquittal* to one case of unjust *conviction,* still the mere rarity of the occurrence is no excuse for a

[46]For an example of such a decree, see Krause, Op. cit., p. 213.

[47]See, for example, *People v. Flack,* 125 New York, 324; also the Illinois case cited in Green Bag for June, 1912, p. 321.

failure to acknowledge the principle and to remedy the evil. It makes the individual hardship, when it does occur, seem all the more distressing. That there have been numerous cases of this kind besides the recent Toth case in Pennsylvania and the Beck case in England there is no doubt, notwithstanding the unauthentic returns from wardens collected by the American Prison Congress and reported in this Journal (May, 1912, p. 131) to the effect that there are but few cases of unjust execution of innocent persons.[48] The whole matter of compensation for unjust convictions for felonies and lesser crimes is well worth further study, to the end that within measurable time remedial legislation may cure this defect in our social institutions.

Appendix: Continental Statutes.

Spain—Penal Code of 1822, chap. 12. In force for 15 months. Articles 179-181 deal with indemnity for innocent persons. *Revue Penitentiaire,* v. 19, 1895, pp. 568-9.

Article 179. Every individual who, after having been the object of a criminal proceeding, shall have been declared absolutely innocent of the crime or fault to which the proceeding is due shall be immediately and completely indemnified for all the injuries and wrong experienced by him in his person, reputation and property, and there may not be required of him for this purpose any costs or expenses, and, if he desires, a fiscal attorney shall be charged with representing him in this demand for indemnity as if it concerned a claim advanced ex officio. However, wherever it is not impossible the indemnity shall be fixed in the same sentence which declares the accused absolutely innocent. If this proceeding is not possible the right to indemnity shall be declared and the indemnity fixed as it is prescribed in the code of procedure.

Art. 180. If the criminal action has been instituted by virtue of a private accusation the indemnity shall be at the charge of the accuser; and if the judge has co-operated by *dolus,* ignorance or negligence in the injustice of the information, he will incur the same responsibility in solido.

Art. 181. If the proceeding has been instituted ex officio and it has as its cause the *dolus* or fault of the judge the indemnity shall be integrally charged to said judge. If the judge on the contrary has acted in conformity with the law and it results from the information that the individual accused was absolutely innocent, the indemnity shall be given by the government either in money or under the form of an honor or recompense according to the circumstances of the person, which will be determined by the sentence, but it shall always be effective and sufficient to extend to all the injuries, wrongs and annoyances experienced by the innocent person.

Bâle-Ville (Baselstadt)—Law of December 9, 1889, on the indemnity accorded to those who have been unjustly incarcerated. *Annuaire de Législation Etrangère,* v. 19, 1889, pp. 685-6.

Art. 1. When a person has been incarcerated by order of the authorities,

---

[48]A large collection of cases of unjust executions and sentences of life imprisonment has recently been published by Justizrat Dr. Erich Sello: *Die Irrtümer der Strafjustiz und ihre Ursachen,* Berlin, R. v. Decker's Verlag, 1911. Volume I, 523 p. Quarto.

if the proceeding instituted against him has not ended in the remanding of the accused to the courts, he has a right at the end of the examination to an indemnity proportioned to the wrong which has been caused him and the duration of the incarceration, provided that there has been no fault on his part.

Art. 2. The claims for indemnity based on article 1 of the present law must be brought within fifteen days of the end of the proceeding which led to the incarceration, under penalty of being rejected. If the release and termination of the examination are the work of the police, the police must pronounce on the indemnity. Otherwise the claim is addressed to the authority which remands the individual.

Art. 3. Appeal is allowed against the decision of the police or other authority by making, within seven days from liberation from detention, a written complaint, with the grounds stated, to the president of the tribunal or the court of appeal.

Art. 4. The commission of the court of appeal, in article 31 of the law relating to the opening of criminal procedure of November 4, 1841, shall pass upon the complaint presented in accordance with article 3 of the present law.

Art. 5. The commission decides after having heard the authority charged with pronouncing the remanding or the police, and heard sufficient testimony on the basis of the amount of the claim to indemnity.

If the commission rejects the complaint the claimant may, under the head of expenses be compelled to pay up to one hundred francs.

Art. 6. The accused persons who have been liberated by a competent judge may demand of the state an indemnity proportioned to the wrong which has been caused them by the order of incarceration, and to the duration of the detention provided, nevertheless, that they shall not have been incarcerated by their fault.

Art. 7. When a criminal proceeding is reheard by the terms of articles 121 and 130 of the code of criminal procedure and results in an acquittal, or when it is recognized that the accused deserved a less penalty than that inflicted upon him, he may claim an indemnity proportioned to the pecuniary damage of all kinds which has resulted to him from the detention he has suffered (detention during the examination and detention as a penalty) provided, nevertheless, by his conduct he has not deserved condemnation.

Art. 8. The claim for indemnity based on the provisions of articles 6 and 7 of the present law may, as a general rule, be awarded immediately after the publication of the decree by the same tribunal which has ordered the liberation of the individual, or the diminution of the penalty. The claim must be decided after the public authorities have been heard.

By exception the tribunal may postpone the decision. The injured person may likewise demand a delay of fifteen days during which he may present his demand for indemnity. After that period all claim to indemnity is barred. The tribunal decides in last resort on the demands of indemnity submitted to it.

Art. 9. The competent authorities shall fix freely, taking account of all the circumstances, the amount of the indemnity which ought to be accorded by the terms of the present law.

Art. 10. The demands instituted by the terms of this law, pass to the heirs after the death of the principal claimant.

Art. 11. No demand for indemnity can be directed against the officials who in the exercise of their functions have ordered a detention pending trial, or a detention as penalty. On the other hand, the state may reimburse itself from its guilty employees in case of gross negligence for the amount of the indemnity which it has had to pay in conformity with the provisions of the present law.

Art. 12. Paragraph 63 and 101 of the code of criminal procedure of May 5, 1862, on indemnities due to convicted persons are abrogated from the day the present law enters into force.

Mexico—Penal Code of Dec. 7, 1871.

Art. 344. If the accused has been acquitted by the court, not because of failure of proof, but because his complete innocence of the crime with which he was charged has been established, and if he had not by his previous conduct provoked the presumption of his guilt, this shall be expressly stated in the judgment of acquittal; and when the accused demands it, the amount of his damage and lost profits which the proceeding has caused him shall be fixed in the judgment, after the district attorney has been heard. In this case the civil responsibility is paid out of the general indemnity funds, if by section 348 the judges do not appear responsible or are without sufficient means to pay.

Art. 345. The unjustly accused has a right of action against his unlawfully complaining witness or informant.

Art. 348. The judges and other public officials, employees or officers are civilly liable for arbitrary or wrongful arrests which they have ordered; for illegal prolongation of imprisonment, for injuries caused by ignorance or tardiness in the transaction of their business; and for all misdemeanors or crime which they commit in the exercise of their functions and whereby injury is caused to others.

Portugal—Penal Code of June 14, 1884, Art. 126, Sec. 6 and 7.

Sec. 6. The judgment of acquittal on appeal from a conviction entitles the wrongfully accused person (if he demands it) to an equitable indemnity for the injury which he has suffered through his imprisonment, if the penalty has not been a money fine. If the penalty has been a money fine already paid, it shall be refunded to him. The refunding and the indemnity are charged to the state.

Sec. 7. The judgment of acquittal shall be published in the Official Gazette on three successive days and in duly authenticated form, shall be fastened to the door of the district court where the unjustly convicted person resides, and on the door of the district court, where the conviction has taken place.

The Rehabilitation of duly acquitted persons in Portugal. Decree of Feb. 27, 1895. The law of June 14, 1884, revising the penal code enumerates the means of bringing about rehabilitation. *Revue Penitentiaire,* v. 19, 1895, pp. 920-21.

Article 11. If the accused is declared not guilty the new judgment shall declare void the judgment of conviction without reference to the provisions of the penal law and must rehabilitate the condemned before society, permit him to again occupy his legal status before conviction, as soon as the judgment shall have secured binding force. An extract of the judgment shall be published in the Official Gazette on three consecutive days and attached to the door of the court in the jurisdiction of the domicil of the rehabilitated person and to the door of the court of the jurisdiction in which the conviction was pronounced. Mention in the judicial statistics must be suppressed.

The public minister must furnish the legal means.

Art. 12. The judgment must award to the condemned person, if he requests it, a just indemnity for the injury suffered by the execution of the penalty, if there exist in the proceedings sufficient elements to appreciate this injury. In the contrary case, the indemnity must be fixed in an ordinary proceeding according to the legislation in force. If the penalty has been a fine and already paid the judgment must order its restitution.

Art. 15. It shall be permitted to revise and rehear the proceedings and judgment of a deceased convicted person, observing the previous provisions.

Art. 16. The only persons competent to demand this revision are the parents, descendants, spouse and brothers and sisters of the convicted person.

Sweden—Law of March 12, 1886, Concerning Indemnity to be Awarded against the State to Those Innocently Arrested or Convicted. Lag, angaende ersättning af allmänna medel at oskyldigt häktade eller dömde; given Stockholms slott den 12 Mars 1886. Svensk Författnings-Samling. Number 8, 1886. Translated into French in *Annuaire de Législation Etrangère,* v. 16, pp. 591-2.

Article 1. When an individual shall have been arrested as guilty of a crime and the prosecution against him shall have been subsequently abandoned, or the accused shall have been acquitted, there *may* be awarded to him, or in his default, to his wife or abandoned children, to be borne by the state, an indemnity for the suspension or restriction of his means of existence resulting from the deprivation of his liberty, if it results from the proceedings that the crime for which he has been prosecuted has not been committed, or that its author was another than the accused, or that from all the circumstances it could not have been committed by him, and if in the two latter cases he cannot be considered as an accomplice.

This indemnity shall not be awarded to him who has sought by flight or otherwise to escape the examination or to prevent the discovery of the truth by the suppression of evidence or objects, nor to him who intentionally by an untruthful statement made in court or elsewhere, or by falsely denouncing himself, or in any other way shall have been the cause of the proceedings which have been instituted or prosecuted against him.

Article 2. When an individual condemned to forced labor or prison or to fines, converted into a penalty depriving him of liberty, shall have suffered the burden of his penalty in whole or in part and after a new inquiry or proceeding made in the regular form, he shall have been acquitted, or condemned to a penalty less than that which he has already paid, there may be awarded to him, or in his default to his wife or abandoned children, to be borne by the state, an indemnity for the suspension or restriction of his means of existence resulting from the execution of the penalty, or of that part of this penalty from which he shall have been subsequently released, if he has not intentionally by an untruthful statement made in court or elsewhere, or by denouncing himself falsely, or in any other way, caused the penalty he has suffered to have been pronounced against him.

Article 3. A request for indemnity within the provisions of this law shall be addressed to the King and shall, to be examined, be presented to the Minister of Justice within a period of a year beginning in the case provided for in article 1 from the day when the decision to abandon the prosecution or acquit the accused shall have become *res judicata,* and in the case of article 2 from the day when the judgment pronouncing the acquittal of the accused or his condemnation to a penalty less than that already suffered shall have acquired the force of *res judicata.*

Article 4. When an indemnity shall have been awarded within the terms of this law to an individual imprisoned or condemned in violation of the law, the State shall have the right of recourse against him or those who shall be responsible for the imprisonment or judgment.

Norway—The law of criminal procedure of July 1, 1887 (Jury law) Lov om rettergangsmaaden i straffesager, 1 Juli, 1887, No. 5, Sections 469-472. Norsk Lovtidende, 1887, p. 200 at pp. 285-6.

Section 469. When an individual is acquitted by a judgment after having already paid a penalty under previous conviction he shall on demand be paid from the Treasury, an indemnity for the damages which he has suffered by reason of the executed judgment.

For damages suffered during detention pending trial a person who has been discharged from prosecution, or who is acquitted by judgment, shall, on his demand, receive indemnity from the Treasury, if he successfully rebuts the proofs on which his guilt was predicated.

If the discharge from prosecution or the acquittal is based upon the fact that the transaction can not be brought within a provision of the penal law, or that punishment is excluded or suspended by reason of a circumstance recognized by the law, the court shall decide according to the circumstances of the case how far such indemnity is due.

Sec. 470. Indemnity is never to be granted where the accused by confession or otherwise through intentional conduct had provoked the judgment of conviction or the prosecution against himself, nor for detention pending examination which has occurred because the accused has attempted to flee or has so acted that the conclusion had to be drawn that he has sought to remove traces of the deed, or induce others to bear false witness, or to suppress their testimony.

Sec. 471. The fixing of the indemnity mentioned in section 469 may be demanded in the judgment or in the decree by which the case is terminated.

If this has not occurred or if the prosecution is abandoned without judgment or decree the accused may, within a month after the receipt of the notice, bring his demand before the court which had jurisdiction of the criminal prosecution, or if this cannot be done, before a court which might have had original jurisdiction over the case. The decision takes place by decree after the prosecuting attorney shall have been given an opportunity to defend the interests of the Treasury. If the Treasury is charged with a liability such as is here in question, it can make the claim which the accused would have had by virtue of section 466.

Sec. 466. "For negligent or otherwise improper conduct, so long as they are engaged on a case, public officers as well as private attorneys may be punished with fines, in so far as no greater penalty is by law applicable in the case, and damages are charged to them for the benefit of the person injured by their action. For the damages charged to a public officer, the State is equally responsible.

The State is not, however, responsible to a defendant for duties which an attorney according to section 107 should fulfil."

Sec. 472. If appeal is raised against a judgment on which this chapter provides legal liability the highest court, *ex officio,* examines the question of liability in so far as the decision of this question depends on the ground of appeal; but further examination takes place only in so far as the appeal on this matter has been demanded by one of the parties. * * *

Denmark—Law of April 5, 1888, on Indemnity for Unjust Detention and Conviction and on the Payment in Certain Cases of the Expenses of Appeals Instituted Officially. (Lov om Erstatning for uforskyldt Varelaegtsfaengsel og Straf efter Dom samt om Udredelse i visse Tilfælde of Sagens Omkostningeri offentlige Straffesager, *Samling af Love of Anordninger,* vol. 11, 1886-90, pp. 242-244). (Translated into French in *Annuaire de Législation Étrangère,* v. 18, 1888, pp. 752-754).

Article 1. He who, after having been subjected to detention pending trial, shall be subsequently acquitted or released without his case having been prosecuted to judgment, has a right to indemnity to be fixed by the judge for the wrong, injury, and pecuniary losses which he has suffered, by reason of being deprived of his liberty, when it results necessarily from the explanations furnished that he was innocent of the wrongful act for which he was detained.

An equal right to such an indemnity belongs to him who has been subjected to detention pending trial by reason of inculpation in an act forbidden by a criminal law, but not involving a penalty greater than a fine or simple imprisonment.

Article 2. The right to indemnity above mentioned ceases when the accused has by his conduct provoked his detention pending trial. Nevertheless, when the judge recognizes that the suspected conduct of the accused may have been due to fear, annoyance or excusable error, he may award him an indemnity reduced in proportion.

Article 3. If the case goes to judgment without any accusation against the accused, the latter may, if he desires, demand that the indemnity due him be fixed by judgment pronounced when the case terminates. Nevertheless, the superior authority (in Copenhagen, the director of police) shall be advised in time sufficient to defend the public Treasury.

In all other cases the demand for indemnity for detention pending trial shall be the object of a special civil suit against the State. The summons shall be served on the prefect (in Copenhagen, the director of police) and on the examining magistrate who conducts the proceedings.

The claimant may bring his case before the tribunal of first instance in the place where he has been detained or directly to the superior court having jurisdiction over the examining magistrate, provided that it be not the Supreme Court. This action shall be without expense for either party, and the defendant charged with the interests of the State shall likewise take charge of the interests of the examining magistrate.

When the criminal action or judgment on the detention is appealed to a superior judge, the claim for an indemnity may be formulated and the judgment may be requested in the course of the appellate action. In that case the public minister is charged with defending the interests of the examining magistrate and those of the Treasury.

The decision of the judge of first instance on the demand for indemnity for detention pending trial may be appealed from by the accused as well as by the public minister without limitation of amount.

Article 4. Every action for indemnity for unjust detention pending trial shall be brought within a year from the day when the accused had knowledge of the circumstances on which he bases his demand. If his demand is considered without basis, he shall be condemned to pay the expenses of the case.

Article 5. When a penalty pronounced by the judgment has been paid or expiated in whole or in part and it is regularly proved that the penalty was not justified, the condemned person has a right to an indemnity against the public Treasury for the wrong, injury, and pecuniary losses resulting to him.

The action for indemnity shall be instituted before the tribunal of first instance which had jurisdiction of the criminal case, service to be made on the superior authority and on that one or those of the judges who pronounced the conviction, or directly before the court immediately above, provided that it be not the Supreme Court. The provisions of article 3 concerning the actions for indemnity for detention pending trial shall apply moreover to the actions here in question.

Article 6. The right of action for pecuniary losses, after the death of the accused, passes to his spouse and to his descendants.

Article 7. The indemnities awarded in execution of the present law shall be paid by the Treasury, which shall have recourse against the judge when the latter shall have been guilty of abuse of authority, negligence, or other inexcusable fault.

Article 8. In case of acquittal of the accused, and in general in all cases where the action ends without resulting in a conviction, the expense of the penal action prosecuted officially shall be borne by the Treasury, unless it shall have been occasioned in whole or in part by an illegitimate act imputable to the accused.

Austria—Law of March 16, 1892, Number 64, Reichsgesetzblatt, 1892, pp. 477-8.

Law concerning indemnity for unjust conviction.

§ 1. He who has been legally convicted of a criminal act in accordance with the provisions of the code of criminal procedure, if on a new trial, the discontinuance of the prosecution or the rejection of the charge results, and furthermore in all cases in which acquittal subsequently takes place, may demand of the State an indemnity for the pecuniary injuries suffered by reason of the unjust conviction.

The claim is not permissible when the convicted person has intentionally brought about the unjust conviction or in case of a verdict obtained by contumacy has failed to make objection or take exception.

§ 2. Assuming the presence of the conditions of § 1, the claim may after the death of the convicted person be brought, or if begun by him continued, only by his spouse, children and parents, and only to the extent that these relatives are by his wrongful conviction deprived of support which was due to them from the accused.

§ 3. The claim is barred after three months from the day on which under sections 1 and 2 the claim might have been first brought.

§ 4. The claim is to be brought by written request or protocol before the trial court of first instance which rendered the verdict of conviction and is to be made as definite as possible.

§ 5. The court is officially to undertake the necessary proceedings to establish the facts on which the claim is based, and may take the necessary proofs. All the circumstances for and against the claim are to be considered with equal care. Witnesses and experts may be called and oaths administered where necessary.

§ 6. When the inquiry is closed, the claimant is to be notified that he may make further statements in writing to justify his claim, for which purpose he is to have 14 days' time. The claimant may see the papers in the case.

§ 7. The sealed documents together with an opinion of the court is to be laid before the Minister of Justice who may request a supplementary inquiry or further explanations. The Minister of Justice takes jurisdiction over the claim and fixes the amount of the indemnity.

§ 8. The claimant has a period of 60 days to appeal from the finding of the Minister of Justice to the Supreme Court. The period can not be extended under any circumstances, nor can the extension be granted for default. The appeal does not require the signature of an attorney.

§ 9. The proceedings in the matter regulated by this statute and the relevant memorials are free from fees and postage.

§ 10. The law does not apply to convictions pronounced before the coming into force of this act.

France—Law of June 8, 1895, on the Revision of Criminal Judgments and Indemnities to the Victims of Judicial Errors. Bulletin No. 1706, *Bulletin des Lois,* 1895. This law is substituted for chap. 3, book 2, title 3, of the Code of Criminal Procedure, Articles 443-447.

Articles 443 to 445 inclusive deal with the procedure for reopening a conviction for a criminal act. Article 446 deals with the matter of indemnity for the innocent victim of errors of criminal justice and reads as follows:

Article 446. The decree or judgment of reversal whence results the innocence of a convicted person may, on his demand, award him damages for the injury caused him by the conviction.

If the victim of the judicial error is deceased, the right to demand the damages belongs under the same conditions to his spouse, ascendants and descendants (in a direct line).

It shall not belong to relatives of a degree further removed than would involve a material injury resulting to them from the conviction.

The claim for indemnity may be made at any stage of the procedure for the reversal of the original judgment.

The damages awarded shall be against the State, except that the latter has recourse against the civil person, the complaining or informing witness or false witness through whose fault the conviction shall have been pronounced. The damages shall be paid as expenses of criminal justice. The expenses of the appeal for reversal shall be advanced by the appellant up to the order of the court taking jurisdiction of the claim for indemnity; the expense after that order shall be paid by the Treasury of the State.

If the decree or definite judgment on appeal pronounces a conviction, the condemned person shall be compelled to reimburse the expenses to the State, or to those who demanded the appeal, if there are such.

He who demands the appeal for reversal of the first judgment and loses shall be held to pay all the expenses.

The decree or judgment on appeal whence results the innocence of a convicted person shall be posted in the city where the conviction was first pronounced; in the place where the judgment was reversed; in the community or place where the crime or misdemeanor shall have been committed; at the domicil of those who demanded the appeal; and at the last domicil of the victim of the judicial error, if he is deceased, and shall be officially published in the *Journal Officiel,* and its publication in five newspapers, at the choice of the appellant, should be ordered besides, if he requests it.

The expenses of publicity here provided for shall be borne by the Treasury.

Hungary—Code of Criminal Procedure, December 4, 1896, *Gesetzsammlung,* 1896, pp. 664, et seq. Indemnity in cases of unjust arrest, detention and punishment. Sections 576, et seq.

§ 576. He whom the court has legally acquitted of the charge against him or who has been discharged from prosecution, has a claim to indemnity when he has suffered arrest or detention for an act;

First, which he has not committed;

Second, which has not been committed at all;

Third, which he has indeed committed but which in the legal sense is not a punishable act.

§ 577. An indemnity for a temporary arrest or detention pending trial can not be claimed by a person who

First, has attempted to flee or has fled;

Second, has made a false confession or false avowal of the crime;

Third, to remove evidence of the deed, has sought to induce a witness or fellow accused to bear false witness or an expert to give a false opinion, or sought to suppress the testimony or opinion as the case may be.

§ 578. He who on the basis of a valid legal judgment has been deprived of his liberty or paid a money fine or from whom such fine has been exacted has a claim for indemnity;

First, when on rehearing of his case he is legally acquitted by a valid judgment;

Second, when on the rehearing or new trial a lesser penalty is prescribed against him than the one which he has already borne on the basis of the first judgment now declared invalid.

§ 579. An indemnity can not be demanded by one who

First, has made a false confession or a false avowal of the crime;

Second, who in the principal proceeding has intentionally suppressed the proofs upon which the court in the rehearing bases its judgment of acquittal;

Third, who in the proceedings establishing his guilt has not noted objections and appealed against the verdict;

Fourth, he who has voluntarily entered on his sentence as found in the lower court before that judgment has obtained legal force. (See § 505, paragraph 2; sec. 549, paragraph 1).

§ 580. Indemnity is made by the State.

The indemnity covers a commensurate monetary compensation embracing the sum which the convicted person has paid as money fine and as court costs, the value of the objects which had been confiscated from him on the basis of section 63 of law 5 of the year 1878, and the sums which he has earned during the period of his wrongful imprisonment. Moreover, the court order establishing indemnity is to be published in the *Official Gazette* and in the official paper of the district where the court sits, or in a newspaper within the immediate vicinity, at the expense of the funds of the court, and is to be publicly displayed by the local authorities of the jurisdiction of the court and of the domicil of the accused, at a place designated by them.

§ 581. The claim to indemnity is barred when the individual does not make known his claim within six months from the time of notice served on him of the decree discharging him from prosecution, or of the judgment of acquittal.

§ 582. Those who by law or legally recognized custom have the right to demand support from the accused having such claim to indemnity, may in case of his declining to sue make a claim set forth in § 580 for this purpose. They may, if the accused has brought his action within the period prescribed in § 581, request the continuance of the proceedings; if, however, the unjustly accused has died before the expiration of that period without bringing his action for indemnity, these persons may within six months from the day of his death request the institution of the proceedings.

§ 583. In cases where a valid judgment establishes that an individual who has suffered a death penalty would have been legally acquitted, those dependents who had a right to support from him may, if they are dependent upon this support, bring an action for pecuniary compensation for the support of which they have been deprived. With reference to the publication of the decree awarding indemnity the provisions of the last paragraph of § 580 are to be applied with the modification that the decree is to be publicly displayed by the local authorities of the last domicil of the accused, and, also, if requested by them, in the domicil of his relatives, if they reside at another place. In the case of this paragraph the period prescribed in § 581 is to be reckoned from the day on which the decree discharging him from prosecution, or of acquittal, comes into legal force.

§ 584. The action for indemnity is to be brought in the court before which the criminal proceedings were brought in first instance, or in the judicial circuit in which that court of first instance belongs.

§ 585. The proceedings for indemnity may be instituted verbally or in writing.

§ 586. The court must investigate the data necessary to establish the indemnity through official channels, and may demand evidence from both the wrongfully accused and from the public prosecutor.

The court may call witnesses and experts. Before the end of the investigation the wrongfully accused is to be informed that his remarks and motions must be handed in in writing within eight days.

§ 587. At the end of the investigation the court places its findings before the royal Kurie, or highest court, which, in case it decides that the claim for indemnity is justified, sends the papers to the Minister of Justice. On the basis of the findings of the royal Kurie, the Minister of Justice fixes the amount of the indemnity.

§ 588. To the extent of the amount of the indemnity the State has a subrogated right against all those whose actions or omissions have contributed to the facts making the indemnity payable.

Against the judge, court officials, or public prosecutor the State has a subrogated right only in case it is legally established that their actions or omissions which served to bring about the indemnity may be regarded as an official breach of duty or a punishable act. * * *

§ 589. He who by false complaint or false testimony, or a public officer who has wrongfully brought about the arrest, detention or conviction of another, owes full indemnity for all injuries to property which the convicted or detained person has suffered in so far as the claim for indemnity is established (§ 587), and the damage *exceeds* the sums awarded in accordance with § 580.

A person having a right to this indemnity may instead of the indemnity demand smart-money up to the amount of 2,000 kroners, which amount the court at its discretion may fix.

Germany—Law of May 20, 1898, Concerning Indemnity for Persons Acquitted on New Hearing or Retrial. *Reichsgesetzblatt*, p. 345.

§ 1. Persons who are acquitted on a new trial, or by the application of a milder penal law, have a lighter sentence imposed, may demand indemnity from the Treasury if the earlier penalty has been executed in whole or in part against them. The new trial must establish the innocence of the convicted person of the deed charged to him, or with respect to the circumstance justifying the application of a greater penalty, or it must show that a well-founded suspicion no longer exists against the accused.

Besides the convicted person those who are legally dependent upon him for support have a claim to the indemnity.

The claim to indemnity is not permissible when the convicted person has intentionally or by gross negligence provoked the earlier conviction. Failure to note an appeal is not to be considered as negligence.

§ 2. The substance of the indemnity due to the accused is the pecuniary damage suffered by execution of the sentence. Those entitled to support have the right to compensation to the extent that they were deprived of support during the execution of the sentence.

§ 3. The indemnity is to be paid from the Treasury of that State of the Empire before whose court the criminal proceeding took place in first instance. Up to the amount of the indemnity thus paid, the Treasury is subrogated to the rights which the accused had against third persons, because their unlawful transactions led to his conviction.

§ 4. With reference to the duty of the Treasury to award indemnity, the appellate court in which the new trial takes place issues a special decree.

The decree is to be drawn up by the court simultaneously with the judgment. It is not to be published, but it is to be served on the person. There is no appeal from the decree. It goes out of force if the judgment of acquittal is reversed.

§ 5. He who makes a claim on the basis of the decree awarding indemnity from the Treasury must bring his claim forward within three months after that decree has been served, by application to the public prosecutor. The application is to be handed to the superior court (*Landgericht*) in whose district the judgment was rendered. The highest administrative board of the State (*Landes-*

justizverwaltung) decides on the application. The decision duly drawn up is to be served on the claimant according to the provisions of the code of civil procedure.

Against the decision appeal through legal channels is permissible. The complaint is to be brought within a period of three months after service of the decision. For the claim to indemnity the civil chamber of the superior court (*Landgericht*) has exclusive jurisdiction without regard to the value of the matter in litigation. Until the final decision on the claimant's application the claim is not assignable or pledgable.

§ 6. For such matters as in first instance are within the jurisdiction of the Supreme Court, the Treasury of the Empire is chargeable with the indemnity instead of the State Treasuries. In these cases instead of the public prosecutor of the superior court, the public prosecutor of the Supreme Court is substituted, and in place of the highest authorities of the State administration, the Imperial Chancellor is substituted.

Germany—Law of July 14, 1904, concerning indemnity for unjust detention pending trial. *Reichsgesetzblatt,* page 321.

§ 1. Persons who are acquitted in criminal proceedings or who are discharged from prosecution by decree of the court, may demand indemnity from the State Treasury if the proceedings have shown their innocence or shown that no well-founded suspicion lies against them. Besides the arrested person those whom he has legally to support have a claim for indemnity.

§ 2. The claim to indemnity is not permissible if the arrested person has intentionally or by gross negligence caused his detention. The failure to note an appeal is not to be considered as negligence.

The claim may be rejected if the act of the accused subjected to examination involves an infamous or immoral act, or was committed during a state of drunkenness which excluded the exercise of free will, or when it appears from the circumstances that the accused had prepared to commit a felony or lesser crime.

The claim may also be rejected if the accused at the time of his arrest is not in possession of his civic rights, or was under police surveillance, or when on the basis of sections 181a and 362 of the penal code, he was placed within the last two years under the surveillance of the police authorities. The same is true if the accused has been punished by sentence to the penitentiary and since the expiration of the sentence three years have not yet elapsed.

§ 3. The substance of the indemnity paid the arrested person is the pecuniary damage suffered by his detention. If, before the issuance of the order of detention, an arraignment or preliminary arrest has taken place, the claim for indemnity will include the period of arrest preceding the issuance of the order of detention.

Those entitled to support are to receive indemnity to the extent that they were deprived of support by reason of the detention.

§ 4. On the duty of the Treasury to make compensation a special decree is drawn up by the court at the same time as it hands down the judgment of acquittal. If on appeal from the judgment acquittal is decided anew the appellate court must draw up a new decree on the indemnity.

The decree is not to be published, but is to be notified by personal service as soon as the decree of acquittal has secured legal force. It can not be appealed from. If the duty of the Treasury to make indemnity is recognized the decree is also to be notified to those entitled to support who are not in the household of the accused, in so far as their residence is known.

These provisions are equally applicable when the arrested person by order of the court is released from prosecution.

§ 5. The decree holding the State responsible for indemnity loses its force when a new trial is ordered to the disadvantage of the acquitted prisoner, or when the complaint in the principal action is reopened against the prisoner against whom prosecution had been discontinued. If the indemnity has already been paid it may be demanded back by the State.

§ 6. He who brings a claim on the basis of a decree holding the State liable to indemnity must prosecute his claim within six months after service of the decree, by application to the district attorney of the superior court within whose circuit the proceedings in first instance took place. The highest administrative board of the State decides on the application. Its findings regularly drawn up are to be served upon the claimant in accordance with the provisions of the code of civil procedure.

Appeal against such decision is permissible through the legal channels. The complaint is to be brought within three months of the service of the administrative decision. For these actions the civil chambers of the superior courts have exclusive jurisdiction regardless of the amount of the matter in litigation. Up to the time the administrative decision takes effect legally the claim is not assignable.

§ 7. The indemnity is paid out of the Treasury of the State of the Empire within whose court the criminal proceedings in first instance took place. Up to the amount of the indemnity paid, the Treasury is subrogated to the rights which the indemnified person had against third persons, because by their illegal acts they led to his detention.

§ 8. If a new trial decides against the acquitted person, or the complaint against a person against whom prosecution has been discontinued is again taken up, the decision of the administrative authorities, as well as the payment of indemnity may be suspended.

§ 9. In matters within the jurisdiction of the Supreme Court in first instance the Imperial Treasury is substituted for the State Treasury.

In this case in place of the public prosecutor of the superior court, the public prosecutor of the Supreme Court is substituted, and in place of the highest state administrative authorities the Imperial Chancellor is substituted.

§ 10. This law applies equally to persons acquitted in proceedings in military courts. * * *

§ 11. [It applies also to the consular courts].

§ 12. The provisions of this law are applied to the nationals of a foreign state only to the extent that by the legislation of their state or by treaty duly published in the *Reichsgesetzblatt* reciprocity is accorded.

Chapter 4

Convicting The Innocent
Sixty-Five Actual Errors Of Criminal Justice

By Edwin Montefiore Borchard
with the Collaboration of E. Russell Lutz[1]

Convicting The Innocent: Sixty-Five Actual Errors Of Criminal Justice was published in 1932 by the Garden City Publishing Company, Inc., Garden City, New York. The text and chapter headings are unchanged, but the pagination has been reformatted for a 6"x9" page size from the book's original 5-3/8"x8" page size. The original page breaks are marked with the succeeding original page number enclosed in brackets [ ]. For example, in the text where the original page number 27 begins, it is marked as [27]. Everything *after* that point was on page 27 in the 1932 edition, until the reader comes to [28], at which point page 28 began. All references to page numbers in the text and in the footnotes at the end of the book refer to the original page numbers that in the text are indicated in brackets [ ].

Convicting The Innocent's table of contents is organized so its first chapter begins as page one, so the book's page numbers are not continuous with the rest of this compilation.

---

[1] E. Russell Lutz performed much of the research for the book. See e.g., Alice M. Robertson Collection, "Lutz, E. Russell. to/from Alice Robertson. 1929. In reference to a criminal case of Charner Tidwell and similar cases," McFarlin Library Digital Collections, The University of Tulsa, http://www.lib.utulsa.edu/digital/robertson/Series_II/transcriptions/AR2_05_07_815.asp (last viewed July 15, 2013)

Convicting The Innocent

Sixty-Five Actual Errors Of Criminal Justice

By Edwin M. Borchard
Professor Of Law In Yale University

With the Collaboration of E. Russell Lutz
Research Assistant

Convicting The Innocent: Sixty-Five Actual Errors Of Criminal Justice

By Edwin Borchard
with the collaboration of E. Russell Lutz

The text and graphics in this edition were published in 1932 by: Garden City Publishing Company, Incl; Garden City, New York. The text and chaper headings are unchanged, but the pagination has been reformatted for a 6"x9" page size from the book's original 5-3/8"x8" page size. The original page breaks are marked with the succeeding original page number enclosed in brackets. For example, in the text where the original page number 27 begins, it is marked as [27]. Everything *after* that point was on page 27 in the Garden City 1932 edition, until the reader comes to [28], at which point page 28 began. All references to page numbers in the text and in the footnotes at the end of the book refer to the original page numbers that in the text are indicated in brackets [ ].

To

John H. Wigmore

And

Felix Frankfurter

PREFACE

ALTHOUGH my major interests lie in an aspect of the law somewhat remote from criminal law, I have nevertheless long urged that the State or community assume the risks of official wrongdoing and error instead of permitting the losses resulting from such fault or mistake to be borne by the injured individual alone. Among the most shocking of such injuries and most glaring of injustices are erroneous criminal convictions of innocent people. The State must necessarily prosecute persons legitimately suspected of crime; but when it is discovered after conviction that the wrong man was condemned, the least the State can do to right this essentially irreparable injury is to reimburse the innocent victim, by an appropriate indemnity, for the loss and damage suffered. European countries have long recognized that such indemnity is a public obligation. Federal and state governments in the United States ought to adopt the same policy, instead of merely releasing the innocent prisoner from custody by pardoning him for a crime he never committed and without any admission of error or public vindication of his character.

A district attorney in Worcester County, Massachusetts, a few years ago is reported to have said: "Innocent men are never convicted. Don't worry about it, it never happens in the world. It is a physical impossibility." The present collection of sixty-five cases, which have been selected from a much larger number, is a refutation of this supposition. Inasmuch as the conditions described are of interest primarily to the American public, American cases, mainly from the twentieth century, have, for the most part,[1] been chosen for publication. Fifty cases, by reason of their importance or some striking characteristic, have been used as principal cases; the other fifteen, more concisely reported, follow thereafter. Together, they present an interesting cross section of American life. They come from all sections of the country and, by states, may be grouped as follows: California, 8; New York, 8; Massachusetts, 7; Illinois, 4; Alabama, Minnesota, and Mississippi, 3 each; Georgia, Michigan, Missouri, New Jersey, Ohio, and West Virginia, 2 each; Arkansas, District of Columbia, Florida, Indiana, Iowa, Kentucky, Maine, Maryland, Oklahoma, Pennsylvania, Texas, Vermont, Virginia, and Wisconsin, 1 each; England, 3. Statistically they embrace the following charged crimes: murder, 29; robbery, swindling, or larceny, 23; forgery or counterfeiting, 5; criminal assault, 4; writing of obscene letters, 2; accepting a bribe, 1; and prostitution, 1.

---

[1] There are three English cases.

In the cases chosen for inclusion, the innocence was established in various ways: by the turning up alive of the alleged "murdered" person; by the subsequent conviction of the real culprit; by the discovery of new evidence demonstrating in a new trial or to the Governor or President, as the basis for a pardon, that the wrong man was convicted. There are, in practice, many cases in which pardons are granted without indication or admission of an erroneous conviction—although it seems fairly evident that the prisoner was actually innocent—presumably in order to save the prestige of prosecuting officials or for some other reason. Such cases could not be used for this collection.

The sixty-five cases, although susceptible of dramatic presentation, are set forth in simple narrative form to indicate how the error occurred and how it was later discovered and unraveled. The causes of the error are, in the main, mistaken identification, circumstantial evidence (from which erroneous inferences are drawn), or perjury, or some combination of these factors. Inasmuch as the cases reported constitute a representative group, I have ventured to draw from them certain conclusions indicating the necessity for reforms in criminal procedure. These I have endeavored to present in a concluding chapter, with reference to the cases reported. In that chapter I have undertaken a somewhat detailed analysis of the facts disclosed by the cases presented and suggested certain simple reforms in criminal procedure which might tend to mitigate if not prevent similar errors hereafter. In the original edition, published by the Yale University Press, there were included a technical analysis, as a basis for American legislation, of the statutes of European countries providing indemnity for wrongfully convicted and arrested persons, and a draft statute for use in the United States.

The cases were taken somewhat at random, for cases of this type are not systematically reported. The research was usually begun from a clue often afforded by a governor's pardon, by the report of a trial, or by a newspaper item, and was then pursued by an examination of the record and by correspondence or interview with the attorneys for the prosecution and defense and sometimes with the presiding judge, governor, or pardon board. An earnest effort has been made to present an accurate account of the facts; after each case in the original edition there will be found a bibliography of the principal sources employed and of the persons to whom special acknowledgments are due.

Aside from this indebtedness in particular cases, there are numerous individuals without whose generous aid this collection would not have been possible. First of all, I desire to express to Mr. E. Russell Lutz of Washington, D.C., my former student and collaborator, the deepest appreciation for his painstaking and indefatigable research in many of the principal cases reported. To Mr. Chalmers Hutchison of Fort Worth, Texas, a special debt has been incurred for his personal investigations in Massachusetts, New York, and other states. Mr. Robert Horton of Washington, D.C., was helpful in revising several of the narratives. Mr. George A. Benedict, Deputy Public Defender of Los Angeles, was extraordinarily considerate in furnishing detailed information in a number of California cases and in revising the drafts. Mr. Bert Wentworth, handwriting expert of Dover, New Hampshire, was generous in making available his file of newspaper clippings, which furnished a lead for several of the most striking cases in the book. Mr. James A. Finch, Pardon Attorney of the Department of Justice, was gracious in granting access, under departmental regulations, to the files of the Department in the Federal cases reported. Mr. Douglas Arant of the Alabama Bar was of exceptional assistance in securing information and facilitating contacts in the Alabama and Mississippi cases. Mrs. Mildred Maddox Lutz gave important aid on several cases. I cannot refrain, moreover, from expressing my immeasurable gratitude to the many district attorneys, police officials, defense attorneys, and other public-spirited citizens to whom acknowledgment is given in each individual case, and who, without any other thought than the service of truth and justice, gave so unstintingly of their time and effort in uncovering elusive facts. To the Institute of Human Relations, Yale University, special thanks are due for an appropriation which enabled the investigation to be completed; and to Messrs. Davidson, Donaldson, and Rollins of the Yale University Press, for valuable editorial advice.

Finally, a word of explanation of the dedication: Professor John H. Wigmore of Northwestern University first displayed his unremitting interest in this subject some twenty years ago by writing an introduction to an article, reprinted as Senate Document 974, Sixty-second Congress, third session, entitled, *State Indemnity for Errors of Criminal Justice*. To the persuasion of Professor Felix Frankfurter of Harvard University I owe my willingness to suspend my preoccupation with other interests and to devote the necessary time to the completion of this undertaking. Both Messrs. Wigmore and Frankfurter have distinguished themselves as American leaders in the reform of legal procedure and have made special contributions to the present subject.

E. M. B.

New Haven, Connecticut
January 1, 1932

Table of Contents

Seventeen Witnesses Identified Him

Herbert T. Andrews

IN the summer and fall of 1913 there was a flood of forged and bad checks in Boston, Massachusetts. These were turned over to the Police Department, and particularly to Inspector Conboy, but the efforts to apprehend the forger were unsuccessful.

Sometime in October, 1913, Inspector Conboy received from a Boston merchant a check for $30 which had been given him for a purchase by one Herbert T. Andrews. The check was signed in Andrews' own name. The merchant had received this check some weeks before but had not cashed it. When he did deposit it for payment, it was returned by his bank stamped "no account." The merchant thereupon turned the check over to the police. Inspector Conboy located Andrews on November 1, 1913.

Herbert T. Andrews was cashier for a large Boston store. He was well thought of by his employers as well as by his neighbors and many friends. He lived happily with his wife and baby on Hemenway Street, Boston. Just after he had returned home from his work on the first of November and was sitting down to his supper, there came a knock at the front door. It was Inspector Conboy and Special Officer Lyons with the message that Andrews was wanted at headquarters. Without permitting him to finish supper, the officers took Andrews to the Back Bay Station where Captain Good, after asking a few questions, sent him to police headquarters. Andrews' fingerprints and photograph were taken. The arrest of Andrews seemed like a lucky stroke, for this gave the police a genuine check irregularity to be compared with the numerous bad checks lately passed in the city. Andrews was officially charged with forging and uttering over forty checks. He was held for a hearing in the lower court, and was placed in the Tombs. The court decided that there was probable cause to hold him for indictment by the Grand Jury. The charge based upon the returned $30 check marked "no account," because of [2] which he was arrested, was dismissed by the court for the reason that it was shown that Andrews had $36 in the .bank at the time the check was drawn and for some time thereafter, but had later drawn three small checks which had closed out his balance.

In the short time between his arrest and his appearance in the lower court the Police Department had, however, obtained identifications of Andrews' photograph from the victims of a number of the forged and bad checks which had been turned over to them.

Following the session in the lower court, Inspector Conboy spoke to Andrews and asked him why he had not pleaded guilty to the charges of forging and uttering checks. Andrews replied that he was innocent, whereupon the inspector told him that witnesses had been found to prove his guilt. Later when Andrews' father was endeavoring to plead for his son, the inspector stated that he was absolutely sure of his man and that he had never made a mistake in forty years. Many of the victims absolutely identified Andrews' photograph as that of the person who had passed the checks, others thought that possibly he might be the man, and still others could not identify him at all. The Police Department then arranged for a "show up." They took Andrews to police headquarters and after standing him at one end of a room brought in a number of his alleged victims. Andrews later said that the police officers took down the testimony of those who identified him and disregarded that of those who said he was not the man. After this experience, Andrews was taken to the Charles Street Jail where arrangements were made by his father and wife for his release on bail.

The Grand Jury considered the evidence against Andrews and returned an indictment against him covering forty- three counts of forging and uttering bad checks. The trial was set for February 10, 1914. During the time Andrews was out on bail awaiting trial, further checks were passed in and around Boston of exactly the same character as those attributed to Andrews. When Andrews appeared for trial on February 10, 1914, two additional charges were brought against him and his bail was raised from $1,200 to $4,000. Andrews, unable [3] to raise this additional amount, had to return to jail and await trial, which was postponed from day to day until finally on February 23, 1914, he was tried for three days before Judge Chase of the Superior Court of Suffolk County. The state was represented by Thomas D. Lavelle, Assistant District Attorney of Suffolk County, and the prisoner, by Frank M. Zottoli, attorney at law of Boston, Massachusetts.

The defendant's family and his attorney had made strenuous efforts to prove that the alleged forgeries and utterances of checks had not been committed by Andrews. In the effort Andrews' resources and those of his father were exhausted, and they went into debt to friends. They hired the Burns Detective Agency with no success. Mr. Zottoli endeavored to enlist the services of an eminent handwriting expert, who proved unable to help, in view of his opinion that Andrews' admitted handwriting and that on the forged checks was very similar, and in view of the further fact, as later discovered, that a police inspector had informed the expert that he had witnesses who had seen Andrews write the very checks for which he was being tried.

Seventeen witnesses, men and women, took the stand and identified Andrews as the man who had passed the checks upon them. Many of them were positive in their identifications and there was little that the defendant could do but deny all knowledge of or connection with the checks, and deny that he had ever seen any of the witnesses who testified against him.

Andrews' attorney did his best to break down the various identifications but was unable to do so in the eyes of the jury, for they returned a verdict of guilty of uttering bad checks on seventeen counts. He was acquitted on all of the other counts, including all counts based on charges of forgery, because the state did not have sufficient evidence to establish that the checks had been written by Andrews. Andrews was found guilty on February 26, 1914, and on May 18, 1914, was sentenced to fourteen months in the House of Correction at Deer Island.

When Judge Chase sentenced Andrews in open court, Andrews again asserted his innocence, as he had done consistently since the day of his arrest. Attorney Zottoli asked [4] for a new trial, on the ground that a mistake in identity was apparent. He stated to the judge that a friend of his had seen one of the disputed checks and remarked that it was in handwriting similar to that of a forged check which had been passed on him at Salt Lake City. It was well known that Andrews had not been in Salt Lake City. Mr. Zottoli pointed out further that, while Andrews was awaiting trial and sentence, additional bad checks, similar to those upon which Andrews had been convicted, continued to be passed in Boston and the immediate vicinity. Judge Chase did not feel that he could disturb the verdict of the jury merely upon these statements by Andrews' attorney, but he indicated that if evidence were produced to substantiate these assertions he would gladly grant a new trial.

Bad checks, similar to those upon which Andrews had been convicted, continued to appear after his sentence and commitment to Deer Island. When these came to the attention of the Police Department it became quite evident that someone else was passing bad checks. Information obtained by the Detective Agency led to the belief that possibly these checks were passed by one Earle Barnes, formerly of Denver, Colorado. Captain Armstrong detailed Inspector Linton of the Boston Police Department to find Barnes. Through a careful search of hotel registers, Linton traced Barnes to Nantasket Beach. There he found that Barnes was posing as the son of a wealthy man and that he was spending money freely. He paid for purchases with checks, and several of them came back marked "no account." After careful investigation, Inspector Linton arrested Barnes and took him to headquarters, where he admitted that he had under a fictitious name drawn the several checks they held against him. When faced with additional bad checks going back over a period of months he admitted having passed them. The police officials seemed greatly surprised when he admitted his authorship of a number of the checks on which Andrews had been convicted. By comparing Barnes's handwriting with these checks it became apparent that he had been their author. Barnes's confession given on the day of his arrest, June 12, 1914, was reported to Captain Armstrong of the [5] Police Department, who immediately proceeded to the Superior Court to interview Judge Chase. Although Judge Chase was in the midst of a murder trial he took time to hear

Captain Armstrong's statement and ordered the production of Andrews in court as soon as possible. Assistant District Attorney Lavelle, who happened to be prosecuting the murder case, was advised of the facts. Defense Attorney Zottoli was called to court at once so that when Andrews arrived the principal parties to the trial were present. Barnes, by a coincidence, happened just then to be brought into court. Judge Chase heard the parties. Upon motion of Mr. Zottoli, a new trial was granted immediately. Prosecutor Lavelle promptly nol-prossed the indictment and Andrews was a free man. He was cleared entirely of having had any connection with any of the forged or bad checks upon which he had been indicted and tried.

On June 14, 1914, Earle Barnes was arraigned before the Superior Court and pleaded guilty to a number of charges involving the forging an4 uttering of checks. He requested a short sentence, on the ground that he had freely confessed to passing the checks on which Andrews had been convicted and had thus aided in righting the wrong done Andrews. Judge Chase admitted this, and sentenced Barnes to eighteen months in the House of Correction at Deer Island.

• • • •

WRITING about this case some ten years later, Prosecutor Lavelle observed, concerning the appearance of the two men in Judge Chase's court on June 12, 1914:

> As the two men stood at the bar I wondered how so many persons could have sworn that the innocent man was the one that had cashed the bad checks. The two men were as dissimilar in appearance as could be. There was several inches difference in height and there wasn't a similarity about them. To this day I can't understand the positiveness of those witnesses. I know that they felt they were swearing to the truth. I know that the police felt that the man was guilty. So this was a case 'where "seeing was not believing," as the reverse of the old adage goes.

• • • •

THIS is a clear case of mistaken identity. It would seem, however, that a little care on the part of the police could [6] have avoided the tragic error committed. An identification by photographs is rarely conclusive. It seems not unsafe to infer that the police were instrumental in persuading the seventeen witnesses to identify Andrews. When bogus checks began to appear after his arrest and during his detention for trial and sentence, it must have been apparent that another check passer was at large. It is not usually too difficult for the police to find a congenital passer of checks, especially when he operates in the same neighborhood for a time. He leaves visible traces. The record discloses no serious effort to unravel the problem created by the new checks until after Andrews' conviction, and not until then does the appearance of the new checks seem to have weakened the confidence of the police in the guilt of Andrews. Under the circumstances this appears like gross negligence. The case exemplifies the zealousness of the police for convictions. Though it was apparent that Andrews was not of criminal type and had never been arrested before, he was treated on the theory that he must be guilty. Andrews later described vividly the horrors of the several jails in which he was lodged and the awful criminals and degenerates with whom he was herded. From the first, he, like other accused persons, was treated like a guilty man. For the suffering to which he and his family were exposed, not to speak of the expense incurred in trying to prove himself innocent, no attempt was ever made to compensate him. It must be recorded that when it became patently obvious that the police had gotten the wrong man, Captain Armstrong and the prosecution moved quickly to undo their error. The case of Andrews resembles that of Greenwald (p. 79). Whereas in the Greenwald case six victims identified the wrong man, in the Andrews case, there were seventeen quite a commentary upon the reliability of identifications, especially in a case where the resemblance proved to be most remote, if not indeed nonexistent. Andrews paid a heavy price for the petty oversight of over-drawing his bank balance. Perhaps this is the moral of the case, if there is any.

• • • •

Acknowledgments: Mr. Frank M. Zottoli, attorney at law, Boston, Mass.; Mr. Bert Wentworth, Dover, N.H. [7]

Denied A Defense

Adolf Beck

THE peculiar chain of circumstances and coincidences which led to the distressing misfortunes of Adolf Beck began in 1877 with the conviction of one John Smith on a charge of larceny.

Smith was found guilty of defrauding several women of jewelry by posing as an English nobleman to gain their confidence. His method of operation is described in the testimony of one of Smith's many victims, Evelyn Emily Miller, as follows:

> ". . . About 5 p.m. on 28th January, 1895, I was in Bond Street, when the prisoner said, "Did I not meet you at a ball last night?" I said he might have done so, but that I did not remember him. He said he was sure he had met me, and that he would be delighted if I would allow him to lunch with me at my house next day. I said he might. He said he was not quite sure whether it would be the next day or the day after, but that he would send me a telegram in the evening, signed "Wilton, Carlton Club." I gave him my address and we separated. The same evening I had a telegram signed "Wilton, Carlton Club," stating that he would be with me at two tomorrow. He came at two next day, and had lunch with me. He said he had a house in St. John's Wood, and the lady who had been acting as housekeeper had just left. I asked who he was and he said he was the Earl of Wilton. I said I would consider whether I would go to his house in St. John's Wood. He offered me the position; he said he would come a day or two after and arrange details; that after the sitting of Parliament he was going on a trip to Italy and would like me to go with him, and that I would want a new outfit. He asked for a piece of paper, in order to give me a list of dresses. I gave him the paper and he wrote out a list, which has been destroyed. . . . The tailor-made dresses I was to get from Redfern, and the other gowns from Russell & Allen. He said I should have to pay something on account, and he would give me a check. He took a checkbook, in which there were not many checks, from his pocket, and filled up this check for £30. . . .
>
> He said also that he would give me some jewelry, and asked me to let him have one of my rings to get the size of my finger. I asked him to take the size in cardboard. He said he preferred having the ring. I was wearing some rings, but I did not care to part with them, so I borrowed a diamond horseshoe ring worth £7 or £10 which I gave him. He was with me about one and a quarter hours. Before he left he said he had a pensioned-off coachman who lived [8] near me, and he wanted to take him some money, and he had not any change. Could I lend him £2. I believed about the pensioned coachman,

and I lent him £2. He said I could deduct it out of the £30 check. He said a commissionaire would bring the ring back that evening. The ring did not come. . . ."

Smith, of course, never returned after such a visit. He went on to his next victim. The police began to receive more and more complaints about him from various women, but he could not be found. Finally, however, one of his victims recognized him on the street and succeeded in bringing about his arrest. He was indicted, tried, convicted, and sentenced to five years' penal servitude.

• • • •

ADOLF BECK was what would be described today as a promoter, principally of questionable mining properties. Never with a large amount of money in his possession for any length of time, his creditors suffered, and his character, as painted by witnesses at his trials, was not entirely enviable. This circumstance in itself apparently carried considerable weight with the jury.

Beck was born in Norway in 1841. He was fifty-four when arrested by the London police December 16, 1895. This was fourteen years after Smith had been released from prison upon the expiration of his sentence. Smith had passed from the interest of the police and his whereabouts in 1895 were unknown to them.

On this mid-December afternoon Ottilie Meissonier, a woman who had been defrauded of several rings and two watches, met Beck on the street and accused him of robbing her. He protested, but she was insistent and dogged his footsteps until she found a policeman to arrest him.

After the woman told her story at the police station, Beck was held in custody until a number of women—ten or eleven—called at the station house and identified Beck as the man who had robbed them after telling the same story about St. John's Wood, the housekeeper, the new clothes, and the jewelry.

A man who read about the case in the paper and recalled the Smith case nineteen years before, informed the police [9] that he believed Beck was the ex-convict Smith. An ex-police constable, Spurrell, who arrested Smith in 1877 was brought out of retirement and identified Beck as Smith, and this identification was confirmed by another officer who had worked on the Smith case.

Beck's indictment was the result. He was brought to trial at Old Bailey in March, 1896. He was tried for misdemeanor only, though there were also four felony indictments on file against him in which it was charged that he had been convicted in 1877 under the name of Smith. These indictments were postponed until next session and were subsequently dismissed when a *nolle prosequi* was entered after conviction on the misdemeanor charge.

The Crown's case rested on the testimony of ten women who claimed to have been victims of Beck's guile. Each told substantially the same story as that related by Evelyn Emily Miller, and each identified Beck as the criminal. The defense, of course, relied upon mistaken identity, but in the face of the confident and numerous witnesses called by the Crown the jury could hardly do otherwise than find Beck guilty. He was immediately sentenced to seven years' penal servitude.

• • • •

THE special Parliamentary Committee of Inquiry which later examined the case in detail pointed out that Beck "was convicted on evidence from which everything that told, or might be thought to tell, in his favor was excluded. His case was never tried."

This forthright criticism related to the refusal of the court to admit as evidence any testimony which the defense wished to offer establishing (1) that documents offered in evidence as having been in Beck's handwriting were actually in the same hand as those attributed to Smith in 1877, and (2) that Beck was in South America in 1877 and for several years thereafter.

The defense expected to show upon cross-examination of the Crown's handwriting expert that the calligraphy was the same in both sets of documents. This would mean that Smith was the perpetrator of the latest frauds, thus proving [10] that the witnesses and police were wrong in identifying Beck.

This cross-examination was about to begin when its tenor was noted by the prosecution and an objection raised and upheld by the court. The Common Serjeant (judge) ruled that evidence on the question whether the defendant was or was not the man convicted in 1877 was not admissible on the ground that it related to another and distinct issue and one calculated to mislead the jury.

The Committee of Inquiry was inclined to admit that perhaps the court was right in asserting the principle but that

> the statutory inhibition debarring the prosecution in certain cases from referring to a previous conviction does not debar the prisoner from introducing it, if it is in any way material to his defense. . . . But there is a broader principle underlying the whole question, namely, that evidence adduced by the prisoner relevant to his defense cannot be excluded, although it be relevant also to a collateral issue which is not under trial. . . . There can be no doubt whatever that in this case it was relevant to the main issue. It was the first step in a train of reasoning leading to the conclusion that Mr. Beck was not the man. Two crimes were committed by one and the same man. Mr. Beck could not have committed the first. Therefore he did not commit the second.

The court, ignoring this principle, undermined the foundation of the defense in an instant, so that nothing was left except the bare assertion that Beck was not the criminal. His counsel was denied the opportunity to establish this as a fact.

Immediately after conviction, Beck petitioned the Home Office for relief, saying he had been identified by mistake. This petition and several subsequently presented were all denied until in May, 1898, his counsel demanded that the case be reopened. For the first time the Home Office responded somewhat favorably, and a most remarkable bit of hitherto undisclosed evidence was brought to light.

It was found that Smith was examined by a doctor at Portland prison in 1879, while serving his sentence, and that this physician in his written report on Smith's condition stated that Smith had undergone circumcision. Beck was [11] examined immediately and was found not to have been circumcised.

This seemed to the defense convincing evidence of Beck's innocence, but the Home Office refused to do more than allot Beck a new prison number. He had been given Smith's old number when he entered prison and it carried the sign of a second offender. The new number indicated a first offender. This technical maneuvering had no practical effect upon Beck's plight.

Beck completed his sentence and was released in July, 1901. Three years later, July, 1904, he was again arrested. Again he faced charges similar to those upon which he had been convicted in 1896, but this time he had been trapped by the police.

A woman named Pauline Scott had been swindled by a man of apparently aristocratic circumstances, and the old story was repeated—the house in St. John's Wood, the housekeeper, the new clothes, and the jewelry. After telling the police her story, which corresponded in detail with the complaints of other women recently victimized, she was taken to a spot on Store Street, Tottenham Court Road, near Beck's new lodgings.

She and the police who accompanied her waited. Presently Beck appeared. He wore a silk hat and was dressed accordingly, resplendent from tip to toe. Pauline Scott identified him at once. Once more came the procession of women, each confident that here was the man—the mannerly gentleman who stole from them with unabashed deceit. Indictment followed. Then the same kind of trial. Indeed, the two were practically identical in all respects save one. This time the court had certain misgivings as to the guilt of the defendant and sentence was reserved until further inquiry into the case could be made. And here, Beck's luck began to turn.

Early in July two actresses—Violet and Beulah Turner—had been swindled and there was much in the newspapers about the operations of the thief.

On the afternoon of July 7, a pawnbroker named Lawley sent a clerk to call a policeman. Said the clerk to the officer: "There's a man pawning some rings in my master's shop [12] and Mr. Lawley would like to have you come and look him over. There's been a lot in the newspapers about ladies' rings of late, you know."

The well-dressed man in the pawnshop failed to satisfy the policeman with his answers to various questions concerning the rings he sought to dispose of and he was taken to the police station for further questioning.

He said his name was William Thomas and that he was innocent of any wrongdoing. The suspicions of the officers were aroused, however, and several of the women who had lost their jewelry were called to view the prisoner. They not only identified him but the rings in his possession were likewise claimed. On the basis of this evidence he was indicted, tried, and found guilty.

Then he confessed. He admitted that he was John Smith and that he was responsible for the frauds for which Beck had been twice convicted.

Beck was pardoned of both convictions July 27, and later was granted by Parliament £5,000 for his wrongful imprisonment. This he soon spent, and in February, 1906, he was sued for £220 due his late solicitor's trustee in bankruptcy. He told the court, "I have no money, my lord." In December, 1909, he was in poverty and was admitted to Middlesex Hospital suffering from pleurisy and bronchitis. There he died December 7.

• • • •

THE flagrant mistake made by the police, the court, and the Home Office in Beck's case had the important result of inducing Parliament to establish the Court of Criminal Appeal, which has power to review the facts as well as the law in cases of indictable offenses. This much-needed opportunity for review of the facts should be afforded in felony cases in all the states, but thus far only a few have established it, and then only in capital cases.

Parliament granted the indemnity, because the inquiry had established gross negligence in the administration of justice. The case aroused indignation, for closer attention to the factors indicating Beck's innocence would have [13] disclosed the truth. Beck did resemble Smith somewhat and that doubtless led the victims of the swindler to identify him. But without the help of a complacent if not negligent police and a mistaken judge they could not have accomplished his conviction and imprisonment. At least Parliament did what it could to right the wrong by a substantial indemnity, which could not be compensatory of the injury done but at least restored Beck to good standing with a chance to start anew. [14]

A Corpse Answers An Advertisement

The Boorn Brothers

THE Boorn children did not conduct themselves with the requisite sobriety and dignity to satisfy the standard of propriety firmly established and adhered to in 1812 Manchester, Vermont. They were three—Jesse, Stephen, and Sally—and to the austere Yankee folk of Manchester they were a little wild and somewhat reckless.

Sally married Russel Colvin, and from all accounts it seems that Russel was not distinguished for his intellectual accomplishments; in fact it was said in some quarters that he was slightly feeble-minded. It was generally agreed that he was eccentric, and in this respect he was noted particularly for his habit of suddenly disappearing, to be gone as much as eight or nine months at a time. On several of these periodic excursions he took his favorite infant son, carrying the child on his back.

So when Russel disappeared in May, 1812, no one thought it strange, and practically no one was interested in his peregrinations. Sally was away on a visit when her husband disappeared. When she came home she asked her father and brothers where he had gone. No one could give a satisfactory answer.

It seems that there had been a serious quarrel in the family immediately before Russel disappeared. Lewis, one of Russel's children, had been present and said later that his Uncle Stephen had threatened to kill him if he should mention the quarrel.

Knowledge of the disagreement came through the statements of Thomas Johnson, who had bought the old Boorn place before Russel disappeared. Johnson said that he had been crossing a field the day Russel vanished and saw Jesse, Stephen, Russel, and young Lewis, Russel's son, engaged in a heated quarrel. Johnson did not interfere, he said, but went on; and when he returned later the group was still there, but their tempers seemed to have subsided somewhat. That was the last Johnson saw of Russel.

It was known, before this argument, that ill feeling [15] existed between the Boorn boys and Colvin. But no one ever took it seriously, and a possible connection between this enmity and Russel's disappearance was not suspected. As weeks passed, however, and one aspect after another of the case provided material for town gossip, the villagers began to entertain pointed suspicions. -People began to recall certain peculiar remarks they had heard the Boorn boys, or members of the family, make from time to time concerning the missing Colvin. Someone said he had heard one of the boys say that Colvin was dead; another reported that one of the boys stated that they "had put him where potatoes would not freeze." So the suspicious began to look warily upon Jesse and Stephen.

Finally, Thomas Johnson's children came home one afternoon with an old dilapidated hat they found in the field near the Boorn place. Johnson recognized it as the hat he had seen on Colvin the day of the argument in the field.

Time was passing. Almost seven years had now elapsed since Colvin had disappeared.

In the spring of 1819 occurred one of the most remarkable incidents in the strange case. Amos Boorn had a dream. Uncle Amos was an old man. He seems to have followed the case with interest, and it had, of course, made a great impression upon his mind. In the dream, Russel Colvin appeared at Uncle Amos' bedside. He told the old man that he had been murdered and said that if Uncle Amos followed him he would show him where he had been buried. The tomb was described as an old cellar hole, about four feet square, over which a house had stood. Three times the dream was repeated, and Uncle Amos described the visions as they had taken place. Here, then, said the superstitious, was proof incontrovertible that Colvin had been slain. The more practical may have been impressed, but they were not convinced until another coincidence brought them confidently into the camp of the superstitious, certain that murder had been done.

Fire destroyed an old barn on the Boorn place. The embers were hardly cold before it was gossiped that perhaps the barn had been burned to conceal evidence of Colvin's [16] murder. Then came the third and final incident in the remarkable chain that was growing tighter and tighter about Jesse and Stephen.

A lad and his dog were walking near the Boorn place one day, when the dog stopped and began digging furiously into the earth under an old stump. Bones were unearthed and summarily pronounced human. The patience of the community snapped and action was demanded. Truman Hill, grand juror of Manchester, responded. On April 27, 1819, nearly seven years after Colvin disappeared, Jesse Boorn was arrested and brought before the Justice of the Peace for examination.

The examination lasted from Tuesday until Saturday. During this time the community was searched for evidence. The old cellar hole of which Uncle Amos dreamed was opened and disclosed a large knife, a penknife, and a button. The button was of peculiar style, with a flower design in the center. This and the penknife were identified as Colvin's. No one knew who owned the big knife. The bones from beneath the stump, when compared with an amputated leg imported from a nearby community, were found not to be human bones. This decision threatened to end the investigation, and it would probably have been dropped but for the fact that on Saturday, Jesse

Boorn charged his brother, Stephen, with the murder. Jesse then repeated what he said was the story Stephen had told him.

It was to the effect that Stephen and Russel were working in the "Glazier lot" and got into a quarrel. Stephen struck Colvin with a club and fractured his skull. Jesse said he did not know what had been done with the body, but he mentioned several places where it might possibly be found.

The next day Sunday people turned out for miles around in great excitement to search for Colvin's remains. Cellar holes were opened up, stumps overturned, and the hillsides scrutinized carefully. Nothing was found.

On Monday a warrant was issued for Stephen's arrest. He had gone to New York some time before this, and Grand Juror Hill, with Samuel Raymond, started for New York to arrest him. He was located easily, and on the way back [17] his captors urged him to confess. He was told that the evidence was strong enough to bring conviction, but he continued to protest his innocence. The examination was continued on May 15, when the three got back from New York. Stephen and Jesse were brought face to face, and still Stephen denied that he was guilty.

In jail with the brothers was one Silas Merrill, a forger. When the Grand Jury met in September, Merrill was presented as the chief witness against the suspects. Merrill told a colorful story. He said Jesse had confessed to him in jail that Stephen and Colvin had had a fight; that Stephen struck Colvin but the blow did not kill him; that later Jesse and Stephen, assisted by their father, Barney Boorn, carried Colvin, who was still unconscious, to the old cellar, where Barney Boorn cut his throat, after which he was buried there. Merrill said Jesse told him that about eighteen months later he and his brother dug up the remains and took the bones to the old barn which had burned. After the barn was destroyed, some of the bones were again gathered up, pounded into dust, and thrown into the river. Others had been picked up by Barney Boorn and hidden in a hollow stump.

Needless to say the jury was impressed by this gruesome recital. And it did not suffer from attempts of the defense to break it down by showing that Merrill had been promised leniency if he would tell it in court. (After telling the story he was allowed freedom to roam about the town.)

The defense also pointed out that this so-called confession did not corroborate the one made by Jesse after he had been arrested in May.

Still another "confession" was to be made before the case was settled. Before the trial started in November, the town was once more thrown into a furor when it was learned that Stephen admitted his guilt and blamed Colvin for initiating the fatal quarrel. Stephen did not implicate his father or Jesse. He told of the fight with Colvin and how he was killed. He said he hid the body under some bushes in a fence corner and returned after dark to bury the corpse, not in the cellar, but near it. He told how he later removed the bones to the [18] old barn, and how, after the barn burned down, he threw some of them into the river and put others in the old stump. He did not, however, mention powdering them.

The trial was held in the Congregational Church, as the court room was too small to accommodate the great number of people who wanted to attend the proceedings. The full bench of the Supreme Court sat as then required in capital cases.

The court heard most of the story told in the preceding pages, and Stephen's confession was introduced to discredit Merrill's story.

Despite the ability of the defense attorneys Richard Skinner, former Justice of the Supreme Court; Leonard Sargeant, afterward Lieutenant-Governor; and Mr. Wellman the jury returned a verdict of guilty and the Boorn brothers were sentenced to hang on January 28, 1820.

• • • •

AFTER a petition for pardon had been submitted to the Legislature, Jesse's sentence was commuted to life imprisonment. Stephen's plea was denied. It seemed that nothing could be done to save him.

But he was to save himself. In a conversation with Mr. Sargeant one day, he suggested that an advertisement be published in an attempt to locate Colvin. Mr. Sargeant told him that this would do no good if Colvin had been murdered. Stephen protested his innocence and Mr. Sargeant promised to advertise.

A complete description of Colvin was published in the Rutland *Herald*. The article stated that if Colvin could be located, the lives of innocent men could be saved. The article was republished in the New York *Evening Post* of November 29, 1819, and started a series of events as strange as those which had led to the convictions.

The day after the article appeared in the *Post*, it was read aloud in a New York hotel. James Whelpley, a former resident of Manchester, was present. He knew Colvin and told a number of anecdotes about him. Mr. Tabor Chadwick of Shrewsbury, New Jersey, happened to be standing [19] near by, and the story made a deep impression upon him. It finally occurred to him that a man answering Colvin's description was living with his brother-in-law, William Polhemus, in Dover, New Jersey. Mr. Chadwick wrote the *Post*, saying that the man who lived with his brother-in-law appeared to have once been a resident of Vermont, for he occasionally spoke of Manchester, mentioned the names Boorn, Jesse, etc., and seemed to have considerable knowledge of the town and its people. Mr. Whelpley saw Mr. Chadwick's letter in the *Post* and decided to go to Dover and investigate.

Mr. Polhemus was informed of the mission, and it was agreed that nothing should be said to Colvin until Mr. Whelpley decided whether he recognized him. When Colvin came in from work he looked sharply at Whelpley, but said nothing. Presently Whelpley called him by name. Colvin said there must be some mistake; that Colvin had been his name once, but that he was another man now. By gradually drawing him out, Whelpley became convinced that there was no doubt as to his identity.

Colvin would not consent to go home, however, and only after considerable persuasion would he return to New York with Whelpley. By a ruse Whelpley got him onto a boat bound for Troy. As Troy was not far from Manchester, Colvin finally agreed to return to his old home.

The arrival of Whelpley and Colvin in Manchester was a festive occasion. After Colvin had been greeted by his former friends and neighbors, he and Stephen were brought face to face. Seeing the fetters on his brother-in-law, Colvin asked, "What is that for?"

"Because they say I murdered you," Stephen replied.

"You never hurt me," said Colvin. "Jesse struck me with a briar once, but it did not hurt me much."

When Sally was brought to him, Colvin said merely, "That is all over with," and would have no more to do with her.

To set the brothers free by due process of law, the case was reopened, they were allowed to plead again, and the [20] state's attorney entered a *nolle prosequi*. In 1820 they petitioned the Legislature for compensation and were refused.

• • • •

THE Boorn case is included in this collection because it is a classic in American jurisprudence. It was probably not an appropriate case for state indemnity, because the conviction of the two brothers was to some extent brought about by their spurious confessions. What prompted them to do this—except possibly the hope of escaping execution—is hard to say. Possibly seven years under suspicion and accusation had so preyed upon their minds that they were no longer fully accountable for their thoughts or acts.

Essentially the conviction was induced by public superstition and excitability. Colvin's long disappearance, associated with the quarrel with the Boorn boys, and general knowledge that the relations between Colvin and the Boorns were not friendly, served to arouse the credulity of the community and to break down what should have been a normal skepticism induced by Colvin's previous manifestations of *Wanderlust*. The dream of Amos Boorn served to give exceptional weight to the finding of the bones. When they were proved to be not human, one might have supposed that the suspicion would die. Then Jesse Boorn revived the suspicion by his extraordinary statement that Stephen had confessed murdering Colvin. All the irrelevancies of rumor and fancy were then revived to connect the Boorns with the case; and doubtless to escape execution, Stephen made his confession, though his statements to Jesse differed materially from it, and both contained improbabilities which should have put any court or jury on guard. It seems curious that a state which was willing to spend considerable sums to try to convict a person for an alleged crime committed years before and which at best was an unsolved mystery, should not have been concerned with the expedient of spending a part of the money to advertise for the missing man. Only the imminent fear of the gallows seems to have stimulated Stephen to think of that measure. Even this simple device, which finally unraveled the mystery, would have failed [21] but for the curious concatenation of circumstances which brought about the reading of the advertisement in a public hotel at which was present a man who had known Colvin, and another who knew where he was employed. The links in the chain which disclosed the truth were as accidental and fortuitous as those which led to the mistaken conviction. [22]

THEY FORGOT TO FINGERPRINT HIM

Payne Boyd

ONE traveling through the southern part of West Virginia on a summer's day will always remember it as a land of contrasts—beautiful rolling hills, the homeland of the "mountaineers," dotted with squalid, colorless mining communities, swarming with laborers who spend most of their time underground picking coal for shipment to the industrial centers of Pennsylvania and Ohio.

In May, 1918, there lived in Modoc, Mercer County, West Virginia, a certain negro miner named Cleveland Boyd. He had been one of the small group of negroes to invade this mining district, which was manned principally by Italian workmen. Boyd had proved himself to be rather a quarrelsome fellow, though he was popular among the negroes. He had won and married Charlie Boston's daughter—a mark of distinction.

When Cleveland Boyd was haled before Squire H. E. Cook on Christmas Eve, 1917, and sentenced for participation in a drunken brawl, he boldly threatened that he would get even with the Squire. On May 30, 1918, he was again arrested by the sheriff—this time on vagrancy complaints. Squire Cook sentenced Boyd to thirty days' imprisonment (or road work) and fined him $25. As the Squire and the deputy sheriff, A. M. Godfrey, were preparing to take the prisoner to the jail at Matoaka, Boyd made a special plea that he be permitted to go to his home, about a hundred yards up the tracks (the trial was held in the offices of the coal company), to exchange the new shoes he was wearing for older and more comfortable ones. The request was granted. The Squire, deputy sheriff, and prisoner went to Boyd's shack. Boyd entered while the Squire stood on the porch and the deputy sheriff out front. In a flash Boyd reappeared in the doorway firing a revolver. The Squire crumpled, mortally wounded by two shots in the chest, and the deputy sheriff ran for his life.

The shooting attracted attention, but before aid arrived, Cleveland Boyd had fled to the hills. [23]

Squire Cook belonged to one of the oldest and best families of Mercer County, and there was widespread indignation at this cold-blooded murder. The murderer was well known by numerous citizens. A description was prepared and broadcast so that police authorities might be on the lookout.

Six years later, in the spring of 1924, the police of Richmond, Virginia, arrested a negro on an inconsequential minor offense. He gave his name as Payne Boyd of Winston-Salem, North Carolina. As usual, records of persons wanted were checked, and to the surprise of the police, this prisoner fitted the description of Cleveland Boyd which they had received from Mercer County six years before. The Richmond police mailed a photograph of their man to Princeton (Mercer County seat), and the authorities came to identify him. Boyd was lined up in the Richmond jail with other negroes and was promptly identified. Thereupon he was surrendered to the officials of Mercer County and taken to Princeton, where he was lodged in jail on May 2, 1924. The unsolved murder of 1918 was revived as the principal talk of the county. On Sundays and holidays hundreds of people visited the Princeton jail to see the prisoner. Some said that he was positively Cleveland Boyd. Others were absolutely certain that he was not. Many could not be sure, after the lapse of six years. The prisoner always denied that he was Cleveland Boyd, and that he had ever been in Mercer County before. Nevertheless, upon the positive identification of some prominent local citizens, he was indicted for the murder of Squire Cook.

He was brought to trial on February 5-8, 1925, before Judge George L. Dillard in the Criminal Court of Mercer County. Walter V. Ross, the prosecuting attorney, was assisted by special counsel, H. G. Woods, and by A. J. Lubliner, assistant prosecuting attorney. John Kee and C. B. Martin represented the defendant. A verdict of guilty of first-degree murder was returned, but the court set the verdict aside on technical grounds and ordered a new trial. The second trial was held from April 29 to May 2, 1925. A verdict of guilty was again returned and sentence of life imprisonment was pronounced. [24]

In both of these trials the facts concerning the murder committed by Cleveland Boyd were conceded by all. The only issue was whether the prisoner before the court was Cleveland Boyd. Of the twenty-six witnesses introduced by the state, twenty-four testified on matters of identity and swore that they had known Cleveland Boyd in 1917. Eight of these twenty-four persons were positive in their identification of the prisoner—two of them testifying that Cleveland had a scar over his left eye (a remnant of which could be found on the prisoner), and three testifying that Cleveland had a scar under his left jaw (as did the prisoner) resulting from a mule kick while working in the mine. Four of the twenty-four identification witnesses of the state believed that the prisoner was Cleveland Boyd, while the remaining twelve testified that he looked the same, but they were not sure enough of it to swear that he was Cleveland Boyd. The state's witnesses were public officials, mining company supervisors, and some men who had worked with Cleveland Boyd.

The defense called thirty-nine witnesses, thirty-one of whom had known Cleveland Boyd and testified with absolute conviction that the prisoner was not he. Many of the defense witnesses were negroes, admittedly intimate with Cleveland Boyd before he left the community, such as his father-in- law, the minister who married him, persons present at the wedding, neighbors, fellow workmen, etc. They testified as to the points of dissimilarity between the two, as to height, weight, complexion, hair, lips, feet.

The defense, by six additional witnesses from Roanoke and Winston-Salem, and the defendant himself, endeavored to prove that he was Payne Boyd, born and reared in Winston-Salem, and that he had lived in these two cities only. The scar on the prisoner's neck was said to be the result of a childhood attack of scrofula; and the defendant himself testified that the scar over his eye came from a wound received in a stone quarry while with the American army in France. The prisoner was said to have lived in Roanoke and Winston-Salem during the spring of 1918 and up to the date of his enlistment in the army, July 15, 1918. Certified [25] copies of Payne Boyd's draft registration card, draft questionnaire filled out in Roanoke before the date of the murder (May 30, 1918), and honorable discharge certificate dated July 16, 1919, were submitted in support of this alibi. The defendant, on the witness stand, denied that he had ever been in Mercer County before and that he had ever been in a coal mine. He had never seen any of the fifty-five witnesses at the trial who had known Cleveland Boyd but who differed about him.

With this evidence before the court it seemed evident that there was a person, Payne Boyd, separate and distinct from the murderer Cleveland Boyd. The jury had to decide, however:

1. Whether the prisoner was Cleveland Boyd
   (a) and that he really had no connection whatever with Payne Boyd, but was only endeavoring to use the latter's records, or
   (b) that he might have been Payne Boyd before coming into Mercer County in 1916, and returned to Winston-Salem to use that name for enlistment in the army on July 15, 1918, after committing the murder on May 30, 1918, and using some other Payne Boyd records for events prior to May 30, 1918.

or

2. Whether the prisoner was Payne Boyd, and had no connection with Cleveland Boyd and the murder of Squire Cook.

As related above, the prisoner was found guilty at both trials, and after the second trial, Judge Dillard imposed a sentence of life imprisonment. An appellate court set the verdict aside, and, upon motion, a change of venue was granted. The next trial was ordered for Cabell County. It was held in October, 1925, in Huntington, before Judge Thomas R. Shepherd. Prosecutor Via of Cabell County joined with Prosecutor Ross of Mercer County in submitting the case.

At about this time Garfield Rose, fingerprint expert of [26] the Huntington Police Department, became interested in the case. He took the fingerprints of the prisoner. These were compared with the prints of Payne

Boyd on record in the War Department in Washington, and found to be exactly the same. Thus, it was established to the satisfaction of all that the prisoner was Payne Boyd of Winston-Salem and Roanoke, with a war record just as he had always claimed. Other new data were also received corroborating Payne Boyd's story that he had no connection whatever with Cleveland Boyd. This evidence was all submitted to the Cabell County jury, which returned the following verdict on October 13, 1925: "We, the jury, being convinced that the
prisoner at the bar is Payne Boyd and not Cleveland Boyd, find him not guilty. ..."

Payne Boyd was released immediately, having spent a year and a half in custody and gone through three trials because to some people he looked like Cleveland Boyd.

• • • •

IT may seem difficult to explain why any jury should have convicted Payne Boyd when, of the fifty-five witnesses produced, only eight were positive that he was Cleveland Boyd. Thirty-one were positive that he was not Cleveland Boyd, twelve said he looked like Cleveland Boyd but they would not swear, and four merely believed that he looked like Cleveland Boyd but entertained doubt. The explanation probably lies in the fact, not unusual in similar cases, that a murder having admittedly been committed it seemed necessary to avenge it, and the prisoner presented a sufficiently close resemblance to the criminal to warrant the jury in resolving any doubt against him. The fact that a change of venue was granted might indicate that the appellate court considered that local prejudice was operating against the accused. Just why the fingerprint method of identification was postponed until the third trial is not easy to understand, for it was available to both sides from the beginning. At least his war service helped Payne Boyd to establish his identity beyond challenge, and with the verification of his other assertions that he had always been in Roanoke and [27] Winston-Salem, especially in May, 1918, when the murder was committed, it became apparent that he could not have been the guilty Cleveland Boyd. It took one and one-half years to establish that fact to the satisfaction of the judicial authorities of West Virginia, during which time an innocent man was incarcerated. Payne Boyd appears never to have been indemnified for the wrongs he suffered at the hands of the people of West Virginia.

• • • •

Acknowledgments: Mr. Douglas C. Tomkies, Huntington, W.Va.; Mr. Garfield Rose, Huntington, W.Va.; Mr. L. T. Reynolds, Princeton, W.Va. [28]

HANDWRITING "EXPERTS"

William Broughton

ON Washington's Birthday, 1900, the City Recorder of Atlanta, Nash R. Broyles, received a letter which he considered so obscene that he immediately turned it over to the Federal authorities. The letter reflected most pointedly upon Mr. Broyles's moral character and was signed "Grant Jackson."

There lived in Atlanta a negro, Grant Jackson by name, and he was known to the City Recorder. On February 23 he was arrested. On February 24 his "partner," William Broughton, was picked up while on his way to visit Jackson's mother.

Broughton was arrested because, as two policemen explained conveniently, whatever mischief involved Grant Jackson must of necessity involve Broughton, so close was their friendship in the eyes of the authorities. Other than this the police had no reason for arresting Broughton. Both he and Jackson denied writing the letter, or having any knowledge of it whatever.

As a result of this makeshift method of crime detection, the case against Jackson collapsed when it was discovered that he was unable to write, but the police were equal to the occasion and proceeded on the theory that Broughton must have been the author, as it was shown that on at least one occasion he had served as voluntary amanuensis for his friend in composing a bit of personal correspondence.

To demonstrate that Broughton could write, the police persuaded him to write a note to his mother, asking her to send him some clothing at the jail. This stratagem gave the authorities a sample of Broughton's handwriting to compare with the Broyles letter. The chirography, they concluded quickly, was the same in both. Broughton's indictment followed as a matter of course.

At the trial Broyles not only appeared as a witness but qualified as a handwriting expert by saying that a number of cases involving handwriting had come before him when he was United States Commissioner in Atlanta. Thus [29] equipped, he was able to inform the jury that there were incriminating and unmistakable similarities between the writing in the letter he had received and the note Broughton sent to his mother.

If there were similarities it was undeniable that there were also dissimilarities. This, however, did not stump the prosecution. Broyles testified that they could be explained by the fact that the defendant was a "very sharp, intelligent negro and he knew what he was arrested for and he was trying to disguise his handwriting" when he wrote the note to his mother.

Broyles's expert testimony was supported by that of two other witnesses who were likewise accepted by the court as experts one because he had had long experience in bank work and the other because he was traveling auditor for the Standard Oil Company. They saw the similarities but were unable to corroborate Broyles's characterization of the defendant, as they did not enjoy his acquaintance. The City Recorder had the advantage in this respect, for he had sent both Jackson and Broughton to jail at various times for a variety of misdemeanors.

Broughton testified in his own defense and denied knowledge of the letter until told of it by the police and said frankly that he held no grudge against Broyles for his frequent commitments to jail.

The experts prevailed and the jury found Broughton guilty, the court sentencing him to five years in prison, a fine of $500, plus costs of prosecution, which, it may be added, were considerable by comparison with Broughton's visible resources.

• • • •

BROUGHTON had not been long removed from the scene when, much to Recorder Broyles's consternation, he received a letter from one Charley Mitchell, mailed at Birmingham, Alabama. Broyles knew Mitchell to be an Atlanta negro. Mitchell, curiously enough, wished to inquire about the Broughton case, saying he numbered the unfortunate convict among his friends. He also informed the astonished [30]

Broyles that another friend of his, a woman Becky Lou Johnson—was the author of the obscene letter.

This all seemed very strange to Recorder Broyles. Presently a second letter arrived from Mitchell and moved Broyles to act. It appeared to him that the similarity in handwriting that convicted Broughton was as nothing compared to the likeness between the chirography in the obscene letter and in Mitchell's letters.

It began to appear that the wrong man had been sent to prison, so Broyles wrote to Mitchell, saying he was very much interested in Becky Lou's alleged part in the case and would like to discuss it with Mitchell—would he please come back to Atlanta for a conference with the City Recorder?

It appears that this gesture filled the unsuspecting Mitchell with a feeling of considerable importance and inflated his ego to such an extent that he walked quickly into the trap Broyles had set, and admitted that he—not Becky Lou nor Broughton—was the author of the troublesome letter. And it seemed that twenty cents was at the bottom of the whole case. He and Jackson had had an argument over the twenty cents—a loan—and a scarf pin. The argument was not settled to Charley's satisfaction and he threatened to even the score with Jackson, which he did by signing the letter with Jackson's name, he, too, erring in the matter of Jackson's illiteracy.

Subsequently he was indicted, tried, and found guilty. He was sentenced to five years and costs of prosecution, and it may be pointed out as one of the vagaries of justice that he was fined but $100, whereas Broughton had been assessed $500.

So it was that after serving a little less than two months of his sentence, Broughton was pardoned on May 18, 1900, to return to his friends in Atlanta.

• • • •

THIS extraordinary mistake was due to the impregnable assurance of Recorder Broyles that Broughton must be the guilty letter writer. Before that apparent certainty, all improbabilities vanished. Corroboration by equally competent [31] "experts," plus Broughton's tarnished record, overcame any doubts the jury might have had. Only Mitchell's urge to write letters saved Broughton from serving out his term. After the receipt of Mitchell's letter, Recorder Broyles's prowess as a handwriting expert stood him in better stead and he was enabled to catch the guilty man and thereby release the innocent. [32]

The Wrong Name On The Death Warrant

J. B. Brown

H. W. GORDON'S job at Tilgham's Mill in Palatka, Florida, required that he arise early in the morning and start for work shortly after five o'clock. His regular walk to work led him at about 5:30 through the shop yard of the Florida Southern Railway. As he was passing through the yard on the morning of October 17, 1901, he stumbled upon the body of a dead man. It was still before dawn. He immediately hastened to get the section foreman, J. J. Hunter, and together they returned to examine the body. As day was breaking a large group of railway men gathered around the body, which was identified as that of their fellow workman, Harry E. Wesson. Wesson, an engineer on one of the freight trains, had been shot at close range in the back of the head, and apparently had been instantly killed. His pockets were turned inside out—indicating that the motive for the murder had been robbery. Wesson's money had not been discovered by his murderer, however, for a roll containing $130 was found hidden under his overalls. A few feet from the body a .38 caliber pistol was found. One shell had been fired. Near by was a woodshed—an ideal hiding place for one intending to waylay another.

Wesson had been the engineer on Conductor F. R. LeBaron's freight train which had arrived in the Palatka yards just before four o'clock in the morning. He had shunted cars around on various tracks in the yard, and at 4:10 had put his engine into the roundhouse. There he met Night Watchman H. B. Scott, and together they went to the foreman's office, where Wesson registered at 4:19. Wesson and Scott left the office together. Shortly after, a report, as of a pistol, was heard about a city block from the office, but nothing was thought of it until the corpse was found. Scott said that he and Wesson separated outside the foreman's office, Wesson starting home with his lunch pail, and he to inspect Locomotive 32 and then to go to the roundhouse. This was the last time Wesson was seen alive. It was over an hour later that his body was found by Gordon. [33]

An autopsy was made by Dr. W. H. Cyrus and Dr. Welch. A .38 caliber revolver bullet was taken from the victim's brain.

There was a great deal of public excitement and indignation in Palatka over the atrocious murder. Sheriff R. C. Howell and his deputy, R. L. Kennerly, lost no time in rounding up a number of suspects and in putting them in the Putnam County jail—among them being Lucius Crawford, the regular yard night watchman, who lived in the yards; Harry Landon, a switchman; and Phil Sterges. At five o'clock in the evening, Jailer Hagan was standing on the jail porch, when he noticed a colored man come up to a crack in the fence and call for the prisoner Crawford, who was in the jail yard. Hagan said that it was J. B. Brown—a former brakeman on one of the Plant System trains and that he heard Brown say to Crawford, "Keep your mouth shut and say nothing." This was reported to the sheriff, and in less than an hour Brown was arrested. The possible connection of each of these prisoners with the murder was closely investigated.

It was reported that bad feeling existed between Brown and the murdered engineer. Conductor LeBaron said that in Ocklawaha during the August just past, he had censured Brown for the lax way in which he was coupling some cars, and had pulled him from between the cars and slapped him. Brown hit back at LeBaron with a sealing iron, whereupon the latter called for Wesson, who came running from the engine with a pistol which he gave to LeBaron. Brown then ran away, and he never worked again on LeBaron's train. A porter, Edward Ponder, said that sometime in September, Brown told him about this fracas and said that he was going to get his pistol, which was in Hagan's Bar at Palatka, and kill Wesson. It was not denied that on the night prior to the killing, Brown had passed by Hagan's Bar, but it was not clear whether he entered or not.

Brown, under questioning, accounted for his time on the evening of October 16 and the morning of October 17 as follows: He spent the early evening of the sixteenth at the house of Glover, a restaurant keeper, where he was staying. [34] Later in the evening he went to Nunberg's, where he took part in "a little game" with Glover, Nunberg, and Sanders. The game broke up at about eleven-thirty, and from there he returned to Glover's, passing Hagan's Bar, and went to bed. He slept there all night until "sun-up," when he arose, washed, and went down to "the caboose" and joined in a game of cards with Wilson, Vick, English, Davis, and Johnson. After six o'clock, he went to the store to buy some sugar for Davis, and on his way back learned of Wesson's murder. A short time later, he returned to Glover's, and stayed there the rest of the day until the time of his arrest, helping around in Glover's restaurant.

The officers found a motive for the murder in the trouble between Brown and Wesson, and so investigated him thoroughly. Harry Landon reported that, on October 16, Brown was without money, and tried to borrow a quarter from him. When the loan was refused, Brown was reported to have replied, "Never mind, I'll catch 209 away from here tonight, that's the train going south to meet 208." "Two hundred eight" was Wesson's train. At the card game in the caboose the following morning, after the murder, Brown had a handful of money. Some of the players said that when Brown arrived at the caboose he was all excited, that he took Jim Johnson over to one side, and that they whispered to each other. All these bits of circumstantial evidence against Brown were carefully noted, and he was kept in jail. The other suspects were released.

One day a prisoner, Brown's cell mate, Alonzo Mitchell, called the sheriff, and told him this story: Brown had just confessed to him that he and Jim Johnson plotted to kill Wesson for his money, and they had waylaid him by the woodshack, where Brown had shot him with Johnson's pistol. Brown took Wesson's money, $4.75, and Johnson took his watch and the pistol. Henry Davis, another cell mate in the prison, corroborated Mitchell's story and said that he had heard Brown confess.

With this testimony in their possession, the officers delayed no longer. State's Attorney Syd L. Carter presented the case to the Putnam County Grand Jury, which returned [35] a first-degree-murder indictment against Brown and Johnson. Brown was placed on trial before Circuit Judge W. S. Bullock on November 19, 1901. The prosecuting attorney was assisted by B. P. Calhoun. Brown was defended by A. M. Allred and John E. Marshall. The prosecution submitted the testimony establishing the circumstantial evidence against Brown, and the prisoners Mitchell and Davis testified to the confessions. On cross-examination of Mitchell, the defense attorneys endeavored unsuccessfully to show that Mitchell had been placed in jail for the purpose of obtaining a confession from Brown.

Brown testified in his own behalf, going in detail over his alibi. Glover supported Brown's alibi by testifying that Brown slept at his house on the night of October 16, that the only way Brown could leave the house was through his own room, and that Brown did not leave until sun-up. In rebuttal, the sheriff and the deputy sheriff testified that they had talked to Glover when Brown was arrested, and that Glover had then said that he did not know when Brown had left the house, because Brown was gone when he awoke.

In testifying further, Brown denied that he had made to Edward Ponder a threat against Wesson's life and denied owning a pistol. He admitted his quarrel with LeBaron, but denied that he had ever had a cross word with Wesson and that there was any hard feeling between them. He said that on the evening before the murder he had not gone to the roundhouse, but a state's witness in rebuttal testified that he saw him there. As to the money Brown produced at the card game in the caboose after the murder, it was said that Glover gave him a dollar and that Brown had won some money in the game at Nunberg's the night before, and several witnesses corroborated this. The prosecution endeavored to submit in evidence a transcript of testimony taken at the coroner's inquest, in which Brown was reported to have denied that he had any money in the caboose game; upon defense objections, however, the court refused to admit any record of the coroner's evidence, inasmuch as Brown, admittedly, had refused to sign the statement because he said it was incorrect. Thereupon, the reporter at the coroner's [36] inquest was called, and she testified from memory to certain statements made by

Brown at the inquest contrary to his testimony at the trial.

Brown denied that he had gone to the jail fence on October 17 to talk to Crawford. Jailer Hagan claimed to have recognized Brown by the sound of his voice and by seeing his back. As to the confession, Brown absolutely denied ever having made it. He admitted that Mitchell had tried to get him to confess the murder. Other persons who had also been in the prison testified that Mitchell conferred with the authorities at times while he was locked up with Brown and that they had heard Mitchell try to get Brown to confess, but that Brown always said that he was innocent.

The trial lasted two days, and on November 20, 1901, a verdict of guilty was returned. On the following day, Judge Bullock sentenced Brown to be hanged, the defendant's motion for a new trial being overruled. Upon an appeal to the Florida Supreme Court, the conviction and sentence were affirmed.

• • • •

ARRANGEMENTS were made for the hanging of the convicted Brown upon a specially built gallows. Brown was led to the gallows, and the rope adjusted about his neck. Hanging formalities proceeded, but to the great astonishment of all, when the death warrant was read, it ordered the execution of the foreman of the jury which had found Brown guilty. It is perhaps needless to remark that no one was hanged on that warrant.

Brown's attorneys placed the case before the Governor of Florida, with a plea for a commutation of the sentence to life imprisonment. The plea was granted.

In the spring term of the Circuit Court of Putnam County, 1902, the case against J. J. Johnson, who had been jointly indicted with Brown, was, on the motion of the State's Attorney, nol-prossed.

Life imprisonment, however, was not to be the fate of J. B. Brown. Early in 1913, J. J. Johnson, in a deathbed confession, admitted that he alone had shot Wesson, and [37] that Brown had had nothing to do with it. Realizing the unreliability of many such confessions, the officials checked carefully all corroborating details and became convinced that Johnson really was the guilty man, and that Brown was innocent.

On October 1, 1913, a full pardon was granted to Brown by Gov. Park Trammell and the Pardon Board upon the recommendation of Judge Bullock and the prosecuting attorney, "in order to rectify, as far as possible, a gross miscarriage of justice. . . . the conviction was obtained upon perjured testimony and in the excitement of the heinousness of the crime and the zeal of private interest."

After serving twelve years for a crime of which he was innocent, Brown was given his liberty, but he was then physically disabled. Sixteen years later, in 1929, when Brown was "aged, infirm, and destitute," he was once again remembered by the state of Florida. In consideration of what was called "faithful service . . . during the period of this wrongful imprisonment," the Legislature appropriated $2,492 for Brown's relief, to be paid in $25 monthly installments. This action was taken at the instance of Representatives W. D. Carn of Marion County and T. C. Douglas of Putnam County. Brown is now (1931) living in Marion County drawing his monthly relief from the state of Florida.

• • • •

BROWN was the victim of perjured testimony and circumstantial evidence. The Governor in his pardon admitted that the public excitement at the heinousness of the crime and the zeal for vengeance had a material bearing on the unhappy result. Suggestion doubtless influenced those witnesses who remembered "facts" connecting Brown with the murdered man and with conduct supposedly indicating guilt. The prosecution did come close to the real criminal when they obtained the indictment of Johnson, but instead of seeking to prove his guilt they unfortunately concentrated their misdirected efforts upon Brown. Brown came as close to execution as Purvis (p. 206). The intervention of an improperly [38] drawn death warrant proved to be equally providential. But for Johnson's deathbed confession, which was amply corroborated, Brown would have spent the rest of his broken life in the penitentiary. As it was, perhaps Florida deserves commendation for recognizing the legitimacy of Brown's claim upon the state for the miscarriage of justice of which he was the sufferer.

• • • •

Acknowledgments: Hon. W. S. Bullock, Ocala, Fla.; Hon. T. C. Douglas, Putnam County, Fla.; Hon. W. D. Carn, Ocala, Fla.; Mr. Charles Ausley, Tallahassee, Fla. [39]

OUT OF THE MOUTHS OF BABES

Louise Butler and George Yelder

THE "Black Belt" of Alabama is a well-known section of the sunny South. Whether this belt derives its name from the dark prairie soil or the preponderance of negroes to be found there is one of the traditional issues for street-corner and grocery-store debates. Lowndes County is in the very center of the black belt.

On a plantation in this county, on the southern bank of the Alabama River, lived Louise Butler, with her coal-black fourteen-year-old niece, Topsy Warren, her own daughter, Julia May Dickson, aged twelve, another niece, Anne-Mary Smith, aged nine, and a small son. Louise Butler, a plump light-brown negress, had enjoyed various amours and mothered this family, although still free from the bonds of matrimony. In 1928, she had won the affections of George Yelder, a lean colored gentleman about fifty-five years old, who lived near by with his wife and two grown daughters. George was a regular caller at Louise's house and she was exceedingly jealous of his attentions.

One day upon her return from a visit to Montgomery, Louise discovered that George had visited her house during the day, and found only Topsy at home. When he left, Topsy was the proud possessor of a new half dollar. Louise's jealousy was violently aroused when she learned of this and she administered to this fourteen-year-old interloper a severe beating, even threatening to kill her. Strangely, Topsy was seen no more. The rumor passed that Louise had done away with Topsy, and it gained such credence that the state law enforcement department at Montgomery telephoned to Deputy Sheriff "Buck" Meadows to investigate the matter thoroughly.

Meadows visited Louise's shanty when she was away and found there her twelve-year-old daughter Julia and nine-year-old niece Anne-Mary. In a short while they confided in him an account of the full details of the horrible and cold-blooded murder of poor Topsy. Julia said that Louise had beaten Topsy unmercifully on the afternoon of her return [40] from Montgomery when she learned of the half dollar Topsy had. Later in the day George Yelder came by and during a very short stay he and Louise had quite a personal "fuss" of their own, during which George threatened to whip Louise with some "plow-lines." They apparently made peace before he left, and shortly after dark George again appeared at the home of Louise Butler. After a short conversation they both went out in the yard near the woodpile, carrying a small lamp. Julia said that her mother, Louise, then called to her and told her to go outside the yard down into the edge of the roadway, and to stand there and call if anyone should approach. As she proceeded to obey her mother's command, she heard her mother or George call to Topsy to come out to the woodpile. Topsy went out of the house at about the same time that Julia went to stand in the roadway. She had no sooner stationed herself in the roadway than she heard Topsy cry out, and in just a minute or two thereafter her mother called to her to come. She obeyed, and when she reached the woodpile, Topsy was lying on the ground—dead. They dragged Topsy's body up close against the chop log and placed one of Topsy's arms across the log and demanded that she chop it off with the ax or they would kill her. Julia said that in this manner both of the dead girl's arms were severed from her body; that she was then ordered to go into the house, look behind a trunk, and bring a large sack and a string which were kept there. This she did. Her mother and George then placed the corpse in the sack—putting the trunk or body in the sack first and poking the arms in afterward. They then tied the sack, and left the premises, lugging the gruesome burden, in the direction of the Alabama River, which was not more than a half mile distant. They soon returned from the direction of the river empty handed, having been gone just long enough to have been to the river and back. They then came into the house, and Julia said she was ordered to build a fire in the stove, whereupon her mother cooked some supper for "Mr." George. When George and Louise returned from the trip to the river, George stopped by the woodpile and brought the ax into the house and washed it. [41]

Anne-Mary told the sheriff that she had told her Auntie about Topsy having the half dollar and saw Topsy whipped for it. She was lying in the bed next to the wall that night when she heard Topsy scream out back of the house. She quickly arose and peered through a crack in the wall and saw "Mr." George holding the light and her mother strike Topsy with the ax. Then "Mr." George passed the light to Louise and he took the ax and struck Topsy. Topsy fell down dead right at the woodpile. Anne-Mary then related, in impressive concordance with the testimony of Julia, how Julia was forced to cut off the arms of Topsy, and how the body was sacked and lugged away. When asked how she could tell which way they went off with the body, she stated promptly that she saw which way the lantern went. She said that when Louise and George returned to the house, George stopped by the woodpile for the ax, and brought it into the kitchen and washed it in a pan of water.

These stories seemed incredible to the sheriff, but the children appeared to be intelligent and did not vary their stories in the least under his questioning. Consequently, the only thing he could do was to arrest Louise upon her return home. Louise denied that she had done any more to Topsy than to give her a good whipping, after which Topsy disappeared, and she didn't know where the child had gone. This was suspicious and Louise was taken to jail to await a preliminary hearing. A few days later, while being questioned, she suddenly confessed that she had killed Topsy, and that she and George had tied an old automobile casing to her body to be sure it would sink when thrown into the river. Louise led the sheriff and the plantation owner, her landlord, to the river's edge where she said the body had been thrown into the water. She showed them a growth of vines in which she said she and George had become entangled while trying to get to the river. Louise repudiated this confession almost immediately and stoutly maintained her innocence.

At the preliminary hearing, Julia and Anne-Mary told their stories under oath, and the sheriff related the repudiated confession. Louise was bound over without bail for action by the Grand Jury, and George was then arrested. [42] The following week, there was a preliminary hearing for him. Julia and Anne-Mary, placed on the witness stand, adhered strictly to their former testimony. George was ordered back to jail without bail. Louise had been brought into court that afternoon, with the idea that she might again make the confession which she had made to the sheriff. This, however, she did not do. When the time came for her to be led back to jail, the child Julia began to cry and asked her mother, "Mama, ain't you going back home with us this evening?" She seemed to be very much distressed that her mother was to be denied that privilege. On that occasion, the solicitor told the child that the mother was being confined in jail because of the facts which Julia had told in court, and that if those facts were not true, now was the time to say so. The child, sobbing and holding to her mother, replied: "Deyshore done it." The mother was soon parted from the child and carried back to the jail.

The cases were submitted to a Lowndes County Grand Jury, which returned indictments against both Louise and George on April 17, 1928. The defendants were arraigned the same day. Since they were unable to employ counsel, the court assigned Mr. R. L. Goldsmith, an able attorney of Whitehall, Alabama, to defend them.

Separate trials were held before separate juries in Judge A. E. Gamble's court. Louise was tried on April 24 and George on April 25, 1928. The prosecuting officers were Calvin Poole and Joseph R. Bell, capable public officials. Mr. Bell describes the court scene in this way:

> When the time for the trial of these cases came to hand, the Court House and adjacent grounds were packed and crowded to their fullest limits with colored citizenry. It was as though a pall of darkness had settled over and around the Temple of Justice. It is a fact, strange to relate, that although the defendants were of their own race, the greater portion of the spectators wished for their conviction and punishment. The throng was tense, hushed and expectant, and the day being mildly warm, the odor of the courtroom was most oppressive.

At Louise's trial, the full testimony already related was presented to the jury. In support of her "not guilty" plea, [43] Louise maintained her innocence and denied having any knowledge of what had happened to Topsy. The jury returned a verdict of guilty. The following day George was tried and the testimony of the state's witnesses repeated. George endeavored to establish an alibi by the testimony of his wife and daughters, who stated that he was at home with a "lame back" on the night of the murder. The prosecuting officers attacked the credibility of this story, and the jury found George guilty also. On April 26, 1928, both defendants were sentenced by Judge Gamble to serve life imprisonment in the Alabama State Penitentiary.

• • • •

WITHIN a week after George and Louise had been sent to the penitentiary, a rumor reached the sheriff's office that Topsy was alive, and living with some relatives in Dallas County, some twenty miles away. The sheriff investigated and found the rumor to be true; he found Topsy "hale, hearty, and as black as ever." Mr. Bell relates that

> when Topsy was brought into Hayneville for identification, she was stared at, and regarded by the colored population, even as one who had returned from the dead. It would have been laughable had it not been so pathetic. Her body was examined, and was found to still bear the scars from the beating she received, but there was no evidence showing that she had ever been deprived of her arms nor that her skull had been crushed. Her identification was complete, and steps were immediately taken to have George and Louise restored to liberty.

Judge Gamble and Solicitor Poole were summoned from Greenville and they investigated the reappearance personally. Pardons were granted by the Governor in the latter part of June, 1928.

• • • •

GEORGE told Mr. Bell that he will never be the same again, for a man cannot know what it means to be tried for one's life when innocent, unless one has been through the ordeal.

• • • •

THIS is a case of perjury, fitting into circumstantial evidence. The disappearance of Topsy lent credence to the [44] horribly fantastic explanation of the two children. It is remarkable that two illiterate children could adhere so closely to a manufactured tale, embellished by vivid imaginations, throughout several exacting cross-examinations. It was the impregnability and consistency of the two children which finally persuaded the authorities to believe their stories and to put Louise and George on trial for their lives. Sheriff Meadows later stated that he was reliably informed that the two children had been coached every day for a week by a young man who had unlimited influence over them and worked with them at a dairy and who had a grievance against George Yelder. He had concocted the story soon after the rumor of Topsy's death began to spread. Possibly the trial authorities derived some support from Louise's repudiated confession, which, however, played no part in the trial. What persuaded Louise even momentarily to admit the crime and what induced the children to swear away the life of Louise, who apparently had their affection, it is impossible to say. Sheriff Meadows suggests that in her ignorant way Louise felt she would curry favor by doing what was desired and that the "white-folks" would help her out for telling such a hair-raising story. Had Topsy not been found, Louise and George would have been incarcerated for life. Fortunately for them, their martyrdom was limited to a few months.

• • • •

Acknowledgments: Miss Jozy Dell Hall, Washington, D.C.; Mr. Douglas Arant, Birmingham, Ala.; Mr. D. C. Leatherwood, Hayneville, Ala. [45]

Bag Snatcher

Benjamin Collins

DURING July, August, and the early part of September, 1928, there were about forty successful and unsuccessful attempts at bag snatching from women in Somerville, near Boston, Massachusetts. The snatcher confined his efforts to no particular part of the city, requiring only that the scene be a poorly lighted thoroughfare or a side street. Such a reign of terror existed among the women of the city that the police put about fifty plainclothes men on the case.

The method of operation was practically the same in all instances. The snatcher usually chose Saturday night for his activities. He never molested men or boys and did not hesitate to use violence if resistance were made. Secreting himself behind a fence or hedge in a yard having easy access to the street, he remained hidden until his intended victim had passed. Then he crept after her and, at an opportune moment, snatched the bag. Immediately after obtaining it, he dashed back into the yard in which he had been concealed and through it into an alley or street a block away. Often, though not always, he discarded the bag, keeping only the contents.

The snatching was always done from behind, so that the victim did not get a clear view of the snatcher.

The descriptions of the snatcher, as given by the victims, were practically the same except for a few details. The man always wore a cap, looked about thirty years old, and usually appeared in working clothes. Some remarked upon his speed and agility in making his get-away as contrasted with his stocky build.

So when, on September 1, another bag was snatched from the hands of Miss Mildred King of West Somerville, and a man named Benjamin F. Collins—who in height and build and cap fitted the reputed description—was found on the street a few blocks away twenty minutes thereafter, it was believed that at last the elusive criminal had been caught.

Upon being questioned by the police, he stated that he [46] worked as a dishwasher at the Woodbridge Hotel on College Avenue in West Somerville, and that, as it was a hot day, he had gone out on the street to a soda fountain to get a glass of ginger ale. He was searched, and only five or ten cents was found on him, though Miss King's purse had contained $5.25 in money, and a $10 fountain pen. Collins' room was then searched, but none of the stolen purses could be found, nor any of the articles said to have been in them.

But as Collins happened to answer the general description of the thief, he was taken to the Somerville police station and held for identification by the victims. Several of them came, and identified Collins as the man who had taken their purses. Collins was presented to each woman separately, and each said that he was the man.

The police did not believe that they had the right man, as the circumstances of the case were in Collins' favor. None of the goods had been found in his possession. He was well liked and trusted where he worked, and had no criminal record, though not much was known about him, as he had recently come from Lowell and was a rather quiet and unobtrusive person. He gave his age as forty-five, and it was established that he was the sole support of his aged mother. Officer Augustin J. Fitzpatrick, who had charge of the investigation for the Somerville police, repeatedly told Assistant District Attorney Richard S. McCabe, who conducted the prosecution, that he did not think that Collins was the man they were hunting.

But as five of the victims had positively identified Collins as the culprit, he had to be brought to trial. Three indictments were returned against him by the Grand Jury on September 10, one charging larceny and two robbery. There were seven counts in the larceny indictment, in which he was accused of having grabbed the hand bags of seven women between the fifteenth of July and the first of September. The hand bags were valued at from $3.00 to $7.00 and contained various amounts of money, ranging from $1.75 to $27.00, and numerous trinkets, fountain pens, notebooks, and other articles. On the robbery indictments, he was charged with taking a $2.00 hand bag and $5.00 in money from one [47] woman, and a $5.00 hand bag, $3.00 in money, and two sets of rosary beads worth $4.00 from another woman.

Collins was kept in the Somerville jail from the time he was arrested on September 1 until the time of his trial on October 23. He was unable to raise the required $10,000 bail. The delay in his trial was due to the fact that Collins' original attorney was taken sick and was sent to a tuberculosis sanatorium. He was then represented by Hon. Francis C. Zacharer of Lowell.

At the trial several of the witnesses did not appear against him, one because of old age, and another because of sickness. However, both of these had identified him at the police station. The identifying witnesses were Carrie M. Decker, Cecelia Ketter, and Mildred King of West Somerville, and Marion P. Jackson and Catherine Davis of Medford. They all positively identified Collins again, Mrs. Decker being particularly positive, so much so that the others may have been influenced by her assurance.

Collins took the stand in his own defense and denied that he had taken their bags and reiterated what he had said when arrested, namely, that he was employed as a dishwasher at the Woodbridge Hotel and had left only for a few minutes to buy a glass of ginger ale. Margaret Gleason, who also worked at the hotel, corroborated the statement that he had been at work all morning, as did Florence A. Fitz, another hotel employee. Arthur F. Downs of Lowell appeared for him as a character witness. Officer Fitzpatrick also testified to Collins' original story when arrested and to the fact that none of the bags or their contents had been found on Collins or in his room.

The jury found him guilty on one robbery charge, not guilty on the other, and guilty on four counts of larceny; and on October 23 he was sentenced by the judge of the Superior Court for East Cambridge, Massachusetts, Hon. Patrick M. Keating, to two and a half to three and a half years on the robbery charges.

• • • •

ON the Saturday following the sentence, October 27, another hand bag was grabbed from a woman in the same general [48] neighborhood where the others had been taken. This time, after a hot pursuit, the man was shot by the police while trying to escape. His name was George Hill. He had on him some of the stolen articles.

Hill's room in Medford was searched, and many of the hand bags which had been taken, as well as many of the trinkets, were recovered. For example, one bag had contained two books of stamps and a notebook with a loose five-cent stamp inside. These were found in Hill's room.

On the Monday following, October 29, these facts were brought to the attention of District Attorney Bushnell; and the District Attorney and his assistant, Mr. McCabe, who had tried the case, went to the state prison and informed Collins that a motion for a new trial was being drawn by his attorney, and that the District Attorney would nol-pros the case.

On the thirtieth of October, Collins was brought into court, a motion for a new trial on the larceny charge was allowed, and then a *nolle prosequi* entered by the District Attorney. On the robbery charge on which he had been sentenced, a habeas corpus petition and a motion for a new trial were filed and allowed, and the District Attorney entered a *nolle prosequi.*

Later Hill was brought up for trial and pleaded guilty to having taken the bags of the women who testified against Collins. He was sentenced to the state prison, where he died of septic poisoning as a result of his wound.

After Collins' release, various news items appeared reporting the comments of the five women who had identified Collins. Three of them still maintained that Collins was the man who had stolen their bags; the other two thought they might be mistaken.

The police records of each of the men read as follows:

Collins	*Hill*
48 years	30 years
5 ft. 6-1/4 ins.	5 ft. 6-1/2 ins.
173 lbs.	176 lbs.
light complexion	dark complexion
brown hair	black hair
blue eyes	brown eyes
prominent nose	Very prominent nose

[49]

Both men were further described as having worn dark clothes and gray cap. Collins walked in a shuffling manner, while Hill was very active, having a quick gait and athletic appearance. Collins was of the easy-going, indifferent type, while Hill was of arrogant, sarcastic disposition, and was considered one of the most despicable criminals known to the department. When he was told that an innocent man was in prison because of his activities, he still denied that he was responsible for the crimes, and only confessed when confronted by overwhelming evidence.

A bill was introduced in the Massachusetts Legislature to compensate Collins to the extent of $1,000 for the injury that had been done him, but the compensation was denied, one argument being that the state could not be required to bear expenses which ought properly to fall upon the counties.

• • • •

AGAIN we have a case of sheer mistaken identification by the victims of a crime, as in the Beck, Greenwald, and Preston cases. The opportunity for observing Collins must have been of the most fleeting kind, yet the positiveness of witnesses is sometimes, as in this case, in inverse ratio to their opportunity for knowledge or to their reliability. In this case, contrary to the usual rule, it was the police who were skeptical, and yet, but for the reoccurrence of the same crime, manifestly by another offender, as in the cases of Andrews, Beck, and Greenwald, it is doubtful whether Collins would have been freed. It is unfortunate that the Legislature was unwilling to repair the damage done by the courts of the state.

• • • •

Acknowledgments: Hon. Richard S. McCabe; Hon. J. D. McLaughlin. [50]

"TAXI"

Condy Dabney

CONDY DABNEY arrived in the little mining town of Coxton, Kentucky, in January, 1925, looking for work. He was a young man of thirty-one, with a wife and two children. Not knowing whether he would find employment in Coxton, he had left his family at home in Coal Creek, Tennessee.

Dabney was used to working in the coal mines that were numerous in this section of Kentucky and Tennessee. It was not long before he found work in a mine near Coxton. He soon established a reputation as a quiet man with a good disposition, though somewhat taciturn. He had no police record and as far as anyone knew he had never been in trouble with the authorities of Tennessee or Kentucky.

Soon after he went to work Roxy Baker, a sixteen-year-old Coxton girl, disappeared. The community was mystified and somewhat excited. Just before the Grand Jury met to investigate the disappearance three Coxton men disappeared. No one could account for their whereabouts. The Grand Jury, however, did not involve them in the Baker case and no indictment was returned.

About the first of July, Dabney gave up his job in the mines, bought an old Ford, and began running a taxi in and about Coxton. He had been driving this taxi but a month when the community was again aroused to a high pitch of excitement. Three women disappeared. Two of them were married, and nothing was ever heard of them again. The third was Mary Vickery, the fourteen-year-old daughter of E. C. Vickery. The Grand Jury met once more and this time there were two definite suspects William Middleton and Condy Dabney who were reported to have been seen taking Mary for automobile rides.

Despite the testimony of many witnesses, the Grand Jury again failed to indict. Middleton and Dabney were released and the investigation failed to turn up any pertinent evidence. But Dabney's troubles were not over.

In September, Dabney left Coxton to return to his family [51] in Coal Creek. He had been told, according to statements he made later, that one of his children was sick and for that reason he wanted to find work near Coal Creek.

There are a number of mine shafts around Coxton, some of them old workings. Those that have been abandoned are sometimes used as hiding places for the storage of whiskey or as convenient places for operating stills.

United States Marshal Adrian Metcalf had been told that there was a still hidden in one of the shafts on Ivy Hill, near Coxton, and on the twenty-first of October he set out to look for it.

In the course of his search Marshal Metcalf came to the old Bugger Hollow shaft, an abandoned working. In the dark he stumbled over a pile of stones in one of the passageways and near them he found some clothing. His suspicions were aroused and he called in several other men. Presently they had unearthed the body of a girl. An old black winter coat had been thrown around it. There was no other clothing except pink bloomers, a hat, shoes, and stockings.

The body was badly decomposed, but it was thought to be that of a girl perhaps between twelve and fourteen years old. Mary Vickery had been missing about two months and the discovery of the body brought an insistent demand that the Vickery case be reopened. It was generally believed that the body found in the old Bugger Hollow shaft was Mary's. As the weeks passed various stories went the rounds of the perturbed little town and gradually suspicion began to point more and more impressively toward Condy Dabney. Perhaps the tales which did most to involve Dabney were woven out of material supplied by one Marie Jackson, who finally became the principal witness against him.

So incriminating were the stories that the Kentucky authorities twice visited him at his home in Coal Creek to question him, but each time they returned apparently impressed by his protestations of innocence.

Though he knew, of course, something of the strength of the suspicions in Coxton concerning him, he returned to the Kentucky town in March. Soon after his arrival he was examined by the Grand Jury and on the eighteenth of March [52] an indictment charging him with the murder of Mary Vickery was returned.

Mary's father seemed certain that the body found in the old mine was that of his daughter. At the trial his positive statements indicated clearly that there was no doubt in his mind concerning the identification.

He told of going to the mine after the body had been found and picking up a ring which played an important part in establishing the girl's identity. The defense suspected that the ring had been planted, but other witnesses testified that they had seen it at the mine and one of them testified that he saw Vickery pick it up. It was covered with decayed flesh and a friend of Vickery's carried it on a stick, being unwilling to touch it.

Vickery said he also found some flesh and hair in the mine and a piece of a stocking with a darn in it that he remembered seeing in Mary's stocking. He identified it by its form, which he described as being like the letter *L*. He identified the hair as of the same color as his daughter's, saying it was "sandy like and bobbed, and very fine."

The ring, he said, was one he bought for Mary in Knoxville, Tennessee, for her birthday, June 7. Asked if she had ever run away from home before, he replied in the negative and denied the suggestion that the girl did not get along with her stepmother.

On cross-examination Vickery testified that he did not attend the funeral and that he allowed the county to bury the body. Pressed for an explanation, he hesitated. Before he could reply, Dabney's attorney, G. G. Rawlings, suggested: "You did not know that was your girl, that is what you started to say, wasn't it?"

"At the present time I wasn't perfectly sure," Vickery replied.

G. J. Jarvis, counsel for the prosecution, took the stand and testified that Vickery stated at the undertaker's, where the body had been taken after its discovery, "That is my girl." Another witness testified that Vickery had said he was not sure it was his daughter. There was conflicting testimony as to the color of the hair found in the mine. One witness [53] said it was brown; another described it as black and very coarse.

Then came Marie Jackson, upon whose allegations the state had leaned heavily to obtain an indictment. Her story, briefly, was as follows:

About seven o'clock the morning Mary Vickery disappeared, she and Mary stopped Dabney's taxi as it came up to them on a road just outside of Coxton. Marie ordered Dabney to drive them to town, where they arrived about ten o'clock (though the distance seems to have been but four or five miles). Dabney, she testified, took them to Marler's Restaurant, where she got out. Dabney then drove away with Mary and did not return until one o'clock. When he came back, she said, all three of them drove out to Ivy Hill, Mary sitting in the front seat with Dabney. At the hill they got out of the car and sat down on a log in a clearing. After they had talked a little while, according to Marie, Dabney told her to go around behind the hill as he wanted to talk to Mary alone. She said she went away and sat down at a place from which Dabney and Mary were visible to her. She told the court that she saw Dabney hug the girl, who protested, and then strike her with a stick. Mary fell to the ground and the witness said she saw Dabney attack her. She then told how Dabney walked around the hill, came back, and finally found her. He told her, she said, that if she ever mentioned what had happened he would burn her at the stake and that if he was prevented he would have someone else do it. She said Condy then took the body into the mine while she fled from the scene.

She testified that she met Dabney next day and rode with him as far as Pineville, on her way home. She did not mention the murder, fearing that he might attack her.

This story appears to have impressed the jury greatly, though other witnesses offered testimony that conflicted with it in several respects.

Three girls—the Stewart sisters and a Miss Smith—whose testimony was substantially in agreement, testified that they saw Dabney and Mary Vickery between two and four on the afternoon she disappeared. The Stewart sisters said that [54] they were walking along the road with Mary to their grandmother's about two o'clock, when Dabney came along, with a woman in his car, and asked them if they wanted a ride. They refused. Soon after, William Middleton and Otis King came along and all three of the girls rode with them for a while, the two sisters finally leaving Mary in the car talking with Middleton and King.

This was substantiated by Middleton, who set the time as being about four o'clock. King said he did not know Mary Vickery but that he found out later that it was she who had been in the car. The mother of the Smith girl, who said she saw Dabney and Mary together, testified that she saw Mary before that with the other two girls and two men. This testimony accounted for Mary's time between two and four o'clock of the afternoon she disappeared and contradicted the testimony of Marie Jackson, who said that she and Mary and Dabney were on Ivy Hill from one o'clock until nearly dark.

Another witness said he talked with Dabney after getting off the train in Coxton one morning and inquired if Mary had been found. Asked what Dabney had replied, he testified: "I believe he said there wasn't much use hunting for her—going any ways off to look for her, he didn't think she was very far off."

The state also offered as a witness one Claude Scott, with whom Dabney had spent some time in jail while awaiting trial. He said he had known Marie Jackson fifteen years; that he had talked to her while in jail; and that he delivered a letter to Dabney from Marie. He said Dabney offered him fifteen dollars to testify in the case, and, to use his own words, " . . .he tried to make me remember stuff that Marie Jackson should have said through that window to me; while he was sitting there he tried to make me remember stuff I never heard her say and she never said to me."

Finally Dabney took the stand in his own defense. He told a straightforward story of his movements from July, 1925, to March, 1926. He said he did not remember ever carrying Mary Vickery in his taxi, but that he might have done so, as he carried many people he did not know. He said he knew [55] Marie Jackson, and had taxied her occasionally with men. He said he did not know Marler's Restaurant, and that he had never been on Ivy Hill. He called Marie Jackson's testimony false and said he left Coxton because he had received a letter saying his little daughter was ill. When he got home to Coal Creek he worked at various jobs during the late fall and winter and was at all times available to police officers, he said. He testified that he had been arrested on suspicion in the Vickery case but was later released. He told the court that he did not refuse to return to Coxton and he denied that he returned in March only after hearing that the Grand Jury declined to indict him. He insisted that he was innocent and knew nothing whatever about the disappearance of Mary Vickery.

On March 31, 1926, the jury returned a verdict of guilty and recommended life imprisonment. A motion for a new trial was overruled. An appeal was taken. On the same day Dabney was sentenced to be confined for life at hard labor in the state penitentiary at Frankfort.

• • • •

AS Dabney was without funds and had had to take the pauper's oath, a transcript of the testimony was printed at the state's expense and filed with his bill of exceptions, May 19. His appeal to the Kentucky Court of Appeals was pending, almost a year later, when on a night in March, Patrolman George S. Davis noticed, quite by chance, the name of Mary Vickery on the register of a hotel in Williamsburg, Kentucky.

The name sounded familiar to Davis. He thought he had heard it before. He asked about it and was told that Mary Vickery had lived in the hotel at one time. He was told that she had gone across the Cumberland River to visit friends. He soon found her and recognized her at once; and the story she told Davis was quite different from the imaginative tale Marie Jackson had spread upon the record.

Mary said she left Coxton, August 23, 1925, with five dollars in her pocketbook, because she couldn't get along with her stepmother. She had gone to the train in a taxi. [56] She did not know the driver, but the description she gave fitted Dabney. She was sure she did not know Marie Jackson. From Coxton she said she went first to Livingston, where she worked as a waitress, then to Berea, where she worked as a maid. From Berea she moved on to Mount Vernon and finally to Cincinnati, where she found work in a woolen mill. She admitted that while in Cincinnati she had heard that someone had been convicted of murdering her and was told that she should go home, but it was some time before she decided to do so. She informed Davis that she was then on her way back to Coxton.

Her return to Coxton led to an immediate pardon for Dabney and the appointment of G. J. Jarvis as a special investigator to inquire into the conduct of Marie Jackson. True to form Marie offered more stories about the Vickery case, all untrue. Jarvis was quoted in one newspaper account as being of the opinion that Marie Jackson testified against Dabney to get a $500 reward that had been offered, but other accounts have it that Marie wanted Dabney to leave his wife and children and live with her. He would not consent and for revenge she testified against him.

As a result of Jarvis' investigation of the Jackson episode, she was convicted of false swearing, and on the same day (March 27) it was reported that Mary Vickery was married to C. E. Dempsey by Rev. H. C. Davis of the Baptist Church of God in Coxton.

• • • •

READING the cold record, it seems hard to understand why a jury should deduce from so much conflicting testimony a conclusion of Dabney's guilt. Perhaps Dabney's directness and apparent indifference operated against him, rather than in his favor. So far as personal credibility was concerned, there should have been but little question he had been an inconspicuous, unobjectionable citizen. Marie Jackson, the state's star witness, had not been. Why she should have been believed, and not he, is hard to say. Perhaps unfavorable inferences were drawn from his six months' return to his home in Coal Creek, Tennessee, shortly after Mary Vickery's [57] disappearance. But if Marie Jackson was believed by the jury, the testimony of the Stewart girls and Miss Smith must have been disbelieved, for the Jackson story was quite inconsistent with theirs. The father's identification of a decomposed body was also none too certain, and the difference among the witnesses as to the color of the hair should have aroused suspicion of the accuracy of the identification. But it was assumed that murder had been committed, and someone must apparently be required to suffer for it. Piecing together every unfavorable inference, however inconsistent, and refusing to give weight to evidence in Dabney's favor, the jury became sufficiently convinced that the murder could and should be charged to Dabney. Perjury and too easy credulity, operating on minds predisposed by the circumstances of time and place to believe the worst, rather than official or judicial incompetence, were responsible for a grievous miscarriage of justice. [58]

EVEN THE POLICE AREN'T SAFE

Evans and Ledbetter

ON August 30, 1929, Harry D. McDonald was arrested by the sheriff of Los Angeles County on a charge of conspiracy to violate the Wright Act in receiving stolen property. McDonald admittedly had a criminal record for felonies. Nevertheless, he surprised the District Attorney by confessing numerous conspiracy transactions involving over fifty officers of the Los Angeles Police Department. McDonald implicated most of these guardians of the law in schemes of bribe taking to prevent prosecutions.

Two of the officers so charged by McDonald were Walter E. Evans and Miles H. Ledbetter, officers in the Department of Detectives. McDonald's confession concerned twenty-five or thirty stolen diamonds which he had purchased from one Jack Hawkins in August or September, 1927. About a year later, McDonald was questioned about these diamonds by Officer Reavis. McDonald said that he thereupon telephoned his friend Patrolman Ledbetter, who called at his place of business, nominally a bathhouse, at which time Ledbetter said that he would talk the matter over with Detective Lieutenant Evans, and call again the following day, Saturday. Evans and Ledbetter were said to have called on Saturday, and, stating that Jack Hawkins had confessed to the San Francisco police that he had sold the stolen diamonds to McDonald, demanded $1,000 to hush the matter up. McDonald said further that the matter was thereupon hushed, and that, on the day following, he paid $750 in currency to these two officers. Mrs. McDonald and Elizabeth Pierce, a maid at the McDonald place, corroborated the fact that $750 had been paid to the officers. McDonald set the date of this transaction as sometime around October 1, 1928.

McDonald, his wife, and the maid were called before the Grand Jury to repeat their stories, and Evans and Ledbetter were consequently indicted on the charge of having received a bribe of $750 from McDonald upon their agreement [59] not to arrest and prosecute him on a charge of receiving stolen property. They were called for trial before Judge William C. Doran in the Los Angeles County Superior Court. Deputy District Attorney William R. McKay represented the state, and Alfred F. McDonald and Theodore C. McKenna represented the defendants.

The only additional testimony against the defendants was on the admitted fact that Mrs. McDonald and Mrs. Ledbetter were friendly. Evans and Ledbetter both testified in their own defense. They admitted calling at McDonald's place on a Saturday and on a Sunday in 1928, but said that this was on July 7 and 8, 1928, and concerned the Oswald diamond robbery; they also maintained that they knew nothing and had heard nothing of any diamonds McDonald said he had purchased from Jack Hawkins; and they denied absolutely that they had ever received $750 from their accuser. In rebuttal, both Mr. and Mrs. McDonald testified that, on the Sunday prior to July 4, they had moved to a bungalow at Venice, California, and that McDonald was not in Los Angeles for the two weeks thereafter. The case was submitted to the jury, which, apparently believing the McDonalds rather than the defendants, returned a verdict of guilty. They were sentenced on November 7, 1929. Their conviction was affirmed on appeal, and their motions for new trials, on the ground of newly discovered evidence, denied. On July 2, 1930, they started to serve their terms in San Quentin.

• • • •

INVESTIGATIONS of the matter were, however, continued by the authorities. No record could be found that Hawkins had made any statement to the San Francisco police regarding stolen diamonds or that such a matter had been reported to the Los Angeles police.

The daily detective reports in the files of the Police Department, which were admittedly genuine but which for some reason were not accepted in evidence at the trial, showed that on June 16, 1928, two valuable diamond rings had been stolen from Mrs. Nick Oswald. Detective Lieutenants Stone and Evans were assigned to the case. They started a [60] systematic investigation. On Saturday, July 7, Mr. Oswald telephoned to detective headquarters to say that he suspected McDonald, remembering that McDonald on one occasion had greatly admired the very diamonds that were later stolen.

On July 7 and 8, Lieutenant Stone was off duty, so Evans requested Detective Captain Vernand to assign some detective who knew McDonald, to assist him in the investigation. Ledbetter was chosen, and together he and Evans went to McDonald's place. McDonald denied any knowledge of the Oswald diamonds. Yet McDonald told the officers that he might be able to find a clue to the missing diamonds if they would call the following day. They called on Sunday, July 8, and received a "tip." On Monday, July 9, Stone reported again for duty, and he and Evans continued the investigation until July 25, at which time the case was closed. Ledbetter was on the case, therefore, for only two days, July 7 and 8; and he had been taken to McDonald's place by Evans, and not as the result of a call from McDonald, as the latter testified. It was further discovered that on July 9 McDonald had signed the safety-deposit record of the Bank of America, at the branch at Main and Washington Streets, Los Angeles, a day when both Mr. and Mrs. McDonald swore that he was out of town. It was found that the maid, Elizabeth Pierce, had not entered the employ of the McDonalds until after August 8, so that she could not have been present on July 7 and 8. These disclosures and other facts later discovered, coupled with McDonald's previous record of felonies, convinced the authorities, including the District Attorney, the Advisory Pardon Board, and Governor C. C. Young, that the testimony of the McDonalds and their maid was wilfully false and that, in truth, Evans and Ledbetter were entirely innocent of the charges made by McDonald. On January 5, 1931, Governor Young granted them full and unconditional pardons, and they were forthwith given their freedom.

But this was not the end of the matter. Defense Attorney Theodore C. McKenna presented petitions to the California State Board of Control for indemnity under the California [61] statute of 1913, providing indemnification for erroneous convictions. The Board recommended to the Legislature that Evans be compensated in the sum of $4,533.36 and Ledbetter in the sum of $3,313.39, which they duly received.

• • • •

THE convictions of Evans and Ledbetter rested solely upon the perjury of the prosecuting witness, his wife, and maid. We have seen that the police occasionally conspire, by suppression of evidence, to convict an accused person of tarnished character. In the present case the actors are reversed. Why it was not possible to establish the true facts at the trial is hard to explain. It is not understood why the police records of June and July, and particularly of July 7 and 8—the dates when Evans and Ledbetter did call upon McDonald—were not admitted in evidence. Taking advantage of the fact that the police officers did call upon him, but by misrepresenting the dates and the purpose of the call, McDonald swore away the liberty of two police detectives. The perjurers were sufficiently impressive before the jury to overcome the truthful stories of the officers. Subsequent developments confirmed the accuracy of the officers' account of the transaction and the complete error of the conviction. They received at least some compensation for the misfortune and, through that compensation, public vindication. Although there appear to be some people in Los Angeles who question the advisability of compensating the two police officers here under consideration, the editor feels justified in accepting the record made by the state officials as evidence of their innocence.

• • • •

Acknowledgments: Hon. Webb Shadle, Assistant Secretary, State Board of Control, Sacramento, Calif.; Hon. George A. Benedict, Deputy Public Defender, Los Angeles, Calif. [62]

JUSTICE BY ELIMINATION

Floyd Flood

ABOUT twelve miles southeast of East St. Louis, Illinois, there lies in St. Clair County the snug little town of Freeburg. At 2:15 on August 23, 1924, the drowsy afternoon peace of Freeburg was violently broken by the daring holdup of its First National Bank. A Flint car carrying six men drove up before the bank; four men entered, armed with revolvers. They ordered the president (Russell E. Hamill) to enter the vault, covered the cashier (Miss Susie Wolf) and the bookkeepers (Miss Minnie Hoist and Miss Emma Wolf), and escaped with over ten thousand dollars in cash and currency. They left town in the Flint car, speeding toward Fayetteville.

Police officers took up the trail immediately and traced the car to the Mississippi River, where it was found abandoned. Some of the stolen currency consisted of new $5.00 and $10.00 national bank notes of the looted bank which had not yet been placed in public circulation. It was therefore possible to broadcast a definite description of these notes through banking channels in the nearby states. Shortly afterward, some of the currency was spotted at the bank of Jonesboro, Arkansas, and led to the arrest of two men there who gave the names James Breene and Ralph Southard. Much of the loot taken from the Freeburg bank was found on this pair, and they were promptly returned to the St. Clair County Jail at Belleville, Illinois.

At about this same time the police authorities in St. Louis, Missouri, notified the Illinois authorities that Floyd Flood, a painter and chauffeur, was under arrest, and that he fitted the description of one of the bandits. It is not clear just why Flood was apprehended. The arresting officers told one of Flood's attorneys that he had been taken up because he was a "bad egg," although he had no criminal record. Flood claimed that the arresting officer had a grudge against him because his girl friend had refused the officer a date, after which the officer threatened to "make it tough on her sweetheart." No charge appears to have been entered against [63] Flood in St. Louis as a ground for his arrest. The police authorities merely noticed that Flood seemed to fit the description of one of the Freeburg bandits, and they so notified the Illinois authorities.

In view of the information furnished by the St. Louis police, Misses Susie and Emma Wolf went to St. Louis to identify the suspect. They were told that one of the robbers had been captured. At police headquarters, Flood was placed in the "show-up cage," a contrivance about ten feet square which enables identifying witnesses to examine suspects under flood lights, although the suspects are unable to see the witnesses. The police forced

Flood to turn his coat collar up, put on a cap not his own and pull it down over his eyes, stretch his hand forward and say, "Stick 'em up." The police had been informed that one of the bandits, so attired, had thus acted. Under these conditions the two women identified Flood as the bandit who had covered them during the robbery.

Flood was indicted, jointly with Breene and Southard, for the robbery, and they were tried before Justice George A. Crow in the St. Clair County Circuit Court on December 2—5, 1924. The case was prosecuted for the state by Hilmar C. Lindauer. Flood was defended by Attorney Joseph B. McGlynn of East St. Louis. Indisputable testimony was adduced connecting Breene and Southard with the robbery. According to the testimony of the witnesses, including the bank president, Breene was the bandit who forced the president into the vault. Southard was definitely identified as the driver of the Flint car. President Hamill was unable to identify Flood. The Misses Wolf and Miss Hoist, however, did positively identify him. Among the numerous other witnesses who identified Breene and Southard as having been among a group of men who had been seen camping near Freeburg on the night prior to the robbery, only two, August and Clem Wesnusky, youthful Freeburg coal miners, asserted that Flood was in the group.

In view of Flood's contention that he had not been in Illinois for over a year, his defense, naturally, was an alibi. It was to the effect that on the morning of the robbery, he [64] arose late, had breakfast at 9:30, after which he went into the garage at the rear of his house and worked on his machine until 12:30, when his family had dinner. After that, he returned to the garage and worked there until about 2:30 o'clock. Between 2:00 and 2:15 he called up the Yellow Cab Company, for which he drove a taxi, to request leave (he was supposed to report for duty at four o'clock). His request was denied. He reported at the Cab Company office for work at 3:30 and checked out with his cab at four o'clock. The defendant took the stand in his own defense, and his testimony was corroborated by his father, mother, a visiting aunt and cousin, several neighbors, and several employees of the Cab Company.

The jury apparently gave little credence to the alibi testimony, for it returned a verdict of guilty against Flood, as well as against Breene and Southard. On December 18, 1924, a motion for a new trial having been denied, Flood was sentenced to serve from ten years to life in the Southern Illinois State Penitentiary. Breene and Southard received like sentences.

• • • •

WHILE Mr. McGlynn was preparing a writ of error, Breene sent a message to him from the penitentiary requesting an interview. Mr. McGlynn granted the request. Breene and Southard thereupon confessed their part in the robbery and said that four other men, whom they refused to name, had assisted, but that they did not even know Floyd Flood. A little later, two more of the gang were caught in Ohio, and they named the six participants as Breene, Southard, John Lyons, Benjamin Ingram, Arthur Richardson, and Brice McConnell. They made an affidavit that they had never heard of Flood, and that such a person had had no part in the affair. They said that after the robbery, the gang took the loot out into the woods, divided it, and then scattered. When Susie and Emma Wolf were informed of these developments, they admitted the possibility of a mistake in their identifications. An application for a pardon was filed, but Mr. McGlynn had an uphill fight of over a year, against the opposition of the Bankers Association, before a pardon [65] could be obtained. It was necessary to account for every one of the six robbers and to obtain their convictions or confessions before final action freeing the innocent man was taken. Finally, all six were caught and convicted, whereupon the Bankers Association helped Mr. McGlynn to secure the long overdue pardon for Flood. On January 21, 1926, Gov. Len Small commuted Flood's sentence to expire at once, on the ground of his innocence.

• • • •

THIS mistake in identity was largely induced by the power of suggestion exerted by the St. Louis police upon the Misses Wolf. To pick up Flood on the merest suspicion, to state to these ladies that one of the bandits had been captured, to dress him up to fit the known description and compel him to act the part, was too persuasive to resist. Notwithstanding the consistent testimony of numerous alibi witnesses that Flood was in St. Louis at the very moment the robbery occurred, the jury preferred to believe the affirmative evidence of the Misses Wolf and Hoist against the overwhelming contradictory evidence. Again it is observed that an identification by the victim of a violent crime is given preponderant weight. Flood was ultimately saved by the fact that the crime was a joint enterprise, and that all the culprits were accounted for, so that by elimination, an innocent man, as in the New Jersey case of Sweeney, could be weeded out and his innocence established.

• • • •

Acknowledgment: Mr. Joseph B. McGlynn, East St. Louis, Ill. [66]

THE KEY TO ROOM 31

"Frenchy" Ameer Ben All

ON the southeast corner of Catherine Slip and Water Streets, on the Manhattan water front of the 1890's, there flourished the East River Hotel, a squalid drinking place and bawdy resort. At nine o'clock on Friday morning, April 24, 1891, the night clerk, Eddie Harrington, made his rounds of the hotel rooms, routing out all those who had not already left. Most of the rooms had been vacated. Room 31, however, was still locked. He rapped lightly—no reply; louder knocks—no reply. Eddie applied his master key to the door. Peering in, he was petrified by the ghastly sight of the mutilated body of "Old Shakespeare," a dissolute woman of sixty, a habitué of the neighborhood. She was a former actress, and received her nickname because she frequently quoted the Bard's plays when tipsy. Her name was Carrie Brown.

Eddie, greatly excited, rushed to the first floor to spread the news and call for the police, who soon arrived, accompanied by newspaper reporters. The coroner took charge of the body.

An examination of the body showed that the woman had been strangled, atrociously slashed by a filed-down cooking knife, which was found on the floor by the bed—and upon her thigh was cut the sign of the cross. As a murder this was a challenge to Chief Police Inspector Thomas Byrnes, who was justly proud of his record for solving crime mysteries. The cross on the victim's thigh gave the case a special significance. It was the mark of "Jack the Ripper," the notorious London murderer who had baffled Scotland Yard by his nine brutal killings of women in the streets of London from December, 1887, to January, 1891. The New York Police Department had chided the London police about the "Ripper" and boastfully let it be known that if the latter appeared in New York with his evil doings, he would be in the "jug" within thirty-six hours.

On April 25, 1891, the day after the murder, the New York newspapers headlined the arrival of "Jack the [67] Ripper." Inspector Byrnes and his force concentrated upon solving the crime. Investigation showed that "Old Shakespeare" had arrived at the hotel at about eleven o'clock with a male companion half her age, who gave a name which was written down by the clerk as "C. Knick." They were assigned Room 31, to which they repaired with a tin pail of beer. Several of the hotel hang-abouts saw the man and were able to supply descriptions of him a medium-sized, stocky, blond, seafaring man. This man vanished and was never apprehended. The police combed the water front for him in vain.

Some of "Old Shakespeare's" acquaintances were found, among them Mary Ann Lopez, who had a frequent visitor known in the neighborhood as "Frenchy." Although a decided brunet, Frenchy's general appearance was otherwise not greatly different from the description given of the man who spent the night in Room 31; so Frenchy was arrested, among numerous others, for questioning. He professed not to be able to speak English. Many languages were tried on him until it appeared that he spoke Algerian Arabic—he was an Algerian Frenchman, named Ameer Ben Ali.

On April 25, Frenchy was a suspect. On April 26, the newspapers carried a police statement that he was probably implicated as being a cousin of the murderer. On Wednesday, April 29, the case was still unsettled, with the police apparently at sea. Detective Kilcauley of Jersey City reported to the police that a conductor employed on the New Jersey Central was very sure he had carried the murderer to Easton on his train. All the while, Frenchy was kept in the star cell at the police station.

On April 30, Inspector Byrnes gave several reporters the news that the case against Frenchy was complete, and that the police were convinced that he was the murderer. It was admitted that Frenchy was not "Old Shakespeare's" companion during the fatal night, but it was said that Frenchy had spent the night in Room 33, across the hall from the murder chamber, and that after the other man had left, Frenchy had crept across the hall, robbed his victim and killed her, and then crept back into his own room. As [68] sketched by the Inspector, the evidence against Frenchy consisted of blood drops on the floor of Room 31 (the murder chamber), and in the hall between Rooms 31 and 33 (Frenchy 's room); blood marks on both sides of the door of 33, as if the door had been pushed open by bloody fingers and then closed; blood marks on the floor of Room 33, on a chair in that room, on the bed blanket, and on the bedtick (there were no sheets). Blood was said to have been found on Frenchy's socks, and scrapings from his finger nails indicated the presence of blood. His explanations as to how the blood got on him were investigated and found to be false. Some of Carrie Brown's professional sisters said that Frenchy consorted much with "Old Shakespeare" and occupied Room 31 with her only the previous week.

On this same day (April 30), Frenchy, who by this time was called Frenchy No. 1, to distinguish him from other "Frenchies" involved in the case, was arraigned before Judge Martine and was formally committed to jail for the murder. Since the prisoner was unable to employ counsel, Judge Martine appointed Levy, House and Friend as his counsel. On May 1, Frenchy was removed to the Tombs.

At about this time it was learned that the prisoner had served a vagrancy term in March and April in the Queens County Jail and that two of his fellow prisoners there, David Galloway and Edward Smith, had reported that Frenchy had a knife like the one used in the murder.

On Wednesday, June 24, 1891, Frenchy's trial opened before Recorder Smyth. An interpreter from his own Algerian village had been found in New York. The state was represented by Assistant District Attorneys Wellman and Simms, and the police force by Inspector Byrnes and four officers. In addition to evidence bearing upon the facts as related by the Inspector to reporters on April 30, the prosecutors called many witnesses from the lowest stratum of New York life, to prove that Frenchy had been living a sordid life, and, particularly, that he was accustomed to staying at the East River Hotel and to wandering from room to room at night. On cross-examination, the credibility of these witnesses was thoroughly attacked. [69]

The climax of the trial came on Wednesday, July 1, when District Attorney Nicoll himself took charge of the trial and called Dr. Formand of Philadelphia as an expert witness. Dr. Formand testified that he had made tests of samples of the blood found on the fatal bed in Room 31, in the hallway, on the door to Room 33, inside Room 33, and on Frenchy's socks, and found that they all contained intestinal contents of food elements, all in the same degree of digestion—all exactly identical. This led to the direct inference that all of these bloodstains resulted from blood flowing from the abdominal wound of the deceased. The Doctor stated that he would be willing to risk his life upon the accuracy of his tests. Dr. Austin Flint and Dr. Cyrus Edson corroborated Dr. Formand's testimony, and concluded the case of the state against Frenchy.

On July 8, the defense opened. After calling Constable James R. Hiland of Newtown to prove that when Frenchy was arrested, in Queens County, he had no knife, the defense counsel put the defendant on the stand. He was asked about his life history, his eight years of service in the French army, and his movements in this country. Finally he was asked, "Did you kill Carrie Brown?" These words had hardly been translated into Arabic when Frenchy jumped to his feet, lifted his hands over his head, looked skyward, and fairly screamed in Arabic—he appeared to be having hysterics. No one could quiet him. Finally he sank back into his chair exhausted, and the translator gave the gist of Frenchy's plea: "I am innocent. I am innocent, Allah il Allah [God is God], I am innocent. Allah Akbar [God is great]. I am innocent. O Allah, help me. Allah save me. I implore Allah to help me."

Frenchy made a bad witness, at times appearing to understand English and again pretending not to understand questions even when interpreted into his own tongue. He consistently denied killing "Old Shakespeare," but he became badly tangled up time and again upon cross-examination.

The defense called several medical experts to testify that the substances found in the various blood exhibits did not necessarily all come from the intestine, but that they might [70] have come from other parts of the body. Each of these experts, however, was forced to admit that Dr. Formand was at the top of his profession and that they had high regard for his opinion.

The prosecution added an interesting bit of evidence by showing that Frenchy's tallow candle had been burned for more than an hour in Room 33 on the night of the murder, implying that he had been sitting up for some definite purpose. Testimony was submitted to show that he left the hotel at five o'clock the following morning, and that he "slinked" out of the door in a guilty manner.

The jury soon returned a verdict of guilty of second-degree murder. The Inspector and the prosecutors were much disappointed; but it was apparent that a compromise had been made by the jury. On July 10, 1891, Ameer Ben Ali was sentenced to Sing Sing for life.

The newspapers and the public had taken great interest in the case. The newspapers reported fully the testimony of each witness and the case was avidly followed by thousands. There was little disapproval of the verdict.

Newspaper men, among them Jacob A. Riis and Charles Edward Russell, who had been assigned to the case from the very beginning, were far from satisfied that this presented a true solution to the murder, and felt that it could never be unraveled until the police had found the man who had gone to Room 31 with "Old Shakespeare." However, the public authorities rested when Frenchy went to Sing Sing to spend the remainder of his days—soon to be transferred to the hospital for the criminal insane at Matteawan.

• • • •

PERSISTENT rumors drifted back to New York among seafaring men that the murderer had quietly gone to sea, bound for the Far East. These tales could never be substantiated.

At the turn of the century, however, brighter days came to the penniless Frenchy. An application for a pardon on his behalf, based upon new evidence, was submitted to Governor Odell. It was established that just prior to the murder a man answering the description of the murdered [71] woman's companion had been working for several weeks at Cranford, New Jersey, that this man was absent from Cranford on the night of the murder, and that several days thereafter he disappeared entirely. In his abandoned room was found a brass key bearing a tag 31 (the key exactly matched the set of keys at the East River Hotel) and a bloody shirt. From evidence previously adduced, it was quite certain that the murderer had locked the room when he left it. There never was any evidence to connect Frenchy with the key. The principal evidence against Frenchy had been the reported bloody trail between the two rooms, which, even as testified to at the trial, consisted of very small and faint blood marks. There were submitted to Governor Odell numerous affidavits of disinterested persons, described by the Governor as "persons of credit, some of whom had had experience in the investigation of crime," to the effect that these persons had visited the hotel room on the morning following the murder, and prior to the arrival of the coroner, and that after careful examination they had found no blood on the door of either room or in the hallway. It was to be inferred that the bloodstains, found by the police on the second day following the murder, had been made at the time of the visit of the coroner and the crowd of reporters when the body was examined and removed. It was further pointed out that even according to the police testimony there was no blood on or near the lock or knob of the door to the murder chamber which the murderer presumably unlocked, opened, closed, and relocked. This new evidence in the Governor's opinion demolished the case against Frenchy.

The application for executive clemency was based solely upon the ground that Frenchy was innocent. The Governor concluded his report on the case, after reviewing the facts, as follows: "To refuse relief under such circumstances would be plainly a denial of justice, and after a very careful consideration of all the facts I have reached the conclusion that it is clearly my duty to order the prisoner's release."

Frenchy's sentence was commuted on April 16, 1902, and it is understood that the French Government arranged for his transportation back to his native Algerian village. [72]

• • • •

FRENCHY'S conviction was apparently due to the zealousness of the New York police in seeking to sustain their boast that the murders which had baffled the London police would not be left unsolved in New York. In Frenchy they found a helpless scapegoat, and there is some ground to believe that the case was worked up against him by insufficient attention to the obvious operative facts. Why no better effort was made to trace the woman's companion or to account for the missing key to Room 31 is not easy to understand. That key was also the key to the mystery. As to the blood spots in the hall and on the door of Room 33, the conclusion seems inescapable that they were not there when Clerk Harrington discovered the murder. How they got there, we shall not venture to say. Let it be assumed that careless visitors dragged the blood around. Nor is it clear how the blood got on Frenchy; there is something very strange about that, which the testimony leaves vague and uncertain. Some of the reporters thought that there was no blood originally on Frenchy, or, if there was any, that it had nothing whatever to do with the murder. The evidence of the experts also seems to have been untrustworthy. In spite of the neatly woven case against Frenchy, the jury evidently had grave doubts, for in such a case a verdict of second-degree murder is not natural. It was manifestly a compromise between a belief in guilt and innocence. Frenchy was also penniless and the assigned counsel could not command the funds to run down the man who had occupied Room 31. The fact that entirely disinterested persons unraveled the mystery attests the weakness of the prosecution's case and justifies the inference that Allah had apparently not altogether deserted Frenchy. [73]

They Went Hunting

Galindo., Hernandez, Mendival

EVERYTHING was quiet in the First National Bank of Arcadia, California, as the noon hour was drawing to a close on April 5, 1922. No customers were there. The president of the bank, Mr. Dunham, was standing at the teller's window checking some slips. Cashier Hatterscheid and Bookkeeper Stover were in the cages working on their accounts. Miss Montgomery, another bookkeeper, was due back from lunch in a few minutes. Suddenly bank routine was interrupted by a crisp command—"I mean business." The speaker was standing at the teller's window of Mr. Dunham, who understood the real meaning of the words when he glanced up and saw the barrel of a pistol pointed at him. Two other bandits carrying guns were covering Hatterscheid and Stover. They, with Mr. Dunham, were ordered to lie down in a row on the floor, face down. While one bandit stood guard over them, the other two began their work. At this moment Miss Montgomery appeared and was immediately ordered to join the others. A customer (Marshall Dessem) entered the bank and was promptly ordered to join the ranks on the floor.

In some haste and rather awkwardly, the bandits rifled the money drawer and the safe. They addressed remarks to each other occasionally, using perfect English. The whole proceeding took but a few minutes. The loot was stuck into two canvas bags, whereupon the three bandits quickly retreated through the front door of the bank and entered a Chevrolet touring car, in which a fourth man had been waiting at the curb. Mr. Dunham immediately notified the police and reported that the robbers had taken about $2,800 in currency and silver, $3,720 in bonds, and $2,700 in American Express travelers' checks. None of the bandits wore a mask.

The countryside was immediately warned by the police siren at Monrovia, a few miles east of Arcadia, that criminals were being hunted. A few minutes later Virgil Barlow, a farmer living several miles south of Arcadia, saw a [74] Chevrolet speed by his place, plunge into a washout, and disappear. Barlow got into his own car and went to look- for the Chevrolet. He found that it had been driven about three-quarters of a mile farther on and was standing unoccupied across the bridge on Chicago Park Island in the San Gabriel River.

When the car passed his farm he had seen four or five men in it, and he decided that they might be the men sought by the police who had sounded the siren. He notified the police at once, and Constable James L. Quipple was sent to investigate.

He discovered that the radiator of the Chevrolet was still warm. The license plates had been torn off, and on the rear seat were a number of paper wrappers, used for wrapping coins. It was found that the car had been stolen. Neither Barlow nor Quipple could find a trace of the recent occupants.

An hour after the holdup four Mexicans were arrested while driving through San Gabriel Valley toward Los Angeles in a Ford. Five guns were found on them, and in the back seat were two canvas sacks. The Mexicans at first gave aliases, but were finally identified as Faustino Rivera, Broulio Galindo, Jose Hernandez, and Salvador Mendival. They said they had rented the Ford in Los Angeles that morning and were in San Gabriel to pick oranges. The revolvers, they said, were for rabbit shooting.

The police doubted their story and took them at once to the bank at Arcadia, lined them up in front of the bank's employees, and asked if they were the robbers who had been there an hour before.

Dunham and Marshall Dessem, the customer who had entered the bank during the holdup, could identify only Rivera. Hatterscheid identified Rivera and Galindo. Miss Montgomery was positive about Galindo, and Stover said he recognized Galindo and Hernandez. None of them identified Mendival, so it was supposed that he was the man who had stayed outside in the car. He was partially identified by G. A. Cane, a telephone-company employee, who was working near by. Cane said Mendival's complexion resembled that [75] of the man he saw sitting in the Chevrolet. The Mexicans' car was examined by the bank employees, and Hatterscheid claimed that he found a silver dollar on the back seat.

On further police investigation, it was discovered that Galindo and Hernandez had been previously convicted of felonies; and several days after the holdup a scarf pin was taken from Galindo and identified by Miss Montgomery as one she had seen on one of the bandits.

In May the four were indicted, and on September 27 three of them were brought to trial—Rivera having died in jail. It was the theory of the prosecution that the Mexicans had used the Chevrolet to escape from the bank, driven it to the island, where the Ford had been left, changed cars, and started back to Los Angeles to return the Ford, which they actually had rented the morning of the robbery. The two sacks found in the car were partially identified as those used by the robbers, as were two men's caps and the five guns.

The defense could find but one alibi witness, and he testified that Galindo was in San Gabriel at the time of the robbery. Several character witnesses testified for Mendival. The prosecution was unable to explain how it was possible for these men who had to testify through an interpreter to use such fluent English as described and quoted by the bank employees. Neither was any attempt made to explain what became of the loot, though the defendants were captured within forty-five minutes of the holdup.

The three men denied any knowledge of the crime and stuck to the story of their innocent excursion to San Gabriel to pick oranges. Just before the case was given to the jury, Galindo, through the interpreter, told the court:

> This is an outrage that the people of the bank and the community want to do to us. It is an outrage, an injustice, because we haven't done anything. They have caught us with some weapons; we have delivered them to the officers; they have found some bags that were in the automobile. They have found these bags in the automobile, they have returned those bags, those sacks to us that we might put them into our pockets. And when they arrived at the bank they took us inside and they placed the weapons out in front of us so that they could be seen, and they asked a young lady there and a young man, who was also there, if we were the parties concerned, [76] and the young lady began to look at us and said that I resembled some one; that I resembled that I had a white face and that I looked like the man that was there, and then one of the policemen, a fat man who testified here yesterday, was standing at the side and nodded to her in an affirmative way so that she might say that it was I who was there. This is really an injustice. We haven't committed any crime. That is all.

The jury found all three guilty, and on November 6 Galindo and Hernandez were sentenced to from one year to life and taken to Folsom. On November 9 Mendival was sent to San Quentin for a term of one to ten years.

• • • •

SOON after the trial a Mr. Jack Thomas appeared at the office of the Deputy District Attorney, Mr. Burke, and informed him that the Mexicans had had nothing to do with the Arcadia holdup, and he named as the guilty men Frank Sullivan, W. F. McMahon, Tom Gray, and Eddie Burns. He told the Deputy District Attorney that he knew these men and that they had told him that they were the actual bandits.

Almost simultaneously, these four men happened to be arrested in Los Angeles on a liquor charge. It was then found that Sullivan had used a United States bond for the purchase of liquor and that this bond was one of those taken from the Arcadia bank in the holdup. Six hundred dollars in travelers' checks stolen from the bank were found buried at a ranch in Artesia. This had been done by Tom Gray. Gradually a complete chain of evidence was forged by the authorities linking these four men with the Arcadia crime, although there was a time early in the investigation when they were released for lack of evidence.

Finally, however, the story was unraveled, and in 1924 the four were indicted, together with E. S. McCardia and Sam Fair, who were also indirectly involved. A former Los Angeles policeman, Hubert Kittle, and David McGregor were indicted for receiving stolen goods in connection with the disposal of the travelers' checks under a forged name. Kittle committed suicide before the trial. The others were convicted. [77]

As soon as the indictments against the real criminals had been brought in, the District Attorney and Sheriff Treager, who always suspected that a mistake had been made and continued the investigation, took steps to bring about a governor's pardon for the Mexicans. On May 2, 1924, Mendival was pardoned. Hernandez was pardoned May 26, and Galindo, on September 30. They had served practically two years for a crime of which they were innocent. They received no compensation.

What became of Galindo and Hernandez is not known. Mendival, who had always had a good record, discovered that the position he held before his arrest had been taken by someone else. When he entered prison he had left behind him a wife and a young baby in the little house he was buying on the instalment plan. When he returned they had vanished, apparently driven from their home by poverty.

• • • •

THIS is another case of circumstantial evidence supported by mistaken identification by the victims. The obvious facts which pointed to the complete innocence of the men were apparently disregarded by the police, the prosecution, and the jury, namely, that the men spoke no English, whereas the robbers spoke perfect English; that they were in a Ford car, and not in a Chevrolet; and that the loot was not found on them one-half hour after the crime. Those who commit robbery or theft usually have the money on them, if caught immediately, or prove to have changed their normal habits of spending, if apprehended later. The identification was misguided, as it so often is, by preconceptions and assumptions and by the keen desire to avenge a crime and fasten it upon someone who might plausibly have been guilty. There is some indication that the police were not disinterested or impartial. The fact that two of the men had been in the toils of the law before undoubtedly counted heavily against them. There were so many palpable and avoidable slips in the administration of justice in this case, however, that the state should have offered an indemnity even without a [78] petition. Mendival's life seems to have been ruined by the ghastly episode. So far as can be discovered, no indemnity was requested under the California law from the State Board of Control. [79]

"Copper-Riveted and Air-Tight"

Irving Greenwald

IN January, 1924, a number of money-order blanks were stolen from post-office substation No. 28, located in a drug store in Buffalo, New York, by a man who came into the store to use the telephone. The telephone booth was situated near the cage which inclosed the small post office. The man was of not unusual appearance, probably between five and a half and six feet tall, and around twenty-five years of age; and other than that, he was described as having blond hair and blue eyes. No particular thought was given to him until the blanks were found to have disappeared. The postal authorities were notified, and the usual procedure was followed to arrest the culprit.

The stolen blanks began to appear in New York in February and March. Some man came into the store of the A. Taylor Trunk Works on the twenty-first of February, bought some goods, and cashed one of them. He received $65 cash in change from the clerk, John Gravich. The money order purported to have been issued in Buffalo, New York, on February 17, at post-office substation No. 28, and bore the name of W. Gallagher, the postal clerk at that substation. This order bore the number 32,469.

The next orders appeared about March 21, 1924. One of them, for $75, was cashed in Wanamaker's store. Some goods were bought from a clerk, Miss Elizabeth A. Colby; and when the money order was presented, the man was sent to the credit department, where Mr. Noble, credit man for Wanamaker's, approved cashing it. This one bore the number 32,475. The third money order was given to R. J. Melamede, of Reynolds & Melamede, druggists at 275 Amsterdam Avenue, bore the number 32,457, and was for the amount of $25. Another was passed the same day to C. Stiefel, a clerk in the Schwartz Brothers' jewelry store at 1454 Broadway. It was for $75 and bore the number 32,476. Various dates were placed on them, but all purported to have been issued at substation No. 28 in Buffalo. The man gave the name of J. C. Alderman. [80]

The post-office inspectors followed the trail closely, with Inspector Gurnie Smith in charge. At the end of March they brought about the arrest, on Wall Street, of a man who fitted the general description of build and weight given by the several persons who had been tricked. He had blue eyes and blond hair. Detectives tapped him on the shoulder, addressed him as J. C. Alderman, and told him to come along with them for examination. He asked the detectives what kind of game they were playing. When assured it was not a game he still thought it very amusing and willingly consented to accompany the officers. He merely insisted that his name was Irving Greenwald and that he had never heard of Alderman.

The detectives were unconvinced, and he was taken into custody. Some or all of the clerks from the stores which had been imposed on were called to identify him as the man who had passed the forged money orders. They identified him as the man, and things became more serious. On April 11, the grand- jury indictment was filed against him for passing and uttering forged money orders purporting to have been issued by the postmaster at Buffalo, and in violation of Section 218 of the Federal Criminal Code. He was indicted on four counts, one for each of the four money orders.

The Hon. J. Joseph Lilly, at one time Assistant United States Attorney in New York, had known Greenwald and his family for a long time, and Greenwald asked that Lilly defend him. Mr. Lilly investigated the case against Greenwald. He had been associated with Hon. James Johnson, the Assistant District Attorney who had charge of the prosecution of Greenwald, and was told that the identification of Greenwald by the several clerks, the credit man, and the druggist, was positive and that they would all swear that Greenwald was the man who cashed the money orders—that the case against Greenwald was "cast-iron, brass-bound, copper riveted and air tight." As Mr. Lilly knew that Johnson was not addicted to exaggerated statements, he went to Greenwald, who was confined in the Tombs Prison, and advised him that, if he was guilty, it would be best to plead guilty and thus perhaps obtain the court's mercy. But Greenwald [81] stoutly asserted his innocence, and flatly refused to plead guilty, although he did not have a single witness to call in his behalf. He had no money with which to hire experts to prove that the handwriting on the forged money orders was not his. Possibly that would have been of little avail in the face of his very positive identification by the Government's witnesses and of the fact that the indictment was for uttering and passing forged money orders, not forging them.

Accordingly a plea of not guilty was entered for him on April 14. The trial was set for the twenty-first of April, and was concluded on the twenty-second. Greenwald took the stand in his own defense and completely contradicted the Government's witnesses; but to no avail, for the jury, after remaining out only a few minutes, returned with a verdict of guilty. That same day he was sentenced to seven and a half years in the Federal penitentiary at Atlanta, Georgia, two and a half years each on three of the four counts on which he had been indicted, one having been dropped. Greenwald, when questioned by the court, vehemently and stubbornly asserted his lack of knowledge of anything in any way connected with the crimes; but Judge Francis A. Winslow gave him practically the maximum sentence possible, after a denunciation for his persistence in maintaining his innocence. In a few days Greenwald was taken to the Atlanta penitentiary.

• • • •

SOON after Greenwald was imprisoned, other stolen money orders began to appear in Philadelphia and New York, and Inspector Gurnie Smith was again put on the trail. The money orders in Philadelphia were passed under practically the same circumstances as those in New York, and by a man who answered the description of the man who had passed them in New York. Within sixty days of the time Greenwald had been convicted, Mr. Lilly was called to the office of Assistant District Attorney Johnson and informed by Mr. Johnson and Inspector Gurnie Smith that apparently Greenwald was not the man who had passed the forged money orders, but that another man then in custody was the [82] real criminal. The money orders which had been passed in Philadelphia and New York bore the same forged signature of W. Gallagher, the name of the Buffalo postmaster, and bore numbers very close to those which had been passed earlier in New York. Two of them were: 32,474 and 32,481.

To make sure that the actual culprit had been captured, the witnesses who had testified against Greenwald were again called to identify this second man, Richard Barry, who also used the names W. H. Ford and John Derby. Barry had given the names of the places where he passed money orders, and had told just how they had been stolen in Buffalo. When presented to the witnesses, he told each of them the circumstances under which he had cashed the money orders, described the goods he had bought, and described his actions as well as their actions and appearance at the time. All save one of the witnesses now identified Barry as the man who had passed the money orders. The only one who did not change his identification was the postal clerk in Buffalo, but he was not present at the time Barry was being investigated. Except for the blond hair and the blue eyes, there was no material resemblance between Greenwald and Barry. Upon the information of the witnesses who had once identified Greenwald, Barry was indicted on the same counts as Greenwald, and on June 23, 1924, pleaded guilty and was sentenced to three years in the Atlanta penitentiary.

Now two men were in Atlanta for a crime of which one only could have been guilty. Barry disclaimed knowing or ever having known Greenwald, and it was clear that only one of them stole the money orders from the post office in Buffalo, and only one man had passed them in New York. To secure Greenwald's speedy release from prison, Mr. Lilly made a motion for a new trial upon the ground of newly discovered evidence. This was done within the ninety days allowed under the fifth General Rule of the United States District Court, in which the case was tried, and under the authority of R.S. 918 and Judicial Code, Section 269. At the hearing of the motion, the affidavits in support alleging that Barry and not Greenwald was the criminal were conceded to be true by the District Attorney; but the application was

[83] denied by Judge Winslow upon the authority of the case of *U.S. v. Howe*, 280 Fed. 815, which holds that it is doubtful whether the court has the power to rescind its judgment and grant a new trial after a sentence of imprisonment has been in part executed. The court, it is believed, misconceived the purport of that case. But as the application for a new trial is addressed to the discretion of the District Court, no appeal from its denial could be taken to the Circuit Court of Appeals. This technicality caused considerable further delay and left open only one avenue for Greenwald's freedom a presidential pardon.

On August 7, 1924, Irving Greenwald was given a full and unconditional pardon by President Coolidge, on the ground that he was "innocent of the . . , offenses of which he was convicted."

• • • •

THIS is another case of mistaken identity. It is not unusual, either in the fact that four or five persons identified the wrong man, or that the resemblance was very slight. The emotions of the victim of injury, fraud, or deception create a predisposition to believe the worst of a person brought before him as the probable offender, especially when there is no alternative suspect. Motive is a persuasive interpreter of probabilities and possibilities, which under the passion of injured pride easily become "certainties." When two alternative offenders are presented, impartial judgment, discretion, a balancing of evidence and truth have a better chance. So it proved in the Greenwald case. Postal Inspector Gurnie Smith was perhaps a little more sure than was justified, and may well have exerted an unconscious influence upon the victims to identify Greenwald. He is to be given credit for admitting his mistake, and opening the road to the correction of the error. Judge Winslow was excessively technical, if not, indeed, perhaps wrong on his legal grounds, in prolonging Greenwald's detention by refusing him a new trial and compelling resort to the President's pardon. Judge Winslow's denunciation of Greenwald when pronouncing sentence, though conceived in good faith, proves to have [84] been rather unfortunate. Greenwald was restored to society, but the injury done him by the administrative machine has never been repaired.

• • • •

Acknowledgments: Hon. J. Joseph Lilly, Office of the Corporation Counsel, Municipal Building, New York City; Hon. Robert B. Watts, Assistant United States District Attorney, New York City. [85]

THE MAN IN THE BROWN COAT

William Habron

THE bar at the Royal Oak in the little town of Whalley Range, near Manchester, was busy on a Saturday night in July, 1876. The usual Saturday night gathering was drinking and arguing in an atmosphere of smoke and the blended odors of strong liquors.

Prominent among the patrons' of this inn were the brothers Habron—William, John, and Frank. They were employed on the Deakin farm.

William was a powerful youth of twenty-two—tall, broad, pugnacious, and capable with his fists. William's encounters with other patrons of the place were famous throughout the community, and no one knew William's *penchant* better than Constable Cock, whose beat passed the door of the Royal Oak.

It was the proprietor's custom to call upon the able Cock to pacify Habron and his chance opponent on the frequent occasions when the fray threatened to wreck the furnishings of the inn.

On this particular night Cock was uneasy. It was near ten and nothing had happened. Cock felt it should. There was drinking in the inn. Habron was there. Trouble was in the air.

The previous week he had been called in by the proprietor when William broke loose with his fists, and after he had quieted the principals he said to Habron: "Look here, Habron, I'm tired of this. The next time you raise disorder here I'll have you up before the Magistrate."

Habron did not take the threat kindly. His prestige was being challenged before an audience. If he failed to answer they would think he was afraid of Cock, so he growled: "It'll be a sorry day for you, the day you arrest me."

The tables were turned. It was now up to Cock to make good his threat. This made him uneasy. He did not want to start a feud with the Habrons; still he felt that these repeated outbursts of violence must be stopped. He was in a, quandary, but his doubts were soon settled. [86]

About ten o'clock he was passing the inn and heard sounds of fighting. Without waiting to be called he ran into the bar and there saw William and another man pounding each other furiously. He stepped between them, placed Habron under arrest, and took him to the station.

It so happens that this time William was not to blame. He had gone to the inn determined to control himself. He had been moderate in his drinking and conducted himself with exemplary propriety for one of his aggressive character. And it was this very moderation that started the trouble. Another young farm hand, inspired by liquor, interpreted William's unusual attitude as evidence of weakness and decided that it was an appropriate time to pick a fight. And this is what Cock did not know.

So well substantiated was the contention that William was blameless that the magistrate dismissed the case next day. This rather complicated matters in William's mind, for Cock had made good his threat and also done him a serious injustice, so he forced his way through the spectators in the court room and walked up to Cock.

"I promised you a sorry day if you ever ran foul of me," he said. "I'll do you in for this."

"Oh, you're all bluster and wind," Cock replied. "I know you."

Near midnight Cock was murdered.

Cock was walking along his beat with another constable, James Beanland, and John Massey Simpson, a law student. It was ten minutes of twelve. They stopped at a corner to talk a few minutes and then Simpson went on his way. Soon after, Beanland left to follow a man who had passed the three while they were talking. The man disappeared in the shadows and a minute later two shots were fired.

Simpson had gone but a short distance. He ran back and found two carters pulling up their horses; Beanland was in the middle of the road whistling for help, and Cock was lying a few yards from where the two men had left him.

He had shouted, "Murder, I'm shot, I'm shot," when the bullets hit him, but he could not say who fired them; a few minutes later he died. [87]

Police Superintendent Bent joined the group around the dying man. Bent was told that the man Beanland started to follow was dressed in a brown coat, pot hat, and walked with a stoop. "I suspect it's that Will Habron," he said.

Bent and several constables started for the Deakin farm. As they approached the cabin in which Habron and his brothers lived, they saw a candlelight flicker for a moment in the window and then go out.

Bent knocked. "We are armed and will shoot unless you light up and show you mean to give no trouble," he called out.

Again a candle was lighted. The brothers were getting out of bed and dressing hurriedly. William opened the door.

"William Habron, John Habron, Frank Habron, I arrest you in the name of the law for the murder of Constable Cock," Bent announced.

"We were in bed at the time," William replied.

Bent noted this remark in his book and asked, "Where are your boots?"

The soles were covered with fresh mud. Bent wrapped them up to take with him. He searched William's clothes and found two percussion caps of revolver caliber. He ordered the brothers to dress and saw that William put on a brown coat and a pot hat, and on the way to the station he noticed that William walked with a decided stoop.

The brothers were lodged in jail. Bent returned to the scene of the murder carrying one of William's boots. Near the spot where Cock fell were boot tracks. They showed a sole with rows of nails down each side and two rows in the middle. The number and position, he found, corresponded with the number and position of the nails in William's boot.

The community was excited by the murder and news of it spread rapidly. Presently two clerks from a store in a village near by came to Superintendent Bent and said a man had priced revolver cartridges in their store the afternoon before the murder. They believed they were such cartridges as those used to kill Cock. The clerks said their customer had worn a brown coat and a pot hat.

Habron was pointed out to them. [88]

"That's the man," said one clerk.

"It looks rather like him," said the other.

At the preliminary hearing William and John were held for trial. Frank was released. The two brothers were tried in Manchester. The prosecution's case was strong. The incidents related above were skilfully handled by the prosecutor. His examination of the brothers was conducted so adroitly that he soon had them contradicting themselves and making a very bad impression upon the jury.

The defense was hard put to answer, but made a desperate fight. Mr. Deakin testified that William was a hard worker and very peaceful on the farm. He explained the presence of the percussion caps in William's vest by saying he had given the vest to William and often carried such caps in his clothes so that those found by the police were probably his.

The defense also pointed out that whoever priced the cartridges described by the two clerks did not buy them, and this the clerks admitted.

The threat against Cock and his murder the same night were said by the defense to have been merely an unfortunate coincidence and not proof that Habron was the killer. The boot print was hard to refute, but as Bent had made neither photograph nor cast of it, the judge and the jury were unable to determine the resemblance for themselves and had to rely solely upon Bent's testimony.

The prosecution was unable to offer in evidence the weapon used in the murder, though a careful search had been made at the scene and among the possessions of the Habrons. This point was emphasized by the defense as well as the fact that William's style of boots and their nails were common among farm hands as well as the brown coat and the pot hat.

But the jury was not convinced. After deliberating several hours they returned a verdict of not guilty for John and guilty for William, with the recommendation of mercy because of his youth.

The court asked William if he had anything to say before sentence of death should be passed and he answered, "I am innocent." [89]

The court then put on the black cap and sentenced him to be hanged. On leaving the dock the prisoner raised his hands and repeated, "I am innocent."

• • • •

COCK had been murdered about midnight August 1, 1876. Habron was sentenced November 28, 1876. The Crown accepted the jury's recommendation and William's sentence was commuted to life imprisonment at Portland Prison.

On the day William was sentenced a spectator caused considerable disturbance in the gallery by his aggressive attempt to get a place near the front. He forced his way through the spectators, ignoring their emphatic protests, until he reached the edge, where he announced, "I came all the way from Sheffield to see this trial."

This man was Charles Peace, later revealed as one of the most brutal, clever, and dangerous criminals in English police history.

Charles Peace was hideous physically as well as mentally. He had a skull like a monkey, with an undershot jaw, a thick, flat nose, and eyes set deep in his head. His skull was bare in front but thick with hair at the sides, which formed a deep oval across the crown. At the time of Habron's trial Peace was forty-four.

His principal occupation was crime—crime of all kinds; and though he had been in prison several times it is certain that he escaped punishment for scores of offenses. His hobby was the fiddle and with it he earned a little money playing in saloons, at parties, and on the street. He often wandered over the country paying his way with this violin. He dabbled in picture framing, wood carving, singing, composing, writing poetry, teaching Sunday school, and inventing.

The night after William Habron was sentenced to death, Albert Dyson, a civil engineer, was murdered at Banner Cross and Charles Peace was the killer. Some time before this, Peace became acquainted with the Dysons, who then were his neighbors in Darnall, a suburb of Sheffield. He had become enamored of Mrs. Dyson, an Irishwoman of twenty-five, and had urged her to leave her husband. Despite his [90] facial handicap and his character, Peace exerted a powerful influence over certain women and Mrs. Dyson was r one of them.

As the result of his persistent pursuit of Mrs. Dyson, her husband determined to be rid of him; and after Peace grossly insulted him on the street one day he swore out a warrant for his arrest. Peace learned of this move and went to Hull before the warrant could be served.

He kept close watch on the Dysons' movements, however, and on the night of November 29, 1876, he returned to murder Dyson. This he did in Dyson's home, in the presence of Mrs. Dyson, and then escaped.

Two years later he was living under the name of Thompson at 5 East Terrace, Eveline Road, Peckham, London, S.E., supposedly engaged with Mr. Brion, a neighbor, in the invention of a method for "raising sunken vessels by the displacement of water within the vessels by air and gases."

He was popular among his neighbors and entertained frequently at musical parties, proud of his collection of violins, banjos, and numerous other instruments. He attended church regularly and had at his home an odd assortment of dogs, cats, rabbits, canaries, parrots, and cockatoos and was "curious as to why a Christian nation should support the very un-Christian Turks against the Christian Russians."

He always went to bed early "but not to sleep for he 'worked' by night and most successfully."

His household included Mrs. Peace, known as Mrs. Ward, and her son, Willie. These two lived in the basement. Upstairs Peace lived with "Mrs. Thompson," alias Susan Grey, a woman he had picked up in his wanderings with his fiddle. She was addicted to the frequent and extensive use of strong drink, with the result that Peace was constantly complaining of her liquor bills, which, he said, often ran as high as £3 in two days.

The acquaintances he made in Peckham were valuable to him. He was entertained and was always careful to observe the layout of the rooms in the homes he visited and to scan well the locks on doors and windows.

The community was soon plagued by an epidemic of [91] burglary. It spread to others near by. Presently the whole country was talking about it, but the police could not find the burglar.

The night of October 10, 1878, Constable Robinson was patrolling his beat in Blackheath, a lonely London suburb, when he saw a light moving about a room in the home of J. A. Burness in St. John's Park. Robinson knew that the Burness' retired early so he called the constable on the next beat, Girling', to investigate with him. As they were about to start Sergeant Brown came along. He sent Robinson and Girling to watch the back of the house while he went up to the front door and rang the bell.

The light went out. A window on the first floor opened. Robinson and Girling saw a man climb out with a bundle under his arm. As Robinson started after him the man turned and said calmly, "Stop, or I'll shoot."

Robinson jumped for him and the man fired. The fifth bullet shattered Robinson's elbow but he grappled with the burglar and with his good arm managed to strike the man squarely on the chin as the latter drew a long knife. The man dropped to the ground, and as Brown and Girling came up Robinson collapsed from loss of blood.

The prisoner was taken to the station and revived. He was booked as a mulatto and refused to give his name, but the police soon discovered that his dark skin was a disguise applied with walnut juice.

With the arrest the epidemic of burglaries ceased. The prisoner, who gave the name "John Ward," was convicted and sentenced to life imprisonment for assault with intent to murder Robinson.

For some reason he wrote his friend Brion and asked him to call at the prison. Brion came and immediately identified "Ward" as Thompson and from this his actual identity was discovered. He was taken from prison and tried for the murder of Albert Dyson. On February 4, 1879, he was convicted and sentenced to death.

Peace then began a pious preparation for death. He wished to confess his manifold sins and called for the Reverend Littlewood to hear his story and there was then unfolded the tale of Constable Cock's murder. [92]

Peace was the man in the brown coat and pot hat. His was the hand that pulled the trigger. He told the story in such detail that the authorities, at first skeptical, finally undertook a very thorough investigation and substantiated his assertions one by one until they were completely satisfied that no one but the actual murderer could have had such an intimate knowledge of the crime.

Cock, it seems, had interrupted Peace on one of his nocturnal adventures, and met a fate which Robinson barely escaped.

After three years in prison William Habron was granted a free pardon and was voted by Parliament £500 indemnification. On February 25, 1879, Charles Peace was hanged.

• • • •

THIS was a case of circumstantial evidence exclusively. Habron's threat directed at Constable Cock and the latter's murder immediately thereafter turned public suspicion naturally upon Habron. Whether Inspector Bent was altogether accurate in his report on the boots was later seriously doubted. The prosecution, convinced of Habron's guilt, discredited all the evidence pointing to his complete innocence. The jury were convinced by the prosecution's clever construction of its theory of guilt and fell into the same trap of blindness to the factors indicating innocence. But for Peace's insatiable appetite for crime, it is quite possible that Habron would have served out his life term. Peace's confession was also a matter of good luck for Habron. Confessions are always looked upon with suspicion, but this one was so authentic in every detail that the Home Office was thoroughly convinced and recommended the appropriation of £500 as indemnity to Habron for his erroneous conviction. [93]

"HELL HATH NO FURY"

Hess and Craig

AT about 1:30 in the morning of January 7, 1929, Deputy Sheriff J. W. Dugan of Herculaneum, Jefferson County, Missouri, was aroused by the ringing of his telephone. Lifting the receiver, he heard an anguished voice asking for help. It was Virgil Romine, at the Artesian Park Filling Station near St. Louis, moaning that he had been shot and urging the sheriff to hurry over. In a few minutes, the sheriff had reached the filling station. Shortly thereafter, L. H. Jones, owner of the station and of the attached restaurant, and Dr. O. E. Hensley arrived. They found Romine sitting in a chair in the restaurant suffering intensely and bleeding profusely from fresh bullet wounds in the abdomen. Perspiration was pouring from his face. Blood smears were on the floor. The furniture was flung around in the room, indicating a violent scuffle. Romine, in agony, begged to be taken to a hospital.

While Dr. Hensley was administering first-aid treatment, Romine gave directions to Mr. Jones concerning the delivery of his property to his mother, in case he should die. He signed a check for $700, payable to his mother, and requested Mr. Jones to deliver it to her.

Sheriff Dugan urged Romine to tell how he had been shot and who did it. The wounded man related that three or four men and a woman—all dressed in overalls and caps—stopped at the restaurant and ordered food. One, a tall, slim man, ordered a hamburger sandwich. When Romine went to the kitchen to prepare it, this fellow followed him and shot him. In the ensuing scuffle, Romine got his gun and tried to defend himself. His own wounds were so grievously painful that he didn't know what followed. Sheriff Dugan went into the kitchen and saw the hamburger still sizzling on the stove. Romine added:

> I can't tell you their names but you can find out. It is the same fellows I had trouble with up here a couple of weeks ago over the slugging of a slot machine and I run them away that night and they ran off and left their automobile here. They settled it with Mr. [94] Jones and he finally let them take their machine away. The fellows were often seen around old lady Vinyard's place.

Dr. Hensley took Romine to a St. Louis hospital in an ambulance. He had been mortally wounded, however, and lived only a few hours.

Mr. Jones remembered two boys who had come to him a couple of weeks earlier and who had admitted that they had slugged a slot machine for seventy-five cents. They paid Mr. Jones seventy-five cents, and he in return gave them a written message to the person in charge of the filling station so that they might get their detained car. At 2:30, Sheriff Dugan went to the Vinyard place, about half a mile up the road. There he found the Vinyard daughter sitting with a friend in a car in front of the house. Mrs. Vinyard was still up. She showed the sheriff to a room where two boys were asleep with her son, Jimmie. They were Alvin Craig and Walter Hess, about nineteen years old, of Crystal City. The boys, awakened, said that they had left Crystal City late that afternoon to visit Jimmie. They picked up a ride and arrived at the Vinyards' around six o'clock. After playing cards for a time, they all went to bed and had been there ever since. Mrs. Vinyard confirmed the statement that they had not been away from the house that night. The boys readily admitted that they had had trouble with Virgil Romine a short time before over slugging a slot machine and that they had fixed it up with Mr. Jones, the owner. Sheriff Dugan arrested the boys, since Romine had said positively that his assailant was one of the boys who had slugged the slot machine. Furthermore, these boys had rather bad reputations.

The following morning, a crew of men working for the State Highway Department about a mile north of the filling station found overalls and a pair of trousers, both of which bore bloodstains. They were thrown on a fire and burned. A little later, a white shirt was found with a bloody sleeve and a colored shirt with a hole in it and a bloody splotch. These shirts were turned over to the St. Louis Police Department.

The county officers shortly thereafter received word that Leo Bassler of Ste Genevieve, Missouri, and Dewey [95] Grieshaber of St. Louis had been in the Artesian Restaurant, after one o'clock on the fatal night; they had stopped for some sandwiches and coffee. They related that just before they left the restaurant, three young fellows, roughly clad, and a girl dressed in men's clothes, entered the restaurant, sat down at a table, and ordered food. One of the men was rather heavy, but the other two were very young and weighed only about 130 pounds. One of these young fellows left the table to play the slot machine, and just as Bassler and Grieshaber were leaving, he ordered a "hamburger." This lad, they said, wore a blue shirt, overalls, a cap, and a dark coat. Neither Bassler nor Grieshaber could identify Hess or Craig as among this party, but their descriptions of the two slightly built men fairly well suited the accused boys.

In addition to this information, John Bechler, County Treasurer and a respected citizen of Jefferson County, reported that he had heard Walter Hess make the statement that on the morning of the murder he saw the headlights of an automobile coming toward old lady Vinyard's house, and had said to his comrade Alvin, "Here comes the law." Walter denied making any such statement.

On January 14, 1929, just one week from the date of the murder,

Prosecuting Attorney Charles W. Green filed an information against the boys in the Circuit Court of Jefferson County, charging them with first-degree murder. At the trial, which took place on April 18-19, 1929, before Judge E. M. Dearing, the Prosecuting Attorney was assisted by R. E. Kleinschmidt. The prisoners were defended by Attorney Albert S. Ennis. Mr. Ennis endeavored to exclude, as inadmissible hearsay, the testimony of Sheriff Dugan and Mr. Jones as to what Virgil Romine had said about his assailants. The court, however, admitted this testimony as a dying declaration. The defense attorney also sought to establish alibis for both Hess and Craig, by the testimony of Mrs. Tiney Craig, mother of Alvin; Mrs. Hess, mother of Walter; and Mrs. Vinyard. Further, he showed that no other murder or shooting had occurred in the vicinity at that time, thus raising the implication that the bloody clothes found by the road crew must have been discarded by the [96] bandits, and that one of the bandits, at least, must have been rather badly wounded. Neither Hess nor Craig had any wounds. The defendants testified in their own behalf, but to no avail. The jury found both boys guilty of second-degree murder, Judge Dearing having given instructions to the jury on both first- and second-degree murder, over the objection of the defense. On June 10, 1929, each defendant was sentenced to a ten-year term in the Missouri State Penitentiary.

Pending appeal, Craig was admitted to bail, but Hess, unable to raise bail, had to go to the penitentiary.

• • • •

THE appeal was never heard by the Supreme Court of Missouri. Before the expiration of the year provided for the perfection of the appeal, one Mamie (Babe) Woolem went to the police in St. Louis and volunteered the information that she had accompanied her former sweetheart, Louis Taylor, and two of his friends, Radford Browning and Joe Muehlman, to Herculaneum on the night of January 6, 1929, when the restaurant keeper at the Artesian Filling Station had been shot. She stated that Taylor had done the shooting. The three men named were immediately arrested. Taylor strongly denied knowing anything about the case. The police then required Taylor to put on the blue shirt in which a bullet hole had been made; a scar, giving every evidence of having been a bullet wound, was found on his body at the exact spot left by the hole in the shirt. Taylor also, thought the police, answered the descriptions given by Bassler and Grieshaber. Upon these developments, Taylor broke down and confessed that they had intended to rob the station and that he had done the shooting. Browning and Muehlman then also confessed.

Taylor, Browning, and Muehlman pleaded guilty in the May, 1930, term of the Circuit Court. Taylor was given a life sentence, and the other two ten years each. Mamie Woolem maintained that, while she had been along on the trip, she knew nothing about the intention to rob the filling station. Taylor, however, turned state's witness against her [97] and testified that she had planned the holdup herself and had supplied him with the gun used in shooting Romine. She stood trial, was convicted, and was given a life sentence.

With the disclosure of these facts, the whole situation was submitted to Governor Caulfield of Missouri, who granted pardons to Hess and Craig on the ground that they were innocent men.

• • • •

IT appears that when the St. Louis police received the two shirts on January 7, 1929, they established a sharp lookout for a wounded man. None was found. It later developed that Taylor, who had shot Romine and had been wounded by him, was at the time a soldier stationed at the Jefferson Barracks. Upon returning to St. Louis, Mamie Woolem dressed his injury, a flesh wound only, in her rooms; Taylor reported at the Barracks the next morning and asked for a few days' leave of absence on the plea of sickness. This was granted without examination. During his leave, Mamie dressed the wound and cared for him. He was sufficiently recovered, upon the expiration of his leave, so that no one ever learned of the wound. The identity of the bandits was completely concealed until Taylor, over a year later, permitted his amorous attentions to wander afield, a fact which incited Mamie to retaliate by "squealing."

• • • •

THE misfortune of Hess and Craig was due to an extraordinary concatenation of circumstances, including the defective powers of observation of the unhappy victim of the crime, Romine. Although he had probably never before seen Taylor and his gang, he seemed to believe that they were the same people with whom he had had trouble on account of the slot machine some weeks before. That was primarily the cause of Hess and Craig's undoing, for they happened by a curious chance to be at the Vinyards' place on the night the sheriff called and readily admitted the slot-machine incident at the filling station, though neither of them resembled Taylor. Romine said the man who shot him was tall and slim, but Taylor was neither. Even Bassler and Grieshaber, though [98] they could not identify Hess and Craig, did not correctly describe Taylor as the man whom they heard order the "hamburger." It is hard to explain County Treasurer Bechler's testimony that he had heard Hess refer to alleged oncoming lights as "Here comes the law." Possibly the boys made foolish remarks. The statements of Romine and Bechler, the mere presence of the two boys at Vinyard's house, the fact that they had had trouble about the slot machine, and that they thereby became associated in Romine's mind with his assailants, taken together with the boys' slightly tarnished reputations, overcame in the jury's mind the evidence of the bloody shirt, which could hardly have been discarded by Hess and Craig, the inability of Bassler and Grieshaber to identify them, and the rather well-established alibis that they had not left the Vinyard house that night. They might have remained in the penitentiary for ten years, but for the vengeance of a woman scorned. The bandits had covered their tracks exceedingly well, and though the police were on the lookout for a wounded man, Taylor's being a soldier and his extra-curricular method of hospitalization enabled him to escape detection. Without Mamie's efficient help, the mystery would have remained unsolved; yet her effort in the cause of "justice" also served justly to entangle her as a life tenant of the state. The Hess and Craig case exemplifies the danger of conviction for first-degree murder on circumstantial evidence; only the prosecutor's belief that he might not be able to sustain that charge induced his request for the alternative second-degree charge, which under the circumstances was equally erroneous.

• • • •

Acknowledgments: Charles W. Green, Prosecuting Attorney, Jefferson County, Mo.; Albert S. Ennis, Festus, Mo. [99]

FARMER BARNHILL'S HORSE SALE

Everett Howell

ALBERTUS JANSSEN, cashier of the Exchange State Bank of Golden, Adams County, Illinois, usually arrived at the bank to open it for the day's business at eight o'clock. When he opened the bank on August 20, 1928, there was nothing unusual to indicate that this was to be a red-letter day in his life. According to his custom, he started arranging the books. In a minute a stranger entered the bank. To Mr. Janssen's cordial "Good morning," the stranger produced a revolver and ordered him to open the safe. Just then a confederate entered the bank and closed the front door, so that Janssen had little choice. He unlocked the safe. The robbers stuffed a large number of bank notes into a black bag they were carrying. Cashier Janssen was gagged, bound, and left in the vault. As the bandits were leaving the bank, James Garrison, a customer, entered the door, and was forced at pistol's point to retire to the rear of the bank and join the cashier in the vault. Then the robbers fled, having taken with them, it was later found, $4,305.

The burglar alarm at the bank was sounded immediately, and a fleeing Whippet sedan was traced by John Bedale, F. W. Witler, and W. F. Secman as it left Golden in an easterly direction at a high rate of speed. The trail was lost at the end of a hidden lane deep in the woods on Missouri Creek near a farm formerly occupied by one John Barnhill. At this spot they found torn bits of paper which were perfectly dry, although there had been a heavy dew that morning. Upon these bits of paper there were pencil markings. Sheriff Kenneth Elmore examined the spot carefully and found more bits of paper. Fitting them together, he had a sheet of paper bearing an outline plan of the plundered bank sketched in pencil on the back of an advertisement. Evidently, the culprits had dropped these bits of paper at this spot after the robbery. The printed side of the paper bore the announcement of Farmer Barnhill's horse sale.

Barnhill did not have a good reputation in Adams County. Upon finding the suspicious bits of paper, the [100] officers ordered his arrest. As more evidence was found, the authorities became certain that Barnhill had directed the scheme though he had not appeared at the bank. Handwriting experts found that the writing accompanying the sketch of the bank on the bits of paper found near Missouri Creek was exactly the same as on one of Barnhill's checks. Anna Woerman, an employee of the bank, and Eleanor R. Gronewald, as well as Cashier Janssen, remembered seeing Barnhill, in the spring of 1928, take down one of his horse-sale bills from the wall of the bank and make notes on the reverse side while examining the layout of the bank.

These circumstances strongly indicated that Barnhill was implicated in the holdup. He was located in Peoria and was continuously shadowed, while his friends and associates were watched. Finally he was arrested, but denied any knowledge of the affair.

While these facts were being developed, investigations were pressed to locate the two young men who had actually entered the bank and stolen the money. A number of persons saw the Whippet car standing in front of the bank, and then speeding out of town just before the burglar alarm sounded. Henry J. Gerdes had sold some gasoline to the operator of the car just before it drove up to the bank. Gerdes got a good look at the man. Samuel R. Woerman and Frank F. Winkle were with Gerdes and saw him, too. Henry Schuster was near by when the bandits came out of the bank with a black bag, entered the Whippet, and drove away.

All these people, in addition to Cashier Janssen, had seen the bandits in broad daylight and therefore were of assistance to the police. The descriptions given led to Everett Howell of Farmington, Illinois, who was arrested in Peoria about two weeks after Barnhill; he had been seen with Barnhill a number of times during the time Barnhill was being shadowed. His record was none too good, though not criminal. Barnhill and Howell denied knowing each other. Witnesses of the Golden robbery were brought to Peoria to determine whether Howell was one of the participants. Howell was positively identified by gasoline-station owner Gerdes and his companions, Woerman and Winkle, and by [101] Henry Schuster, as the man who had driven the Whippet. Cashier Janssen was positive that Howell was the one who held him up with the pistol. Customer Garrison was not sure that Howell was one of the robbers, but said that he looked like one of them.

The testimony thus collected was presented to the Grand Jury of Adams County, which returned an indictment against Howell and Barnhill on September 20, 1928, just one month after the crime had been committed, and within the succeeding month they were called for trial before Judge Fred G. Wolfe in the Adams County Circuit Court. Neither defendant took the witness stand, but Howell's attorneys, Hartzell and Cavanagh of Carthage, Illinois, produced a number of witnesses to establish the alibi that on the morning of the robbery, Howell was in Fulton and Peoria counties, dozens of miles away from Golden. Richard Whitney saw him at 7:00 a.m. on the Peoria-Farmington highway. Dr. William Glover, Ed Larson, and Policeman George Greenwell saw him in Canton, Illinois, seventy miles from Golden, at eight o'clock, the hour of the robbery. He had gone there to call at Dr. Glover's office.

Between nine and ten o'clock, he was seen back in Farmington, only ten miles north of Canton and about eighty miles from Golden, by his neighbors,

Dr. and Mrs. William Plummer, who had known Howell all their lives, and by Mrs. Charles Thomas, William Settles, and William J. Aiken.

The jury, apparently believing the witnesses from Golden rather than those from Farmington and Canton, returned a verdict of guilty against Howell, as well as Barnhill. On October 17, 1928, Judge Wolfe sentenced them each to the state penitentiary for terms of from one year to life. Appeal bonds were furnished and the cases appealed to the Illinois Supreme Court.

Before the appeal was completed, Barnhill made to the sheriff a full confession of his part in the robbery, but said that Howell had nothing whatever to do with it. He named Gilbert Ammerman and Peter McDonald as the ones who had committed the actual holdup and admitted that he had met these young men in Chicago and induced them to come [102] to Adams County for the purpose of holding up the Exchange State Bank.

McDonald, a nineteen-year-old lad, was soon apprehended in Chicago and confessed. Ammerman was located driving a taxicab in Indianapolis. When arrested, Ammerman stoutly maintained his innocence until he was confronted by the confessions of Barnhill and McDonald, both of whom he admitted knowing. He then made a complete confession covering all the details of the case. McDonald and Ammerman were taken to Quincy, where they both pleaded guilty before Judge Wolfe on July 23, 1929, almost a year after the holdup. Ammerman was sentenced to the state penitentiary for a term of from one year to life, and McDonald, because of his age, was sent to the state reform school.

The Supreme Court of Illinois affirmed the conviction of Barnhill, but, upon the appearance on December 11, 1929, of Attorney-General Oscar E. Carlstrom to confess error as to Howell, the case against Howell was remanded to the Adams County Circuit Court, "for such other and further proceedings as to law and justice shall appertain."

On January 25, 1930, Judge Wolfe ordered a new trial, and the State's Attorney dropped the case. Everett Howell left the County Court on that day a free man but only after an expensive sixteen months' fight to clear his name.

• • • •

THE Howell case is not unusual. Again a jury lent greater weight to the identifications of the overwrought victims and witnesses of a crime of violence than to the testimony of sober-minded and disinterested persons who positively saw the accused at other places and thus established a perfect alibi. Howell and Ammerman bore but a slight resemblance. Yet five people, including the principal victim, were positive that Howell was the guilty bandit. One of the witnesses had seen him in a passing automobile, one of the least reliable, if not worthless, opportunities for identification. The seven witnesses who swore to having seen him in Canton and Farmington the morning of the robbery were impliedly stamped as perjurers by the finding of the jury. Possibly the greater [103] indignation and vehemence of the witnesses from Golden carried the day against Howell. But for the fortunate confession of Barnhill, after his conviction, completely exonerating Howell, and implicating Ammerman and McDonald as the robbers, and but for the confession and conviction of this pair, Howell might now be serving his one year to life sentence in the penitentiary.

• • • •

Acknowledgment: Mr. J. Leroy Adair, attorney at law, Quincy, Ill. [104]

Fishing Creek Farce

Frank Howell

FISHING CREEK meanders down from the hills of Wetzel County, West Virginia, to join the Ohio River, dividing the towns of Brooklyn and New Martinsville. Here and there along its course are found small mountaineer homes, with their kitchen gardens and a cow or two. The men of these homes usually work at mining, farming, or odd jobs.

One of these small homes, near New Martinsville, was occupied in September, 1929, by Frank and Norma Howell, tenants of C. W. Edgell, who lived with his own family about one hundred yards farther up the stream. With the Howells lived the three children of Mrs. Howell by a former marriage—Eldora, Ronald, and Betty Lehew, aged fourteen, twelve, and ten.

Norma Howell appeared to be much interested in discussing with neighbors the newspaper accounts of the robbery on September 5 of Jack Cotts's filling station, situated on the Waynesburg Pike, about three miles east of Moundsville. Norma observed that, since the robbers were reported by Cotts to have been a tall, gaunt man and a short, heavyset, round-faced woman, descriptions which almost exactly fitted her husband and herself, John Arnette, Chief of Police of New Martinsville, would try to lay it upon them as he was always trying to get Frank "in bad."

• • • •

THE record is not clear as to how they got there, but on September 12, 1929, several days after Norma's statement, Frank and Norma Howell found themselves in the jail at New Martinsville charged with the robbery of Cotts's filling station. Mr. Cotts came to New Martinsville and positively identified them as the bandits. They were at once transferred to the Moundsville jail, and Prosecuting Attorney J. Lloyd Arnold began the preparation of the case. This was comparatively simple in view of the positive identification of the pair by Cotts and the definite way in which he recalled the facts concerning the affair. [105]

Cotts was a farmer who operated a Standard gasoline station on the Waynesburg Pike. Near eleven o'clock on the night of September 5, 1929, he was locking up his station when a large closed car drove up, occupied by a man and woman who asked for some "Esso." Cotts unlocked his Esso pump and supplied three gallons, all that was needed to fill the tank. When he entered the station room to get some change, the man followed and asked for some soft drinks. Cotts went to his ice chest and got out the desired two bottles of "Orange," when he was ordered to "stick 'em up." He turned to find himself covered by two revolvers, the second one in the hand of the woman standing in the door. The bandits took thirty dollars in bills from Cotts's hip pocket, and about twenty-seven dollars in cash from the register. The woman kept him covered while her companion got the car started, then she backed out, and they fled. Cotts grabbed his revolver, ran to the road, and emptied his gun at the retreating car, but it had gotten away to a flying start. Cotts at once reported the holdup to the police, but no one was captured that night.

The *Wheeling Register* of the following day, in reporting the incident, said that the car was a dark Buick sedan. When Cotts appeared before the Grand Jury, and later at the criminal trial of the Howells, he testified under oath that he did not see what kind of car the robbers were driving, since he saw only the rear of the car where he supplied the gas. The car, he testified, was a dark-colored, two-seated, closed car.

Circumstantial evidence also developed against the Howells. On the evening of September 5, the three Lehew children went to the movies with their own father. Also, Howell's landlord, C. W. Edgell, reported that on the evening of September 5 Howell had promised to get him some crawfish, for fishing bait, and that the next morning when his son went to get the bait, Howell did not have it, excusing himself by saying that he had gone up the Ohio River (which was in the direction of Moundsville) . Edgell also reported that Howell was very dilatory in paying the rent and sometimes was several months behind, but that on [106] Septemher 7, two days after the robbery, Norma Howell had paid him $10.00.

Although the Howells absolutely denied any knowledge of the holdup or having been near the Cotts place, they were jointly indicted by a Grand Jury in Marshall County and brought to trial before Judge James F. Shipman, in the Circuit Court of Marshall County, on November 4, 1929. The prisoners were unable to employ counsel, and the court appointed J. B. Rickey and John M. M. Fitzsimmons of Moundsville to defend them. Upon motion of counsel, separate trials were granted. Frank Howell was tried first. The general circumstances implicating Howell were established. It was shown that he was the owner of a closed Ford and possibly of another car. The exact identification of Howell's cars was not developed, as the prosecutor's case rested upon Cotts's positive identification of Howell. Cotts had seen the bandit hatless under a good light at the time of the robbery—only about two months before the trial. From the witness stand, he pointed to Howell and said, "That is the man right there." He testified that he had no trouble at all in identifying the defendant or his wife, saying, "I couldn't be mistaken."

The defense was an alibi. Both of the Howells testified that during the day of September 5, Frank assisted George Coburn to move. This was corroborated by Coburn. After returning home from work about seven o'clock in the evening, he remained there with Norma. Mr. Coburn called upon them between eight and nine o'clock to see about some business. The three children, having spent the evening at a movie with their own father, returned about nine o'clock, when the whole family went to bed. None of the family left the house all night. Clarence Lehew, Norma's former husband, and the three children corroborated that part of the alibi pertaining to them. Both of the Howells denied ever having seen Cotts prior to their arrest, and knowing anything of his gasoline station. Howell claimed that Edgell's rent had been paid earlier than Edgell said, and that the crawfish incident had occurred in August. He also denied owning a revolver. [107]

In cross-examining the Howells, the prosecutor introduced intercepted letters admittedly written by the Howells, while in jail awaiting trial, to various persons, suggesting how they should testify. Having no counsel then, the prisoners were apparently trying to handle their own cases in their own way. Over the objection of defense counsel, these letters were read to the jury.

After the defense rested, Prosecutor Arnold recalled Norma Howell and asked her to identify a small black hat and a black coat. She testified that these articles belonged to her. Then Mr. Cotts was recalled, and he identified them as having been worn by the woman robber. Sanford Wright testified that Howell had once told him that he had a .38 revolver and "said he had a notion sometimes to use it." Jess Greathouse testified that he had heard Norma comment on the similarity of Frank and herself to the description of the robbers given in the newspapers. He reported Norma as saying, "Probably me and Frank done it." On cross-examination, he admitted that he took this as joking on her part.

With this testimony, the case was submitted to the jury, which returned a verdict of guilty. In sentencing Howell to the maximum penalty, fifteen years, Judge Shipman is reported to have said that he was determined to break up the constantly increasing robberies in Marshall County. Howell's only reply was: "Judge, you are sentencing an innocent man."

On November 6, 1929, Norma Howell was tried before a second jury on the same charge, on the same testimony, and was acquitted, despite Cotts's positive identification. This, to say the least, was a peculiar result, inasmuch as a great deal of the detailed testimony connecting her husband with the robbery concerned Norma's hat and coat.

As Norma was leaving the Marshall County Court House she was arrested on a charge of robbery at Cadiz, Ohio, where an inn owned by W. A. Willett had been held up by a tall, slim man and a short, stout young woman. She maintained her innocence and refused to go to Ohio voluntarily. She was extradited and then indicted and tried in the Harrison County Court. She was later acquitted and returned [108] at once to West Virginia, where she found employment as a waitress in a restaurant to support her three children.

• • • •

IRENE CRAWFORD SCHROEDER and Walter Glenn Dague, two notorious convicts awaiting execution in the state of Pennsylvania for the murder of Highway Patrolman Brady Paul, confessed on January 5, 1931, that they had committed the robbery of the Cotts filling station as well as the one at Cadiz. Prosecuting Attorney Arnold, Mr. Cotts, Defense Attorney Rickey, and others went to the Newcastle (Pennsylvania) jail to hear the confessions, which were recorded in an exhaustive affidavit describing every detail of the holdup at Moundsville and of the movements of the pair before and after. After this conference there remained no doubt in anyone's mind, including Mr. Cotts's, that Irene Schroeder and Glenn Dague were the guilty bandits and that the Howells were absolutely innocent. There was a remarkable likeness between the two couples. With commendable speed, the appropriate officials recommended the pardon of Frank Howell. Governor Conley granted it on January 14, 1931.

Several days later, January 19, 1931, Chauncey D. Hinerman introduced a bill in the West Virginia House of Delegates providing compensation for Howell in the sum of one thousand dollars, on account of his erroneous conviction and imprisonment for over fourteen months. The bill passed the House on February 6, 1931, but failed to receive action by the Senate Finance Committee prior to adjournment of the 1931 Legislature.

One of the leading newspapers of the state commented editorially as follows:

> No amount of money will compensate for the mental suffering Howell endured through his fourteen months of false imprisonment. Under the law, he is barred from suing the state and collecting damages. The just and decent thing for the state to do is to act promptly and voluntarily and compensate Howell, not make him fight for what is due him.
>
> The brand of a felon is no light matter and fourteen months is a long time to remain cooped up in a cell for a crime the prisoner [109] did not commit. Suffering was intensified by the fact that Howell all the while did not know but what he would have to serve out the full fifteen years.
>
> Our only objection to the Hinerman bill for restitution is the niggardliness of the sum. It ought to be for several times the amount stipulated. Five thousand dollars would not be excessive. It is due Howell and the state would not be hurt by paying him more.

• • • •

THIS mistake was due to a conjuncture of erroneous identification by the victim of a robbery, plus circumstantial evidence. Hostile witnesses interjected enough unfavorable circumstances into the case to make the identification seem unimpeachable, whereas the alibi, perfect in itself, was in the main supported by self-serving or possibly interested witnesses. Why so little emphasis was laid on the car, a fundamental factor in the case, is not clear, for the Howells possessed no such car as was involved in the robbery. What doubtless weighed most heavily with the jury was the positive and persistent identification by Cotts. Perhaps the physical resemblance between the Howells and the guilty pair may to some extent excuse Cotts's mistake. Fortunately for the Howells, Irene Schroeder and Glenn Dague, nationally notorious murderers, had the grace, just a few days before their execution in Pennsylvania, to make a complete and irrefutable confession that they were the guilty participants in the Moundsville holdup. No one but the guilty persons could have given so accurate a description of every incident connected with the affair. Cotts then admitted his mistake, and was instrumental in having justice ultimately done. Although the judicial machinery thereupon moved swiftly to undo the wrong which West Virginia had inflicted upon the innocent Howells, it did not move as effectively as it should have, for the 1931 Legislature adjourned without making the compensation provided for in the Hinerman bill.

• • • •

Acknowledgments: Douglas C. Tomkies, Huntington, W.Va.; Vincent Legg, Secretary to the Governor, Charleston, W.Va.; Albert G. Jenkins, State Pardon Attorney, Charleston, W.Va. [110]

"Dogskin" Does Ten Years

John A. Johnson

No. 2, South Francis Street, Madison, Wisconsin, was the home of hard-working Martin Lemberger and his family, which consisted of his wife, their three children—Alois, aged nine, Annie, aged seven, and Martin, Jr., aged six—and their little fox terrier. Very early on the morning of Wednesday, September 6, 1911, the community was startled to learn that little Annie Lemberger had disappeared. The police were called in by the parents. Chief of Police Shaughnessy, Detective Boyd, and several officers answered the summons.

Mrs. Lemberger told the police that, at ten o'clock the night before, she had put Annie in her cot by the window. When she arose early in the morning to prepare her husband's breakfast, she found Annie's bed empty and she couldn't be found anywhere. The two boys slept in another bed in the same room and the door leading into the parents' room had been left ajar. Upon retiring, Mrs. Lemberger said, she had locked all doors and windows, and in the morning, she found them all locked, excepting the one by Annie's empty cot. On examination, a triangular piece was found to have been broken out of the windowpane, and the lath window prop was found outside on the ground, broken in two. Mr. and Mrs. Lemberger both said that Annie must have been taken out of the window. The police found footprints outside.

An immediate search started, for the little girl and for her abductors. Vacant lots, factories, culverts, manholes, and nearby marshes were searched. No tangible clues were found. The city of Madison became aroused. Many clues and rumors came to the officials, as happens in most mysteries, but their investigation led nowhere. Mrs. Lemberger felt sure that gipsies had kidnapped Annie. Her husband said that he had consulted a spiritualist who said that Annie had been kidnapped and carried away in a covered wagon and was being held a prisoner west of the city. These suggestions proved as baseless as the rest. Finally, Chief Shaughnessy appealed to the citizenry through the newspapers: [111]

> We have had nothing of the kind before in Madison that I know of. I want to appeal to every citizen who can possibly spare the time to be on hand next Saturday morning at eight o'clock to take part in an extensive hunt. We must find the girl if alive, or her body if dead.

Sheriff Brown came into the case and made use of T. J. Barto's trained bloodhound. After getting the scent from some of Annie's clothing and at her cot, the dog followed it a short distance and lost it at a street crossing. On a retrial, the dog followed the same trail, bolted across the street, and went, according to Barto, on a "dead scent" toward Lake Manona. The dog repeated this several times. This was extraordinary, for it was two days after the disappearance, during which time there had been rain. This led Barto to believe that the girl's body had been taken to the lake the night before Thursday night.

On Saturday an enormous searching party answered the appeal for assistance. The indignation of the community was running high. Private contributions were made to obtain expert detectives, and official rewards were posted. That day the body of little Annie was found by George Younger in Lake Manona.

The autopsy of Doctors Purcell and Dean disclosed a wound back of the left ear, and at that point a clot on the brain which had probably caused death or unconsciousness before the girl was thrown into the water, for no water was found in the lungs. The discovery that Annie had not been criminally attacked, or more seriously injured, increased the mystery, especially in the search for possible motives for the crime.

The private subscriptions made it possible to retain the W. J. Burns Detective Agency, which assigned shrewd and experienced Edward L. Boyer to the job. He went to Madison at once. It had been reported that the hole in the windowpane was too small even for a woman's hand to get through, so it was thought that possibly a group of boys might have committed the crime; and thorough investigations were made along this line.

Among the many disconnected leads pursued, the police arrested John A. ("Dogskin") Johnson, neighborhood [112] loafer, barroom hanger-on, and public character. He had been one of the first to hear of the story and had followed all of the excited crowds in the searches. He even nosed around the undertaking parlors, until he aroused Coroner Lynch's suspicions. After an all-night grilling, through which John- son asserted his innocence, he was released. Johnson was rearrested, however, when the police learned of his past record of arrests two commitments to insane asylums for taking liberties with girls, and one sentence for the nonsupport of his wife and two daughters. He was thoroughly questioned, but stoutly maintained his innocence through hours of rapid-fire and relay examination. To sustain him, there was his alibi that he had gone to bed at about nine o'clock on Tuesday evening, September 5, and had not left the house until six o'clock the next morning. His wife, who really supported the family, verified this, and said that he couldn't have left the house without her knowledge that night because she had sat up with a sick daughter. The daughters, Bertha and Selma, both confirmed that fact. Nevertheless, the authorities kept hammering at "Dogskin," with the efficient help of Detective Boyer, but Johnson would not give in.

On Wednesday, September 13, 1911, Johnson was taken to Judge Donovan's court room, where District Attorney Nelson read the charge to him. Johnson pleaded not guilty. Ten thousand dollars bail was set, and the trial continued to September 25. The court assigned Emerson Ela to defend the prisoner.

A short time after being returned to jail, Johnson called Turnkey Foye, who took him to the authorities, where he made the following statement:

> I had been drinking hard the last two months and on this night I went to bed drunk. Sometime after one o'clock I awoke and wanted another drink of whisky. I got out of bed and dressed quietly and crept downstairs and got my shoes from behind the stove. When I got outside I put them on with the intention of going to some saloon close by and begging for a drink.
>
> I walked up Francis Street as far as the Lemberger house which is four doors away from my home. When I reached there I remembered I had often looked into the window of the little cottage and seen the Lemberger children going to bed. Some devilish impulse caused me to step over to the window and reach my hand through [113] the broken pane and raise it. I lifted Annie out without making any noise and the cold air awakened her and she saw me and yelled, "Johnson !" I hit her with my fist and began to run. She kept making a noise and I kept hitting her until she was limp in my arms. By that time I had reached the middle of the vacant lot and I laid her down in the weeds to catch my breath and get my bearings.
>
> In a few seconds I began to realize what I had done and I thought I had better throw the body into the lake. I walked to the bay, five blocks away, and by keeping in the shadows of the barns and fences I got there without any one seeing me. I threw the body as far as possible out into the water and then ran home. I took off my shoes and put them back and got upstairs without waking any of the family. I want to plead guilty and make this confession so I will be taken to prison today.

Johnson insisted that the trial be held immediately, that he be sentenced and taken to Waupun penitentiary that day.

The various officials were quietly called together. Attorney Ela explained to the defendant the seriousness of the plea; yet he persisted in his confession and his desire to change his plea to guilty. Thereupon, Judge Donovan of the Municipal Court for Dane County sentenced Johnson to life imprisonment at hard labor, with the anniversary of the murder, September 5, to be spent in solitary confinement.

Johnson was slipped out of a little-used side door of the courthouse, secreted in a car by a blanket, and rushed out of Madison before the populace knew of the rapid turn of affairs. When about ten miles out of town, he was permitted to come up from under the blanket. When he reached the penitentiary he appeared to be greatly relieved. To Sheriff Brown's, "Well, Johnson, here is where you will spend the rest of your life," Johnson is said to have replied: "I don't care. The mob didn't get me anyway. I know I did not kill Annie Lemberger."

Although the city of Madison had been most indignant over the murder, there did not appear to be much enthusiasm over the trial and sentencing of Johnson as was quite evident from the newspapers. The question arose at once whether or not an innocent man had not been "railroaded." Johnson wrote letter after letter from his prison cell, starting immediately upon his arrival at Waupun, asserting his [114] innocence and alleging that he had pleaded guilty solely to save himself from death at the hands of the mob which, the officers said, was after him. In view of his past record and the belief that he was not entirely sound of mind, his pleas were not taken seriously, until August, 1920, when former judge A. O. Stolen became interested as the result of a pleading letter from Johnson to look into his case. Mr. Stolen interviewed Johnson and, after studying the record, became thoroughly convinced of his innocence. Upon petition, on September 14, 1921, Gov. John Elaine appointed the late Rufus B. Smith as commissioner to conduct a hearing on Johnson's pardon application. At the hearing Johnson was represented by Mr. Stolen; Theodore G. Lewis, District Attorney for Dane County, represented the state. The hearings started on September 27, 1921, and continued during six days of tense excitement for those attending the trial, the public, and the press. It was rumored about that Mr. Stolen was going to prove who the actual murderer was, thereby freeing Johnson from guilt. The granting of a pardon was obstinately opposed by the state.

Mr. Stolen began by proving that the hole in the windowpane at Annie's bed was far too small to admit the hand of a man, and that since the whole area of the Lemberger house was not over twenty feet square, any intruder from the outside must have awakened some of the family or the dog. Then he called Mrs. Johnson and the two daughters to establish the alibi that Johnson had retired at ten o'clock on September 5, 1911, and had not left the house until six o'clock the next morning. These witnesses were cross-examined by District Attorney Lewis and their testimony remained unshaken.

Johnson was then called to the stand, and the hearing room settled into perfect silence. Johnson was a ready witness and told of the third-degree methods that had been used on him by the police. It appears that the officers had learned that on one occasion Johnson had seen a negro lynched strung up with a rope, riddled by bullets, cut down, and stabbed. This had made a deep impression on his unstable mind, and the mention of it made Johnson cringe. [115]

Johnson told Commissioner Smith that the officers informed him that there was a mob outside the jail just waiting to get at him. In this ruse, Sleuth

Boyer of the Burns Agency took a prominent part. He said that he was warned to keep away from the jail windows, because men were on nearby buildings waiting for a chance to get a shot at him. Johnson said that he was livid with fear of being lynched, and, when Boyer said that he could escape lynching by making a confession, which Boyer helped to prepare, that he availed himself of what seemed to him his one chance of getting safely into the Waupun penitentiary before the mob could get him and tear him to pieces. He said that he always told the officials, even Judge Donovan, that he was innocent, as he had maintained for days under the most grueling pressure. It was hard for the Commissioner to believe this statement, especially in view of the denials by court attaches and the fact that the Commissioner had known Judge Donovan personally. District Attorney Lewis attacked Johnson's whole story of third-degree methods by producing the testimony of the officials attached to the courthouse, and of Defense Attorney Emerson Ela, men of high standing in the community, all of whom contradicted Johnson and insisted that Johnson had not displayed any fear and that the plea of guilty was not the result of duress. Mr. Nelson, the District Attorney at the time of conviction, however, testified that he had always been morally certain that Johnson was not guilty and that he had urged Johnson not to plead guilty if he were really innocent, but Johnson had persisted. With this testimony, Johnson's chances of winning a pardon seemed rather slim.

Then one night, just before the hearings were about to terminate, Attorney Stolen received first an anonymous letter and then a telephone call. Mrs. Mae Sorenson of 612½ West Johnson Street offered to tell who killed Annie, if she would be protected from the murderer. Stolen at once called Judge Hoppman, who got out of bed and opened his court at midnight to take Mrs. Sorenson's testimony, and to issue warrants for the persons named by her. The man she named had been attending the hearings daily. [116]

When the hearing convened on the last day, Mrs. Sorenson was called to the stand. The crowded audience had no inkling of what she would say, but after the first dozen words or so, the whole room was electrified. This was her story: She was a good friend of Mrs. Lemberger and on the morning of September 6, 1911, went to console her on the disappearance of Annie. She found Mrs. Lemberger in the kitchen burning a bloodstained nightgown of Annie's. Blood spots were on the bed sheet and pillow slip. Mrs. Lemberger was weeping bitterly and finally fainted. As she was regaining consciousness, she cried, "Martin, Martin, why did you do it?" On the day of Annie's funeral, little Alois Lemberger told Mrs. Sorenson that his father, in company with other men, had been drinking heavily on Tuesday evening. Annie had risen to get a drink, and on passing through the kitchen, was asked by her father to hand him the poker. She couldn't find it. In a drunken fury, he struck her behind the ear with a beer bottle and she fell against the stove unconscious. Lemberger then carried her to her cot, and later she was found dead by her mother. The body was then hidden in the basement and the next night a negro named Davis was hired to take the body to the lake.

The Lembergers were called to the stand and they denied the truth of Mrs. Sorenson's story. Martin Lemberger, however, was arrested as he left the stand and charged with second-degree murder; his wife and son were arrested and charged with perjury.

At Lemberger's preliminary hearing, January 5, 1922, his attorneys, Hill and Spohn, relied on Section 4629 of the Wisconsin code, which provides that a charge of second-degree murder is outlawed in ten years. Reluctantly, Judge Hoppman felt obliged to dismiss the charge; and Lemberger was released the same day.

In the meantime, on December 13, 1921, Commissioner Smith rendered his report to Governor Blaine, and recommended the granting of a pardon to Johnson in the following words:

> "Upon the hearing before me, no testimony was offered by the present District Attorney tending to show Mr. Johnson's guilt, [117] except the testimony of his confession and his plea of guilty. The District Attorney who was in office at the time of the conviction, was a witness at the present hearing, and was interrogated by me as to whether or not at the time of the conviction the State had any evidence of Mr. Johnson's guilt. The response of the District Attorney and the other evidence adduced satisfies me that the State and the prosecuting officer at the time of Mr. Johnson's confession had absolutely no evidence tending to show his guilt of the crime. There was testimony that he hung around the undertaker's establishment, to which the body of Annie Lemberger was carried, and some vague testimony that he was seen near the shore of Lake Manona, apparently looking through the bushes near the shore of the lake, but I cannot be made to believe that these matters were or are sufficient to raise even a suspicion of his guilt. . . .
>
> An attentive consideration of all the testimony taken before me and of all the facts and circumstances attending the disappearance of Annie Lemberger, has produced the profound conviction in my mind that Mr. Johnson was not guilty of the crime. There is much in Mr. Johnson's previous history which would tend to show a tendency on his part to take liberties with little girls, but I regard that as having little bearing here, because I am satisfied that the person committing this horrible crime, did not misuse this little girl in that respect. There is some vague testimony about some quarrel between Mr. Lemberger and Mr. Johnson some time previous to Annie's disappearance, but there is nothing in it which shows any adequate motive for this crime. There is so much in the situation in that house, that night, which shows that it would have been almost impossible

for a person from the outside to open that window and take that child out, that I cannot believe that the crime was committed by any one from the outside in the way in which it is now claimed the thing was done. When it is considered that if some one from the outside opened that window and took the child out, and killed her, that the noise necessarily occasioned by so doing would probably have alarmed Annie or some of the other children or Mr. and Mrs. Lemberger, or the dog, it seems to me that the theory of the District Attorney involved so many difficulties and so many improbabilities, that it ought not to be entertained, unless there was some evidence connecting Mr. Johnson with the matter.

Much stress was laid by Mr. Lewis upon the credit to be given to Mr. Johnson's confession. It is of course clear that ordinary people do not ordinarily accuse themselves falsely of the commission of crime. If Mr. Johnson were a man of ordinary strength of character, and of ordinary prudence and sagacity, I should find it difficult to disbelieve him when he stated that he committed this offense. But I find that he was and is far below the ordinary individual in mentality. The testimony establishes in fact, to my satisfaction at least, that he was a man conspicuously weak, weak almost to the [118] degree of irresponsibility. There was no sufficient reason why he should have feared mob violence, but I am satisfied that he got that idea into his mind, and did fear it, and I am satisfied that groundless fear suggested to him the idea, that by admitting this crime, he could be at once taken to Waupun and escape the mob violence, which he so much dreaded. Mr. Johnson, I am sure, did not tell the truth upon this hearing when he testified that he told the District Attorney and the presiding Judge that although he pleaded guilty, he was not guilty in fact, but the testimony satisfies me that he did feel the fear which he now describes, and that that fear caused him to take the foolish course he did take.

Under all the circumstances of this case, I am constrained to recommend that pardon be granted to Mr. Johnson."

Governor Blaine concurred in Commissioner Smith's conclusion that Johnson did not kill little Annie Lemberger, and commuted his sentence to expire at once on February 17, 1922. He had spent over ten years in the penitentiary for another's crime.

Mr. Stolen applied for compensation under the Wisconsin statute of 1913 which allows compensation to innocent persons erroneously imprisoned. The state board administering the statute denied Johnson's claim on December 5, 1922, on the ground that he had contributed to his conviction and imprisonment, and therefore he was excluded from the benefits of the statute. An appeal from this decision was taken to the Circuit Court of Dane County, which sustained the ruling of the Board on March 21, 1923. In 1925 and

1927 bills to compensate Johnson were introduced in the State Legislature, but they failed of enactment. In 1929, over three thousand persons signed petitions requesting the Legislature to grant the compensation, but nothing was accomplished. Of recent years, Johnson has been employed by the city of Madison. When last heard from in 1929, he was in ill health and aging rapidly.

• • • •

FROM the investigation conducted by Judge Stolen, it is not to be doubted that the most extraordinary pressure was brought to bear to produce a confession from Johnson and thus solve the "mystery." When Detective Boyer learned of Johnson's obsession on lynching, he evidently conceived the [119] idea of staging a continuous mob scene and thus preyed on Johnson's weak mind until he finally caved in. But the state, especially in view of the District Attorney's doubts, might have been more astute. Any number of facts pointed to the impossibility of the crime having been committed from the outside the small aperture in the windowpane, the fact that nobody heard the window opened or the girl removed, not even the terrier, who usually barked at the faintest sound, the fact that the girl had evidently been dead before she was taken from the house and before she reached the lake and that she had not been assaulted. There was- no reason at all to connect Johnson with the crime; but the need for a scapegoat seemed to furnish the necessary motive for pinning the crime upon the poor fellow. A community does not like to be baffled, and when some plausible culprit is caught in the toils, especially if his record is unsavory, social pressure demands a conviction. Detective Boyer and the court officials had these factors on their side. In face of them, Johnson's alibi, though absolutely sound and true, was ignored, and he was psychologically "beaten" into a confession. It is strange that so many persons in the Lemberger household could stand for ten years the torture of having sent an innocent man to the penitentiary for life, but the fear of the consequences of telling the truth was doubtless as powerful to produce silence as a different fear was to produce from Johnson a confession of guilt. It is true that the Wisconsin law denies indemnity to those who contributed to their conviction, and Johnson's confession comes within this category. But it does seem that a confession extorted as was Johnson's should not have been given the same weight as a voluntary confession. This is a matter not for a statute, but for the discretion of administrative authorities, who might well have exercised it in favor of Johnson. [120]

"ALL I CAN DO IS EXPRESS PROFOUND REGRET"

Edward A. Kimball

EDWARD A. KIMBALL was in trouble, a new experience for him. Activities which might arouse the suspicions of the police were distinctly alien to the placid routine of his life, yet he suddenly found himself in a police station charged with grand larceny the theft of $15,000 from Michael Funicielo of New York.

His replies to the questions asked him by the two officers who examined him disclosed an almost incredible story, utterly inconsistent with the allegations made by Funicielo.

Kimball had been waiting for a train at the Pennsylvania Station in Baltimore on June 10, 1926, when Funicielo, accompanied by a policeman, came running into the station, picked Kimball out of the crowd, and told the policeman that he was the man who had robbed him at the Emerson Hotel a few hours before.

Denials were unavailing against the claims of the excited Italian and his positive identification. Consequently Kimball was pushed into a patrol wagon and taken to the police station.

He told the police he was on his way to Philadelphia, where he planned to visit the Sesquicentennial celebration. He had come directly from the Emerson to the station and he repeatedly denied that he had ever seen Funicielo before in or out of the Emerson.

He said he had no occupation.

"I have no business, but I am interested in different things. I belong to societies, read a great deal, and am interested in things of that kind."

He was forty-seven years old and had an annual income of between $7,000 and $8,000 from an estate left by his father. He was married and had a twenty-three-year-old son, a student at Bowdoin College.

He was a deeply religious man, a student of philosophy, an ardent supporter of the Salvation Army, and was known to many of its representatives as Brother Kimball. He wrote on religious subjects, and his father had written a book [121] called *Signs of the Times*, which dealt with the second coming of Christ.

Kimball's grandfather had been a successful Salem sea captain and trader. He left a fortune of $600,000, part of which the accused had inherited two years before his arrest.

Everything about Kimball made it difficult to believe the serious charge against him. Funicielo, however, remained positive in his assertions that Kimball was the man who had robbed him.

Funicielo had come to Baltimore from New York, June 8, with a friend, one Costello. Their original destination had been Washington, where Costello said they could buy whiskey permits and resell them at a huge profit. Funicielo was the proprietor of a successful trucking business in New York. Costello had persuaded him to raise $15,000 for the purchase of the whiskey permits. While they were on the train Costello received a telegram saying that he should stop first in Baltimore for a conference.

They left the train at Baltimore and went to the Joyce Hotel. After engaging a room they walked to a nearby restaurant for breakfast. During the meal Costello found a wallet under the table. It contained a large amount of money in bills, some notes which appeared to be tips on stock investments, a picture of the owner, whose name appeared to be Moyer. The wallet also contained a telegram addressed to Moyer at the Emerson Hotel.

It was decided to return the wallet to Moyer so the two men went to his room, No. 1618 at the Emerson. Moyer was exceedingly grateful and offered Costello a reward of $100, but it was refused. Moyer then suggested that he might be able to give his new friends some tips on the stock market which would prove valuable.

The three men walked down to the stock exchange; Funicielo was left outside while Moyer and Costello went in to place their order. They came out in a few minutes and said $200 had been invested and all three returned to Moyer's room. Half an hour later Moyer was notified that his stock was going up. He hurried back to the exchange and soon returned with $400 cash. After a brief conversation he said [122] he was going back to the exchange and he took Costello with him. When they returned they showed Funicielo $1,200, supposedly the result of the second investment.

And so it went until Moyer claimed to have invested $60,000, which was soon converted, so he said, into $181,000. About four o'clock Moyer left for the exchange to collect his money and he returned presently with a man he introduced to Funicielo as "Mr. Rose, manager of the stock exchange." Rose carried a small black bag from which he produced $181,000 cash, saying that was what Moyer had made.

He then told Moyer that before he could turn it over to him Moyer must put up $60,000 in cash to show that his investment had been legitimate and that he had had that much money when he placed his order. He said he would give Moyer twenty-four hours in which to get the cash.

After Rose left, Moyer confided to his friends that he could not lay hands on so much cash. He could get part of it and if the other two, Costello and Funicielo, would lend him the balance he would prove his gratitude in a substantial way.

Funicielo at first refused, but the temptation was apparently more than he could resist. That night he and Costello went back to New York. Funicielo drew $5,000 from each of three accounts in which his wife also had an interest. She at first flatly refused her consent, but was reluctantly persuaded by her husband, who explained that he was investing in a new partnership.

Back in Baltimore they met Moyer in his room. He had what money he could raise. Costello went ostensibly to a telegraph office and collected the funds he claimed to have sent for and Funicielo turned over his $15,000.

Moyer now had $60,000 in cash. Costello was intrusted with the delivery of it to Rose. Ten minutes after he left the room he called up and said Rose was busy and he would have to wait. Moyer and Funicielo waited some time. Then Moyer's "employer" called him and he excused himself, saying he would return soon.

Funicielo waited several hours. No one came. Finally, he [123] became suspicious and went to the desk to inquire for Moyer. At just that moment he saw a man getting into a taxi in front of the hotel whom he recognized as Rose. He ran out of the hotel, jumped into a cab, and ordered the driver to follow the taxi ahead. At the station he met Police Sergeant William Curd, excitedly told his story, and pointed to Kimball as the swindler. Kimball was arrested.

Kimball answered his inquisitors frankly. He said he arrived in Washington about 5:00 p.m., June 8, and engaged a room at the Willard Hotel. He was on a sight-seeing trip and spent the next day taking bus rides around Washington, returning to his hotel late in the afternoon. He checked out about 4:30, he said, caught the 5:30 to Baltimore, and arrived at 6:30, going direct to the Emerson, where Room 1615 was assigned to him.

In the morning he went sight-seeing in Baltimore and spent the afternoon visiting Annapolis on a Gray Line tour. He returned to the city in time to check out of the Emerson at 6.05 to catch the train to Philadelphia.

His bag was searched but it was found that he traveled very light. It contained nothing but the bare necessaries and a Bible, which he said he always carried with him. He had about $32 and a ticket to Philadelphia.

He told the police that he had been graduated from Boston University in 1911, had studied law and worked in the office of a Boston lawyer for two years, the only position, because of chronic ill health, he had ever held. He had studied medicine and taken courses at Columbia University. His home was at 200 West Fifty-eighth Street, New York City, and his wife was traveling in Europe.

Despite the fact that his story appeared to be true in every detail, he was held, and on June 28 an indictment charging larceny of $15,000 was returned against him.

His knowledge of legal procedure in such a predicament was very slight, and it was several days after he was arrested before he considered bail. He communicated with his bank in New York and a lawyer was sent to see him and arranged bond for him. [124]

The case came on for trial before Judge Eugene O'Dunne and a jury in

Baltimore, November 10, 1926.

The state relied principally upon Funicielo's testimony until Joseph Elsie of Canton, Ohio, was put on the stand by the State's Attorney. He was a surprise witness and his story appears to have created an impression upon the jury favorable to the prosecution's cause.

Elsie testified that on April 27, 1925, he had been induced to go to Chicago by Costello, then using the name of Madison, where he met Moyer, introduced as one Mills.

Elsie said these two men introduced to him one "J. W. Rose, of the National Stock Exchange for the Rothschild boys." This man, said Elsie, was the present defendant. He was as positive in his identification of Kimball as Funicielo had been at the station. Elsie said that one thing about Kimball which helped to identify him was the glasses he wore; Funicielo also had singled out the glasses as a distinguishing mark.

Elsie had lost $17,000 in a swindle alike in all respects to the one by which Funicielo had been victimized. Every detail, practically, was identical with the exception that Costello and Moyer used different names.

This testimony was admitted in toto by Judge O'Dunne, over the objections of the defense,

> for the purpose of enabling you [the jury] to get some additional light on whether the intent with which the transaction was done here, if you find it was done whether the intent was to defraud or not. In other words, you cannot try a man here for a crime which he committed in Chicago, but if the evidence is of such a character as to satisfy you of a similar form of operation, from which you can infer that as to the one that is under inquiry here, the intent was to defraud, and not satisfactorily explained, then you can treat it as admissible for that purpose and for that purpose only.

Kimball took the stand in his own defense, repeating the story he told the police. His testimony was corroborated by his wife, his son, and an old friend, Rudolph E. Gruge, vice-president of Merck & Company, manufacturing chemists.

It was pointed out by the defense that Kimball was a type of man much more likely to be the victim of a swindle than [125] the perpetrator of the offense, and consistent with this contention was his wife's description of him as a "literary loafer."

Questioned as to what she meant she replied:

> I have had to manage everything since I was married. I have been married 25 years, tomorrow. I was married at 17 and became a mother the same year and I have been the man of the family ever since. I never know in the morning what he is going to do before the

day is over. He does what he wants to do and what he feels like doing.

Another indicative exchange occurred during questioning about the glasses he wore, those which both Funicielo and Elsie had referred to. On redirect examination it was said that the defendant needed glasses to read the fine print in the Bible he always carried with him. The court ordered him to put on his glasses and read from his Testament.

He chose the following passage:

> Truly my soul waiteth upon God. From Him cometh my salvation. He only is my rock and my salvation. He is my defense. I shall not be greatly moved. How long will ye imagine mischief against me. Ye shall be slain, all of you, as a bowing wall which ye be and as a tottering fence.

Kimball's wife, his son, and Mr. Gruge all denied that he had been in Chicago in 1925. Hotel records substantiated the story of his stay at the Willard and that he had paid his bill there shortly before 5:00 p.m., June 9. The books of the Emerson Hotel corroborated his testimony that he occupied Room 1615 at 6:45 the same evening.

Despite this alibi the jury, after deliberating about an hour, returned a verdict of guilty. When the foreman had announced the finding Judge O'Dunne said: "Gentlemen, I hope you have convicted the right man but I am personally satisfied that you have made a terrible mistake."

The jury was then discharged and Judge O'Dunne retired to his chamber. The jurymen, perturbed by his remark, sent word that they wanted to confer with him but he replied that the verdict was enrolled, the jury dismissed, and nothing further could be done at that time.

Kimball's friends were convinced of his innocence and as [126] a result a motion for a new trial was filed November 12, 1926, with twenty-five exhibits which established definitely, and to the satisfaction of the eleven justices of the Supreme Bench of Baltimore, that Kimball was not in Chicago, April 27, 28, and 29, 1925, the dates on which the transaction involving Elsie had taken place. It was shown in the exhibits accompanying the motion that Kimball was in New York on April 27, 1925, and that on that day he and Mrs. Kimball visited their safe-deposit box at the National Park Bank, 214 Broadway. It was shown through their signatures in the bank's records that they had had access to the vault that day.

Other exhibits showed conclusively that Kimball was also in New York April 28 and 29.

The motion was granted on the strength of this mass of detailed exhibits, and on January 7, 1927, the new trial came on for hearing before Judge O'Dunne. State's Attorney Herbert O'Connor entered a plea of "not guilty confessed."

In closing the case Judge O'Dunne apologized to Kimball for the injustice he had suffered and said:

> I am of the same opinion regarding this case as the State's Attorney. I told the jury which brought in a verdict of guilty that a great mistake had been made. Since then new evidence has been found which justified my statement.
>
> I am sorry, Mr. Kimball,, that the State of Maryland does not provide for restitution when a man is unjustly convicted of a crime.
>
> In France and other countries such restitution is provided for, but not in Maryland. All I can do is express profound regret and the greatest admiration for the heroic support given you by Mrs. Kimball during your trial.

"God bless you, Judge," said Mrs. Kimball.

• • • •

IT would be hard to find a more preposterous mistake than Kimball's conviction. Yet it was all plausible enough. The positive identification by Funicielo, supported by his fellow victim, Elsie, swept away all those doubts which should have troubled the jury, as they did Judge O'Dunne. Had the [127] Judge had the power, he would have set aside the verdict, but in Maryland, only the Supreme Court of eleven judges, *en banc*, can do that, by granting a new trial. Probably the fact that Kimball had no accountable occupation, as well as the coincidence that he occupied a room in the Emerson near Moyer's, influenced the jury against him. But a more innocent, unworldly man it would be hard to find, and one would suppose that the jury would have realized that. On the contrary, his strange and detached character doubtless contributed to his undoing. Twelve good men and true could not understand him. His case indicates how possible it is for any man to be taken from the streets and to be placed in jail and suffer the tribulations of the damned. Possibly Kimball's religious philosophy helped him to bear with fortitude a predicament which must have been harrowing and tormenting. Although he escaped the penitentiary, it took a considerable expenditure of time and money to enable his family and friends to prove him innocent. Not every victim of the law's mistakes has such means and funds at his disposal. As Judge O'Dunne points out, Maryland should have compensated Kimball for his undeserved sufferings. Needless to say, it did not do so.

• • • •

Acknowledgments: Judge Eugene O'Dunne; Mr. Leigh Bonsai; Mr. J. Richard Standiford. [128]

Poison Pen

Oscar Krueger

IN December, 1910, a very respectable young woman, who was then boarding at 51 Third Avenue, New York City, advertised for a position in the New York Journal. Her name was Miss Waschack. In reply, she received an obscene letter couched in such language that it cannot be reproduced. Miss Waschack, naturally, was disturbed over it, and showed it to the people with whom she was boarding. She was advised by them to take it to Anthony Comstock, the founder of the Society for the Prevention of Vice in New York City. The letter, dated December 10, 1910, and signed by "Ed," had been posted at Branch Post Office, Station Y, at Twenty-third Street and Fourth Avenue. It contained an improper proposal, with the suggestion that, if Miss Waschack desired to accept it, she should insert a notice in the personal column of the New York Journal, stating where they should meet.

Mr. Comstock determined that this was a matter which should not be permitted to rest. He inserted a notice in the Journal, as directed, stating that the place of the meeting should be at Fourth Avenue and Twenty-third Street at one o'clock on December 19. Under the directions of Mr. Comstock, who was standing close by and watching the entire proceeding, Miss Waschack went there and waited on the corner waited until fifteen minutes past one, but no one approached. She noticed a man on the opposite side of the street who seemed to be watching her, so she began looking at him. He didn't approach. Thereupon she crossed the street and strolled slowly by him and on up the sidewalk. The man followed her for a couple of blocks, and finally accosted her, without using any name. She asked him if he was "Ed," and he replied, "Yes." She then asked him if he was the man who sent her a letter, and he said, "No," whereupon she told him that he was not the man she was looking for. He, however, was not in a mood to be dropped so abruptly. He decided to speak up, and said, "Well, I sent you the letter." Miss Waschack mentioned circumspectly the proposition [129] made; and his replies were as vague as her references to it. He made a "date" with her, however, to meet later that afternoon, and they parted.

Miss Waschack went to the appointed place, but the man never appeared.

Some days later, this man was arrested upon the complaint of Mr. Comstock. His name was Oscar Krueger, and it was learned that he lived near Fourth Avenue and Twenty-third Street with his wife and two children. He was a well-built man of Teutonic type, about five feet ten inches tall, and rather good-looking. He was employed usually as a painter or plasterer, or at some kindred occupation, on various construction jobs, and before his arrest in December, 1910, had never been arrested. He was induced to write "Waschack" on an envelope. This was compared with the handwriting in the obscene letter, and it looked like the same. Handwriting experts were called in by Mr. Comstock for consultation. They proclaimed this writing, and other letters written by Krueger, similar to that in the objectionable letter. The matter was laid before a Federal Grand Jury, which indicted Krueger on December 27, 1910, on the charge of depositing in the mails a lewd, lascivious, obscene, and unmailable letter, in violation of Section 211 of the Federal Criminal Code.

Krueger was arraigned in the District Court for the Southern District of New York on January 25, 1911, and entered a plea of not guilty. He was tried before Judge James L. Martin on February 2, 1911. The testimony against the defendant was entirely circumstantial. Mr. Comstock and Miss Waschack both related the circumstances of Krueger's accosting her on the street. The various samples of handwriting looked similar; and an alleged handwriting expert, who shall be nameless, testified that the two writings were the same. Krueger seems to have offered but little evidence. He flatly denied having written the incriminating letter or knowing anything about it. He produced no handwriting expert. He explained that he followed the prosecuting witness on December 19 because she was evidently trying to "pick him up," to see what would happen. He did not [130] fulfil the "date" made at that time because he did not desire to do so.

The jurymen evidently placed little credence in his story, in view of the expert testimony on the handwriting and the other circumstantial evidence. They found him guilty of the charge, and Judge Martin sentenced him to serve eighteen months in the Federal Penitentiary at Atlanta.

• • • •

PROTESTING his innocence, as he had from the very day of his arrest, Krueger was sent to Atlanta. He wrote letters continually to the President and the Attorney-General maintaining that it was an outrage to keep him in prison for an offense he knew nothing about. The letters made some impression. He was advised to apply for a pardon, and he did make three applications. The first two were refused. The third application was presented about one year after he arrived at Atlanta; and on being referred to the United States Attorney in New York for investigation and report, it happened to come to the attention of Hon. Daniel D. Walton, then an Assistant United States Attorney. He became interested in the case and made a thorough investigation. He obtained the samples of Krueger's handwriting, and the letter which Miss Waschack had received. He had them reexamined by other handwriting experts, particularly by the late William J. Kinsley, who pronounced the two handwritings different, though to the lay observer they might have indicated some similarity.

On the basis of this second examination of the writings and a thorough reinvestigation of all the testimony in the case, the District Attorney's office strongly recommended that Krueger be pardoned on the ground that he was not the person who had written the obscene letter and sent it through the mails. The pardon was vigorously opposed by Anthony Comstock, who attacked the United States Attorney and Mr. Walton for their conclusions and recommendation. It is understood that Mr. Walton's recommendation to the Attorney-General included a suggestion that, in view of the undoubted injustice suffered by Krueger, compensation ought to be awarded to him. [131]

On January 18, 1912, Oscar Krueger was released from the Atlanta Penitentiary on a full and unconditional pardon granted by President Taft, after an imprisonment of nearly a year for a crime committed by another.

• • • •

KRUEGER'S predicament arose out of circumstantial evidence, backed by the corroborative testimony of a person who professed to be a handwriting expert. Anthony Cornstock, that zealous "Roundsman of the Lord," evidently considered Krueger's continued incarceration part of his divine mission, for in spite of Mr. Kinsley's positive declaration that the two writings could not have been the work of the same man, Comstock vehemently opposed Krueger's pardon and denounced those who favored it. Comstock's sincere, though often misguided, fanaticism induced in him gullibility and carelessness in fastening so serious an offense on an innocent man, and these characteristics were combined with exceptional stubbornness and unwillingness to admit error. He and the lady were eager to believe that the handwritings were those of the same person, and Comstock seems to have found an obliging "expert" who agreed with them. Krueger could not afford to engage a handwriting expert, and apparently the government prosecutor did not feel disposed to do so. Had he, however, retained Mr. Kinsley at the trial, instead of on the application for a pardon, much suffering and injustice would have been averted. Krueger owed his ultimate pardon and release to the conscientious investigation of Mr. Walton, who took the trouble to retain an impartial and noted expert. Inasmuch as the whole case turned essentially upon the identity of the handwritings of the letter writer and of Krueger, it seems unfortunate that the government prosecutor and the jury relied solely on the "expert" furnished by Mr. Comstock. There is much to be said for publicly employed experts who shall not be considered witnesses for either side. What happened to Krueger's family during his imprisonment or to Krueger after his release is not known.

• • • •

Acknowledgment: Hon. Daniel D. Walton, New York City. [132]

Knight Of The Road

Hugh C. Lee

CHARLES H. FITE, the postmaster in the village of Priors, Polk County, Georgia, was held up in the post office at the point of a pistol at eleven o'clock on the morning of September 15, 1923. The intruder took 165 blank United States money-order forms, a money-order dating stamp, and a metal cutter used in preparing marginal notations on issuing money orders. Van Underwood, a fourteen-year-old boy, who was in the post office during the robbery, was forced to stand by and keep quiet. The robber made a successful escape.

Mr. Fite immediately notified the Federal authorities of the occurrence, and a search for the culprit was begun. The investigation was placed in the hands of Post-Office Inspector Clyde Fleming of Atlanta. Only four days later, September 19, 1923, one of the stolen money orders was filled out and passed in Nashville, Tennessee. Fleming immediately followed the trail. In conferring upon the case with local authorities in Nashville, and in checking over former money-order forgery suspects in the Nashville district, it was recalled that in June of the previous year one Hugh C. Lee, about thirty-five years old, had been apprehended in Nashville while passing a forged money order on some blanks which had been stolen from the post office at Snowden, Virginia. Lee was also at that time wanted by the authorities of Tennessee. In October, 1922, he had been tried on the Tennessee charge of larceny, and had been convicted and sentenced to the state penitentiary for a term of from three to ten years. In December, 1922, he had made his escape from the penitentiary.

The photograph and description of Lee, with those of other suspects, were exhibited in Nashville to the person who had cashed the forged money order from the village of Priors, and were identified as those of the man who had passed it. The writing on the order did not agree in all details with the known writing of Lee, but there were some points of similarity. Consequently, Lee's photograph was [133] sent to Priors for identification. Postmaster Fite could not identify the picture, but fourteen-year-old Van Underwood did, and several others said that they had seen a stranger around the town about September 15 who looked like the photograph of Lee. In certain middle-western towns where forged Priors money orders were being passed, Lee's picture was likewise identified. The investigators now felt convinced that they were on the trail of the right man. Lee's pictures and description were advertised, after a Grand Jury, under Foreman George S.

Reese, had, on November 19, 1923, returned an indictment against him for the Priors post-office robbery.

In October, 1924, over a year later, at Emporia, Virginia, Lee was arrested on this indictment and returned to Rome, Georgia, for trial in the United States District Court, Northwestern Division, Northern District of Georgia. The indictment was brought against "Hugh C. Lee, alias R. C. Lester, alias R. C. Moore, alias R. C. Johnson." United States District Attorney Clint W. Hagar had Lee arraigned before Judge Samuel H. Sibley on November 19, 1924. Lee stated to the court that he was unable to employ counsel, and Judge Sibley assigned Mr. Barry Wright of Rome to defend him. The defendant pleaded not guilty. Postmaster Fite testified to the holdup, but could not identify Lee, with 'any degree of certainty, as the robber. However, the boy Van Underwood testified positively that Lee was the man; and a number of reputable citizens testified to having seen Lee around the neighborhood at about the time of the robbery. A hotel keeper and a waiter from nearby Cedartown, Georgia, testified that Lee had spent the night before the robbery at their hotel. The evidence against Lee was complete, with the exception of the handwriting on the forged money orders, which, as already observed, had only a few points of similarity to Lee's writing. The identifications were evidently considered sufficient to overcome this defect.

In his conferences with the Federal officers, Lee protested his innocence, but it was impossible to find corroboration for his alibi; and in several matters it was found that he made false statements. Lee maintained that he was in Detroit, [134] Michigan, at the time of the robbery in September, but since more than a year had elapsed and he was without funds, he could not furnish proof of the alibi. He absolutely denied having been anywhere near Priors in September, 1923.

Lee did not take the stand in his own defense, possibly because of his known criminal record. The trial was very short, and the verdict of guilty and a sentence to a term of five years in the Atlanta Penitentiary were given on the same day as the trial, November 19, 1924 over a year after the robbery. Lee was delivered to the warden of the penitentiary to start serving his sentence. He was then thirty-seven years old.

Lee had lived in Fitzgerald, Georgia, but he seemed to have become a "knight of the road," being separated from his wife, who lived in Roanoke, Virginia. Because of his record and his apparent lack of respectable connections, no one outside of the court officials appears to have taken much interest in his fate. Mr. Wright, the assigned defense counsel, filed a motion on November 19, 1924, for a new trial, on the ground that the verdict was contrary to the law and evidence, that a continuance should have been granted to allow the defendant to locate and subpoena witnesses, and that the defendant expected to be able to produce evidence within a short time to establish his innocence. Mr. Wright was unable to produce the further evidence hoped for, and, therefore, at his request in open court on January 3, 1925, the motion for a new trial was dismissed.

• • • •

DETECTIVES Kiger and Kiger of Nashville, Tennessee, were trailing one Will Barrett in 1923 and 1924 in connection with some forged checks. In the middle of January, 1925, Barrett carelessly returned to Nashville and passed two additional forged checks which came to the attention of the detectives. They recognized Barrett's handwriting and picked him up at once. Barrett voluntarily confessed that he was the one who had committed the robbery at Priors. Inspector Fleming was called from Atlanta, and he [135] permitted Barrett to go into all the details of how the robbery had been perpetrated, how he was dressed at the time, where he had been, and many other details. It was found upon examination that Barrett's handwriting was identical in every detail with that on the forged money orders. Barrett's written confession was taken. It was learned that he was an escaped convict from the Alabama Penitentiary. Barrett was turned over to the Federal authorities, and was indicted and brought to trial in the United States District Court, Northwestern Division of the Northern District of Georgia, on February 9, 1925, before Judge Robert T. Ervin. He pleaded guilty and was sentenced to three and a half years in the Atlanta Penitentiary. After Barrett was arrested, the lad, Van Underwood, admitted his mistake in identifying Lee, but there was, in fact, a striking resemblance between Lee and Barrett. Postmaster Fite was certain that Barrett was the culprit.

• • • •

THE United States Government now had two men in the Atlanta Penitentiary convicted of the same crime. Everyone connected with the case was convinced that Lee was entirely innocent of the robbery at Priors. Judge Sibley, the District Attorney's Office, and the Solicitor of the Post Office Department recommended to the President that a pardon be granted.

On March 13, 1925, President Coolidge granted the pardon, with the direction that the prisoner be immediately apprehended for trial under an indictment pending against him for the robbery of the post office at Snowden, Virginia. Lee was taken to Lynchburg, where he was placed in jail to await trial. A. J. William, the postmaster at Snowden and the chief witness against the defendant, had, however, died, so that the case against Lee was nol-prossed on January 4, 1926. Lee was then turned over to the state authorities of Tennessee to serve out his old unexpired term.

• • • •

THIS was again a case of mistaken identity, though it would seem that it might have been avoided by a more careful [136] comparison of handwritings. The main identifying witness was a boy of fourteen, whereas the robbed postmaster was doubtful that Lee was the criminal. The facts that Lee had so bad a record and that several witnesses claimed to have seen him in and around Priors at the time of the robbery were handicaps too great to overcome. In view of the cautious attitude of the postmaster and of Lee's positive assertion that he was in Detroit in September, 1923, it might have been possible, notwithstanding the fact that the burden of proof is usually upon the one advancing an alibi, for the Federal Government to have investigated the alibi through its officials at Detroit. Again, Lee's record probably prevented such an inquiry, for there is not much sympathy for a man believed to be a congenital criminal. It is not improper to infer that such a person charged with a crime has, in practical effect, to bear the difficult burden of proving himself innocent.

• • • •

Acknowledgment: Barry Wright, attorney at law, Rome, Ga. [137]

Bootlegger And Child

Harvey Lesher, Mike Garvey, Phil Rohan

ROBERTA SCRIVER could not understand why Mr. Miles, the proprietor of the drug store, did not wait upon customers. She rapped on the counter, and there was no response. She yoohooed, and there was no reply. As she was starting, indignantly, to leave emptyhanded, the father of the druggist arrived. He was as surprised as she that no one was caring for the store. Father Miles looked around, called, then entered the rear room. He was met by the sight of his son lying on the floor, unconscious, bleeding from head wounds. A call for an ambulance was dispatched at once, and the police were notified.

The ambulance hurried the unconscious man to the hospital, where, despite expert care, he died within the hour.

This was on the first of November, 1927. Mr. Miles's drug store was located at the corner of Fourth Avenue and Jefferson Street, Los Angeles, California.

The autopsy surgeon, Dr. A. F. Wagner, reported that he had found an extensive contusion behind the left ear, and underneath it a subdural hemorrhage covering the entire surface of the brain, extending downward into the spinal cord. This might have been caused either with a blunt instrument or by a fall. He also found an abrasion on the right side of the forehead, and a contusion over the left eye.

The police investigators learned that Miss Scriver had reached the store shortly after 10:15 o'clock in the evening, and that as she approached the store she had seen someone come out of the store on a "kind of a trot," throw a bundle into the rear seat of a Hudson, in which two men were sitting, and drive off hurriedly. They learned from Father Miles that he had examined the store cash register and that, while the sales-register tape showed the receipt of thirty-six dollars, there was not a single cent in the drawer. Father Miles also said that when he found his son, he was bound hand and foot with wire. The most complete information came from Eddie Yates, the ten-year-old son of a dentist who lived in the neighborhood. He told the investigators that [138] he was passing the drug store on his way home from a moving-picture show at about ten o'clock when he saw a Hudson car draw up, three men get out, and enter the store. One of these asked Mr. Miles for a cigar, and wanted it free. Miles refused, and when he retired to the room in the rear of the store, the men followed him. In about five minutes they came out hurriedly, got into the car, tossing a bag into the rear seat, and drove away.

The problem of the police was then to find the three men. The ten-year-old youngster thought he could recognize them if he were to see them again. Hence the natural thing for the police to do was to have Eddie attend the periodical "showup" of criminal suspects. At the fourth "show-up" he attended, about a month later, Eddie pointed out two men who had been in the store, and a little later he picked out the third. These men had all been arrested on other charges, ranging from vagrancy to robbery. They were Harvey Lesher, Mike Garvey, and Phil Rohan. They denied any knowledge of the crime on Jefferson Street. This, however, did not raise any doubt in the mind of little Eddie Yates. He was positive in his identification of them.

With the evidence of only a child connecting Lesher, Garvey, and Rohan with the murder and robbery in the Miles drug store, the District Attorney's Office was considering whether or not to submit the case to the Grand Jury, when Howard C. Walton of Los Angeles came forward with a story of events which made the submission imperative. He said that on the seventh or eighth of November, the three defendants were at his home drinking bootleg liquor and wine. Lesher, he said, became so intoxicated that he had to be placed in bed. About 2:30 the next morning, when Lesher was coming out of his drunken stupor, he said, "Why did I kill him?" Later, when the two were alone, Walton asked Lesher what he meant by that, and Lesher replied that he had done the "Jefferson Street job," and that he had killed Miles because he had recognized him after being knocked down.

As in all cases of this kind, some effort was made to trace the Hudson automobile. It was learned that a Mr. Stopp [139] owned a light-green Hudson sedan which had been stolen from a garage on Mariposa Avenue three days before the tragedy on Jefferson Street occurred. One of the garage attendants said that on the day the Hudson was stolen, he had seen Lesher around the garage. This was all that could be learned about a stolen Hudson car or the possible connection of the suspected! men with it.

On December 20, 1927, the Grand Jury indicted each one of the prisoners on the separate counts of murder and burglary. Upon arraignment all three pleaded not guilty and the cases came on for trial January 9, 1928, before Hon. William Tell Aggeler of the Superior Court of Los Angeles County. The state was represented by Deputy District Attorney Tom Menzies, and the defense by Mr. S. S. Hahn of Los Angeles. Each defendant took the stand in his own defense, denying any knowledge of the crime and testifying that they were all three at the home of Lesher the whole of the evening in question, more than three miles away from the Miles drug store. This alibi was supported by the testimony of others, friends and relatives. The conflict between the testimony given by the witnesses for the prosecution, who told their stories as they had been reported to the police, and the witnesses for the defense, had to be decided by the jury. They found against the defendants, and on February 11, 1928, a verdict of guilty on both the murder and burglary counts was rendered against each of the defendants. A motion for a new trial was denied, and the case appealed.

At this stage of the proceedings, Mr. William T. Kendrick and Mr. William T. Kendrick, Jr., of Los Angeles, became the attorneys for the defendants.

The Court of Appeals found no reversible error, and each man had to face the execution of the sentence of the trial court imprisonment for life in the San Quentin Penitentiary.

The Messrs. Kendrick were untiring in their continued efforts to prove the innocence of these men, in which they so thoroughly believed. The appeals of the prisoners for further investigation of the case were so earnest that the District Attorney's Office renewed its inquiries. The case was [140] investigated by a Los Angeles County Grand Jury whose foreman was Hon. John C. Porter, later Mayor of Los Angeles. The result was that a great deal of new evidence was uncovered which tended to discredit the evidence submitted by the prosecution at the trial. It was concluded that Eddie Yates did not arrive at the drug store until about the time the ambulance came and that his testimony was the honest romancing of a child. Walton, an admitted bootlegger, repudiated the testimony he had given at the trial, and acknowledged that he was thoroughly intoxicated himself the evening the three men had been at his home. He said that he had first told the police the confession story to cause the arrest of Garvey and Lesher in retaliation for their rumored intention to "shake him down" as a bootlegger.

Other new evidence corroborated the alibis sworn to by the defendants. Still further evidence raised very serious doubts whether Miles was really tied when he was found unconscious in his store, and whether money had been taken—in this way leading to a conviction on the part of the investigators that quite likely there had been no murder or robbery at all, but that Miles had suffered a fainting spell and in falling had received his injuries.

These developments were submitted to Governor Young, and by him referred to the Advisory Pardon Board of California. An independent investigation was made by this board, and a carefully prepared report submitted to the Governor by its chairman, Lieutenant-Governor Carnahan. The conclusion reached was that the men were entirely innocent of the crime charged, and that they had been erroneously convicted. Immediate pardons for all three were recommended. Upon considering the newly discovered evidence, Judge W. T. Aggeler (the trial judge), Mr. Asa Keyes (the District Attorney at the time of the conviction) , Buron Fitts (the District Attorney at the time of the investigations), Mayor John C. Porter of Los Angeles, and the Rev. Gustav A. Briegleib (pastor of Eddie Yates, who started a personal investigation of the case immediately after the finding of Miles's body)—all concurred in the [141] conclusion that the defendants were innocent, and in recommending that pardons be granted.

The family of Eddie Yates naturally took a keen interest in all of these investigations. The highly commendable position taken by them in this delicate situation was clearly stated in a letter from the father, Dr. Yates, to the Governor:

Dear Governor Young:

I am E. W. Yates, the father of Eddie Yates, that testified in the case of the State against Harvey Lesher, Mike Garvey, and Phil Rohan.

I am informed that these men are being held entirely on the evidence of my boy. I know the boy did the best that he could, and sincerely believes these men were guilty, and has never changed his opinion to this day. But he having never seen these men before, and seeing them at night, under the circumstances there is great possibility of a mistaken identity. So, if his is the only evidence it does not look to me that it would be just or fair to hold them.

I am asking you under these circumstances to consider favorably their release.

Very respectfully yours,
[Signed] E. W. YATES

Governor Young had publicly announced that as a policy, he did not favor the granting of pardons except after suitable parole periods, unless "a very definite presumption of innocence" could be established. In this case he demanded "certainty" of innocence. He found such certainty to exist, and granted the prisoners full pardons on June 20, 1930. They had served about two and a half years of a life sentence.

• • • •

MESSRS. KENDRICK thereupon made an application to the California Board of Control, the first of its kind, for a maximum of $5,000 indemnity for each of the three innocent men, under the Act of May 24, 1913 (chapter 165, Statutes of 1913). The Board rejected the claim on the ground, as reported by the Sacramento Union of December 18, 1930, purporting to quote Mr. Ray L. Riley, State Controller, "that the verdict of guilty was returned by a jury on the [142] basis of evidence presented to the court by the child," and hence presumably the prisoners were not convicted' erroneously. Such a construction of the word "erroneous" is a travesty on the purpose of the statute.

A rehearing was granted by the full Board in the spring of 1931, and on April 30, 1931, the Board handed down an opinion and recommendation to the Legislature, approved by Governor Rolph, denying the claims of Lesher and Garvey, but allowing Rohan $1,692. In the cases of Lesher and Garvey, the Board maintained that they were men of unsavory character, had gambled for large sums, had possessed and sold intoxicating liquors, and had been "charged" with other crimes, for which they had never been tried. Although both had trades, the Board claims that they were not employed at an honest occupation for some months prior to the Miles death. While satisfied that Rohan was entirely innocent, the Board also asserts that it was "unable to determine to its satisfaction whether Harvey Lesher or Mike Garvey did or did not commit the crime of which they were convicted," thus ostensibly reversing the positive finding of innocence by the State Board of Pardons, Governor Young, and other state officials. The Board also adds that it was "not satisfied that Harvey Lesher and Mike Garvey did not by acts or omissions, negligently bring about their arrests and convictions," though it gives no evidence to support this important conclusion. The Board evidently felt that Lesher and Garvey had such poor reputations that they ought not to be compensated by the state for their convictions, notwithstanding the Governor's finding. Unless the Board could show in what definite way Lesher and Garvey had contributed to their own conviction for the murder of Miles, it would seem that its conclusion denying an indemnity is unsustainable. The suggestion that Lesher and Garvey suffered no pecuniary injury for two and a half years' imprisonment seems a mockery. There is nothing in the statute which requires the Board to deny justice to men of questionable character, if (as in this case was established by the Advisory Board of Pardons and by Governor Young) they had not committed the crime of which they were convicted. [143]

By throwing doubt upon and inferentially reversing all the other authorities of the state which had found Lesher and Garvey absolutely innocent of the Miles murder, the Board has done Lesher and Garvey an unnecessary injury.

• • • •

THIS is another case of conviction on what was ostensibly mistaken identity, but proved to be romancing, apparently combined with some perjury. There was nothing but the testimony of the movie-inspired boy of ten and the false testimony of Walton to connect the three men with the Miles case. That two of them were men of deficient character doubtless helped to convict them. There was commendable activity on the part of the authorities in reopening the case and then demonstrating that the men were innocent. The State Board of Control gave an exceptionally narrow construction to the California indemnity statute, which gives rise to the belief that in an amended statute it should be provided that the application for indemnity should be made not to a financial administrative body, but to a judicial or quasi- judicial body, like a Court of Claims. [144]

Pastor Of The Flock

Ernest Lyons

IN the little congregation of colored folks at Reid's Ferry, Virginia, in the summer of 1908, there arose a division over the question of who should serve as pastor of the flock. Rev. James Smith had been the regular pastor for some time, but he was losing the support of many of the members. These members favored the selection of Rev. Ernest Lyons, a younger man, who, on occasion, had been assisting Smith in the preaching. Smith, it seems, lived in the Lyons home, but as the rivalry between them became more intense they developed suspicions of each other and at times had serious quarrels. This was especially true after Lyons began to suspect Smith of intimacy with Lyons' sister-in-law.

On July 31, 1908, the congregation intrusted its funds to Smith to be taken to the regional church conference which was to start the next day in Suffolk the beautiful old tidewater town a few miles away which serves as the county seat of Nansemond County, and is reputed to be the peanut capital of the world. That day Smith and Lyons were said to have quarreled over some of the conference details, and in the heat of the argument Lyons threatened to kill Smith. Nevertheless, they were seen leaving the church together at about six o'clock in the evening. The next day Lyons arrived at the conference, but Smith never did appear. This was especially unfortunate for the members of the Reid's Ferry congregation, since they were unable to make the expected good showing with their $45 conference fund. Lyons reported that he had left Smith shortly after their departure from the church, and that Smith had said he would follow the next day.

Smith completely disappeared and Lyons became the preacher of the church, although many folks, especially Smith's friends, were unconvinced by Lyons' story of their last separation. Their suspicions were confirmed in a very short time when the corpse of a large negro was found in the Nansemond River near the church disintegrated beyond recognition. The body was buried by the county [145] authorities. Rumors immediately spread through the colored community and soon came to the attention of the Commonwealth's Attorney. The corpse was of about the same build and proportions as Smith, and several of the latter's friends identified various articles of clothing found on the corpse as similar to those worn by Smith when last seen. A woman friend of Smith's, who had not seen the corpse, told the authorities that if the body were really Smith's they would find a ring, with a purple setting, on the little finger of the left hand. The body was exhumed and a ring exactly fitting this description was found on the finger mentioned by the woman. The ring could not be gotten off the finger because of its swollen condition, so the finger was amputated by the medical authorities for use as an exhibit in court. The doctors reported further that the autopsy showed that the man had died by violence a blow upon the head with a dull instrument and that he had been thrown into the river when he was dead or dying.

The Commonwealth's Attorney presented this evidence to the Nansemond County Grand Jury, which returned an indictment against Lyons for murder. The trial was called on January 13, 1909, before Judge James L. McLemore of the Nansemond County Circuit Court, and was held in the old Colonial courthouse in Suffolk. The trial attracted a large crowd of people, and despite the strong accumulation of circumstantial evidence against him, Lyons was persistent in his assertions of innocence. Lyons was defended by Robert W. Withers, one of the leaders of the bar of southern Virginia; and the prosecution was in charge of the equally able Commonwealth's Attorney James U. Burgess. The state submitted all of its evidence on the identity of the corpse and on the alleged motive the defendant had for getting rid of Smith. It was also shown that Lyons had told a number of conflicting stories about the disappearance of Smith, declaring at various times that he had seen Smith since his disappearance, in Portsmouth, Norfolk, and Newport News. These statements were shown to be untrue. The defense tried to show that the corpse was not Smith's, that Smith was still living, and that in any event the evidence connecting Lyons with Smith's disappearance was too weak [146] to sustain a conviction. The Commonwealth's Attorney urged the jury to return a verdict of first-degree murder, carrying with it a sentence of death.

At the close of a three-day trial, the jury returned a verdict of second-degree murder, evidently believing that Lyons had killed Smith, but that the crime was an incident of the renewed outbreak of their quarrel. The Commonwealth's Attorney's plea had made such a deep impression upon Lyons' imagination that when the milder verdict of second-degree murder was returned, a look of great relief almost of joy was markedly noticeable upon his face. Instead of execution, he received a sentence of eighteen years in the penitentiary.

• • • •

MR. WITHERS felt convinced of Lyons' innocence. He made a motion for a new trial, which was denied by Judge McLemore. Mr. Withers was not satisfied and requested the Judge to grant a rehearing of the motion. This the Judge agreed to do if Withers would first go to the jail and, after advising Lyons that the motion for a new trial had been denied, ask him for the true story of what had happened. Mr. Withers did this merely to satisfy Judge McLemore. His surprise was great when Lyons confessed that he had participated in the killing of Smith. The details of his confession, concerning the way the crime had been committed, were exactly as the Commonwealth's Attorney had alleged them at the trial, but Lyons implicated many of the members of the church. All of those implicated, incidentally, had been witnesses against Lyons at his trial. The Commonwealth's Attorney had them all arrested.

The next morning, the implicated negroes were lined around the reception room of the jail, and Lyons was brought in. There was astonishment on both sides. Lyons, however, repeated his confession as he had given it the day before. The others were dumbfounded, and so frightened that they could not find words to speak. Finally the Commonwealth's Attorney told Lyons to raise his right hand to heaven which he did and to repeat, "If I have told a lie, may God strike me dead." Lyons dropped his hand without a murmur. The officials were convinced of the falsity of the [147] statement implicating the others, and they were all released immediately. Lyons had lied entirely too often. He was sent to the penitentiary.

• • • •

MR. GEORGE E. BUNTING, the Clerk of the Circuit Court, owned a farm on the Nansemond River, and had known Lyons and Smith well. Although Lyons went to the penitentiary, Mr. Bunting believed that Smith was still alive. He was inclined to give credence to a story passing about that the corpse was that of an unknown negro who had come up the river in a rowboat with another unknown man. The deserted boat was later found near by, and the tracks of only one person could be seen leading away from it. Mr. Bunting investigated the matter privately as opportunity offered from time to time. Although he never unraveled the mystery of the corpse, he did find Smith alive and in the best of health just across the state line in North Carolina. After much urging, Smith was induced to return to Suffolk, where he was produced before Judge McLemore and was identified by a large number of people who knew him. Smith Admitted that when he obtained the $45 conference fund he fled into North Carolina, where he had remained. He had seen the newspaper stories of the trial and conviction of Lyons, but had done nothing because he feared prosecution for having taken the money. He had a ring exactly like the one on the corpse. One calling at the courthouse today will find, in the archives, the ring from the amputated finger. It is a ring made from the cheapest kind of yellow alloy metal and has a setting of purple glass.

Needless to' say, the officers of Nansemond County were thoroughly disgusted with Smith, and possibly with their own credulity. Commonwealth's Attorney Burgess immediately laid the whole situation before Gov. William H. Mann, who granted Lyons a pardon, without delay on April 3, 1912. Lyons had served over three years' for the murder of a man who was still alive.

• • • •

THIS was a clear case of circumstantial evidence. The body of the negro in the river was never really identified as that [148] of the Rev. Mr. Smith, but the disappearance, the quarrel, the supposed motive, and the discovery of the fatal ring with a purple setting on the little finger of the left hand were sufficient to tip the scales against Lyons. The coincidence of the ring probably convinced the last skeptic, but like many other coincidences it was utterly worthless as evidence of guilt. Fortunately, the jury refused to heed the demand of the Commonwealth's Attorney for a verdict of murder in the first degree. The jury did what the law itself should do in all such cases, namely, make impossible the death penalty when the conviction rests upon circumstantial evidence alone. Whether greater zealousness in establishing the truth could have enabled the Commonwealth's Attorney to find Smith in North Carolina, as he was later found by Mr. Bunting, it is hard to say. The eloquence of the Commonwealth's Attorney so unnerved the distressed Lyons, that, alarmed and chagrined at his fate, he not only admitted, after conviction, a crime he did not commit, but implicated unfriendly witnesses whose testimony helped to bring about his predicament. Only the fortunate circumstance that Mr. Bunting took a personal interest in unraveling the mystery saved Lyons from a harsher fate; not all erroneously convicted persons have such good fortune.

• • • •

Acknowledgments: Judge James L. McLemore of Suffolk; Miss Olivera Whitehurst, Deputy Clerk of the Circuit Court. [149]

THE CASE OF THE FAMILY PHYSICIAN

Robert MacGregor

BAD AXE is the county seat of Huron County, Michigan. It is about six miles from the town of Ubly, Michigan, where lived the ill-fated Sparling family. In 1907 this family, living on a small farm, consisted of Mr. and Mrs. John Wesley Sparling and their children, Peter, Albert, Scyrel, May, and Ray. In 1908, Father Sparling died. In July, 1910, Peter died; in May, 1911, Albert; and in August, 1911, Scyrel. This left only Mrs. Sparling, May, and the youngest son, Ray.

These developments did not pass unnoticed in the small communities of Ubly and Bad Axe, especially since the family doctor of the Sparlings was a Canadian who had incurred local ill will by sending some of his patients to Canadian hospitals instead of patronizing the one in Bad Axe, of which the local folks were proud. This physician's name was Robert MacGregor, a man about thirty-five years old. During the illness of Scyrel, the last one to die, Dr. MacGregor called into consultation Drs. Herrington and Conboy of Bad Axe. They apparently noticed symptoms in Scyrel which indicated that possibly the boy was being slowly poisoned. Dr. Conboy conferred with Prosecuting Attorney X. A. Boomhower, at Bad Axe, and, as a result, Mr. Boomhower called upon Dr. MacGregor at Ubly and told him that if Scyrel died there would be a post-mortem and an investigation into the case. After a conference between the prosecuting attorney and Drs. Conboy and MacGregor, it was decided that the boy should have a nurse to watch him. Miss Gibbs was obtained by Dr. MacGregor. Scyrel had fallen ill on August 4, 1911. Dr. Herrington had been called into the case on August 5, and Dr. Conboy on August 7. The prosecuting attorney took notice of the matter on August 8. Dr. Holdship also was called into the case, but Scyrel continued to grow worse and he died on August 14, 1911.

That night Drs. MacGregor and Holdship held a post-mortem, by lamplight, concluding that death had resulted [150] from cancer of the liver. The authorities, however, were not satisfied with this report, and sent certain portions of the organs to the University of Michigan for examination by Dr. Vaughn and Dr. Warthin, who was head of the pathological department. They both found traces of arsenical poisoning, and their conclusions as to the symptoms of the poison upon a dying person agreed with the observations of the attending physicians. It appeared to the authorities, therefore, that Scyrel had died from taking arsenic. The question remained Was the arsenic present as a result of criminal acts, or, as Dr. McGregor explained, were the arsenic deposits left from overdoses of patent medicines which Scyrel had taken, as had his brothers, for an unfortunate diseased condition from which they were suffering?

The investigation was exhaustive. Dr. MacGregor had become the family physician for the Sparlings in 1907. Upon the death of John Wesley Sparling, in 1908, the doctor became a very intimate friend and adviser to Mrs. Sparling, even on business matters, and was known to call at the Sparling home on many occasions. In July, 1909, the four Sparling boys were insured for $1,000 each in the Sun Life Insurance Company, for which Dr. MacGregor's father was an agent in London, Ontario. In January, 1910, three of them were insured for small sums in the Gleaners Insurance Company. Dr. MacGregor was the local examining physician and consequently passed upon the health of the boys for this insurance. Shortly thereafter, the boys exhibited the beginnings of their fatal illnesses.

While the circumstances surrounding Scyrel's death were being investigated, the body of Albert was exhumed and a post-mortem performed. The internal organs were sent for examination to the University of Michigan. Traces of arsenic were found, and Drs. Warthin and Vaughn gave their opinion that Albert's death was caused in substantially the same way as Scyrel's.

An examination of Dr. MacGregor's books showed that, after the investigation was started, he made certain changes to regularize his accounts with Mrs. Sparling. His explanations were not very satisfactory. He was reported, also, to [151] have made various statements which were interpreted to mean that he certainly knew that the boys were poisoned; and other facts were disclosed showing that he had received, presumably in payment of his professional services, part of the money collected on the insurance policies of the deceased boys. Furthermore, MacGregor and his family were living in a home purchased by Mrs. Sparling.

In view of these circumstances, Prosecuting Attorney Boomhower, on January 22, 1912, filed an information charging Dr. MacGregor with the murder of Scyrel Sparling. Mrs. Sparling and Nurse Gibbs were separately charged as accomplices. The case, as might well be expected, caused great excitement in Huron County. Ubly public opinion is reported to have believed MacGregor innocent of the murder charge (though he had not used the best of discretion in his relations with the Sparlings) , but the opinion of much of the county was unfavorable.

Dr. MacGregor was tried before Judge Watson Beach in the Circuit Court for Huron County at Bad Axe. The defendant entered a plea of not guilty. He was defended by Joseph Walsh and George M. Clark, and the prosecuting attorney was assisted by special counsel, E. A. Snow. The trial was held in April, 1912. The prosecuting attorney called witnesses to establish the circumstances developed by his investigation, weaving a net of circumstantial evidence around the defendant. The testimony of the experts from the University of Michigan made a deep impression upon the jury, as did testimony implying too close a relationship between Dr. MacGregor and Mrs. Sparling. Dr. MacGregor took the stand in his own defense and testified at length in regard to the many circumstances brought out against him. The jury did not believe him and returned a verdict of guilty. On June 10, 1912, Judge Beach pronounced a sentence of life imprisonment in the state prison at Jackson.

An appeal was taken to the Supreme Court of Michigan, which affirmed the conviction on January 5, 1914, and denied a rehearing on June 4, 1914. Many of the assignments of error related to the expressions of belief by the prosecuting attorney in his argument to the jury. While the [152] Supreme Court refused to reverse the judgment on this ground, it commented that "certainly the course pursued by the prosecutor was improper and not to be commended." It is fair to say that the state's prosecution of MacGregor was exceptionally vigorous. The convicted physician went to the state prison at Jackson to serve his sentence.

The charges against Mrs. Sparling and Nurse Gibbs were never prosecuted, and were nol-prossed. Mrs. Sparling had always said that her husband and sons died from natural causes, an opinion which was interpreted by the authorities as an attempt to protect Dr. MacGregor.

• • • •

IN a very short time, appeals on Dr. MacGregor's behalf were presented to Governor Ferris, and the Governor instituted a thorough examination of the case. On November 27, 1916, he granted a full and unconditional pardon to Dr. MacGregor on the ground of his innocence. The Governor took the unusual course of having the prisoner brought to Lansing by the warden of the prison and of handing the pardon to him personally. On the day that this was done, Governor Ferris gave this statement to the press:

> For more than two years I have been investigating this case, and have had assistance from some of the best authorities in Michigan, and I am firmly convinced that Dr. MacGregor is absolutely innocent of the crime for which he was convicted, and I am satisfied that in sending him to prison, the state of Michigan made a terrible mistake.

The records pertaining to this investigation are considered confidential, hence it has been impossible to ascertain the grounds upon which Governor Ferris became so firmly convinced. This is unfortunate, especially in view of the fact that some persons still believe that MacGregor was guilty.

Upon gaining his freedom, Dr. MacGregor was joined at once by his loyal wife to start life over again. They made a short visit to relatives in Canada, and then returned to Jackson, where he was promptly appointed as the official physician to the state prison. He held this position until the time of his death in 1928 at the age of fifty- two. [153]

• • • •

THIS case of circumstantial evidence is baffling, because the grounds upon which the Governor reached his conclusion of innocence are not disclosed by the authorities at Lansing. This is an injustice to Dr. MacGregor and to the public, who have a right to know the facts and the basis of MacGregor's vindication. He appears to have been the victim of honest, but overzealous, prosecution, and of a combination of circumstances. The chief circumstance which pointed to his innocence the trifling amount of the insurance, of which he got only his fees appears to have been given little weight. Community opinion, based on extraneous grounds, such as his patronizing Canadian hospitals, may unconsciously have played its part with the jury. On a question of veracity and inferences, prejudice is always a material factor. The experts may have been correct in their finding of traces of arsenic, but it is quite probable that Dr. MacGregor's explanation of their origin was the correct one. Fortunately, only life imprisonment was meted out, so that the error was still susceptible of partial correction; but the five years of the doctor's suffering could hardly be compensated. Toward this end, no effort appears to have been made.

• • • •

Acknowledgments: Mr. X. A. Boomhower, Bad Axe, Mich.; Mr. Joseph Walsh, Port Huron, Mich.; Mr. Harry H. Jackson, Jackson, Mich. [154]

"LOOKING FOR A DOG"

Clarence LeRoy McKinney

AS was their duty, Henry Adams and Emory McCreight, the night police officers in Wilmington, Ohio, made it a regular practice to patrol the dark and questionable places of the town. This duty was brightened for them, on the evening of February 14, 1922, by occasionally slipping into Murphy's Theater, back stage, to see how the musical comedy, George Cohan's *Mary*, was progressing. After the show was out, between eleven and twelve o'clock, and after the two officers had gotten some pie and milk at Zimmerman's restaurant, they started to check over the down-town alleys—and entered the one skirting the post office on Main Street. No sooner had they reached the rear of Gallup's store when they heard a racket at the back of the neighboring hardware store of Murphy and Benham. The officers made out dimly two shadowy figures against the building. Adams called out, "What are you doing here?" "Looking for a dog," came the reply. "You are liable to get in bad in here," answered Officer McCreight, as Adams flashed his light full in the face of the nearest dog hunter. Pistols flashed! The two mystery men fired and escaped in a waiting automobile. Both officers were struck by bullets—McCreight mortally. He died the following afternoon.

Officer Adams was the only one who had really seen the burglars (it was discovered that they had been cutting their way through the rear door of the hardware store), and he had clearly seen only the one upon whom he had flashed his light. This one was^ fairly well built and had heavy eyebrows. He wore a short khaki coat lined with sheepskin, and a toboggan hat. This type of coat was popular among college boys in 1922, but others also wore them. The sheriff and his deputies immediately started checking the known owners of such coats and toboggan hats. Suspects were interviewed and questioned, without success, for over a week. The man hunt was spurred by the offer of a reward for the arrest and conviction of the murderer. The aid of W. H. Jackson of [155] the Jackson Detective Agency in Cincinnati was enlisted by the county.

On February 24, Charles Smalley, a Clinton County farm hand, called at Officer Adams' home to get a description of the burglars. He said that very early on the morning following the murder, he had overtaken two men, whom he knew, sitting in a Ford coupe, which had a flat tire. They tried to get a tire from him. He said that in their car were many gallons of whiskey and they gave him a drink. As Smalley was leaving them, one of the men called, "Smalley, don't you never say a word you saw us on this road this morning." Smalley reported further that these two men usually visited a garage in Highland every Saturday night, and if the officers came out Saturday they could all go over there. Several officers went to Highland on Saturday with Smalley, but the men did not appear. Then Smalley gave the officers their names Clarence McKinney and Jim Bill Reno of Cincinnati.

The following morning, Sunday, February 26, the officers drove to Cincinnati, obtained the cooperation of the local police, and arrested McKinney at his home. Reno was arrested later the same week. Both were lodged in the Clinton County Jail at Wilmington. McKinney and Reno were examined by many people. Ralph Moon and L. O. Carpenter identified them both as having been in Carpenter's Drug Store in Wilmington between ten and eleven o'clock on the night of the murder. One evening at the jail, a sheepskin coat and a toboggan cap were put on McKinney, the lights turned out, and Officer Adams flashed his light in the suspect's face, as he had done on the night of the shooting. From that moment forward, he was certain in his identification of McKinney as the smaller of the two burglars. The case was then submitted to the Grand Jury, which jointly indicted McKinney and Reno. They were also indicted for illegally transporting liquor in Clinton County on February 20, 1922.

The prosecuting attorney elected to try McKinney and Reno on the liquor charge first, in the hope that some facts might be developed in regard to the murder charge. In this [156] he was disappointed, although both men were convicted on the Liquor charge. Then came the trial on the murder charge. McKinney was tried first, the law of Ohio requiring separate trials in cases of first-degree murder. The case was tried before Judge Frank M. Clevenger of the Clinton County Court of Common Pleas and a jury of eleven men and one woman. The trial opened on August 20, 1922, and lasted over a week. The state was represented by the prosecuting attorney, S. L. Gregory, and by special counsel Joe T. Doan; the defendant, by J. G. De Fosset and R. L. Neff.

The case of the state rested upon the positive identification of McKinney as one of the burglars, by Officer Adams, upon the testimony of Moon and Carpenter that the prisoner and his companion, Reno, were in Wilmington on the night of the murder, and upon the statement of Smalley that he had seen them stalled on one of the roads of the county early the following morning. Twelve other witnesses were also called by the prosecution.

The defense counsel announced that the defense was a complete alibi. Over fifteen witnesses from Cincinnati were called to prove that on the night of the murder McKinney and his bride of a few months attended the Queen Anne Moving Picture Theater in Cincinnati, and that Reno was playing poker with friends at the home of his neighbor, George Reuhl. The witnesses were closely and effectively cross-examined by the prosecutors. Many of them remembered well the principal facts about the movements of the accused on February 14, St. Valentine's Day, but could remember little else that occurred about that time. The defendant testified in his own behalf, and on cross-examination the prosecution brought out the details of prior convictions and police difficulties. The testimony left a very definite impression with all present that the accused men were in the illicit liquor business, whereas the defense witnesses indicated that the principal occupation of McKinney and Reno was that of buying eggs and butter, and retailing them in Cincinnati. McKinney was forced to admit that, for days at a time, he did nothing but "monkey around" (he objected to its being called loafing), and that usually he had plenty of money. [157]

In rebuttal, the state presented witnesses to show that immediately after the arrest the defendant and Mrs. Reno had said that the McKinneys and the Renos had attended the Auto Show in Cincinnati on February 14, the night of the murder. At the trial, it was proved that the show had not opened until the fifteenth. Both the defendant and Mrs. Reno denied making such statements at any time, averring that they had attended the show on the opening night, February 15.

The case was submitted to the jury by Judge Clevenger with appropriate instructions. The jury returned a verdict of guilty, with a recommendation of mercy. McKinney was accordingly sentenced to life imprisonment in the Ohio State Penitentiary at Columbus. He submitted to his fate, protesting his innocence.

Reno was not immediately brought to trial on the murder charge, but was held in jail, serving sentence on the liquor charge.

• • • •

MONTHS later, some young men came to the sheriff of Clinton County with a strange story. They reported, in a rather casual way, that one Louis Vandervoort, the nineteen-year-old son of a wealthy Jamestown (Ohio) family, had been bragging that he had shot and killed Me Cr eight. The young men did not believe Vandervoort, for all his bragging. Nor did the sheriff; but as a matter of duty he had Louis arrested and questioned. To the sheriff's surprise, Vandervoort maintained that he had shot McCreight, and named a number of other burglaries in Clinton and Greene counties which he had committed. He even went so far as to tell the sheriff where some of the loot was hidden. The sheriff considered the boy partially insane. Nevertheless, he investigated; to his great astonishment the stolen goods were found where Vandervoort had indicated. Further investigations corroborated Vandervoort's confessions to such an extent that there could be no doubt about their truthfulness. Finally, Vandervoort named his accomplice in the McCreight murder, his nineteen-year-old companion, Walter Bingham. Bingham was immediately arrested. Under questioning, he also confessed. [158]

On February 14, 1923, just one year after the murder, Vandervoort and Bingham were indicted by the Grand Jury; and on February 20 and 21, 1923, they pleaded guilty to charges of second-degree murder and manslaughter, and received appropriate prison sentences.

At this time, McKinney's appeal case was still pending before the Ohio Court of Appeals in Cincinnati from a denial by the trial court of a motion for a new trial. On February 22, 1923, Judge Cushing ordered that the case be returned to the Clinton County Court of Common Pleas and that a new trial be granted. Mrs. McKinney, who had found employment in Cincinnati and had been working hard to raise money to prove her husband's innocence, went to Columbus with the sheriff of Clinton County and there met her husband on February 23, 1923. The sheriff and Mr. and Mrs. McKinney journeyed back to Wilmington together. The new trial was held before Judge Clevenger on February 24, 1923, and the case was nol-prossed by the State's Attorney. In ordering McKinney's release, Judge Clevenger is reported to have said: "You have been a victim of a miscarriage of justice. So far as this Court is able, it has made amends. You are now as free as any man in the state, and I, personally, and in the name of this Court wish you Godspeed."

In view of these developments, the fines in the liquor cases were suspended for both McKinney and Reno as a form of restitution. McKinney had spent five months in the Ohio Penitentiary, on a life sentence, for a murder committed by another.

Queerly enough, before leaving the court room on the day of his release, McKinney admitted to the court that he had been in Wilmington on the night of the murder, with a load of liquor, and that he had endeavored to establish a false alibi, not only to escape conviction for the murder, but also to avoid a possible liquor charge. This attempt at falsification proved to be a costly one.

The newspapers took a great interest in McKinney's case, and it was made the occasion for extensive editorial comment on the operation of criminal courts. One of the leading [159] Cincinnati newspapers printed a statement from a prominent local judge:

> There are many men in prisons all over America who are innocent of the crimes charged against them. But that is the misfortune all of us face. Any one picked up by the police may have to face circumstantial evidence which incriminates him. He may be innocent, but it is the duty of the prosecutor and the jury and the Court to deal with the evidence as presented. If an innocent man is convicted he has no recourse. He has to take the chance that all of us face. It happens infrequently, but when it does it emphasizes the plight of the imprisoned innocent man, without bringing out the fact that dozens of guilty men go free. It is unfortunate, but when such cases happen it is not the fault of our laws, but a trick of fate that cannot be forestalled.

It does not appear that McKinney's case was ever presented to the Ohio Legislature.

• • • •

McKINNEY was the victim of mistaken identity, plus circumstantial evidence. When evidence of his prior convictions was introduced, his plight became critical. When his false alibi broke down, he was lost. By putting on him the khaki coat and the cap, the prosecution openly provoked an identification from Officer Adams. Yet McKinney had nothing to do with the crime. While he had been in Wilmington on the evening of the murder and the next morning, it was for quite a different purpose. The identification was absolutely false. The circumstantial evidence was equally untrustworthy. And yet, but for the corroborated boasting and confession of Vandervoort, McKinney would probably have served out his life sentence. His record made the conviction easy. It has already been observed that only under limited circumstances, where the previous record becomes an important issue in the case, should the accused be asked questions on that point. The question when put by the prosecution is highly prejudicial to the accused and is intended to be so. A question might arise whether the false alibi which was not intended to defeat, but rather to help, justice should deprive McKinney of compensation, under an indemnity statute, on the ground that he thereby contributed [160] to his own conviction. It is believed that it should not be so considered. The untruth of the alibi may have prejudiced the jury, but McKinney can hardly be said thereby to have brought about his own conviction.

• • • •

Acknowledgment: Hon. F. M. Clevenger, Wilmington, Ohio. [160]

Buzzards Over Brindlee

John Murchison

ON Friday morning, August 6, 1920, as he left his home near Guntersville, Alabama, John Franklin McClendon, a white man, told his wife that he was going to Guntersville and then to Smith's Lake to open a soft-drink stand and sell its wares at a picnic to be held at Smith's Lake the next day. When he left his companions at Smith's Lake that night about midnight, he told them that he would be there early the next morning, and set off in the direction of his home.

When he did not appear at the stand the next morning, and when nothing was heard of him for three or four days, a search was begun and continued for five or six days. About ten days after his disappearance, a colored boy who lived in the community reported to one of the searchers that he had seen buzzards flying close to the crest of Brindlee Mountain, which was about a quarter of a mile from the McClendon home. A group of searchers went at once to investigate. As they approached a cave near the top of the mountain, they saw the tracks of a rubber-tired buggy leading to the cave and a bent bush over which the buggy had apparently driven. When they came nearer, they called other searchers to them, as the odors emanating from the cave told them their search was at an end. When they entered the cave, they found a body covered by brush and leaves and partially screened from casual gaze by a quilt. The dead man had been shot twice at close range, as the powder burns on the clothing showed. The body was subsequently identified as that of McClendon by the clothing and the teeth.

The boy who had directed the searchers' attention to the mountain later made a statement in which he said that he had told John Murchison, a colored man, what he had seen, and that Murchison had told him to say nothing about it, as it "might get him into trouble." Murchison also came under suspicion because he was known to have a rubber-tired buggy one of whose stirrups was bent back, and he was also known to have played craps with McClendon. He was placed in jail on the charge of murder. [162]

Later two other negroes, Willie Crutcher and Cleo Staten, were placed in jail on the charge of participating 'in the murder. Their number was increased by the addition of Jim Hudson, G. B. Staten, Alfred Staten, and Ben Nobles, all of them colored. These men were under suspicion because they had been hunting the night of the murder, supposedly in the vicinity of Brindlee Mountain.

They were all indicted for murder in the first degree by the Grand Jury on October 8, 1920, and were arraigned for trial October 11, 1920. Trial was set for October 19, 1920. By agreement it was decided to try Murchison, Crutcher, Hudson, and Cleo Staten together. The trial was held before the Hon. W. W. Haralson, Judge of the Ninth Judicial Circuit of Alabama. The prosecution was conducted by A. E. Hawkins, Prosecutor for the Ninth Judicial Circuit; H. G. Baily, County Solicitor for Marshall County; and John A. Lush of Guntersville, special counsel retained by the representatives of the deceased. The defendants were represented by P. W. Shumate and W. M. Rayburn, both of Guntersville.

At the trial Ben Nobles, one of the men indicted for the murder, testified for the state that he had seen John Murchison shoot the deceased in the back. Nobles asserted that about midnight on the night of the murder he had gone to the schoolhouse grove, in which a game of craps was taking place, that he had there seen Jim Hudson, Willie Crutcher, John Murchison, and Cleo Staten, and that he had seen John Murchison fire the first shot at McClendon, in his back, and Cleo Staten the second. He said that they then wrapped the body in a quilt and took it away. He claimed to have had a clear and unobstructed view of the whole scene.

There was conflicting evidence as to whether or not the quilt in which the body had been wrapped came from the home of Laura Bell Nobles. One witness testified that he knew it was hers because of a certain patch. Yet Ben Nobles, her brother, and the woman who did most of the sewing for the Nobles family did not recognize it.

Nobles and others testified that they had heard Murchison and Willie Crutcher object to the relationship existing [163] between McClendon and Laura Bell Nobles and say that it should be broken up. This may have been considered by the prosecution one. of the motives for the murder.

Ben Nobles and the boy who reported the presence of the buzzards testified that Murchison had warned them to say nothing about the birds.

One witness testified that on the night of the murder he had heard shooting on the mountain, two shots perhaps a minute apart. He lived about a half mile from the schoolhouse near which the shooting was supposed to have taken place. Various witnesses testified that they had seen Crutcher and Hudson carrying weapons about the time of the murder.

The defense was based on alibis. All the defendants denied on the stand that they were present at the crap game and that they were in any way connected with the murder.

Various witnesses established the fact that both Murchison and Jim Hudson had gone to a meeting at the schoolhouse, which had broken up between ten and eleven o'clock. Some testified to having accompanied Murchison to his home, and his wife testified that he had not left during the night. Part of the same evidence established the fact that Jim Hudson had spent the night at the home of Nancy Staten, a relative.

The other defendants claimed to have been hunting with horses and dogs on the night of the murder and produced witnesses who had seen or heard them hunting until two or three in the morning. All this evidence, however, pointed to the fact that they had been hunting near Black's Gate, not Brindlee Mountain.

One of the searchers who assisted in removing the body from the cave testified that the clothing found on the body did not show shot holes in the back, but in the front.

The defense offered evidence to show that Ben Nobles, as well as another man who had left the county shortly after the discovery of the body, and others also, had rubber-tired buggies, and that the stirrup on Murchison's buggy had been bent long before the murder took place.

There was some evidence that, after the murder was discovered, a bloodstained mattress was seen at the Nobles [164] home, where both Ben Nobles and Laura Bell Nobles lived. Medical evidence established that the stains were not blood.

It was testified that Laura Bell Nobles was not married, but had a child.

Upon this evidence, on October 21, 1920, the jury returned a verdict of guilty. The four defendants were sentenced to life imprisonment and immediately began their sentences.

• • • •

AFTER he had served about two. years of his term, Willie Crutcher was killed by falling rock in the mine where he worked. Jim Hudson died of tuberculosis, after having served three and a- half years.

In April, 1926, while Murchison and Cleo Staten were still in prison for the murder of John McClendon, and. after Myrtle McClendon, the widow, had remarried, Otis McClendon, a nephew of the dead man, made a confession to his mother. He stated that the wife of the dead man had confided to him her desire to kill her husband, and had promised him, in return for his aid, forty acres of land, a pair of mules, and a home as long as she had one, and that they had shot McClendon as he entered his own home, the wife firing the first shot and he the second. He described how they had wrapped the body in an old quilt from the house and taken it to the cave in McClendon's rubber-tired buggy. He told of injuring the stirrup and attempting to repair it. He claimed that he had no peace of mind, especially as Myrtle McClendon had in no way kept her promise to remain loyal to him but had married another man, Cleve King; and he vowed that he was going to kill her, her husband, and himself. After making this confession, he ran from the house to carry out his vow. He did in fact attempt to do so, firing on Myrtle and her husband in their home, but before he could accomplish his object, he was fatally wounded by a shot fired by the husband. He was found crouching at the foot of a tree, with a pistol, the hammer back, in his hand; it was the theory of the officers that he was about to shoot himself when fired on by King.

When affidavits relating these facts were presented to the [165] Board of Pardons, John Murchison and Cleo Staten were at once released on permanent parole, July 7, 1926. Staten, on March 12, 1927, was granted a full pardon, but unfortunately never received it, for he died just a few days before it was issued. A pardon was denied to Murchison by Gov. Bibbs Graves, though Murchison was admittedly innocent, because of a record of bad conduct in prison. At last accounts, Murchison was working for a Mr. Claybrook of Albertville, Alabama, doing chores about the house. In July, 1931, the Alabama Legislature voted Murchison $750 as compensation for his unjust conviction and imprisonment.

• • • •

THIS tragedy was the result of a combination of circumstantial evidence and rank perjury. Possibly Ben Nobles, whose vivid testimony as to things that never happened, may have been induced by fear, an excited imagination, suggestion, or coaching he appears to have been arrested, but not indicted believed what he claimed to have seen. Possibly the fact that all the accused were negroes and that John McClendon appears at times to have associated with negroes, may have directed suspicion easily toward negroes as the authors of the crime. Why the known bad relations existing between McClendon and his wife did not lead to suspicion of the wife is not disclosed. The evidence against the accused, apart from Nobles' testimony, seems so conflicting that it might well have led to a disagreement of the jury. It is not improper to infer that the premature deaths of Crutcher, Hudson, and Staten had a more or less direct relation to their wrongful imprisonment. Alabama made a tangible gesture of contrition and vindication by awarding Murchison $750.

• • • •

Acknowledgments: Hon. C. A. Moffett, President of the Alabama State Board of Administration, Montgomery, Ala.; Mr. P. W. Shumate, Guntersville, Ala.; Mr. Douglas Arant, Birmingham, Ala. [166]

He Stayed Home

Joseph Nedza

SUNDAY evening at the Elks Hotel in East Syracuse, New York, was usually very quiet. Mr. Olmsted must have thought so at 10:30 on December 7, 1930, as he surveyed the lobby from one corner. There on the sofa lay the proprietor, Samuel Meyers, quietly dozing the time away. But not for long. Two brusque figures came into the lobby brandishing pistols. Olmsted immediately slipped out. The bandits, a large one and a small one, stepped over to Meyers and nudged him. Meyers awoke and, upon seeing his predicament, jumped to his feet. He grappled with the large fellow, who was nearer to him. As they struggled for the pistol, it was fired several times, without effect. The smaller bandit hovered about; and when he got a chance he shot at Meyers, hitting his victim in the left side. The bandits then tried to take the diamond stick pin from Meyers' tie, but it was fastened by a special clasp. The bandits fled. They got no loot, but left a wounded man, who was taken at once to St. Joseph's Hospital.

This attempted robbery was reported to the Syracuse Police Department at once, with general descriptions of the men. They were wearing caps. Soon police headquarters received a call from the Pan- Am gas station at 4004 East Genesee Street, which was on the same route but nearer the city of Syracuse. Two men had been there at about 10:50 o'clock, had locked Attendant Frank J. Brady in a closet, and had rifled the cash register of a large sum of money. A few minutes later the police received a call from the Colonial gasoline station at 2974 East Genesee Street, which was farther along on the route from East Syracuse to the city of Syracuse. Attendant Samuel Starks had been surprised by two men with guns, announcing, "We are here, stick them up." Starks was locked in a small closet, and the bandits drove off with the money in the cash drawer. These three reports to the police on Sunday night indicated that the same men had done all three jobs. It also recalled to the detectives the incident of the Friday preceding, December 5, when two [167] men, of similar appearance, had gone to the used-car salesroom of Forsythe & Gale, had taken a demonstration ride in an Oldsmobile landau with Mr. Martin, an auto salesman, and then had stolen the car from Martin at pistol point.

Police Officers Ours, Dolphin, and Forsythe were assigned to these cases. The rogues' gallery was studied, and the pictures of two men withdrawn. The week before, Vincent Starowitz, aged twenty-four, had arrived in Syracuse. Starowitz had just finished his sentence for a burglary committed in Onondaga County in 1927, to which he had pleaded guilty. His partner in that burglary had been Joseph Nedza, then twenty years old, who had been placed on probation. Nedza was known to be living at the Terminal Hotel, an inexpensive boarding house near the New York Central depot. Officer Dolphin took the pictures of Starowitz and Nedza to the hospital on Monday, the day following the attack, and Meyers identified them as his assailants Starowitz as the smaller of the two, who had shot him, and Nedza as the larger, with whom he had fought over the gun.

Officers Dolphin and Forsythe then went to the Terminal Hotel. Clerk William Koss said that neither Nedza nor Starowitz was there, but that Nedza had rented Room 3. The officers returned late in the afternoon and arrested Nedza as he was lunching in the barroom. He accompanied them to his room, where everything was carefully searched but no revolver was found. Nedza was taken to the police station. A short while later, Starowitz was arrested in the New York Central depot. Both men denied any knowledge of the holdup of the Elks Hotel. They had spent all Monday afternoon together, obtaining information for Starowitz about enlisting in the navy. Starowitz had been drinking heavily.

On Tuesday, victims Brady and Starks were called to the police station, where they identified both prisoners. Nedza, during this interview, was dressed up in a gray topcoat and a cap, as it had been reported that the large bandit had been dressed at the gas stations. Mr. Armstrong, from the firm of Forsythe & Gale, also identified them as the men who had gone on the demonstration ride in the Oldsmobile with [168] Mr. Martin. Nedza was taken to the hospital, where Meyers, from his sick bed, identified him in person. However, he was never identified in a "line-up."

In the meantime, Starowitz swore to a statement at the police station in which he confessed his participation in each one of these crimes. He implicated " Jimmie" as his partner. Acting upon some of Starowitz' comments, the officers drove over to Utica with Starowitz and arrested a man named Sherwood. Before bringing Sherwood to Syracuse, he as well as Starowitz was identified by several holdup victims in Utica, so that the Utica police put in a claim for Sherwood. Nevertheless, he was brought to Syracuse, but was almost immediately released to the Utica police for prosecution there, for several of the Syracuse victims failed to identify him.

The county authorities lost no time in presenting the matter to the Grand Jury, which returned a joint indictment against Starowitz and Nedza for an attempt to commit the crime of robbery in the first degree. They were brought to trial before Judge William L. Barnum in the Onondaga County Court in February, 1931. Assistant District At- torney William C. Martin represented the people. Dennis Nash appeared for Starowitz, and Irving Devorsetz for Nedza. The court refused Mr. Devorsetz' motion for a separate trial for Nedza.

The first witness produced by the prosecution was Deputy Sheriff Hoffmire, to identify certificates establishing the convictions of these defendants for burglary in May, 1927. These were admitted, over defense objections, as bearing on the credibility of the defendants. The reason for this evidence was the fact that they had been indicted as second offenders, and this was the method adopted by the prosecution to prove the first offense. The arresting officers and the victim, Meyers, then testified as to their parts in the affair, and that part of Starowitz' alleged confession relating to the Elks Hotel was introduced. He identified his companion as "Jimmie," but claimed not to know his real name. The inference was that "Jimmie" was not Nedza.

Nedza, for the defense, took the stand and related that [169] he spent the Sunday evening in question at the Terminal Hotel and that he was there at 10:30. He was subjected to a grueling cross-examination, but survived it without a single inconsistency or contradiction. Three persons, one of whom had worked in the same factory for twenty years, supported Nedza's alibi, and two others, who had been at the Terminal Hotel until about ten o'clock, testified that he was there at that time. Starowitz, in his own defense, said that at the time of the robbery he was in Utica, more or less under the influence of liquor, playing "rummy." He claimed to remember but little about the "confession," except that it was forced from him and that, though he signed it to be relieved from pressure, he did not know what was in it. He had no supporting witnesses. In rebuttal the prosecutor called the gas-station victims to break down the defendants' credibility further, as each defendant claimed to have been elsewhere at the time of the holdups.

In submitting the case to the jury, Mr. Martin vigorously emphasized the criminal record of the prisoners, the fact that they had been known to be drifting about the country together after their release from prison, Starowitz' confession, and the positive identifications. He discounted the alibi witnesses of Nedza as coming from his close friends at the Terminal Hotel.

After four hours' deliberation the jury found both men guilty, and both received exceptionally long sentences Nedza being sentenced for thirty-five years. Both men were sent to Auburn Penitentiary.

• • • •

MR. DEVORSETZ was firmly convinced that Nedza was innocent, but at the same time he believed Starowitz guilty. He interviewed Starowitz several times at Auburn, and finally the latter agreed to name his accomplice Albert Sherwood. Sherwood, who had been convicted for the Utica holdups, was also serving a long sentence in Auburn. Mr. Devorsetz solicited the cooperation of Prosecutor Martin, and to them Sherwood made a complete and detailed confession. During his earlier term at Auburn, Sherwood had become friendly [170] with a Syracuse convict and had spent some time with him after his release. This man had taken him to the Elks Hotel in East Syracuse, so that Sherwood had had an opportunity to survey the situation. Several months later he encountered Starowitz and struck up the friendship which resulted in the holdups. This was checked very carefully by Mr. Martin, and he became convinced that it was true. Samuel Meyers was taken to Auburn, and he picked Sherwood out of a group of twenty convicts as the man with whom he had had the tussle over the gun. There could no longer be any doubt of the mistake. An application for a pardon was filed with Acting Governor Lehman, which was recommended by the District Attorney and Judge Barnum. Governor Lehman offered to issue an unconditional pardon, but suggested that the best way to erase the judgment of conviction was through an application for a new trial. This motion was duly made and granted by Judge Barnum, unopposed by the District Attorney. Thereupon, all indictments against Nedza were dismissed, and he was freed on May 19, 1931, having served about three months of his term. It is reported that efforts will be made to obtain indemnification from the state for this innocent victim of circumstantial evidence and mistaken identity.

• • • •

NEDZA'S previous experience with the law and with Starowitz, the admitted association of the two on other occasions, and the identifications by persons robbed were sufficient to convince prosecutor and jury that Nedza must have been guilty. Five victims of a holdup identified him, though they seem to have been assisted by dressing up the accused in clothes similar to those the guilty man was supposed to have worn. When the truth was indicated and Sherwood established as the guilty man, Meyers evidently had little difficulty in admitting his error. Yet on the stand, though conceding that he was terribly agitated and excited and therefore could hardly have had a good opportunity for observation, he nevertheless felt absolutely sure that Nedza was the man. Why Sherwood was not taken before Meyers for [171] identification is not clear possibly because other victims did not identify him. In fact, Nedza and Sherwood bore practically no resemblance to each other. The past association of Nedza and Starowitz made it the more easy to discredit the witnesses for Nedza, who were nevertheless telling the exact truth. To open a trial with proof of the defendants' previous convictions and to admit the evidence in order to challenge the defendants' credibility even before they had testified, was highly prejudicial, even if deemed necessary to prove their indictment as second offenders. It colored the whole trial, though the prosecution was most honest. The New York law makes it possible, in the case of second offenders, to prove the prior conviction either during the trial or after the trial, the second offense carrying a more severe penalty. Only the second method seems fair, for it affects the sentence only. The fact that no money was found on Nedza should not have been dismissed as immaterial on the question of his guilt or innocence, though the District Attorney said that no money was found on Starowitz. Only the circumstances that pointed to possible guilt were apparently given weight, and it may be conceded that the circumstances for Nedza were mostly unfavorable. When, through the persistence of Nedza's attorney, the truth was finally established, prosecutor and judge were zealous in seeking to undo the error. Nedza deserves an indemnity from the state, which might in fact do much good, for it appears that he has not necessarily criminal propensities.

• • • •

Acknowledgments: Hon. William C. Martin, Syracuse, N.Y.; Mr. Irving S. Devorsetz, Syracuse, N.Y. [172]

BAIL-JUMPER

Henry Olson

THE citizens of Rockford, Illinois, were horrified by the cold-blooded murder of Floyd Stotler. Floyd and his father, Orville Stotler, were in charge of the Hart Oil Station at the corner of Broadway and Kishwaukee Streets in Rockford at about nine o'clock on the evening of September 6, 1927. Father Stotler had finally found an opportunity, after nine o'clock, to glance over his daily paper, only to be startlingly interrupted by two young masked bandits, who, at pistol points, ordered his son Floyd to "stick them up." Floyd replied, "Put them down and quit your fooling. What is the joke anyway?" One bandit snapped back, "Stick them up, we mean it, stick up."

Floyd grabbed for one of the bandits a shot was fired, and the bandits disappeared through the door into the night, deserting the Chrysler roadster in which they had driven up to the filling station. Floyd slumped to the floor, crumpled and bleeding, in great agony.

Police Officers Lloyd Fry and John Ott, from headquarters, responded to a hurry call. They took Floyd to the hospital, where he received immediate attention. An emergency operation was unsuccessful, and Floyd died.

The Police Department of Rockford and the sheriff of Winnebago County at once began the search for clues. The only tangible bit of evidence at hand was the .22-caliber bullet taken from the body. The Chrysler car was found to have been stolen in Rockford. A number of suspects were picked up and held for questioning. The night of the murder, police officers called at the home of Henry Olson, a twenty-six-year-old mechanic who lived only about a block from the Hart Oil Station. Henry did not have a good reputation among the officers of the law, and they investigated him when Orville Stotler's description of the general build of one of the bandits seemed to fit Olson. The officers questioned various members of the family concerning Henry Olson's whereabouts during the evening. The Olson statements, however, satisfied the police for the time being that [173] Henry had spent the evening at home with his young wife and other members- of his family. Stotler could not give a complete description because the bandits had worn handkerchief masks, almost completely covering their faces, except for holes for the eyes.

Various suspects were brought before Father Stotler for identification. Some he eliminated, but of others he was not sure. These were presented to him a second and a third time, and he studied them from all angles, with caps on and caps off. About a week after the shooting, Henry Olson was added to the group, and Stotler at once identified him as the bandit who had shot his son. Despite the mask, Stotler said that he could identify Henry by his high cheek bones, hollow cheeks, light hair, height, and general build.

With this positive identification, the case against Olson was presented by Prosecutor William D. Knight to a Grand Jury, under the foremanship of George F. Colton, which heard the testimony of Stotler and Physician Sheehe. An indictment for murder was returned against Olson on October 7, 1927, and the case called for trial on October 24, before Judge Arthur E. Fisher in the Circuit Court of Winnebago County. Olson was defended by Attorney Harry B. North of Rockford. The newspapers took a great interest in the case and supplied their readers with sensational news. The community thought Olson guilty.

Both the prosecution and the defense submitted testimony about the general location and situation of the oil station. Orville Stotler's positive identification of Olson was the only evidence connecting Olson with the murder. Defense Attorney North was convinced of his client's innocence and made strenuous efforts by cross-examination over the better part of two days to break down Stotler's identification.

Olson's defense was the alibi that he had spent the evening at home. Mr. and Mrs. Aaron Sanfordson, neighbors of the Olsons, testified that they had seen Olson sprinkling his lawn about six o'clock the evening of the tragedy, and that Mrs. Olson was then out. Emanuel Olson, his father, and Adolph Olson, his brother, said that they knew that Henry was at home at 8:30 and that they heard him moving about the [174] house after nine o'clock, the time of the shooting., Mrs. Sarah Olson, his mother, said that she had spent the evening on the porch of her home with Henry, the defendant, and that shortly after nine o'clock Henry's wife alighted from a bus across the street. Henry went to meet her. Then they all sat on the porch for a short time. The testimony of Mrs. Henry Olson's visit to her aunt, Mrs. Josie Glass, was corroborated by her sister, and by Mrs. Glass; and of her return on the bus, arriving at Kishwaukee and Buckbee Streets just about nine o'clock, by bus driver James Dounett. Mother Olson also testified that while she, Henry, and his wife were sitting on the porch Vito Turciano, a flagman at the Illinois Central station on Kishwaukee Street, came for a drink. Turciano confirmed this and said that when he came to the Olsons' house it was about 9:15. Shortly after this the family went to bed. The prosecutor's objection to the testimony of Henry's wife was sustained by the court so that she was not permitted to take the stand. According to the defense testimony, the first the Olsons heard of the tragedy was when the police called to question Henry during the night.

The defense further tried to weaken Stotler's identification by introducing testimony to show that his description of the bandit just after the murder varied from that given at the trial and also that for some days he was not sure which of several suspects, dissimilar in appearance, was the true culprit.

The case as thus outlined, and after arguments of counsel, was given to the jury with the Judge's instructions. The jury was locked up for the night. In the morning, they reported themselves deadlocked six to six. Since there appeared to be no probability of an agreement on a verdict, Judge Fisher discharged the jury. The defendant was released on bond again until his new trial, which started on February 13, 1928. The jury this time, under Foreman Elvidge, found him guilty of murder, as charged in the indictment, upon practically the same evidence that had been used at the first trial, and fixed the penalty at life imprisonment in Joliet Penitentiary. Mr. North at once made a motion for [175] a new trial, and Judge Fisher permitted Olson to remain at liberty under a $10,000 bond, thus evidencing his doubt of Olson's guilt, despite the verdict of the jury.

Thereupon, Olson vanished from Rockford. It was learned that he had driven with his wife in their car to Chicago and from there had telegraphed the family to come for the car. Henry and his wife disappeared completely. A nation-wide search was unsuccessful. There were rumors about Rockford that the second bandit was Olson's wife and that the escape had prevented her indictment. By the community, Olson's flight was considered an admission of guilt.

• • • •

MR. NORTH, firmly believing his client innocent, continued his efforts to solve the mystery, and one day a fruitful lead came to him. A business man in the city reported that a maid-servant in his family had stated that Olson was not guilty. The police questioned her, but she denied making the statement or knowing anything about it. Later, she was taken by the police for further questioning. She then admitted that she had made the statement, and said that her eighteen-year-old sweetheart, Maurice Mahan, had boasted to her that he and his eighteen-year-old chum, George Bliss, had held up the filling station and that Bliss had done the shooting. These two boys were arrested and, questioned separately, finally confessed. They gave complete details concerning the facts, each corroborating the other, so that there was no doubt as to the genuineness of the confessions. They were indicted and arraigned and entered pleas of guilty before Judge Edward D. Shurtleff, whereupon Bliss was given a sentence of thirty-five years and Mahan, fourteen years, in the state penitentiary.

• • • •

EVERY effort was made to locate Henry Olson and his wife, to give them the good news. The new developments were broadcast through the press and the radio with a message to Olson to return home. After some weeks, Mr. North received a telegram from Olson in New Orleans, where he had [176] finally seen the notice in the newspaper. Upon receiving assurances that the news story was true, the Olsons returned to Rockford. A new trial, his third within a period of six months, was ordered by Judge Fisher, and Olson was acquitted on March 16, 1928.

He settled down in Rockford, vindicated before the law and before the community.

• • • •

THIS miscarriage of justice was due to mistaken identity. The positive identification by Orville Stotler, a victim of the tragedy, outweighed in the minds of the jury the mass of evidence which indicated that Olson was at home at the time of the shooting. The jury evidently preferred to believe that nearly a dozen people were perjuring themselves rather than admit that Father Stotler could have been mistaken. The fact that Olson "jumped" his bail confirmed the community in its belief that he must have been the murderer. As he left the court room, his emotions were a mixture of happiness and righteous indignation. It is perhaps superfluous to add that he was never compensated by the state of Illinois for his ordeal. But he did bring suit against his attorney, Mr. North, for negligence, and the jury returned a verdict in his favor, for $29,250. This was reduced by the court to $7500. That judgment is now on appeal to the Appellate Court of Illinois Second District. Considering the trouble taken by Mr. North, the finding of negligence seems unusual.

• • • •

Acknowledgments: Judge A. E. Fisher, Rockford, Ill.; Mr. H. B. North, attorney at law, Rockford, Ill.; Mr. Lewis F. Lake, Clerk of the Circuit Court, Rockford, Ill.; Mr. Edward L. McCleneghan, attorney at law, Rockford, Ill.
[177]

THEY ONLY WALKED UPSTAIRS

Pezzulich and Sgelirrach

NO. 36 Beach Street, New York City, was at one time a private house, but after 1910 had been used for light housekeeping and furnished rooms. Most of the men who stayed there were Austrians or Croatians who worked for the railroad companies, or on the boats which plied New York Harbor. On the ground floor of the house was a large room, which during the evening hours was lighted only by the faint glow of a single gas light.

In this room, and the one next to it, nine of these laborers all Croatians lived. They slept and cooked their meals in the two rooms. Usually after their evening meal they sat around the dimly lighted room and talked until bedtime. This was what they were doing on the night of March 22, 1919, when the door suddenly opened, and seven masked men walked in, all of them brandishing pistols.

The holdup men went about their business systematically, for each of the men in the room was covered; and to add to the terror of their victims, one of them, Vincent Zic, was hit on the head with the butt end of a revolver, and three shots were fired into the ceiling. During the proceedings, the handkerchiefs, used as masks, dropped from the faces of two of the robbers.

The nine Croatians were carefully searched and relieved of all their money. Frank Zic, a railroad laborer, thirty-eight years of age, was robbed of $1,728, his savings from a lifetime of hard work. John Bonafacto had $85 taken from him, Nick Zic lost $13, and Andrew Androzvick, $15. In six or seven minutes the job was done. The robbers fled from the house to the street, and then separated in different directions, some going toward Varick Street and some toward Hudson Street.

The victims were stunned by the outrage. But Mike Zic recovered a little more quickly than his fellows. He rushed to the front door of the house and ran after the thieves. He chose the group that went toward Varick Street. About a block and a half away, at the corner of Varick and North [178] Moore Streets, he caught up with one of the robbers whom he had not lost from sight, and held him until he was arrested by Policeman Robert Wilson of the Fourth Precinct, who came upon the scene. The prisoner was taken to the station house at the corner of Beach and Varick Streets. There he was identified by Zic as one of the robbers, and gave the name of Frank Strolich, twenty-five years old, a fireman on one of the river boats. Strolich denied having had anything to do with the robbery. He gave his address as No. 408 West Twenty-fourth Street, which was a sailors' and laborers' boarding house run by Mrs. Mary Nazinovich.

Detective James P. Murphy immediately went to that address. Arriving there at about 9:30, in company with Frank Zic, the heaviest loser in the robbery, he met two men coming up the stairs leading to the first floor. They seemed about to leave the place. Despite their protests, he forced them to return to the kitchen and there arrested them, upon the identification of Frank Zic, as two of the other robbers.

The two men gave the names of Frank Pezzulich and Frank Sgelirrach. The former said that he had lived at the house for only three weeks, that he was a marine fireman, having come to the United States from Austria in 1907, and that he was thirty-three years old and unmarried. Sgelirrach, also a marine fireman, said he was twenty-seven years old and unmarried, and had been in this country six years. Both could read, write, and speak English, though not well, and both were unnaturalized. Neither had been convicted before of any offense. They claimed that they knew nothing of the crime, though they did know Strolich, the man already arrested, who lived at the house.

That ended the arrests for that night. The other robbers were not caught, nor were any further suspects captured until December, 1919, over eight months later. But in the meantime, proceedings were begun against the three men who had been arrested. An indictment was filed against them on March 31, 1919. Strolich was the first to go to trial, before Judge Charles E. Nott of the Court of General Sessions, and a jury; and on May 9, 1919, two months after [179] the holdup, he was convicted of robbery in the first degree and sentenced to not less than eight nor more than sixteen years in Auburn prison. This was his first conviction since he had come to the United States from Austria six years before.

Before Pezzulich and Sgelirrach were brought to trial a few weeks later, Assistant District Attorney Owen W. Bohan had Strolich returned to New York to question him further about the holdup, with the idea of using him as a witness against Pezzulich and Sgelirrach.

Then for the first time, Strolich denied that Pezzulich and Sgelirrach had been involved in the robbery, and to substantiate this statement he gave Bohan the names of all the others who took part. He refused to testify in the impending trial and was sent back to Auburn while the police began a search for the men he had named.

Despite this new information, Pezzulich and Sgelirrach were brought to trial, inasmuch as, according to Bohan, three of the robbers' victims had identified them, though the other six were unable to do so. They were identified as the two robbers from whose faces the handkerchiefs had dropped.

Their defense was an alibi, supported by the testimony of seven witnesses. They said they had not worked the day of the holdup because of a strike. They went out that afternoon, they testified, to buy some clothes and then returned to their lodging house and had supper about six o'clock, remaining in the kitchen talking until after nine. When Zic and the detective arrived they were on their way upstairs to their room, they said. All seven witnesses testified that the two had not left the house between six o'clock and the time of their arrest.

The jury returned a verdict of guilty against them, and on June 9 they, too, were sentenced by Judge Mulqueen to eight to sixteen years in Sing Sing Prison.

• • • •

IN December, Lino DePiero was arrested in connection with the robbery, indicted, and tried. Strolich had named him as [180] one of his accomplices and was brought to New York to testify against him. Judge Mulqueen, however, felt that the evidence against DePiero was insufficient and directed an acquittal.

In January, 1920, three men were arrested in Milwaukee for a crime committed there. They gave their names as Tony Blazcik, alias Tonjak; Frank Fratar; and John DeFranza. The Milwaukee police discovered that they were wanted in New York for the Beach Street robbery. Detective James Murphy, who had charge of the New York case, was sent to Milwaukee to return them to New York. Before starting back he obtained a written confession from the three telling of their participation in the New York robbery, a confession signed in the presence of Capt. John T. Sullivan of the Milwaukee police. They named the others, as Strolich had done, but said nothing about Pezzulich or Sgelirrach.

After they were indicted, Blazcik jumped bail and became a fugitive. The other two were brought to trial before Judge Otto Rosalsky and were found guilty, though they repudiated their Milwaukee confession. Strolich had been brought from Auburn and testified against them. Each was sentenced to eight to sixteen years in Sing Sing.

Assistant District Attorney Bohan had been deeply impressed by the Milwaukee confession, which confirmed Strolich's statements, and he became more and more doubtful of the justice of keeping Pezzulich and Sgelirrach in prison. He continued his efforts to get the Milwaukee men to repeat their confession and was finally successful through the diplomacy of Father Cashin, the Catholic chaplain at Sing Sing. The two men admitted their guilt and denied emphatically that Pezzulich and Sgelirrach had participated in their crime.

Mr. Bohan was now convinced and initiated proceedings to free Pezzulich and Sgelirrach. They were released from the penitentiary August 19, 1920, on a certificate of reasonable doubt. Mr. Bohan filed a motion for a new trial, which was granted. Then, in an exhaustive review of the entire case, he furnished the court with a complete story of the injustice done the two men, the statements of Strolich, [181] Fratar, and DeFranza exonerating Pezzulich and Sgelirrach from all connection with the crime, together with the facts that the identifications were made by frightened victims, in an ill-lighted room, with opportunity only for hasty observation, and that Fratar and DeFranza bore a physical resemblance to Pezzulich and Sgelirrach. "The People's witnesses," said Mr. Bohan, "were honestly mistaken." On April 28, 1921, the indictment against Pezzulich and Sgelirrach was dismissed and they were again free men after having served about fourteen months for a crime they did not commit.

• • • •

NOT much that is new can be said in comment upon this case. The conviction was due to an honest mistake in identification by the panic-stricken victims of a robbery committed under conditions which deprived the victims of their normal capacity for perception and observation. Perhaps the District Attorney might have given more weight to Strolich's exoneration of Pezzulich and Sgelirrach, and the jury, to the facts that six of the victims were unable to identify them, that the conditions for identification were not of the best, and that the alibi was substantiated by seven witnesses. But the ways of juries are strange. Possibly the fact that Mike Zic had correctly identified Strolich, whom he had kept in sight, gave undue weight to the identifications made later by the other Zics.

• • • •

Acknowledgments: Hon. Owen W. Bohan, 225 Broadway, New York City; Hon. Lewis E. Lawes, Warden, Sing Sing Prison, Ossining, N.Y.; Hon. R. F. C. Kieb, Commissioner, Department of Correction, Albany, N.Y. [182]

"THE WACO KID"

Willard Powell

IN 1908, Willard Powell, known to turfmen as "the Waco Kid," lived in Denver, Colorado. He owned horses and with them followed the racing seasons from California to Colorado, through Oklahoma and Texas, to Louisiana and Florida. His path in life crossed that of Henry Stogsdill, to his great misfortune.

Henry Stogsdill owned a store and was in the business of stock trading at Cabool, Missouri. One day in March, 1908, he was on his way to examine some stock when a friend, William Scott, came running after him and said, "Would you go and help me make some money if it didn't cost you anything?" Stogsdill replied, "Of course, we are always out for a dollar." Scott then introduced an old acquaintance of his, Billy Connors, who said he had a cousin in Denver by the name of Frank Maxwell, secretary to a group of millionaires. His employers had misused him and Maxwell wanted to get even by getting some of their money, which he knew he could do if he only had the backing of someone with substantial means. Stogsdill was asked to help by going to Denver personally. They said it would not cost him anything and it was intimated that if Maxwell succeeded in his scheme Stogsdill would get a share of the profits. Stogsdill approved the idea and accompanied Scott and Connors to Denver, where he met Maxwell, who explained the scheme. Stogsdill was to meet the millionaires in a hotel room and to bet with them on a private horse race to be run on the outskirts of Denver. Maxwell was going to give Stogsdill $5,000 cash to be used in the betting. As secretary to the millionaires, Maxwell would be permitted to be stakeholder in an adjoining room and as money was brought to him he would slip more into Stogsdill's pockets for further betting. It was planned that when the millionaires had been induced to put up $20,000 or more, the race would be run, a race which, Maxwell said, he would have so fixed that the millionaires' horse would lose. Stogsdill was told, however, that he would have to have something to prove to the millionaires that he was a [183] man of means and a worthy person for them to deal with. Scott prepared a letter which Stogsdill signed and mailed to his bank at Cabool, Missouri, asking for $10,000. The bank refused to send this amount. Thereupon Stogsdill was persuaded to return to Cabool for his money, accompanied by Scott. He got only $3,000, and this by mortgaging all his property. With this money they returned to Denver, met the millionaires at a hotel as planned, and the betting began. Those present were Love joy and two other millionaires, whose names Stogsdill did not remember, Scott, Maxwell, and Connors; and they were later joined by one Tom Rogers, who had charge of the race horses.

The first afternoon the millionaires bet thousands of dollars, and Stogsdill matched them from funds stealthily supplied by Maxwell from the stake as planned. Late in the afternoon the betting session was adjourned until the following day. Next morning Maxwell told Stogsdill that he had learned that the millionaires were going to offer $10,000 to start the day off and that he had only succeeded in obtaining $7,000. He pleaded with Stogsdill to loan him $3,000 for the day. This Stogsdill did, and so his money went into the pot. Shortly after the betting started this second day, and the $10,000 wagers were taken, one of the millionaires, Love joy, demanded a count of the stake, saying that he was $500 short, and that he must have counted out too much on one of the last bets. There was an uproar. Stogsdill saw that if there was a count then, the trickery of Maxwell and himself would be exposed. He was in a quandary, when someone suggested that Maxwell keep the money intact and that they all go out and have the race run. They agreed that the money could be counted after the match the betting sheet showed the amount that should go to the winner.

Thereupon, the whole group drove out in buggies beyond the city limits of Denver and held the race in a secluded lane. At the start, the horse backed by Maxwell and Stogsdill got off to a lead but just before the end of the race the jockey, Murphy, fell off on his shoulder and was apparently badly injured, bleeding from nose and mouth. The [184] millionaires' horse won, placing Stogsdill and Maxwell in a difficult situation, for they realized that as soon as the stakes were turned over to the winners, it would be found that they had not actually put up nearly as much money as they had pretended.

Stogsdill, suspicious that there had been some foul play in the race, which was supposed to have been spiked in his favor, pulled his Colt revolver and started for Connors and the jockey, Murphy. Connors threw up his hands, yelling, "Oh, my God, don't doubt me, don't doubt me" and soon persuaded Stogsdill to put his gun away, saying quietly to Stogsdill that Maxwell, his cousin and stakeholder, wasn't going to pay the millionaires but that he was going to skip town with the money and go to Cabool to hide. Stogsdill looked around and, sure enough, Maxwell had disappeared. Connors then told Stogsdill to leave town as quickly and rapidly as possible. Just then the millionaires came up and Love joy, seeing Stogsdill's gun, drew his revolver and covered him. Passions rose rapidly. Hot words filled the air. Two determined men faced each other with pistols cocked. It was only through the intervention of the others that a real duel was averted and the antagonists were separated. The injured jockey seemed to recover and they all started toward town. It was later found that in appearance only was the jockey injured. He had carried a little sack of red liquid in his mouth which he burst when he faked being thrown from his horse. Stogsdill and Scott went to the station at once and took the first train home, there to await the arrival of Maxwell with the money Stogsdill's own $3,000 and his share of the money gotten from the millionaires.

A week passed and no word came from Scott, Connors, or Maxwell. .Stogsdill knew that Scott was on the Blake farm near Sargent, Missouri, and wrote to him there. He got no reply until April 16, 1908, when he received a message suggesting that he could get back his money and more besides if he would help Scott in finding new victims for the swindle. While Stogsdill evinced some interest in this proposal, nothing came of it and he never got his money back.

Just about this time the authorities received rumors and [185] complaints that organized groups were swindling persons out of large sums of money at Council Bluffs, Denver, New Orleans, Seattle, and other cities. The United States mails were being used in the scheme, and the Post Office Department became interested. J. S. Swenson, one of the department's ablest and most astute investigators, was assigned to the case, and the facts which he uncovered astounded the nation.

In numerous cities, notably Council Bluffs and Denver, it was found that several sporting gentlemen banded themselves together in what was known as a "Millionaires' Club" for the purpose of operating fake horse races, wrestling matches, foot races, and boxing matches. The plan was to have one of their agents, a "steerer," induce someone with ready money, a so-called "mike," or "sucker," who was looking for something for nothing by extracting large winnings on a race or contest, to join with the club's secretary in betting against the club, the "mike" believing that the race or match was to be "thrown" in his favor. After the stakes were put up, with the club's secretary as stakeholder, the event was instead thrown to the club and the "mike" got a dose of his own medicine, just as did Henry Stogsdill. The stage scenery was arranged according to the standing and background of the prospective victim. John C. Mabray was found to be the master mind in the scheme. There was found in Mabray's trunk, which was seized at the time of his arrest in Little Rock, Arkansas, a documentary record of the operations of the gang, showing that millions had been collected by them and that nearly two hundred persons had assisted in one way or another in carrying out the swindle. A long list of victims and the detailed history of each transaction were found. In fourteen cities where the scheme was worked, post-office lock boxes had been rented.

Through this Mabray record about eighty participating agents were located as well as many of the victims. The results of the investigation were laid before a Federal Grand Jury in Iowa, which returned an indictment, on September 23, 1909, against the leader of the organization, John C. Mabray, and approximately eighty codefendants, for [186] conspiracy to use the mails to defraud under Section 5480 of the Revised Statutes of the United States.

Seventeen of those under indictment were called for trial before Judge Smith McPherson in the United States District Court, Southern District of Iowa, Western Division, at Council Bluffs, in the March Term, 1910. The prosecution was in charge of Col. M. L. Temple, assisted by George Stewart and Sylvester R. Rush. The seventeen defendants were represented by nine attorneys. George H. Mayne of Council Bluffs, Iowa, was the attorney for Willard Powell, one of those indicted. For ten days, various swindled victims, from all walks of life and every section of the country, told the court and the jury their tale of woe, each story having the same ending. The scheme had been most cleverly worked out, inducing persons to surrender their money, yet leaving them in such a compromising situation that they were not anxious to report the affair to the authorities. Henry Stogsdill, among the witnesses, told of his experience in great detail. The Government had induced William Scott, the fellow who had "steered" Stogsdill into the swindle, to turn state's evidence and tell the whole story, thereby corroborating Stogsdill's testimony, and also the stories of several other victims he had brought in. None of the persons guilty in the Stogsdill affair, however, was among the seventeen actually on trial, and the defense was prepared to ignore this particular testimony.

No evidence had been produced connecting Willard Powell with any conspiracy. The testimony of Joseph Walker of Denver, and John Sizer of King William County, Virginia, showed that Powell knew and associated with some of those clearly involved in the scheme, but there was no evidence connecting him with the criminal conspiracy now charged.

The well-founded expectation on the part of Mr. Mayne, Powell's attorney, that Judge McPherson would direct a verdict of acquittal for Powell, was shattered on the seventh day of the trial, just before the closing of the prosecution's case, by the recalling of Henry Stogsdill. He pointed out Powell in the court room as being the "Tom Rogers" who was present in Denver during his experiences there. [187] Stogsdill could not give the date of the race any more exactly than that it occurred sometime between March 20 and April 10, 1908, or about the first of April. He did not remember the name of the hotel at which he had registered, but with great positiveness he identified Powell. When Mr. Mayne, on cross-examination, tried to shake Stogsdill's identification of Powell, he testified, "He is the identical man that was there. He is the man." Stogsdill had been attending the trial, he said, and had seen and recognized Powell among the defendants.

This recalling of Stogsdill at the last minute placed the defense at a great disadvantage, since Stogsdill could not fix very definitely the date when he was fleeced, and the only other witness who had testified about this swindle, "Steerer" Scott, had already been dismissed by the court and had left Council Bluffs. The exact date of the transaction was the vital point as to Powell, for his defense was an alibi to the effect that he was in Havana, Cuba, in March,

1908, and that he returned to Tampa, Florida, toward the end of that month, and did not arrive in Denver until after the middle of April. Edward Rice and G. A. Millsap, race-track men, testified that they were in Cuba with Powell and returned to Florida with him about the first of April. J. E. Woods, a horse trainer, said that he was in Denver when Powell arrived with his horses by train about the middle of April.

None of the defendants except Powell produced any witnesses. The case of fifteen of the defendants went to the jury. It returned a verdict of guilty for fourteen of them, disagreeing on one man. In finding Powell guilty, the jury elected to believe Stogsdill's positive identification rather than the testimony of the alibi witnesses.

On March 21, 1910, Judge McPherson sentenced Powell, with the others, to the maximum penalty under the statute, two years in the penitentiary at Leavenworth and a fine of $10,000.

• • • •

THE Stogsdill identification had come so late in the trial of the case, and the association of Powell with the Stogsdill [188] swindle was such a surprise, that the defense did not have an opportunity to obtain further evidence to substantiate the alibi in time to have it introduced before the end of the trial. Soon after the conviction, the hotels of Denver were canvassed by defense counsel, and it was found that Stogsdill, Scott, and Connors had stopped at the Brown Palace Hotel on March 19, 1908. Calculating from this date, according to Stogsdill's own testimony, the race must have occurred on March 28, 1908. The new evidence positively established this date. Certified copies of the passenger lists of the SS. Mascotte showed that Powell, Rice, and Millsap had gone from Tampa to Havana on March 10, 1908, and had returned to, Tampa on that boat on March 26, 1908. Further, a number of postal cards from Powell to his mother, mailed in Havana from March 12 to March 26, were produced. Affidavits of reputable citizens confirmed the fact that Powell returned from Havana to Tampa the latter part of March and stayed in Tampa until April 8 or 10, when he left for Denver with his horses. He arrived in Denver, April 19 or 20.

This evidence clearly established the truth of Powell's alibi, and the error of Stogsdill's identification. All of the new evidence was submitted to Judge McPherson, who, according to the Attorney-General's published report, became satisfied that it was a case of mistaken identity and recommended a pardon. The Attorney-General concurred in this recommendation and on July 12, 1910, President Taft granted Powell a full pardon.

• • • •

THERE is nothing extraordinary about this case of mistaken identity, except the brazenness and cleverness of the scheme for parting victims from their money and the evidence of the number of people whom cupidity can lead into a swindler's trap. Stogsdill was doubtless honest in his identification of Powell and was probably persuaded to his conclusion by his disappointment in not finding any of his "millionaires" or their unreliable "secretary" among the defendants. Powell evidently looked like Rogers. Fortunately [189] for Powell, he had sufficiently ample funds and able counsel to conduct a thorough investigation and obtain documentary records to establish by dates the fact that he could not have been in Denver at the time of the Stogsdill affair. Not all victims of erroneous identification are so fortunate. By speedy work of all those concerned in righting the wrong, Powell remained in the penitentiary less than four months, though his total detention was much longer. Powell was first caught in the mesh because of his associations, but his ultimate conviction was more his misfortune than his fault. Nobody really can be blamed for it; certainly not the prosecution. Stogsdill's mistake turned the wheels of justice against Powell.

• • • •

Acknowledgment: George H. Mayne, attorney at law, Council Bluffs, Iowa. [190]

"The Weasel"

James W. Preston

THE man wore a mask covering the lower part of his face. He walked quietly into the room where Mrs. Dick R. Parsons was playing the piano. She was alone in her home at 906 West Fiftieth Street, Los Angeles.

"Stick 'em up, I want your diamonds," said a voice, and she turned in fright to face the robber. She raised her arms and screamed. Speaking abusively, the robber ordered her to keep quiet. He took the rings she was wearing and demanded that she turn over any others she had in the house.

In the confusion she was unable to remember instantly where she had left the rest of her jewelry and, accompanied by the robber, she looked in several places around the house but found nothing.

The robber became angry at the delay and threatened to kill her if she did not stop stalling. They went into the den to search. The shade on one of the windows was raised. It was dark outside and anyone passing the house could look in and see what was going on in the den.

This thought apparently occurred to the robber and seemed to infuriate him. His abuse became more violent and the menace of his revolver more dangerous. Mrs. Parsons, fearing that he would carry out his threat, made a dash for the door. The robber fired and she fell with a bullet in her back, as the robber fled.

While still in bed in a hospital, Mrs. Parsons was interviewed by the police. She described her assailant as a man about five feet six inches tall, weighing 130 pounds. She said he wore a soft hat, a mask, and had particularly piercing blue eyes the eyes seem to have impressed her deeply and she said they would narrow to "slits" when he looked at her.

The police searched for clues at Mrs. Parsons' home. They discovered that the robber had entered through a window on the first floor, and on the dust of the screen fingerprints were found.

The robbery and shooting occurred on the night of [191] October 18, 1924. A few days later one James W. Preston was arrested by the Los Angeles police for wearing a naval uniform illegally. His fingerprints were compared with those found on the screen. They were not the same. The Los Angeles newspapers, however, carried stories saying that Preston had been identified as Mrs. Parsons' assailant through the fingerprints. The source of this misinformation could not be determined.

Mrs. Parsons read these accounts, and when Preston was brought to her bedside she identified him as the man who had shot her, and saw in him the eyes of the robber which had narrowed so peculiarly when he looked at her.

She also assured the police that Preston's voice, which was admittedly a peculiar one, was the same as the voice that had ordered her to "stick 'em up."

On January 30, 1925, an information was filed against Preston charging him with burglary, robbery, and assault with intent to murder. On March 11 he went to trial. The prosecutor appears to have been extremely doubtful of the strength of his case, for on the first day he asked counsel for the defendant George A. Benedict, Deputy Public Defender if his client would plead guilty to one of the charges. Mr. Benedict refused and the case was continued until the next day. Again the prosecutor repeated the question, received the same answer, and Judge Carlos S. Hardy ordered another continuance until the next day. On the third morning the prosecutor went so far as to say he would dismiss all three counts against Preston if Preston would plead guilty to simple assault.

Mr. Benedict consulted his client on this offer. He told Preston that simple assault carried a maximum sentence of six months, whereas should he go to trial on the three felonies with which he stood charged, the minimum would be eleven years and the maximum, life.

"I didn't do it, and I will not plead guilty to anything," Preston told Benedict immediately. The case went to trial on the felonies.

The only witness offering direct evidence against Preston was Mrs. Parsons. She said on the stand what she had said [192] at the hospital concerning his general appearance, his eyes, and his voice.

Preston took the stand in his own defense and denied every allegation in the information. He said that he had been at Long Beach, twenty-two miles away, at the time the crime was committed; and the defense produced a young woman who testified that she had been with Preston at the beach during this time. Due to her embarrassment, apparently, she was somewhat hesitant in her replies and seems to have raised some doubt in the mind of Judge Hardy as to her honesty; he personally cross-examined her at length.

The prosecution introduced Preston's previous record, and this, perhaps, more than anything else prejudiced the jury against him. He had been convicted of vagrancy, deserted from the army, been dishonorably discharged from the navy, and was finally arrested for wearing the naval uniform illegally. He explained this latter offense by saying that he had been discharged from the navy only a short time before his arrest, that all his clothes had been stolen by a sailor, and having no work or money he had to wear the uniform until he could get civilian clothes.

And, finally, the prosecution showed that he had been in jail during the time that he told the court he had been elsewhere, and this appears to have discredited all his previous testimony.

Not once was the subject of fingerprints introduced, and nothing was presented by the prosecution to show that the fingerprints found at the

Parsons home were not Preston's.

It does appear, however, that someone informed Judge Hardy of the fingerprints confidentially during the trial, but the information conveyed was construed to mean that the prints found on the screen were similar to Preston's.

Mr. Benedict knew nothing of the fingerprints, nor that information concerning the dissimilarity was in the state's files. Nor did he know of what Judge Hardy had been told. The jury likewise was in complete ignorance of this important factor in the case.

On March 14 (Saturday) Preston was found guilty of burglary and robbery as charged. The third count assault [193] with intent to murder the jury ignored and found against Preston on the lesser charge of assault with a deadly weapon.

On Monday, Preston was brought before Judge Hardy for sentence, and there occurred a most extraordinary proceeding.

Judge Hardy submitted Preston to a searching cross-examination, going into many details of his life and conduct and expressing opinions that indicated a bitter prejudice against the defendant.

The following is a fair example of the Judge's sentiments and of this peculiar extra judicial inquisition preceding sentence.

The Court had been urging Preston to admit that he was Mrs. Parsons' assailant.

THE COURT: Despite the fact that your fingerprints were there, and despite the fact that fingerprints are the one infallible identification, still you insist you were not there?

PRESTON: Yes, sir.

THE COURT: Well, the jury did not have that evidence, which the court had before it at the time. I suppose the jurors will probably be glad to know the court had the evidence that you were identified by the fingerprint system. But I think that the identification of you was ample and complete. There are two elements about you that would make it impossible for any person to be mistaken. One is your eyes, as the witness said, or victim; the other is your voice. Any one listening to you testifying on the stand there would be able to identify you in the middle of Africa or in the darkest night. You have a voice that not one in ten thousand has, possibly, or one in one hundred thousand. You are a young fellow yet. You may be able to train out your voice so that you can get rid of certain peculiarities that identify you and always will identify you, in my judgment; but you will never be able to train out your eyes. You committed one of the most serious crimes that can be committed, showing not only an abandoned disposition, to begin with, but a vile and wicked heart, when you shot the poor victim in the back. Well, young fellows like you are doing things of that kind around here, holding people up and shooting them, and expecting to get away. They don't get away. Any legal cause to show why judgment of the court should not be pronounced?

Preston's counsel offered no objection, but it seems that the judge was not quite ready to pronounce sentence. An afterthought occurred to him, and he questioned Preston [194] further as to his education and whether he had ever learned a trade and then offered him the following advice:

> THE COURT: Better keep your hands out of your pockets. You have made the threat that you will never be taken to San Quentin, so the officers will be prepared, and you need not try to start any funny work. You are going now to be sentenced, and you better take your medicine and try to learn your lesson. You are young, and despite the fact that you are going up there for long sentences, just the same you need not abandon all hope. You can look forward to regenerate yourself in your mind and your soul, and then try to come out and make restitution to society by right living. . . .

The sentences ran from eleven years to life and were to be served consecutively. Preston entered San Quentin, March 21, 1925.

• • • •

SERGEANT H. L. BARLOW, fingerprint expert of the Los Angeles Police Department, doubted Mrs. Parsons' identification of Preston from the time that he learned the fingerprints on the screen were not Preston's. As the months following Preston's conviction passed, he carefully compared the fingerprints of all persons arrested with those taken from the Parsons' screen.

In May, 1926, Earl M. Carroll, known as "The Weasel," was arrested on suspicion in connection with several burglaries in Los Angeles. Carroll's fingerprints matched exactly those on the screen. Sergeant Barlow at last had his man.

While being questioned by the police, Carroll expressed the utmost contempt for fingerprint identification and said: "Listen! If I told what I knew about fingerprints an innocent man would be released from San Quentin tomorrow."

Carroll was then confronted with the findings of Sergeant Barlow as to the identity of the fingerprints and was urged to admit his guilt, if guilty he was, so that Preston might be freed.

He was silent a moment and then exclaimed: "I will neither admit nor deny I was on the Parsons job. It's up to you guys to convict me if you can prove I was there. That's what you're paid for." [195]

The detectives proceeded to earn their salaries and in so doing brought about the conviction of Carroll for the Parsons crime.

Preston was granted a full pardon by Governor Richardson, September 2, 1926, after serving eighteen months for another man's offense. A group of public-spirited citizens attempted to obtain indemnification for Preston under the California law, but failed.

The last heard of Preston was on the occasion of his appearance in Oakland Police Court on a charge of vagrancy. His wife accompanied him to court.

Said Preston: "I don't like to say the prison record damned me. What it did was to throw me out of step. I don't seem to have much confidence any more."

Said Judge Edward J. Tyrell: "Society owes you a debt. I don't see why you should be prosecuted. I'll release you to the custody of your wife and wish you good luck."

• • • •

IT is hard to excuse the prosecuting officials for withholding from the jury the vital fact that the fingerprints of Preston did not fit those found on the screen. It is unfortunate that the defense knew nothing about the fingerprints. Judge Hardy, who later acquired unfavorable notoriety in connection with the case of Aimee McPherson, apparently became completely convinced of Preston's guilt by the erroneous information, privately conveyed, that the fingerprints were Preston's. Who it was who gave this information, and for what purpose for it was not placed before the jury it is difficult to say. Judge Hardy did not disclose the name of his informant, though we may be justified in inferring that it was someone connected with the prosecution. The same source may have been responsible for the newspaper stories that the fingerprints were identical. At all events, it cannot be doubted that the newspaper stories exerted a powerful influence upon Mrs. Parsons to identify Preston as her assailant, though she professed to establish the identity by voice and eyes. What doubtless weighed heavily against Preston was his previous record of delinquencies, though he had [196] never committed a major offense. Had the fingerprints been kept out of the case altogether instead of being so maliciously used it is probable that the Judge would have been more impressed with Preston's striking refusal to plead guilty even to simple assault, which would have given him merely a six months' sentence. Whether knowledge of this fact got to the jury is not known. Mr. Benedict is one of the ablest public defenders and doubtless did the best he could. But he could not overcome the prejudicial factors against Preston, and especially the positive identification of the victim, whom a jury is always prone to believe. But even if the fingerprints did not insure Preston's acquittal, as they should have done, they did at least ultimately effect his pardon and vindication, for Carroll's guilt was irrevocably determined by them. Just why Preston did not get the compensation to which California law entitled him is not known, for he would seem to come fully within the terms of the statute. [197]

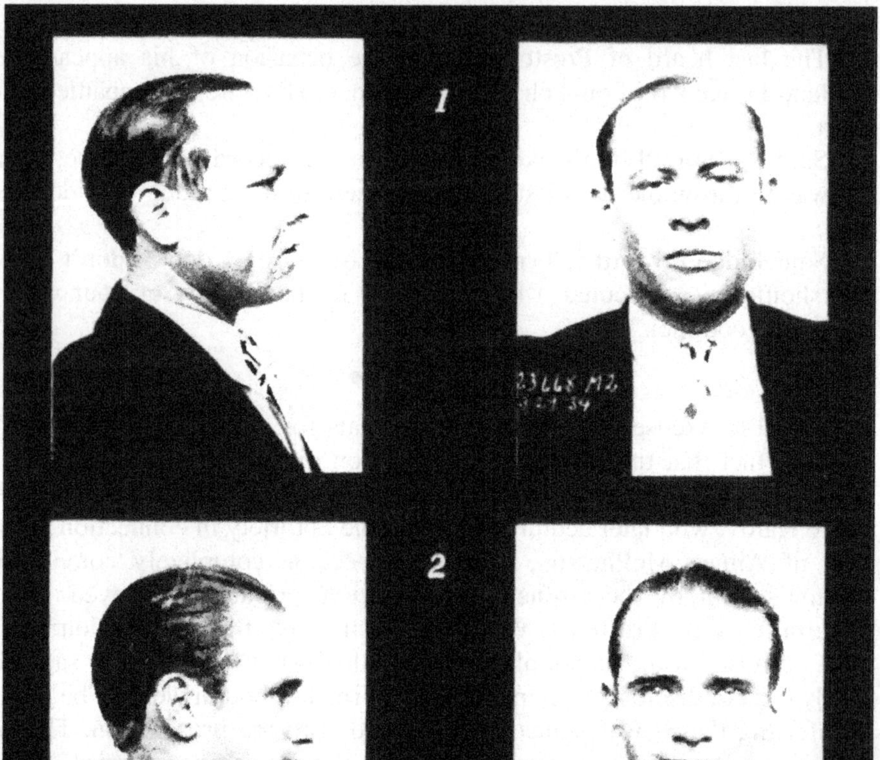

1. James W. Preston, who spent a year and a half at San Quentin for a crime he did not commit.
2. Earl Carroll, alias The Weasel, the real culprit who was finally brought to justice.
3. The finger print of Earl Carroll alias The Weasel.
4. The finger print found on the window screen in the Parson's apartment.
5. The finger print of James Preston.

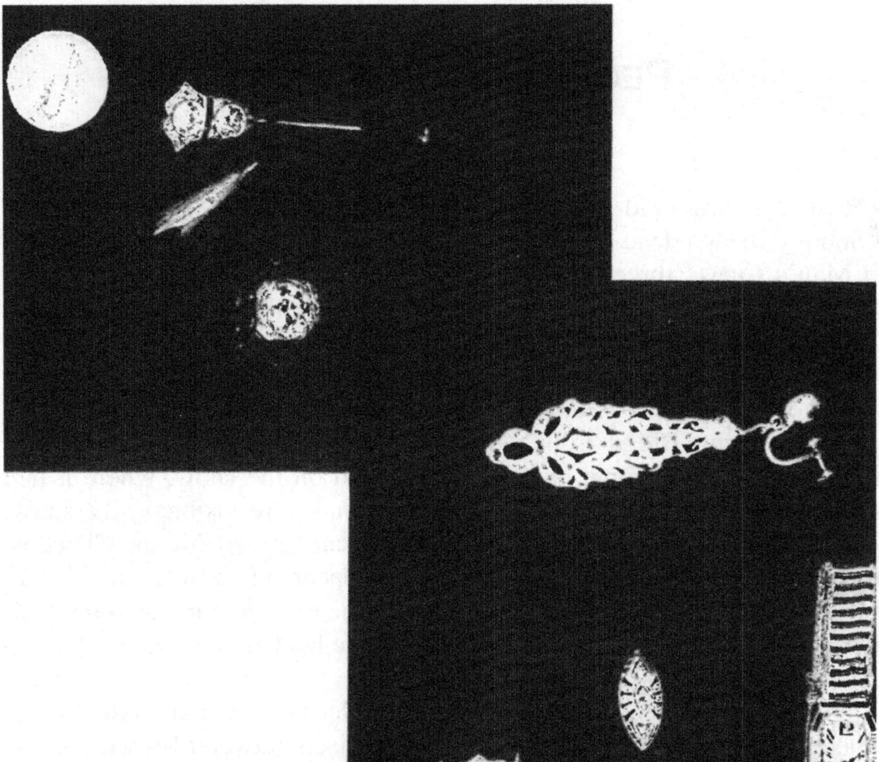

Some of Carroll's loot.

People vs. John Doe

Lloyd Prevost

ON the freezing cold morning of December 24, 1919, farmers found J. Stanley Brown dead in his Dodge sedan on the Drefahl road, just above Dead Man's Curve, three miles west of Mount Clemens, Macomb County, Michigan. The dead man's left hand was grasping the steering wheel, his right hand was hanging helpless, and his hat had fallen from his head. Brown had been shot four times in the back of the head by someone who was within close range. The coroner found that Brown had died at about eleven o'clock the previous night. Blood from the bullet wounds was found on the floor boards of the car, and some had flowed through on the snow, where it had congealed. Tracks leading away from the machine were visible in the snow, indicating that a man had run away from the car toward Mount Clemens. Measurements of the footmarks were taken; it appeared that the murderer had worn rubbers. The lights were still burning on the car when it was found. On Brown's body were found his diamond ring, three bankers' checks for $20.00 each, and $2.00 or $3.00 in currency.

Stanley Brown was twenty-six years old. He had married Ruth Prevost and there were two children. Difficulties had arisen between Brown and his wife which had led to their separation. Brown was suing for a divorce, naming a co-respondent and questioning the paternity of the youngest child. Brown's father had left him about $100,000 in trust, which provided an income of about $250 a month. Several months before Brown's murder, he had received a portion of the principal of the trust fund.

After Brown separated from his wife, he lived with a friend of some years' standing, Lloyd Prevost, first at Brown's own house, then later at the Edison Hotel in Mount Clemens. Lloyd was a first cousin of Stanley's wife and had been raised at Mount Clemens. Lloyd and Stanley were close companions, although Lloyd worked as a mechanic and truck driver for Adams Express, whereas Stanley was not employed, sleeping a great deal in the daytime and spending [198] much time out at night. Frequently, he did not return to his lodgings during the night. In view of their close association, it was not unnatural that, on the morning of December 24, when Brown's body was found, the officers should get into immediate touch with Lloyd Prevost and obtain as much information from him as possible.

Prevost told them that he and Brown had left the Edison Hotel at about nine o'clock or shortly after, driven to Cass Avenue, and stopped in front of Carter's real-estate office, where he had gotten out of the car (about 9:15 or 9:30) and visited for a time with Mr. Graham. Brown drove away and

Prevost said that that was the last time he had seen him. Prevost also said that soon after, he returned to the hotel and went to bed, that he had never owned a gun, and that he had not had one for months. The proprietress of the Edison Hotel and her nephew corroborated Prevost's story that he had not left the hotel after about 9:30, when he retired.

Then the investigators started out to learn everything else they could about Brown's activities on the fatal evening. Prevost had told the chief of police that when he left him Brown was going to visit the Marins. The Marins reported that Brown had called there about 9:15 and had eaten a meal prepared for him by Mrs. Marin, who was also a cousin of Lloyd Prevost. While eating, Brown was said to have told Mrs. Marin that he had a date with Lloyd and that he was going out into the country to get some liquor. The Sunday night previous, Stanley Brown had also visited the Marins and mentioned liquor stored out in the country. Brown left the Marins after ten o'clock, headed for down town.

While the thread of the story of how Brown spent the last hours of his life was being worked out, every conceivable circumstance having a possible connection with the murder was investigated. It appeared that none of Brown's money or securities had been disturbed. The footprints were photographed. Searches were made for guns in connection with each suspect, and all persons knowing anything about the case were carefully interrogated. The Prosecuting Attorney for Macomb County, Lynn M. Johnston, received the [199] personal assistance of the Attorney-General of the state, Alexander Groesbeck, later to become governor, and of Bert V. Nunneley, as special counsel.

It appeared that Stanley Brown had broken off relations with his wife because of her alleged association with other men. Brown and two of these men, taxicab drivers, had had public fights over the matter and they had sworn to get even with him. One of these men, Benjamin Schonschack, was named as corespondent in Brown's divorce suit. Here was an apparent motive; but both men furnished proof that satisfied the authorities that they knew nothing about the murder.

The investigators were told by the nephew of the proprietress of the Edison Hotel that Brown returned to the hotel about 10:30, went up to his room, came down again with Prevost, and that when he last saw them Brown was seated in the car and Prevost was standing outside, both joking about drinking some liquor. Several persons saw the friends at that time.

The proprietress of the hotel finally came forward with the story that Lloyd had not come back into the hotel at 10:30, but that he came in alone, very quietly, at about two o'clock the next morning. Both she and her nephew said that Lloyd had asked them to say that he had come home at 9:30. It thus appeared that Lloyd had misstated vital facts when first questioned. When called upon for further explanations, Prevost replied that he had learned that he was suspected of the murder and that upon advice of counsel, he refused to make any statement on the ground that it might incriminate him. In the preliminary inquiries, as well as throughout the trial, Mrs. Brown also refused to testify on the same ground.

The taxi driver Schonschack reported that he had seen Brown's car headed for Cass Avenue about 10:30, and that it was occupied by Brown and Prevost.

Information was received that on the Sunday night prior to the murder, Lloyd Prevost had a revolver at the Edison Hotel, and that he then requested two young men to procure some bullets for him. There was some indication that [200] this was a .38 revolver, the size which had been used, in murdering Brown. The officials found a .38-caliber revolver in a drawer at the Adams Express office where Lloyd worked, and it was partially identified as the one he had had on the Sunday prior to the murder, although several persons were firm in their statements that the Adams Express pistol had not been out of the cash drawer for many months until turned over to the authorities, and that at that time it was covered with dust.

The chain of circumstantial evidence was drawn about Prevost very closely when Ballistics Expert William H. Proctor of Massachusetts said that the death bullets had passed through the Adams Express gun and that the gun when last fired had been fired four times. The state officers also worked up a theory that the footprints in the snow near the death car might have been made by Prevost's shoes, old army shoes which he admitted wearing on the night in question.

As a motive for Lloyd Prevost to murder his closest friend, it was stated that he had been very friendly with Brown's wife; and one of the latter's friends reported that she had at one time spent a night at the Brown home when Prevost was also there, and that she had seen Mrs. Brown enter Prevost's room at about one o'clock and stay there until four.

These various facts were developed, along with a great mass of other material, in a special statutory proceeding entitled, People of the State of Michigan v. John Doe, a proceeding against no named or particular individual, but one in which all persons were called upon, separately, to tell what they knew about the case. As has been related, upon the advice of counsel, Prevost refused to testify in this proceeding, on the ground that to do so might incriminate him. After innumerable conferences with prospective witnesses, the prosecuting attorney of Macomb County, on March 13, 1920, filed an information in first-degree murder against Lloyd Prevost. On the same day, Prevost was arraigned and "stood mute, and thereupon a plea of not guilty was entered by order of the court." The trial opened on May 14, 1920, [201] before Judge Fred S. Lamb of the Macomb County Circuit Court. The defendant was represented by Lungerhausen, Weeks and Lungerhausen, William T. Hasner, and James McNamara. The trial lasted about four weeks and was fiercely fought by both sides. It seemed evident that Attorney-General Groesbeck was thoroughly convinced of the prisoner's guilt. The passion with which the case was contested at times even affected the judge, who seemed to believe that something was being concealed.

Throughout the trial Mr. Groesbeck persistently wove the web of circumstantial evidence about Prevost. When witnesses were reluctant to answer his questions, he was ever ready with the full transcript of their testimony in the John Doe proceedings to refresh their memories, or to contradict them. These proceedings were in his exclusive possession and were turned over in part to defense counsel only later by order of court. Many of the state's witnesses were closely related to the defendant and it required all of the Attorney General's adroitness to procure the testimony desired.

Lloyd Prevost took the stand in his own defense. He stated that on the night of the murder he had returned to the hotel at about 9:30, and that he went to his room and fell asleep on the bed, dressed. He was awakened after ten o'clock by Brown, who had returned to get a quart of whiskey which was hidden under the mattress. He went downstairs and out to the automobile with Brown. He admitted that he had been in front of the Edison Hotel with Brown at 10:30, as others had testified, and that Brown had insisted that he go along on a "party," but he denied that he had ridden away with Brown. He said that after Brown drove away he went back to his room and to bed, and that he did not leave the hotel again that night. He also said that this was the last time he saw Brown. By this testimony he contradicted the proprietress, who had stated, as her last version of the affair, that Lloyd had returned at 2:00 a.m. the following day, and also the testimony of the taxi driver, Schonschack, who had stated that he had seen Brown and Prevost in the former's car at about 10:30. The credibility of the proprietress was attacked by the production of [202] evidence to show that she had been convicted in Pennsylvania of conducting houses of prostitution, and that of the taxi driver, by showing his enmity to both Brown and Prevost, for he was the corespondent in Brown's divorce action.

As to the pistols, Prevost admitted that he had obtained some bullets for a revolver on the Sunday prior to the murder, but he insisted that it was a .32-caliber gun and belonged to Brown. The gun was produced in court. The prosecution, however, produced witnesses to show that this gun had been in a place inaccessible to Prevost for years past and had not been taken from that place until one week prior to the trial. Defense witnesses testified that the Adams Express revolver had not been away from the office for months until delivered to officials, but this was contested by the testimony of the ballistics expert and somewhat by the testimony concerning a revolver on the Sunday evening preceding the murder. The defense did not have an expert who could forcefully contradict the prosecution's ballistics expert concerning the death bullets and the Adams Express revolver. Defense experts were metallurgists and chemists.

Prevost denied absolutely the alleged incident of Mrs. Brown's coming into his bedroom. He explained that he treated Mrs. Brown as the wife of his best friend and as his own cousin. They were good friends and dined together occasionally, sometimes with and sometimes without Brown. As to the friendship between Stanley and himself, Lloyd testified that they were the closest of friends and that they had been planning to go to Florida to enter business in January, 1920.

The defense endeavored to prove that the footprints of the murderer showed that he had worn rubbers and also that the prints were much larger than Prevost's shoes. Rubbers had in fact been looked for by the prosecution, but not finding any, they fell back on the theory that the footprints were made by army shoes.

Seven of the leading business men of Mount Clemens testified as to Prevost's good reputation for truth and honesty.

From the testimony produced by both sides in court, there [203] seemed to be a strong basis for the impression that the prisoner knew more about the murder of Brown than he had admitted, and for" the impression of the judge that the defense was endeavoring to hide something.

There were other points raised too numerous to narrate. After extended arguments, the case was submitted to the jury on June 4, 1920, and after less than three hours' deliberation, it returned a verdict of guilty of murder in the first degree. On the following day, the defendant was sentenced to life imprisonment, Michigan having abolished the death penalty. A motion for a new trial was denied. The case was appealed to the Supreme Court of Michigan, which, with two dissents, sustained the conviction on July 20, 1922.

Prevost was sent to the state prison at Jackson, where he was assigned to the hospital staff. His proficiency earned him promotion, in five years, to the position of first assistant to the doctor in charge.

• • • •

IN view of Prevost's persistent claims of innocence, and in the light of his exceptional prison record, the case was thoroughly investigated in the fall of 1930 by the Michigan Department of Public Safety, which submitted a full report, including the developments subsequent to the trial. A hearing was held at Jackson by the State Commissioner of Pardons and Paroles, Richard W. Nebel, on December 20, 1930, on Prevost's petition for a pardon on the ground of innocence. The petitioner told the story which he had given at the trial and on all occasions thereafter, and those having to pass upon it were impressed with its truthfulness. It was learned that the proprietress of the Edison Hotel had been convicted of disreputable practices to such an extent that her testimony could be given little weight, especially in view of the fact that her stories had varied. It was admitted that for weeks prior to the trial prosecution witnesses were thoroughly drilled in midnight sessions by the Attorney-General. It was further learned that the corespondent taxi driver who had testified to seeing Prevost driving with Brown at 10:30 on the fatal night had been far from sure of it when first [204] questioned, and in this matter he could be little relied upon because of his antagonism to both Brown and Prevost. Upon reviewing the pistol and the footprint testimony, it was felt to be very flimsy. The Prosecuting Attorney, Lynn Johnston, is reported by Commissioner Nebel to have stated that he "did not believe Prevost was guilty of the crime," and that the conviction was obtained largely through the overawing influence of Mr. Groesbeck with the jury. In addition, convincing information seems to have been presented to the authorities indicating rather pointedly who the persons were who had actually perpetrated the crime. In view of all these facts and circumstances, it was concluded that Prevost was innocent and a pardon on his behalf was recommended. The Governor of Michigan, Fred W. Green, granted the pardon on December 29, 1930.

• • • •

THIS is a case of circumstantial evidence. It would appear from the report of Commissioner Nebel, after an exhaustive investigation by the Department of Public Safety, that there was little to connect Prevost with the murder and that the evidence on which his conviction was obtained was to a considerable extent perjured. The report indicates that the prosecution's witnesses were drilled in their testimony and that the Attorney-General decided to prosecute Prevost only after Prevost declined to state, on the ground of ignorance, who actually committed the crime. The testimony of the proprietress of the hotel as to Prevost's coming back about 2:00 a.m. of the taxi man that Prevost was seen in the car with Brown after 10:30, of the identification of the revolver as the Adams Express revolver, of the allegation that the footprints were made by a shoe and not by rubbers, together with the apparently overwhelming influence of the Attorney General, were enough to convince the jury. The report of the Commissioner indicates that the testimony of the hotel proprietress and of the taxi man was perjured; that the ballistics expert was mistaken, for the Adams Express revolver could not have been the fatal weapon; and that five jurymen in affidavits maintained that they voted for [205] conviction in the belief that the guilty man wore no rubbers, and that had they realized that he did wear rubbers, they would not have so voted. The report shows that the real motive for the murder was to put Brown out of the way before he had divorced his wife, who by the divorce would have been left penniless. Prevost's refusal to talk before trial, whether he knew anything about the killing and whether justified or not, certainly did not help him; in fact, it seems to have aroused the Attorney-General against him. On the whole, the case may be deemed to show that the supposed privilege against self-incrimination is of but little if any help to an innocent man.

• • • •

Acknowledgments: Hon. Ray O. Brundage, Commissioner of Pardons and Paroles, Lansing, Mich.; Mrs. Mary E. Frankhauser, State Librarian, Lansing, Mich.; Professor Hobart R. Coffey, Librarian, University of Michigan Law School, Ann Arbor, Mich.; Professor Edwin D. Dickinson, University of Michigan Law School, Ann Arbor, Mich. [206]

MISSISSIPPI MELODRAMA

Will Purvis

IN the latter part of the last century, following the disruption of the Ku Klux Klan, a strong, closely knit organization called the Whitecaps was formed in the Far South to put down criminality and petty thievery among the negroes. Its members, consisting of mature men, hardened lumberjacks, and young blades eager for excitement, swore in blood never to reveal its secrets. The negroes were terrorized by the Whitecap bands riding through the woods completely shrouded in white, often smeared with blood red. Except in unusual cases violence was little used.

Early in 1893, the band in Marion County, Mississippi, directed its action against a negro servant of one of its own members, Will Buckley. They unmercifully flogged him while Buckley, who knew nothing of their intentions, was absent. Buckley, enraged at this uncalled-for violence and the secrecy with which it was carried out, decided to submit the whole affair and to expose the secrets of the Whitecaps to the next meeting of the Grand Jury to convene at Columbia, the county seat. Rumors of Buckley's intentions soon reached the Whitecaps. When the jury met, members of this organization were there to watch the moves of everyone suspected of having designs against the order. As a result of Buckley's evidence, an indictment was voted against three Whitecaps who were known to have been most brutal in the attack.

On his way home, accompanied by his brother Jim, and by the flogged negro, all on horseback, Will Buckley traveled a forest road which was hardly more than a lane beaten through the heavy underbrush by woodsmen. As the three horsemen, Buckley in the lead, came through a ravine, in which the underbrush was unusually dense, to a small stream over which they had to pass, a shot pierced the stillness. Buckley with a moan swayed in his saddle, then fell to the ground, dead. The assassin, who had been concealed in a blind, jumped out into the road, reloaded his gun, and fired at the others, but they instantly spurred their horses and escaped unscathed. [207]

The road on which Buckley was killed led by the home of the Purvis family. It was generally believed that young Purvis, although but a mere lad of nineteen, was a member of the Whitecaps. Two days after the tragedy, bloodhounds were taken to the place of the murder and after much coaxing, picked up a cold scent which led them in the direction of the Purvis home. A neighbor of the Purvis family, who owned land on both sides of their small farm, and who had repeatedly attempted to gain their holdings, was one of the first to throw suspicion on the boy. Purvis was placed under arrest, taken to the county jail, and thrown into a dungeon used only for desperate criminals. He admitted that three months previous he had joined the Whitecaps, but repeatedly professed his innocence of the crime. The Grand Jury quickly returned an indictment against him for murder.

Excitement and indignation among the people ran high. Repeated disturbances had culminated in this foul murder. They were determined to take drastic action to avenge the murder and to do it without delay. Because mob violence was feared, Purvis was shifted from jail to jail.

District Attorney James Neville, well known for his vigorous prosecutions, had Purvis arraigned before Judge S. H. Terrill of the Marion County Circuit Court in August, 1893. The Purvis family were unable to employ counsel, so the court appointed David M. Watkins, a prominent attorney and a former senator of the state, to defend the prisoner.

Jim Buckley, the state's key witness, testified that he and the negro had witnessed the killing of his brother Will. When asked if he could name the man who killed his brother, he turned toward Purvis, and pointing his finger at him, said, "Will Purvis, there, killed the man." He related that he had been with his brother, Will, at the time he was murdered, that he had dismounted and had taken a pistol from the dying man's pocket and had leveled it at Purvis, who disappeared into the brush. The witness was positive in his identification. This, coupled with Purvis' admission that he belonged to the clan, made a strong case. Purvis in his own defense said that at the time the murder was reported to have been committed, he was talking with Lewis Newsom [208] about the picnic which they had planned for the day. Newsom, a Confederate veteran, who enjoyed the high regard of his neighbors, and others substantiated Purvis' alibi, and further testified to his good character. The defendant's witnesses were all apparently discounted as being "interested," for the jury returned a verdict of "guilty as charged." The brilliant argument of defense counsel could not withstand the state's testimony. When asked by the court if he had "any reason to give why the death sentence should not be pronounced against him," Purvis protested his innocence as he had done many times before. He was sentenced on August 5, 1893, to be hanged on February 7, 1894. In October, 1893, the Mississippi Supreme Court upheld the sentence.

At sundown the night before the execution, Purvis was taken to Columbia under heavy guard. The following day hundreds of curiosity seekers came to Columbia on horseback, in wagons, carts, and buggies; in those days executions were still public spectacles and gala events. When the hour came Purvis slowly mounted the scaffold, the minister close by his side. The crowd, breathless, and expecting a final confession, waited for Purvis' last words. Instead, he said simply, "You are taking the life of an innocent man, but there are people here who know who did commit the crime and if they will come forward and confess, I will go free." Then the rope was adjusted around the boy's neck and tested. The deputy sheriff, seeing an ungainly strip of rope dangling from the knot, cut the rope flush with the knot, while the minister droned his prayer: "God save this innocent boy." When everything was ready, the executioner, taking his hatchet, cut the stay rope holding the trap and the body of Purvis dropped with a sharp jerk. The knot, instead of tightening around its victim, untwisted, and Purvis fell to the ground, unhurt.

An indescribable horror shook the spellbound onlookers. Purvis staggered to his feet, the death mask falling from his head, and, turning to the sheriff, said simply, "Let's have it over with." With his hands and feet still bound, Purvis hopped up the first step of the scaffold before the awed silence was broken. A wave of emotion seized the crowd. [209]

Some ascribed to the incident a significance far beyond its natural import that divine intervention had saved Purvis. The officials again prepared to carry out the execution. One of them, reaching for the rope, found that it was just beyond his reach. From the platform, he called down to Dr. Ford, "Toss that rope up here, will you, Doctor ?" Ford picked up the rope and was about to toss it up, when he instinctively drew back. Ford had been bitterly opposed to the Whitecaps and had often so expressed himself in public, but all along he had refused to believe that Purvis was guilty of the crime charged. Letting the rope fall from his fingers, he said: "I won't do any such a d—n thing. This boy's been hung once too many times, already."

This speech seemed to crystallize the feeling of many. They cried, "Don't let him hang." Another group, hoarse with determination, shouted, "Hang him— he's guilty." The crowd was fairly evenly divided. During the confusion, Rev. J. Sibley sprang up the steps of the scaffold. Immediately all eyes centered upon him. Acting upon an inspiration he cried, "All who want to see this boy hanged a second time, hold up their hands." There was complete silence. Not a person moved. Then Sibley shouted, "All who are opposed to hanging Will Purvis a second time, hold up your hands." Almost all hands were raised. The crowd that had come to see the life wrenched out of a man in full health called for his release. The officers, charged with fulfilling their duty, were perplexed. It was their duty to proceed. Yet how could they go ahead with the execution of Purvis against the will of five thousand excited people? Dr. Ford advised the sheriff to ask for the advice of an attorney. One was called from the crowd. Attorney Foxworth could find no solution except to carry out the letter of the sentence, which stated that Purvis must be "hanged by the neck, until dead."

Again the preparations were made. Special care was taken that the rope would not slip again. When Dr. Ford heard the decision of the attorney, he replied: "I do not agree with you. If I were to call for the help of three hundred men to prevent the hanging, what would you do?" The sheriff realized that in such event he would be helpless. Ford added, [210] "And I am ready to do it, too." Purvis sat by wretchedly, hoping that the whole thing would soon be over. The sheriff, realizing that it would be futile to try to proceed with the execution, loosened the bonds of the prisoner and reconducted him to the jail.

The question whether or not Purvis could be hanged was carried to the Supreme Court of the state. The court decided that the sentence would have to be executed that officials had been careless in securing the knot was no reason that the law should be thwarted; and that, Purvis having been tried and found guilty, to free him would be to establish a dangerous precedent. To commute the sentence to life imprisonment was out of the question because of the deliberate nature of the crime and the direct testimony of an eyewitness. The court ordered that the sentence be carried out on July 31, 1895.

In the town to which Purvis had been removed, indignation over the ruling of the court ran high. On the eve of the day of execution, under cover of night, Purvis was taken from the jail by a group of friends and, with one companion, hidden on a secluded Mississippi farm, where his friends intended to keep him until they could be assured that at least his life would be spared.

Although the official search for Purvis slackened, his case still remained in the public eye, for in the following gubernatorial election, one of the issues was whether or not Purvis, if caught, should be hanged. The candidate in favor of modifying the sentence, A. J. McLaurin, won the election. When he assumed office, Purvis voluntarily surrendered himself, and McLaurin, in accordance with his promise to the people, commuted the sentence to life imprisonment on March 12, 1896.

• • • •

TWO years later the state's star witness, Jim Buckley, who had identified Purvis as the murderer, stated that he might have made a mistake, and that possibly it was not Purvis whom he had seen. This knocked the bottom out of the state's case. Purvis was consequently given a full and unconditional [211] pardon on December 19, 1898. Not long afterward he married a childhood companion, the daughter of a minister. Years passed. Purvis became a prosperous farmer, seven children played around his fireside; yet there was one cloud over his complete happiness he had never been completely vindicated of the murder of Buckley.

In 1917, Joe Beard, an aged member of the community, attended a revival meeting of the Holy Rollers, who among other virtues emphasized the importance of the public confession of sins. At this meeting Joe Beard came forward to join the church and dramatically declared that he had long been suffering under the weight of a terrible sin. He could say no more, but everyone instinctively felt that Beard must have had some connection with the Buckley murder. Shortly thereafter, he became seriously ill and called his minister and several friends to hear the rest of his confession: When in 1893 four Whitecaps met in a solitary part of a forest to discuss Will Buckley's intention of revealing to the Grand Jury the workings of the Whitecap organization, three of them decided that Buckley's death was the only effective means of protecting the other members. The other, a mere youth of nineteen, refused to have anything to do with such a horrible design, and, telling them that he was going to quit whitecapping, left the group and returned home. This was Will Purvis. Not long afterward, a meeting of the local Whitecap chapter decided to punish Will Buckley. Purvis refused to attend and thus incurred the enmity of the clan. In conclave two men, Louis Thornhill and Joe Beard, were chosen by lot to carry out the assassination. They built a brush blind, by which Buckley would pass on his return home, and lay in wait for him. Thornhill fired the shot which killed Buckley. Beard was supposed to have fired also, but because he lost his nerve, the negro and Jim Buckley were allowed to escape.

Beard's confession, which was corroborated by known facts, completely cleared Purvis of any implication in the assassination. The District Attorney was notified of the confession. Beard died before the meeting of the next Grand Jury. By this twist of fate the real murderer could never be [212] convicted, inasmuch as the law of Mississippi provides that a deathbed confession, to have legal effect, must be made before witnesses and be signed. The confession of Beard was never signed. The murderer continued to live alone in a solitary cabin in the woods, but was never again seen in Columbia.

Purvis was thoroughly vindicated, but the fact remained that he had forfeited to the state four valuable years of his life, three of which had been devoted to hard manual labor. In 1920 the Legislature of Mississippi, at the instance of Senator Henry C. Yawn and Representative John A. Yeager, appropriated $5,000 to Purvis as compensation "for services done and performed ... in the State penitentiary under the provision of an erroneous judgment." State Senator Scott Hathran, who had placed the black hood over young Purvis' face at the time of the attempted execution, counted it a privilege to make an eloquent speech in favor of this appropriation. Mr. Yeager wrote Purvis:

> After more than two years of energetic work, I have been able to obtain for you and your family the sum of five thousand dollars, which has a twofold meaning: first, that the State of Mississippi has confessed to a great wrong done you, and now removes all stain and dishonor from your name; second, that the State compensates you in the sum of five thousand dollars for the suffering you have endured. . . .

• • • •

COMMUNITY emotion called for Purvis' conviction and community emotion effected his reprieve. The providential intervention of the executioner, who unintentionally cut too much of the rope, saved Purvis' life and saved Mississippi from a gruesome blunder. The identification by Jim Buckley naturally impressed the jury and the community, for he was present at the scene of the crime, and was practically the only available witness. That his opportunity for observation was the worst possible and that he had an emotional urge to avenge his brother by confirming the guilt of the accused and that there was an original collateral motive which first pointed suspicion against Purvis these facts were left out of account by all concerned. The strange situation caused [213] by the slipping of the rope, the division of the populace, the cooling of the ardor for an execution, the marked rift between the processes of law (which required execution) and public opinion (which demanded reprieve or commutation), the political issue as to Purvis' fate, the armed jail delivery, his voluntary surrender after the election, the repudiation of his identification by Jim Buckley, the Governor's pardon, and then the indemnification by the Legislature, constitute about as much melodrama as one man's life can afford. It took nearly twenty-five years for Mississippi to right this wrong, but the state ultimately did what still could be done to show contrition. Purvis owes his escape from an undeserved death at the hands of the state to sheer good fortune, but his experience may help to bring about necessary reforms in the law.

• • • •

Acknowledgments: Judge J. Q. Langston, Columbia, Miss.; D. M. Watkins, Hattiesburg, Miss.; Mildred Maddox, Washington, D.C.; T. B. Davis, Columbia, Miss.; E. L. Fithian, New Orleans, La. [214]

A MUTILATED BILL

Shannon and Clements

PHIPPS and English were partners in a grocery supply store, wholesale and retail, in the town of Currie, Texas, near the boom oil fields of Mexia. They were men of good reputation. Shannon and Clements, two young men under thirty, ran a small shop about two miles from Currie and were regular customers of the house of Phipps & English.

On Sunday evening, March 15, 1925, at about nine o'clock, English and two of his friends Boone and Kelly in order to while away the time, were playing dominoes at a table near the back of the store, some thirty feet from the entrance. Boone and Kelly could be seen from the entrance, but English was screened by a tall seed box with a crack in it, which permitted him to see something of what was going on in the store.

About nine or nine-thirty, the door of the store opened and a man stepped inside without attracting any attention until he said, "Well, boys, you can stick 'em up." The players were concentrating upon the domino game and did not move at the order. "God damn it, I said stick 'em up !" At this, English became curious, and looking through the crack in the seed box saw a well-built man, wearing a hat, and having a blue handkerchief tied over his face. He was pointing a revolver at the other two players. These men, being unprotected, put their hands up. The robber advanced toward the cash register. English, from behind the seed-box barrier, called out loudly the name of a nearby neighbor, Mr. Meador, when he was ordered to "shut up." A second man with kerchief -covered face and a revolver appeared around the seed box and ordered English's hands up. The first man ordered all three to face the wall. He was obeyed.

As the cash register was being tampered with, English turned and glanced to the right to see what was going on. "Yes, trying to watch, are you? Turn that head back and keep them hands high, or I will come around there and bust your brains out." English got several pistol pokes in the [215] back. The receiver and mouthpiece were torn from the store telephone. This was the sole telephone in Currie. The cash register was rifled, and the domino players were relieved of their change.

"Everything is all right outside, boys!" came the word from a third robber, who put his head in at the door. He was apparently acting as guard; and his face below the eyes was also covered with a handkerchief. The three men withdrew and drove off in a car, taking with them approximately $200.

Phipps, the senior partner, came on the scene about five minutes later, when a small crowd had begun to gather. Although the robbers were masked and had hats on, exposing but little more than their eyes, English informed his partner that he recognized the first of the stick-up men as Clements. Phipps thereupon went out to Clements and Shannon's place. When he arrived, Clements was coming outdoors with a couple of buckets and did not return during the five or ten minutes Phipps was there. Shannon and some other persons were in the shop. Phipps entered into conversation with Shannon, and at Shannon's subsequent trial testified that Shannon appeared excited and nervous, asked how Currie was, what was going on in Currie, and how they were getting along there.

After Phipps got back to Currie, Shannon's name, for the first time, gets into the case. Phipps testified that at about eleven o'clock that night, his partner English told him that the man at the door who had shouted, "Everything is all right outside, boys!" was Shannon. In Phipps's talk with Shannon's attorney, however, just before the trial, Phipps said that English could not^ identify any of the persons who robbed the store except Clements. The trial judge would not permit the attorney to give his testimony; and on this ground, Shannon's conviction, presently to be mentioned, was reversed by the appellate court (284 S.W. 586). English himself claimed that he recognized Shannon at once, though Shannon was masked and hatted, was at the doorsill for only a fleeting moment, and the distance was some thirty feet. He claimed to have recognized him by his build, eyes, [216] and voice. The other players, one of whom had known Shannon for four years, could not recognize the third man as Shannon, though Boone "thought" he recognized the first man as Clements. Kelly could not recognize either one. English, on the stand, could not tell what Shannon had on, except that he had a shirt, collar, and tie.

English had not mentioned Shannon's name to any of the assembled crowd; and he had not mentioned it to his partner Phipps until two hours later, because, he explained on the stand, he did not wish to make it public. At eleven o'clock Sunday night, the telephone having been fixed, he had called up a peace officer of Wortham, a neighboring boom town, to look out for the robbers, who were commonly suspected by members of the crowd to be the Davis brothers, who lived in Wortham. When asked in court why he called up the sheriff of a neighboring town when he knew, as he claimed, that the culprits were right near him, English explained that he wanted all suspects rounded up. His partner Phipps also visited Wortham on Monday morning, spoke to Peace Officer Miles, and did not apparently mention Clements and Shannon. Instead, he asked whether Miles had seen anything of the Davis boys, according to Miles's testimony. When Constable Jones of Currie came to the scene the next morning, English did not say that he thought Clements and Shannon had done the job, English's explanation for the omission being that he did not think Jones, an old, unreliable man, could give them any help.

Neither did he go to the County Attorney on Monday morning, his explanation being that he wanted to be sure before he took any steps.

Monday, about noon, Phipps made his regular rounds among his customers to take orders and collect bills. In the shop of Clements and Shannon, he had a bill of some $10.55 to collect. Shannon paid him in one-dollar bills; and among these bills was one mutilated bill with a cigarette burn, which Phipps claimed to have recognized as one of those in his cash register before the robbery. It had been set aside by him for exchange at the bank. Phipps was now sure that Clements and Shannon were the guilty men, and had them arrested [217] and indicted. The prosecution worked out a theory that the second robber was a man named Halsey, a brother-in-law of Shannon, who occasionally visited them.

Shannon and Clements were tried separately. Shannon claimed that he and Clements had been at their home, in which their shop was located, the entire time from sunset Sunday until Monday afternoon. He explained the mutilated one-dollar bill by saying that when Phipps called he had a twenty-dollar bill, but that he had changed it in the room next to the store with a man named Murry, who gave him twenty one-dollar bills. Murry, Shannon testified, had been in a poker game all night in Wortham before he came to Shannon's place Monday morning. There were four other persons in the room, including Clements, but none of them was apparently called as a witness to verify Shannon's story. Murry was a roving character and could evidently not be located. Phipps, on the other hand, swore that Shannon had not left the store to change a bill, but had paid him from a roll or stack of bills which he drew from a bag under the counter. Shannon had never been indicted, but had once, two months before the Phipps robbery occurred, been arrested for robbery on complaint of a watermelon peddler, been in jail two weeks, and had been then released without trial.

On Shannon's trial, some ten character witnesses were called to testify to Phipps's good character, though the reputation of Phipps was not in issue. Possibly the purpose was to sustain his veracity in the conflict with Shannon's testimony as to the circumstances attending the payment of the $10.55.

Whether Shannon's one arrest had an influence on the jury, it is hard to say. At all events, the jury concluded that Shannon was guilty, and he was sentenced to five years in the penitentiary. The jury evidently believed that the mutilated dollar bill had found its way into Shannon's hands by direct action, and not by the circuitous route Shannon had described. Shannon was released on bond pending the appeal of his case; but after the reversal of his conviction, [218] mentioned before, he was never retried, for reasons which will presently appear.

In the trial of Clements, his identification as one of the robbers was more definite than had been that of Shannon. Clements was also found guilty and received a five-year sentence. His case was also appealed; but on two occasions in 1927 (106 Tex. Cr. Rep. 628 and 106 Tex. Cr. Rep. 631), the appellate court denied his motion for a rehearing. Although defense counsel were certain that Clements had had nothing to do with the robbery, there was nothing further that could be accomplished for him. Protesting his innocence, Clements surrendered himself at the penitentiary.

Within the penitentiary walls, Clements met a man who had been convicted of highway robbery from another county. His name was Blackie Davis. Davis confessed to Clements that he had committed the robbery at the Currie grocery store, and gave his deposition to that effect. The Governor was unconvinced by Davis' admission, and a pardon was denied to Clements. A sixty-day furlough was, however, granted, to enable Clements to locate the accomplices implicated in the crime by the confession of Davis. Leonard A. Wassum was found. He surrendered to the authorities. Haled before the court under criminal indictment for the Phipps & English robbery, he pleaded guilty to the charge and received sentence.

Upon an application indorsed by the district judge, the prosecuting attorney, and all of the jurors who tried Clements, the Governor of Texas granted him a pardon in May, 1929. Clements had served between two and three years for a crime with which he had had no connection.

Clements had suffered humiliation, the loss of his business and reputation, and had incurred great expense. The charge against his partner Shannon was dropped. He shared all of Clements' sufferings, except the years in the penitentiary.

• • • •

IT is not necessary to conclude that Phipps and English were dishonest in giving their testimony. It is quite probable that the deep sense of injury and the eager desire to find [219] the guilty persuaded them to be too easily convinced that the men they accused were indeed guilty. The finding of the mutilated dollar bill sealed their conclusion of Clements' and Shannon's guilt; and what was before then only the faintest suspicion, so faint that English had not even mentioned Shannon's name, became the firmest of convictions. It is not impossible that English rationalized his identification of Shannon from his supposed recognition of Clements. Why suspicion and identification should have turned to Clements is not clear. There may have been some prior grudge. When English mentioned the name Clements, Boone evidently thought he also recognized Clements. Although there was much evidence that Phipps and the crowd thought the Davis boys to be the robbers, pursuit of that trail was dropped after the mutilated dollar bill entered the case. The County Attorney utterly disbelieved Shannon's story of the changed twenty-dollar bill, and impressed the jury. Why witnesses to the changed bill were not called is unclear; possibly they had all moved away. In boom towns in Texas, things are unstable, and permanence of residence is probably an exception. The defense was ably conducted, and the judge was fair. It was the circumstances that were against Clements and Shannon. Phipps and English were altogether too sure of themselves and far too partisan. A gross miscarriage of justice occurred, without inexcusable fault on the part of anybody.

• • • •

Acknowledgments: Mr. T. W. Lovett, Corsicana, Texas; Mr. J. F. Sutton, San Angelo, Texas. [220]

LABOR TROUBLE

Sisson and Sullivan

BRENTWOOD ROAD, Northeast, in Washington, D.C., where James R. Keeton and Judson L. Powers lived, was very dark at midnight, September 20, 1922. The street was lined with shade trees, behind which one might easily hide.

Keeton and Powers were on their way home from work at the Union Station. They were electricians for the Pullman Company. As they approached their rooming house, they saw a man sitting on a lawn across the road. A moment later several men seven or eight sprang out of the shadows and attacked them.

Some months previously Keeton and Powers had applied for membership in the electrical union, but before they were admitted a strike was called and practically all union men walked out. Keeton and Powers, however, continued at their work and provoked the enmity of several militant labor leaders.

In July, shortly after the strike had been called, Powers had been stopped on his way home. After answering several questions asked by the little group of inquisitors, one of them cursed him and struck at him but he ducked and got away.

This man he later recognized from a police photograph as Sullivan, one of those taking part in the September at tack in front of his home. He and Keeton thought another one was a man named Dean, the president of the local electrical workers' brotherhood. A third they recognized as a foreman at the station named Sisson, who though once friendly with Keeton, had later refused to speak to him. The others were unknown to them.

Both were being severely beaten when Powers broke away and ran toward the house. At the door he turned and shouted, "I'm going to get the gun." When he returned with the weapon ready to drive his assailants off with bullets, he found Keeton alone, staggering toward the house moaning and holding his jaw, which was broken in four places and [221] injured in five others. He had been struck repeatedly in the face by one of the men who used half a brick as a weapon. Powers had his friend taken to the hospital and then called the police.

Two days later, as the result of Keeton and Powers' identifications, three men had been arrested Robert W. Sisson, Maurice J. Sullivan, and Earle D. Dean and each offered an alibi.

All three had been in the city the night of the assault. Dean, with the corroboration of members of his family, and a druggist in whose store he claimed to have been late that evening, accounted for his time from 11:00 p.m. until about 1:00 a.m. He denied that he had been near the Union Terminal that night, which contradicted the stories of Powers and Keeton that they had seen him in a lunch room just before they got on a street car to go home, and that he later appeared to be following the street car in an automobile.

He did, however, admit that he had been present the night in July that Powers had been first stopped on his way home. His description of the incident did not agree exactly with Powers' story but it established the fact that there had been trouble at that time.

Sisson's wife said her husband seldom went out at night and that on the night in question he had gone to bed early, that they slept in the same bed together, and that he had gone out but once that night. That was early, she said, when he went to make a telephone call. Sisson told the same story and also said he had never met Sullivan until they had both been arrested.

Sullivan offered the most elaborate alibi. He said he knew nothing of the affair until he read about it in a newspaper the next morning. Several members of his family testified that he went to bed about ten o'clock the night of the assault. His wife said he got up about 11:20 to help her feed their sick child and that she was up nearly all night with the child so that had her husband gone out she would have known it. A physician testified that the child had been sick and it was established that a prescription had been filled for the child next morning. [222]

Sullivan's credibility may have been weakened when it was brought out that he had been previously convicted of assaulting his mother-in-law, though in the present case she testified for him.

Despite their alibis, all three men were found guilty. Sisson and Dean were sentenced to five years each and Sullivan to seven years. A motion for a new trial was overruled, and on an appeal the appellate court on February 5, 1924, affirmed the convictions.

• • • •

THE three men had been at the District of Columbia reformatory at Lorton, Virginia, about a year and a half when Dean informed the authorities that he had a confession to make. He named seven men and said that they and himself were the men who had assaulted Keeton and Powers and that Sisson and Sullivan had had nothing to do with it.

He admitted that he had been in the automobile which Keeton said followed the street car. He said he had followed the two men but a few blocks and then taken a short cut to their home to arrive ahead of them. It also appeared that a man named Smith, one of the assailants, looked like Sisson, which might account for the identification of Sisson.

Sullivan, it was discovered, had been in an auto with one of the assailants about eight o'clock the night of the attack and wanted to admit this at his trial but had been prevented from doing so by the strike committee on the promise that the committee would make a "clean breast" of the affair at the proper time.

All seven men named by Dean pleaded guilty, but got off much more lightly in the matter of sentences than had Sisson and Sullivan. Instead of the five- and seven-year terms given Sisson and Sullivan, respectively, three of the men actually guilty of the crime got three years each, two others were sentenced to two and a half years, and the other two got a year and a half each.

On July 12, 1924, President Coolidge pardoned Sisson and Sullivan, who had spent over a year and a half in the reformatory for a crime of which they were innocent. [223]

• • • •

AGAIN we have a conviction based upon mistaken identification. Keeton saw Dean at the lunch room, and Dean made no effort to escape recognition. Doubtless, Keeton had him firmly enough fixed in mind to recognize him again a quarter of an hour later at the scene of the crime. But his alleged recognition of Sisson and Sullivan was the result of a gross mistake and association with the past. Possibly Smith did resemble Sisson, but Sisson's only possible connection with violence was his refusal to speak to Keeton when they had met some weeks before. There was no other ground for assuming that Sisson would participate in such an assault. Sullivan's identification was even flimsier. Keeton said Powers had pointed Sullivan out two days before—though neither Keeton nor Powers knew his name—as the man with whom Powers had had trouble in July. It is doubtful whether Keeton had ever had a fair look at Sullivan. Powers' view of the supposed Sullivan, at the time of the September assault, lasted but a few seconds, in semidarkness. But the July incident made Powers receptive to associating Sullivan with the September affair. Dean's alibi was deceptive, even if we exclude perjury by the witnesses, possibly because he moved around by motor car and not by foot, as he said. The alibis of Sisson and Sullivan, though apparently air-tight, were disbelieved by the jury, presumably because they were strikers and were thought to harbor grudges against Keeton and Powers, and might, therefore, be presumed to have been present at the assault.

• • • •

Acknowledgment: James A. O'Shea, Washington, D.C. [224]

A Scotch Jury

Oscar Slater

MISS MARION GILCHRIST, a woman eighty-three years old, had made her home for thirty years in Glasgow, Scotland, in the second-floor apartment of the brownstone building at 15 Queen's Terrace. She was in comfortable circumstances and was attended by one servant, Helen Lambie, a girl of twenty-one, who had been with her three years.

Friends seldom called on Miss Gilchrist and relatives, even more rarely. Her only intimate friend, whom she saw frequently, was a Mrs. Ferguson, who had formerly been her servant.

Miss Gilchrist had one interest. She collected jewelry and, at the time of her death, her collection was estimated to be worth about £3,000. This jewelry she kept in her apartment; and looking at the various brooches, pendants, and rings appears to have been one of her intense pleasures. From time to time she had expressed anxiety lest she be robbed and for protection she had placed two patent locks on her front door.

Every evening about seven o'clock Helen Lambie went out to get her mistress an evening paper, with which she returned before doing the rest of her shopping.

On December 21, 1908, the girl went out as usual, a minute or two before seven. At about seven Arthur Adams, who lived with his two sisters in the apartment below Miss Gilchrist's, was startled by "a noise from above, then a very heavy fall and then three sharp knocks."

Adams went up to investigate. Miss Gilchrist's door was closed. He rang three times but got no answer, although he heard a sound inside which he described as the breaking of sticks. He thought that Helen Lambie was engaged in household duties of some kind and so, after listening a minute or two, he returned to his apartment. His sisters, however, were not convinced that all was well for they had heard the sound repeated, and sent him back. He rang again. As he stood listening the servant girl returned from her errands. Adams [225] told her what he had heard. She suggested that the clothesline pulleys in the kitchen had fallen and made the noise the Adams' had heard, despite the fact that the Gilchrist kitchen was not above the Adams' dining-room, in which they had been sitting, and that the old lady had been left in the living room, which was directly above it. It was from this room that the sound had come.

The girl then opened the door, while Adams stood on the threshold. As the girl was going into the kitchen, a well-dressed man appeared and walked quietly out of the apartment past Adams, whose suspicions were not aroused until the man had passed him. Finding the pulleys in the kitchen intact, the girl, at Adams' suggestion, went into the living room to look for her mistress.

There they found the old lady lying upon the floor near the chair in which Lambie had left her. A fur rug was thrown over her head. Nearly every bone in her skull had been crushed by blows. Although still alive when discovered by Lambie and Adams, she died without regaining consciousness.

A number of articles of value in the apartment had not been taken, though they were in plain sight, and nothing was missing except a single crescent diamond brooch worth about £50. The murderer had left no clues.

The only guides the police had were the descriptions supplied by Lambie and Adams of the man who had walked out of the apartment. Adams described him as a well-featured man of the commercial-traveler or clerk type, dressed in dark trousers and light overcoat. He was not sure whether the man wore a mustache, nor could he describe his hat or the color of his overcoat. Lambie's description was confined to the fact that he had worn a round cloth hat, a three-quarter length gray overcoat, and had walked peculiarly.

The police circulars based upon these facts were altered on Christmas Day by reason of details supplied by Mary Barrowman, a girl of fifteen, against whom the man had brushed as he dashed out of the building. She had fixed his age at twenty-eight or thirty years and said that he was clean shaven and had a nose slightly twisted to one side. [226]

There were several discrepancies in these descriptions, such as the color of the overcoat and the shape of the hat.

Late on Christmas afternoon the police came upon a definite clue which led them to Oscar Slater, a German who was shown to have earned his money by the sale of jewels and by gambling operations. He had attempted to sell a pawn ticket on a diamond brooch of about the same size and value as that missing from Miss Gilchrist's home. When the lodgings occupied by Slater and his mistress were raided, it was found that they had left Glasgow the same night for London or Liverpool. Three days later the police discovered that they had sailed for New York on the Lusitania.

Slater was arrested on the dock in New York. His seven trunks were impounded and sealed. Two officers, accompanied by Adams, Helen Lambie, and Mary Barrowman, left Glasgow at once. Adams and Mary Barrowman identified Slater in court at New York as a man exceedingly like the person they had seen on the night of the crime.

The question of extradition was speedily settled by Slater himself, as he volunteered to return for the trial, which began on May 3, 1909. Before that date, however, the prosecution's case had practically collapsed, for it had been established beyond a doubt that the brooch represented by the pawn ticket was not the one missing from the Gilchrist home. It was shown that Slater had owned his brooch for a long time and had been in the habit of pawning it whenever he needed funds. This disclosure was apparently kept from the jury.

The fact that Slater had left Glasgow in what seemed to have been unpremeditated haste was explained by witnesses at the trial who said that the defendant had received two letters on December 21. One, they said, was from a friend in London who informed Slater that Slater's wife had been bothering him for money, and that Slater ought to be on his guard against her, and the other was from a former partner of Slater's, asking him to come to San Francisco.

Upon the return to Glasgow a careful search of the trunks failed to disclose anything of a suspicious nature except a small hammer of such fragile construction as virtually to [227] eliminate it as a weapon capable of inflicting such wounds as were found on Miss Gilchrist's body.

The material elements of the prosecution's case having been explained away, the Crown was forced to rely upon witnesses. There were two sets of these. The first were the three who said that they had seen the murderer Adams, Lambie, and Mary Barrowman. The others were twelve persons who testified that on various dates they had seen a man loitering near Miss Gilchrist's house in a suspicious manner. All of these, with varying degrees of certainty, were willing to identify the defendant as the loiterer.

The Crown produced no evidence connecting the loiterer with the crime. The twelve witnesses did not agree as to his appearance, either as to height, weight, age, features, or dress. The total effect of their evidence did not furnish a fair picture of the man, though the prosecution sought desperately to make the descriptions given approximate the general appearance of Slater.

Testimony showed Slater's movements on the day of the crime. He had given his servant notice. His actions about the time of the murder were not of an unusual nature. He had dispatched communications to a London bank with which he had dealt and to a jeweler who was repairing his watch. Two witnesses testified to having seen him in a billiard-room between 6:20 and 6:40, when he left for his home, which was about a mile from the billiard-room and a quarter of a mile from Miss Gilchrist's house. His servant testified that he had dined at his customary time about seven. The steward of a gambling club testified that he had seen Slater about 9:45 and that he had shown no nervousness or anxiety.

Several acquaintances testified that at that time Slater had a short mustache. Both Adams and Lambie now testified that the man they had seen was clean shaven, though before Adams had not been sure.

When Slater engaged his passage on the Lusitania, he had made no secret of his plans, but had given his true name and address and stated that he would take his berths at Liverpool, which he did. The fact that he later took passage under the name of Otto Sando he explained by saying that he had

[228] good reason to fear pursuit by his real wife, a belief which was shown to have some basis in fact.

What may have convinced the jury finally was later proved to have been an error on the part of the Lord Advocate. In his address to the jury, the Lord Advocate twice pointed out that, after giving his true name at the ticket office, December 25, Slater saw his name and description in the Glasgow papers, with the result that he never went back to the ticket agency but instead, after packing his trunks, remained in the house until time to take the train. The error in this assertion lies in the fact that Slater's name did not appear in the papers on the twenty-fifth and that it was nearly a week later before it was published along with his description by which time he was in mid-ocean.

It was not difficult to demonstrate to the jury that Slater's character was by no means all that the conventions might have demanded, but no actual criminal record was introduced against him. He appears to have suffered several moral lapses and to have been unsteady and rather mobile in his employment.

The fact that Slater did not take the witness stand in his own defense also probably told against him heavily. His counsel felt that he should not testify, for reasons which have never been disclosed. It is possible that he feared the effect upon the jury of any cross-examination which would elicit the story of Slater's amours and general moral depravity.

The jury returned a verdict of guilty after deliberating an hour and ten minutes. Of the fifteen jurors, nine were for conviction, five felt that the Crown had not proved its case, and one favored a verdict of not guilty. Scotch law provides that a majority verdict suffices.

Upon hearing the verdict Slater protested his innocence and complete ignorance of the whole affair. He was sentenced to death.

On May 17 a memorial, signed by twenty thousand persons, was presented to the Secretary of State for Scotland by Slater's counsel, Ewing Speirs, petitioning for a stay of execution. No action was taken on this petition until May 25, two days before the execution was to take place, when a [229] telegram from the Undersecretary of State for Scotland ordered a stay of execution.

On July 8, 1909, Slater was removed to Peterhead, the prison in which he was to serve his commuted sentence of life imprisonment. The interest which had led twenty thousand persons to sign the original memorial continued unabated, but the Crown authorities were slow in granting it formal recognition, although it soon spread to England and gradually gained international prominence.

Not until April 23, 1914, was an inquiry ordered and then the Home Office instructed the Sheriff of Lanarkshire to investigate certain allegations about the case made by a Glasgow detective named Trench. This investigation was held in secret, thereby causing a storm of protest. Two months later the .Government issued a White Paper giving a report of the findings. Detective Inspector Trench, who had an enviable record, was a gold-medal officer, and once had been assigned to guard the person of the King, said that two days after the murder he was ordered to visit Miss Birrell, a niece of Miss Gilchrist, for the purpose of finding out what Lambie had told her when she came to inform Miss Birrell of Miss Gilchrist's death. He reported that Miss Birrell had said that Lambie had named the murderer. As Miss Birrell later denied the story and as Trench's statement was not accepted, the Government decided not to disclose the identity of the person named. It appeared also that the prosecution had been active in persuading the principal witnesses to identify Slater. Trench was, in fact, dismissed from the service, despite his previous exemplary record.

As the years passed, greater and greater pressure was brought to bear on the Government for Slater's release. The late Sir Arthur Conan Doyle was one of the eminent people who interested themselves in Slater's behalf. The public dissatisfaction with the case led to the creation by Parliament of a Court of Criminal Appeal for Scotland which, had it existed before, would have made unnecessary such an inquiry as was conducted by the Sheriff of Lanarkshire.

After serving eighteen years Slater was, in 1927, released on parole. In 1928 he was finally exonerated by this Court [230] of Criminal Appeal after a retrial under a special act and soon thereafter was granted £6,000 by Parliament as indemnity for nearly a score of years' imprisonment for a crime he did not commit.

Slater's counsel in the Court of Criminal Appeal based their attack on the conflicting evidence as to identification and on the Crown's failure to produce all the evidence known to it. Lambie, who had married and gone to America, refused to return for this trial. Mary Barrowman, who was now thirty-four years old, signed an affidavit that she had never meant to identify Slater positively, but had been influenced by the prosecutor. It was largely on her testimony that Slater was convicted. She had received a much larger portion of the reward offered for the capture of the murderer than any of the others who shared it.

• • • •

HAD Slater been tried in England or America, it is probable that he would not have been convicted, for a unanimous jury would have been required. He missed the hangman's rope by just two days. That respite enabled him at least to save his life, though it prolonged his detention to eighteen years. His somewhat unsavory past weighed heavily against him, although no minor factor in the case seems to have been the artificial construction of a case by the prosecution. To coach witnesses to make identifications is a serious delinquency; and it appears not to be unusual. The suppression of the testimony of Detective Trench and the mystery surrounding the person named to Miss Birrell by Lambie as the murderer might almost lead to the conclusion that the Government may have had some ground to believe that Slater was not guilty, although it seems difficult to credit the English or Scotch Government, whose administration of justice ranks high, with such knowledge or belief. Probably the War delayed the exhaustive examination which the Court of Criminal Appeal later made. At all events, Parliament somewhat atoned for an irreparable wrong by granting Slater £6,000 and he, like Beck, may derive what satisfaction he can out of the fact that his misfortunes led to the establishment of a [231] Court of Criminal Appeal, with power to review a jury's findings of fact. Possibly another Beck or Slater tragedy will thereby be avoided. [232]

"MURDERERS" VS. "SUICIDERS"

Stain and Cromwell

THE death of John Wilson Barren divided the little town of Dexter, Maine, into two camps the "Murderers" and the "Suiciders." Barren, though a comparatively young man, was cashier of the bank at the time of his death and had formerly been town treasurer.

About 7:00 p.m., February 22, 1878, he was found lying unconscious on the floor of the bank's vault. He had been gagged with a pail handle, his hands were tied behind him, and his head was cut and bruised in several places. He failed to regain consciousness before he died next morning.

Barren's false teeth were found on the floor, his pen, which he usually kept behind his ear when not in use, was picked up in the coal bin, and a screw driver and an oil lamp were discovered in the vault near the body. What appeared to be cracker crumbs were on the floor.

The authorities had little to work on except these doubtful clues. Someone remembered seeing three strangers in town Washington's Birthday. Others recalled seeing three strangers leaving town that night in a wagon, but no trace of them was found.

Suspects were arrested from time to time early in the investigation, but all were released after being questioned. As activity in the case diminished, the division among Barren's fellow townsmen became more distinct. Strong opinions on the suicide theory were countered with strong ideas about the possibility of murder.

The "Suiciders" based their case on irregularities discovered in the bank's accounts which resulted in a loss of about $700 shortly before Barren's death. There had been a run on the bank the day before the holiday, but this may have been due to general uncertainty concerning the banking situation throughout the state at the time rather than to lack of confidence in a single institution. It was also reported during the investigation that books of a partnership in which Barren was interested had not been properly kept.

These and similar reasons were advanced to sustain the opinion that Barron had killed himself, while the [233] "Murderers" pointed with considerable logic to the condition in which the man was found. They said he could not have gagged himself, bruised and cut his head, tied his hands behind his back, and then taken his own life. There also appeared to be $200 in cash and a $500 bond missing from the bank, and there was never any indication that Barron had had anything to do with their disappearance.

As years passed, however, the suicide theory came to prevail generally; and the community spoke of Barron's death as voluntary, though on two occasions the court found for his estate, on the theory of involuntary death, in suits brought to recover several thousand dollars on the basis of alleged irregularities in his management of certain financial affairs.

Nevertheless, the "Suiciders" were unshaken in their opinion until about ten years later, when, in 1887, Charles Francis Stain appeared upon the scene with evidence he offered as confirmation of the murder theory.

Stain, well known to the police of several New England communities, suddenly announced that a ghost had urged him to tell the story of the banker's death and thus remove from the name the stigma of suicide. Stain's subsequent statement involved his father, David L. Stain, and Oliver Cromwell (Smith), both of Medfield, Massachusetts, and as a result they were brought to trial in March, 1888, for Barron's murder.

Young Stain said the ghost visited him while he was serving time in jail at Norridgewock, Maine. After several visitations, it seems, young Stain was unable to resist its supernatural entreaties and consequently accused his father and Cromwell of slaying Barron.

He said that he had been called to his father's bedside in Medfield one night shortly after the banker's death and that, in a burst of hysteria induced by the weight of his conscience, the elder Stain confessed the murder. His father insisted, the son said, that the murder had not been premeditated but that Barron had been killed when he appeared unexpectedly. Young Stain said his father admitted striking Barron, who fell to the floor stunned, and was then [234] attacked and bound by Cromwell. The elder Stain, according to the son, seemed to have recovered from his spasm next day and warned that mention of what had been said the night before would mean death.

To emphasize this warning, said young Stain, the father threatened to kill him then and there and he saved his life by falling to his knees, begging mercy, and swearing himself to secrecy.

It appears, however, that a feud, known to many people, had existed between father and son prior to this alleged confession. This fact was not introduced at the trial, though there appeared to be very strong reason to believe that young Stain's accusations were based largely on this ill feeling. Cromwell said the feud originated in the father's refusal to send Charles $25 which was necessary to keep him out of jail in Maine. The father replied to the request, Cromwell said, by informing the young man that he would sooner send him a rope to hang with than advance any money.

Many points reflecting Charles's character and his motives, which would have had an important cumulative effect in favor of the defendants, were not introduced; and very little appeared in the record which would tend to discredit the youth's story.

One of the most striking aspects of the proceedings was the remarkable memory repeatedly displayed by prosecution witnesses who quickly recalled superficial events and circumstances then ten years in the past. The prosecution relied principally upon Charles's story and the identification of the defendants by persons who believed they had seen them in Dexter, Washington's Birthday, 1878.

Some twenty witnesses appear to have remembered seeing strangers whom they identified as Stain and Cromwell on that fatal holiday a decade previously. There was no reason to believe that these witnesses had had an opportunity for more than a fleeting glance at the men, and the record does not disclose that they conducted themselves that day in anyway that might be expected to leave a permanent impression.

The identifications were clouded by a profusion of [235] differences concerning almost everything about these mysterious strangers the clothing they wore, their physical appearance, and their features. Testimony on these pertinent points introduced a great confusion of whiskers, smooth faces, mustaches, light clothes, dark clothes, penetrating eyes, expressive faces, tall men, short men, high buttoned coats, and coats open at the neck.

Close examination of this mass of revived and hazy memories disclosed that David Stain had been actually identified as three different men, assuming the details of individual testimony to be correct.

It is difficult to believe that the jury could have assembled even a composite picture of the strangers who had so impressed the citizenry of Dexter. The extremes to which the identifications ran are illustrated by the testimony of two storekeepers. One said he remembered that a stranger entered his store February 22, 1878, and bought a small quantity of cheese and crackers, for which he paid twenty-one cents. The other's memory, going back ten years, recalled that a stranger entered his store the day in question, looked around for a moment, bought nothing, and walked out. Both witnesses believed the defendant Stain was their man.

The defense witnesses proved ineffective for the most part. The jury appears to have felt that they were testifying as friends of the accused and were therefore incapable of telling the truth. Several of them knew Stain and Cromwell well, for they lived in the same small community in Massachusetts. It was impressed upon the jury that neither had a spotless reputation, and that was true, though later evidence would seem to discount a great deal of the ground for the jury's suspicion.

The defense witnesses were called to establish an alibi, and their testimony, if correct, placed both Stain and Cromwell in Medfield, February 22, 1878. Some of them fixed the date through recollection of the theft that day of a horse, an event which occasioned a warm excitement and discussion in the town. The defense used every effort to show that this theft had actually occurred, and it appears that they succeeded. [236]

Several defense witnesses did not make a good showing on the stand, though others appeared highly creditable, but their conduct under questioning and the substance of their testimony apparently failed to impress the jury sufficiently.

So inaccurate was prevailing information concerning the status of two of the defense witnesses that the public understood they were what might be called partners in crime with Stain and Cromwell, whereas it could have been proved that they were bitter enemies of the accused and had been prevailed upon to appear for the defendants only after a great deal of urging.

The defense suffered its greatest setback, however, through an attempt to discredit Charles Stain's accusation of his father and Cromwell. This incident convinced the jury, according to later admissions by several members, that the elder Stain was a forger; and from that point it was apparently but a short step to the assumption that he was a murderer as well.

This occurrence involved a statement in young Stain's accusation that his father, Cromwell, and himself had shipped a team of horses by boat from Boston to Gardiner, Maine. He intimated that the horses had been stolen. To discredit this statement a receipt signed "B. C. Sanborn" was introduced. The receipt was sworn to be the only one known to the steamship company covering horses similar to those described by young Stain as shipped on the boat at the time alleged. It was shown that neither Stain nor Cromwell's name appeared on the paper. At this point the prosecution scored heavily by contending that any name could be signed to a receipt; consequently young Stain's statement stood apparently unimpeached, and the conclusion seems to have been drawn that the elder Stain forged the receipt to hide his identity in making the shipment.

This idea was firmly fixed when, after closing arguments by counsel on both sides, the court permitted the prosecution to introduce several letters written by David Stain. Their handwriting was compared with that on the receipt and pronounced similar.

After twenty hours of deliberation the jury returned [237] verdicts of guilty. Both men were sentenced to life imprisonment for the murder of John Wilson Barren.

● ● ● ●

PETITIONS for a new trial were soon filed on the ground of newly discovered evidence. This evidence, however, concerned further knowledge of the issue on the part of one Baker, a witness at the trial. Consequently it was worthless, for the law then provided that new evidence based upon the knowledge of a person who already had testified could not be used as grounds for a new trial.

More important, however, was the discovery by the defense of B. C. Sanborn of Avon, Maine. Sanborn had been assumed by the jury to be a more or less fictitious person created by David Stain. Quite the opposite now appeared true. It was proved conclusively that Sanborn had shipped the horses in question and had himself signed the receipt.

Yet the court was not satisfied and denied the petition. In a 242-page opinion it was held that the new material would not have produced a different result had it been introduced at the original trial, though the defense contended that proof of untruth in one part of young Stain's statement was a highly important wedge by which to raise the question of the falsity of the entire statement.

An application for a pardon was denied in 1895 but in 1900 the two men were more fortunate. This time the Governor and his Council were presented with a mass of detailed material showing that Stain and Cromwell were absolutely innocent.

Two petitions had been filed for pardons at the same time, one of them by Lewis A. Barker, a son of the defense attorney at the trial. Young Barker had often heard his father repeat his belief that his clients were innocent. This faith had inspired him with an ambition to prove their innocence. He had, accordingly, studied law and was now appearing as counsel in their behalf, sure that his father's faith and his ambition were justified.

An interesting phase of the evidence introduced with the new petitions was a comparison of various witnesses' [238] testimony at the trial concerning the strangers they recalled having seen leaving Dexter on the night Barren was attacked.

Analysis of this testimony disclosed that if the witnesses saw the men when and where they thought they had, the strangers would have pursued an unbelievably erratic course in their wagon. It was found that they must have traveled ten miles the first hour of their flight from Dexter, two and a half in the next six hours, twelve during the next four, and ten during the last hour. It was agreed that this was a most eccentric manner of travel for men supposedly fleeing from the scene of a bank robbery and murder.

Other evidence presented with the petitions showed that a third man accused in Charles Stain's statement—one Billy Scott—had never been described by any witness, nor even found to exist. It was also shown that witnesses who identified Stain and Cromwell had seen pictures of them, whereas there never had been exhibited a picture of the supposed Scott.

The most convincing witness of all, however, was Sanborn. He appeared in person, and there were exhibited at the same time affidavits signed by several jurors saying that they had based their verdict largely on the belief that David Stain forged the shipping receipt.

Finally, there were offered to the Governor a number of letters written by neighbors of Stain in Medfield on or about February 2, 1878, describing incidents which occurred Washington's Birthday and mentioning Stain as having participated in them.

Further evidence tended to discredit Charles Stain's whole story. It appeared that he had voluntarily confessed to a bank robbery in Winthrop, Maine, before he saw the jail ghost. An investigation at the time showed that he had had nothing to do with the affair, and that the men who were guilty were in prison. The defense also discovered evidence that young Stain was apparently in the habit of confessing whatever manner of crime inspired his imagination and that he had finally sold one of his "true stories" to a New York newspaper man.

If proof of young Stain's unreliability had been lacking [239] previously, it was finally supplied by the young man himself, for he suddenly repudiated his testimony at his father's trial and then retracted the repudiation.

On January 1, 1901, Stain and Cromwell were granted a full pardon by Governor Powers on the unanimous recommendation of the Governor's Council. They had spent thirteen years in prison for a crime the state now conceded they had not committed.

As a final demonstration of the instability of young Stain's mental processes let it be recorded that he announced in a newspaper interview the day his father and Cromwell were released that he was very much pleased to hear of the Governor's action.

• • • •

HOW a jury of reasonable men could have relied on the "identifications" of the state's witnesses is hard to grasp. The identifications were so contradictory that they ought to have been utterly discredited. It is obvious that the witnesses could not have seen the same person or persons. On the other hand, the testimony that Stain and Cromwell were in Medfield on Washington's Birthday is almost impregnable. That evidence came from enemies and friends and from impartial witnesses. It is unfortunate that Baker could not tell his whole story and that Sanborn could not be found in time to refute the suggestion that Stain had signed the receipt for the horses and had forged Sanborn's name. Charles Stain's "confession"—even without the clarifying account of the receipt—had been shot so full of holes by internal inconsistencies and external refutation that little if anything should have been left of it. The jury evidently had a hard time convincing themselves of Stain and Cromwell's guilt. The fact that the alibi connected them with a probable horse theft in Medfield did not help the accused. Indeed, what probably turned the scale against them was their somewhat shady record. While they were not professional criminals and had legitimate occupations, they had apparently made occasional amateur excursions into the game of getting something for nothing by the use of nimble legs or wits, [240] though their intelligence was not of a high order. A combination of circumstances which should have operated to establish their innocence, had just enough unfavorable elements to persuade the jury adversely. The gradual wearing away of these elements finally disclosed the case against them as a figment of the imagination, without substantial support. If it proves anything, the case shows how largely identifications are prompted, though not necessarily in bad faith, by a desire to help along the punishment of a suspect.

• • • •

Acknowledgments: Hon. Sidney St. F. Thaxter, now Judge of the Supreme Court, Portland, Me.; Hon. Clement F. Robinson, Attorney-General of the State of Maine. [241]

Governor Whitman vs. Orleans County

Stielow and Green

SEPTUAGENARIAN Charles B. Phelps, a highly respected resident of Orleans County, New York, lived in his farmhouse about one mile south of West Shelby with his housekeeper, Margaret Wolcott. Across the road, in the Phelps tenant house, lived Charles F. Stielow, a farm laborer, with his young wife, two children, his mother-in-law, and young brother-in-law, Nelson Green. These tenants had come to the farm about March 15, 1915.

At five o'clock on the morning of March 22, 1915, Stielow arose as usual to do the chores at the Phelps place. When he stepped out of his home, he found on his doorstep Miss Wolcott, stretched dead and bloody in the snow, clad only in a nightgown. Stielow rushed over to the Phelps house, entered the open kitchen door, and found Mr. Phelps unconscious on the floor. Stielow immediately alarmed the neighbors. Sheriff Bartlett of Albion was summoned and the Medina police notified. Phelps was rushed to a hospital in Medina, but he expired without regaining consciousness. He had been shot three times.

Phelps was known to have kept cash about the house and it was supposed that robbery was the motive for this atrocious murder. The contents of bureau drawers in Mr. Phelps's room were strewn about and his money was gone. Both Phelps and Miss Wolcott had been shot by a .22 revolver.

District Attorney Knickerbocker arrived on the scene at an early hour, gathering facts, and awaiting a bloodhound of Charles Scobell. The hound picked up a scent and followed it to a nearby stream, where it was lost. The dog was unsuccessful in going farther.

As usual in cases of this type, many clues were furnished to the authorities, which they endeavored to check. The Board of Supervisors authorized the expenditure of money to secure the services of detectives. Rewards for the arrest and conviction of the murderer were posted.

On Friday, March 26, 1915, the coroner's inquest was [242] held. Stielow and Green testified that at about eleven o'clock on the night of the murder they heard cries near their house. They arose from bed and looked out of the door but didn't see anyone. They then went back to bed again. A neighbor, Miss Irma Fisher, said that she heard four shots at about eleven o'clock, screams, and the moaning cry, "Charlie, I am dying, let me in," but thought that it was only a quarrel in a family living to the south; and since it soon quieted down, she thought no more of it, until she learned of the murder the next morning.

The Newton Detective Agency of Buffalo, of which George Newton was the head, was intrusted by the county authorities with the task of tracing the murderer. It seemed strange that Miss Wolcott's screams and pleas were so distinctly heard by Miss Fisher, and made no more impression upon the persons in the tenant house. The detectives examined the tenants closely, and discovered that, on the night of the murder, there was a .22-caliber revolver and also a rifle in the tenant house, despite the sworn statements of both Stielow and Green at the coroner's inquest to the contrary. These weapons were found in the possession of Raymond Green, a brother of Nelson. Upon this discovery, the authorities felt warranted on April 21, 1915, in taking both Stielow and Green into custody. Albert H. Hamilton, as expert for the state, said that the four bullets taken from the bodies of Phelps and his housekeeper had been fired from the revolver owned by Stielow. As their investigations proceeded, the authorities became more and more convinced that Stielow and Green knew more about the crime than they had admitted.

When the prisoners were placed in jail, detectives were stationed there also, disguised as fellow prisoners, in an endeavor to learn just what the prisoners knew of the crime.

On the evening of the day of the arrest, Detective Newton received from Stielow a signed statement, denying any connection with the crime. Two days later, April 23, in the county jail, in the presence of Sheriff Bartlett, Undersheriff Porter, District Attorney Knickerbocker, and Detectives Newton and Wilson, Stielow was said to have confessed [243] that he and Nelson Green had committed the murder to get Phelps's money. Many of the statements were made after consultation with Detective Newton in the jail hall. A written statement, including the confession, was placed before Stielow, but he refused absolutely to sign it, saying that it was not true.

With this evidence in his possession, District Attorney Knickerbocker presented the case to a Grand Jury, which returned separate first-degree-murder indictments against Stielow and Green. Stielow was brought to trial at Albion before Justice Cuthbert W. Pound of Buffalo, on July 11, 1915. He was defended by David A. White. Although the prosecutors took over eight days to submit all of the details of their testimony, the great issue of the trial was whether Stielow's alleged confession of April 23 should be received in evidence. Everyone agreed that if this were inadmissible the case against Stielow was very weak. Defense Attorney White sought to prove that Detective Newton had wrung some admissions from Stielow by intimidation and third-degree methods. Both sides submitted considerable evidence on the circumstances surrounding the making of the alleged confession and admissions said to have been made to the sheriff and other officials. Justice Pound admitted the testimony regarding the alleged confession, with testimony on both sides as to how it had been obtained.

In addition to the contention that this was not a voluntary confession, the defense was based upon the alibi that Stielow had not left his home at all during the night of the murder. His wife and mother-in-law supported the prisoner's testimony in this regard. To this was added the testimony of several persons as to Stielow's good reputation and character in the communities where he had lived previously.

In submitting the case to the jury, the Court said: "I will say very plainly to you at this time that if it were not for the introduction of the statement dated April %3rd, and like statements of the defendant admitting his guilt, it would be the duty of the court to direct you to render a verdict of acquittal." The case was given to the jury at 1:35 on July 23 and at 8:15 that evening, it was ready with its [244] verdict—guilty. Evidently, the jury believed that Stielow's confession had been voluntary. Justice Pound sentenced Stielow to electrocution in the week of September 5, following.

Nelson Green's attorneys advised him of the result, and on their advice he pleaded guilty to a charge of second-degree murder. He was sentenced to a twenty-year-to-life term in Auburn Penitentiary.

Attorney White appealed Stielow's conviction to the highest court of New York state, which, in a per curiam decision on February 22, 1916, unanimously affirmed the conviction. The date for his electrocution was set for April 9, 1916.

In the meantime, Stielow, in the death house at Sing Sing, made statements to the officials there which aroused their interest. He denied his guilt and said that whatever he had agreed to while in jail was to save himself from constant badgering by detectives. The officials instituted a private investigation which convinced them that a thorough investigation of Stielow's case should be made before his execution. On the eve of the execution, the Governor granted a stay, but after a motion before Justice Wheeler for a new trial was denied, the date for the death penalty was again set, for July 29, 1916. Mrs. Grace Humiston, attorney at law in New York, became intensely interested in the case. So did a society called the Humanitarian Cult. Further evidence that the confession was not voluntary, and that Stielow had a very immature mind, was submitted to Justice George W. Cole at Buffalo on July 19, 1916, in support of another motion for a new trial. On July 26, 1916, this motion was denied.

The following day, July 27, Warden Osborne's Sing Sing Welfare League forwarded $42 to Mrs. Stielow so that she and her three children, the youngest of whom was born after her husband's arrest, might travel to the penitentiary to see their condemned husband and father. Farewells were said on Friday, the twenty-eighth. Charles Stielow was to die the following morning at 6:00 a.m. Appeals to Governor Whitman were unavailing.

Just after five o'clock on that Saturday morning, the telephone rang in the warden's office at Sing Sing, and Justice [245] Charles L. Guy of

Brooklyn advised the officials, forty minutes before the scheduled time for the execution, that he was issuing a stay, so that he might consider the new evidence submitted before him. By this time a corps of attorneys had become interested in the case and were working feverishly to prevent the execution of one whom they considered innocent. Later the same day, about 7:00 p.m., Justice Guy issued a further stay, with an order to the District Attorney of Orleans County to show cause at Rochester on August 23, 1916, why a new trial should not be granted to Stielow.

Prior to the Rochester hearing, which was held before Justice Adolph J. Rodenbeck in the latter part of September, 1916, exciting developments took place. As Stielow's plight became known, not only additional legal assistance but financial aid became available. This enabled the hiring of detectives to run down rumors concerning an itinerant peddler who had been seen in the Phelps home on the eve of the murder, and who was known to have had a large sum of money after that time. This was considered important on the theory that the best way to establish Stielow's innocence was to find the real murderer. The trail, opened by Mrs. Humiston, led to the peddler Erwin King, who had been arrested in Little Valley, Cattaraugus County, for another crime and who, before seven witnesses, including Surrogate George Larkin, a lawyer of experience and ability, who fully warned King of the possible consequences, made a full confession of his participation, with Clarence O'Connell, in the Phelps murder. This was on August 11, 1916. The Cattaraugus authorities turned King over to the Orleans County Sheriff. Two days later King repudiated his confession, saying that it had been made under duress. It was later learned that George Newton, the Buffalo detective who had obtained Stielow's confession, rode in the auto with King on the 110-mile ride from Little Valley to Albion, where he retracted his confession. Orleans County reengaged Newton at this time to establish the truth of King's alleged alibi on the night of the murder.

Justice Rodenbeck denied the motion for a new trial, principally upon the ground that the evidence presented "might [246] with reasonable diligence have been discovered before the trial and that it is not in fact newly discovered evidence," would not raise a reasonable doubt in the minds of the jury, and that, therefore, it would not affect their decision. King's confession was dismissed from consideration by the Justice as being "only valuable as a psychological study," in view of his retraction and of affidavits that King was elsewhere at the time of the murder. As pointed out by the Justice, he was the tenth judge to pass upon, and to deny, a new trial for Stielow.

Justice Rodenbeck's decision was a devastating blow to Stielow, for his hopes for freedom had risen high when King confessed the slaying. Two weeks later, Stielow was taken to Albany, where the Court of Appeals sentenced him to electrocution during the week of December 11, 1916. This was the third time that he was sentenced to death. It was clear that the courts could find no mistake in the operation of the state's administrative and judicial machinery; yet there remained a conviction in the minds of many earnest citizens that a serious mistake had been made.

Executive clemency remained the only recourse, and the whole matter was fervently presented to Governor Whitman. Fortunately for Stielow, the Governor was an experienced criminal lawyer. Although he had refused to interfere, other than by granting temporary stays of execution, so long as remedies remained in the courts, now that these were exhausted, he set November 28, 1916, for a public hearing on the case. On December 4, following the hearing, he issued a statement, commuting Stielow's sentence to life imprisonment on the ground that, while he believed Stielow guilty, he could not escape the conviction "that there was a possibility, perhaps more than a possibility, that the defendant was not guilty."

• • • •

ABOUT a month later, it came to the Governor's attention that King, who had been arrested for perjury and held in jail in Buffalo, was writing a series of incriminating letters to friends. The New York World, taking an interest in the [247] case, published the letters. The Governor had King brought to Albany for interrogation and became satisfied that King had guilty knowledge of the murder. However, public opinion in Orleans County, which had already spent nearly $50,000 on the case, held King innocent and Stielow guilty. The Governor, who officially stated that no other criminal case where executive clemency had been asked, had so perplexed and distressed him as had this one, decided upon his own course of action in solving the problem. He requested, and received, from the Legislature a special appropriation of $25,000 for an investigation. Mr. George H. Bond of Syracuse, a former District Attorney, an experienced criminal lawyer, and a leader of the state bar, was appointed a special deputy attorney-general for the purpose. Mr. Bond made a most thorough investigation, and his 200-page report to the Governor is a model of methodical and painstaking analysis. Mr. Bond began the investigation in the belief that Stielow was guilty.

Particular attention was given by Mr. Bond to the circumstances of Stielow's confession, the principal basis of his conviction, and to the facts alleged to have been confessed. In addition to the evidence of duress used upon Stielow by Detective Newton, it was found that a dictograph had been used to record the conversations of Stielow with Green, and even with his counsel. Neither the defense counsel, the presiding justice, nor the jury had known of these records. Mr. Bond had them produced, and not a single incriminating remark was found in them. One of the Newton Agency detectives, Sparacino, who spent nineteen days in jail with Stielow in the guise of a prisoner with instructions to get a confession or incriminating evidence, admitted that he did not succeed, that Stielow consistently denied knowing who committed the crime, and that Stielow said that the detectives had tried to get him to sign a statement which was a lie. In later commenting on this phase of the investigation, Governor Whitman said that the Stielow confession "seems to be discredited."

Mr. Bond made a careful study of the ballistic testimony, and engaged the leading experts of the state to make [248] objective tests. He had bullets fired from the Stielow pistol, and then had enlarged photographs made of the bullets as well as of the bullets taken from the bodies of Phelps and Miss Wolcott. The difference was readily apparent. The experts, Mr. Bond, and the Governor concluded that the trial testimony of Mr. Hamilton that the death bullets had come from the Stielow pistol was clearly erroneous. The Governor commented: "It is apparent to any expert, or to a careful observer, that the bullet taken from Mr. Phelps was not fired from Stielow's revolver, but differs in markings from those fired out of the Stielow revolver." It appeared, moreover, that the Stielow revolver had not been fired for some years.

Mr. Bond further demonstrated that Stielow's supposed description of the shooting of Miss Wolcott was a physical impossibility; that the footprints upon which the scent was started could not have been those of Stielow, who was near and had patted the dog when the hunt began, and that the dog did not follow Stielow's tracks made when he notified the neighbors of the crime; that Miss Wolcott, who would doubtless have recognized Stielow in the Phelps house, would hardly have run to his house for protection; that Miss Irma Fisher was mistaken in her report of the supposed repeated prayers of Miss Wolcott to be let in by Stielow, for another resident of the Fisher house remembered no such events and it was physically impossible for a woman with a bullet in her heart to continue such pleadings; that Detective Newton, Sheriff Bartlett, and Undersheriff Porter not only varied their accounts of Stielow's alleged statements from time to time but that the "confession" merely recorded the rumors of how the murder had occurred, rumors which on investigation of the facts were completely exploded.

Probably the most important development during Mr. Bond's investigation, however, was the fact that in December, 1917, Erwin King made a second full and voluntary confession, implicating himself and Clarence O'Connell, a convict in Auburn. O'Connell fired the fatal shots; Miss Wolcott's presence in the house was unknown to them, and she was shot as she ran out of the kitchen door. They [249] followed her, found her dead, and returned to complete the looting. King supplied many details which indicated to Mr. Bond, who was now more familiar with the facts than anyone else, that he was unmistakably connected with the crime. King even accounted for the money taken from Phelps, an omission which had always baffled the authorities in connection with Stielow. King was ready to plead guilty to the charge of murder and to be sentenced. He was arraigned before

Justice Wesley C. Dudley. Since a plea of guilty would be inconsistent with the jury verdict then standing (i.e., the Stielow verdict), Justice Dudley, in accordance with the law, ordered that a "not guilty" plea be entered, and that the matter be submitted to the Grand Jury. Mr. Bond and his assistant, Charles E. Waite, spent nearly two weeks presenting the matter to the Grand Jury. Convinced that a strong prima facie case of murder against King and O'Connell had been presented, the special prosecutors were greatly surprised when the Grand Jury advised the court on December 21, 1917, that it had nothing to report. In informing the Governor about this result, Mr. Bond said that local sentiment was still firm in the belief that Stielow was guilty and that no further public money should be spent to prove that a mistake had been made.

Upon receiving Mr. Bond's report in the spring of 1918, Governor Whitman became convinced that there was gross error in the convictions of Stielow and Green. The fact that Mr. Bond, who in the early days of the investigation thought Stielow guilty, had become thoroughly convinced of his innocence, profoundly impressed the Governor. He commuted Stielow's sentence and on April 16, 1918, ordered him released from the penitentiary, as an innocent man. The same action was taken with respect to Green. Each was free again, after three years' imprisonment and untold agony. Green, now twenty-two years old, returned to farming; and Stielow, aged forty, rejoined his wife and family, and is understood now to be employed in a garage in Buffalo.

• • • •

THE miscarriage of justice in the Stielow and Green cases was due to too keen a desire on the part of the prosecuting [250] officials to pin the crime upon a person they believed guilty, without adequate observance of the many factors which pointed to innocence. Stielow in a way started his trouble by falsifying at the inquest the facts concerning his possession of the pistol and rifle. This was due to the well-meant fears of the womenfolks of his family, who thought it dangerous to admit having had guns on the premises. Stielow at first refused to move the guns, asserting that they had nothing to do with the matter. Had they been left where they were, the chances are that suspicion either might not have been directed toward him or would have been promptly diverted, for examination would have shown that the pistol had not been fired for years. But after moving the guns to the barn, where for some days they were perfectly visible, he followed family advice and gave them to Raymond Green for safekeeping and then denied that he had had guns. This falsehood was discovered. From this point on, according to Mr. Bond's report, the case was built up against him largely by Detective Newton. Nelson Green is described as practically half-witted, and Stielow himself, as of inferior mentality. It did not take much skill to work upon their minds, and shortly after their arrest, April 1, what were called "confessions" had been extracted from them—though Stielow had self-control enough to refuse to sign his. Mr. Hamilton undertook to prove to the jury that the bullets which had caused the deaths came from Stielow's revolver. Had all this evidence corresponded with the real facts, the jury might well have been justified in convicting Stielow. But it was not true. In the month between the murder and Stielow and Green's arrests, they had no money and lived as usual, a circumstance which should have received more attention. Green's plea of guilty after Stielow's conviction was made on legal advice to save him from the electrocution which awaited Stielow. Mr. Bond demonstrated by his scrupulous investigation that every material fact in the alleged confession of Stielow, in so far as it was not patently obvious, actually could not have occurred, and that the bullets could not possibly have been fired from Stielow's revolver. Had the authorities been more eager to establish the truth than to [251] establish Stielow's guilt, in which most of them probably honestly believed, they would have noticed the innumerable leads and clues which refuted Stielow's connection with the affair. The footprints were not Stielow's; the dog paid no attention to Stielow; the description in the "confession" of the salient facts inside and outside the house and the recital of the supposed facts leading up to and following the murder, including the shooting of Miss Wolcott, was manifestly wrong. Stielow was a peaceful individual, and had acted in the most natural manner. Had Stielow been the guilty man, Miss Wolcott would not have sought the protection of his house.

But the general public interest outside Orleans County which the case aroused was apparently responsible for King's escape. Public opinion in the county was incensed at the intervention of the so-called "uplifters" who sought to expose the county's maladministration of justice. Even Mr. Bond, who, as Deputy Attorney-General, directly represented the Governor and who was of the same political party as the local administration, could not, with all the evidence of King's guilt, persuade the 1917 Grand Jury to indict King for the murder, although the vote was divided. A defense mechanism had been set up in Orleans County to prevent the undoing of the Stielow mistake; and though there could not have remained the slightest doubt of King's guilt and Stielow's innocence after the evidence which Mr. Bond disclosed, the press and public apparently rationalized their stubbornness by invoking the great expense that the county had already incurred (the newspapers overlooked the fact that the state had promised to bear the expense of King's trial), the fact that a jury and ten judges had not found Stielow innocent, probably the fact that Stielow's sentence had already been commuted to life imprisonment, and possibly the belief that the Governor could even pardon Stielow. These considerations undoubtedly had much to do with the Grand Jury's yielding to public opinion and refusing to vote an indictment against King. At all events, Stielow and Green were still alive, and the Governor, acting on Mr. Bond's recommendation and his own study of the facts, [252] determined to do what was still possible by restoring these innocent men to liberty. It had cost the state and private agencies large sums to establish the truth, funds which greater initial care in Orleans County might have saved. But at least the maximum wrong was prevented by the narrowest of margins. Compensation was never made to either Stielow or Green.

• • • •

Acknowledgments: Hon. George H. Bond, Syracuse, N.Y.; Mrs. Grace Humiston, New York City. [253]

"Positive Identification"

Percy B. Sullivan

SOON after graduation from law school in 1896, and while hopefully waiting for clients, Mr. Robert F. Davidson happened to be present on arraignment day in the court room of the United States District Court at Indianapolis. The presiding judge was the Hon. John H. Baker. After listening a while to the pleas and the sentences which were imposed, Davidson concluded that it was time to go elsewhere as prospects of business in that court seemed not very promising. He started to leave the room, when Judge Baker spoke from the bench and said, "Sit down, young man, I think I have a case for you in a few minutes." The United States Marshal then brought into the room a tall, slender young man, fashionably dressed and well groomed, notwithstanding the fact that he had spent some time in jail. The charge against him was passing counterfeit money at Evansville, Vincennes, and Terre Haute, Indiana. He entered a plea of not guilty and when questioned by the court, said he had no money with which to employ counsel. The Judge then called Davidson forward and said, "Here is your client," and to the accused, "This is your attorney." The two withdrew to a private room where they conferred, while the Marshal kept guard at the door.

The defendant was Percy B. Sullivan, a graduate of Vanderbilt University and a former adjutant of the Kentucky militia, who had been in the insurance business for some time at Louisville, Kentucky. He came from a prominent Bowling Green family, and was a well-known "man about town."

It developed that Sullivan had not been satisfied with the insurance business in Louisville. In the late summer of 1896 he made a special selling drive, going down the river among the farmers and visiting the cities of Evansville, Vincennes, and Terre Haute, Indiana, and then on to St. Louis, Missouri.

During the time of Sullivan's stay in Evansville, Vincennes, and Terre Haute, a well-dressed young man made [254] purchases in the shops of these cities and paid for them in counterfeit United States currency. This was reported to Maj. Thomas B. Carter of the Secret Service.

Carter's investigators picked up clues which led to Sullivan in the Jefferson Hotel in St. Louis. There he was arrested by the United States Marshal and taken to Indianapolis. Witnesses who in part had identified Sullivan by his photograph were brought from the several cities that had been the scene of the swindle. Some of these persons did not recognize Sullivan. Others positively identified him as the one who had given them the counterfeit money especially Joseph Kunkler and six other persons from Evansville. Sullivan did not attempt to deny that he had been in Evansville, but he stoutly maintained that he had had nothing whatever to do with counterfeit money, and pointed to the fact that he had eighty dollars with him when arrested in St. Louis and all of it was good money. He did not remember having given any money whatever to any of the witnesses who appeared against him or even having seen them.

Based on the positive identification of the Evansville people, United States District Attorney Frank B. Burke submitted the case to the Grand Jury, which, on November 12, 1896, returned an indictment against Sullivan upon the specific charge of having knowingly passed upon Joseph Kunkler a United States silver certificate, raised from two to ten dollars.

It was for arraignment upon this indictment that Sullivan was called into Judge Baker's court and was assigned counsel. The case was called for trial on November 27, 1896. The prisoner was represented at the trial by experienced attorneys, W. L. Dulaney and Clarence U. McElroy, from Bowling Green, Kentucky, who were assisted by Mr. Davidson. The witnesses for the prosecution were positive in their identification of the defendant. In establishing the prisoner's felonious intent in the alleged transaction, Prosecutor Burke produced witnesses from Erie, Pennsylvania, who identified Sullivan as the man who had passed altered currency there.

The defendant took the stand in his own defense, and [255] denied absolutely having had or used any counterfeit or raised currency. He denied being in Erie at the time of the alleged transaction there. On cross-examination, some irregularities in the conduct of his insurance business which had never been made the subject of legal action were brought out in an effort to impeach his credibility. A verdict of guilty was rendered against him by the jury and on December 8, 1896, he was sentenced to four years' imprisonment and fined $100 and costs. Two days later he was brought to the South Prison at Jeffersonville to start serving his sentence.

The exceptional position that Sullivan had occupied in Louisville prior to his arrest was attested by prominent news items appearing in the papers on the day he began his prison sentence. Reporters were sent to interview him, and he spoke freely about his conviction. He said that he was innocent of the charges, and that he had been "railroaded." He was particularly bitter in his denunciation of the District Attorney and the Secret Service for the vigorous manner in which he had been prosecuted. He said that the witnesses against him were wrong in their identification, perhaps honestly, for they had been shown his picture before they saw him.

Sullivan was soon transferred from Jeffersonville to the prison at Michigan City, Indiana.

• • • •

SOME time after Sullivan's conviction Major Carter called Mr. Davidson to his office one day and stated that he had always been in doubt as to Sullivan's guilt; that he believed that at last he had the man who had actually committed the offense for which Sullivan had been convicted; that the man who had just been arrested had admitted passing counterfeit money at Evansville, Vincennes, and Terre Haute about the time charged against Sullivan. Major Carter gave to Davidson a photograph of Tyler, the prisoner who had just been arrested, and a photograph of Sullivan, and suggested that he see the witnesses who had testified at Sullivan's trial, asking them to say which man had passed the counterfeit money; and, if their answers were satisfactory, to secure their affidavits. Mr. Davidson went to Evansville, Vincennes, [256] and Terre Haute and saw most of the witnesses who had testified at Sullivan's trial. Without letting them know which was Sullivan's and which was Tyler's picture, he showed them both photographs and asked them to point out the man who had passed the money. They all promptly pointed to Tyler's photograph and, confronted with the two photographs, they found but little resemblance.

In due course Tyler was convicted and sentenced for these offenses.

Thereupon, the affidavits, accompanied by incontestable evidence that Sullivan had not been in Erie, were submitted to the Department of Justice at Washington in support of an application for a pardon. The trial judge, the District Attorney, and the Secret Service all concurred in the opinion that Sullivan was mistaken for the real culprit and in urging that a pardon be granted. Upon the recommendation of Attorney-General Griggs, President McKinley granted a full and unconditional pardon on May 12, 1898. Sullivan was immediately released, and he disappeared from public notice but for the time being only.

Sullivan spent some years in traveling over the country, participating extensively and successfully in the insurance business and in the promotion of large mining and milling interests in Colorado. Eventually he returned to identify himself with one of the growing cities of Illinois. He entered the land-development, insurance, and banking businesses. In one of his undertakings business rivals learned of the old Indianapolis conviction and were planning to make use of it to Sullivan's detriment. He procured through Mr. Davidson a copy of the pardon record from the Department of Justice, "certified with a gold seal and fastened with a broad band of royal blue ribbon," showing that he was innocent, and fought his rivals to the finish successfully. Mr. Sullivan became prosperous and wealthy. He married, and his children went through college with great credit to themselves and their parents. Today (1931) Mr. Sullivan is one of the prominent public-spirited citizens of this Illinois city, where he has lived for over a quarter of a century. [257]

• • • •

In its setting, the Sullivan case differs in no material respect from the Andrews, Greenwald, and Lee cases. Sullivan's was a clear case of mistaken identity. It does exemplify the dangers of the practice of first exhibiting to the victims of a crime, the prospective prosecuting witnesses of the accused person, a single photograph for purposes of identification. In the case of distant witnesses, the practice may in part be unavoidable, but it should be limited to cases of necessity only and include more than one photograph. The practice is tendentious, for the psychological factors of such an exhibition of single photographs favor identification rather than repudiation of identity. Once an opinion is formed, other emotions, such as pride and stubbornness, make for confirmation of the original identification rather than for open-minded reconsideration. Although Sullivan and Tyler bore but little resemblance, Sullivan was, nevertheless, identified at the trial by those who had first identified his photograph. Only the fact that the real culprit continued his career after the innocent man was in prison enabled Sullivan to escape serving out his sentence. The case also shows that a criminal conviction, even where it does not completely ruin a man, nevertheless is a fearful handicap and can be used by enemies in after years to embarrass the most innocent. Had Sullivan been indemnified by the Government, as he should have been, he would have been vindicated in the eyes of society and would not have had to undertake a campaign to prove to his traducers that he was the victim of a miscarriage of justice.

• • • •

Acknowledgment: Robert F. Davidson, Indianapolis, Ind. [258]

Because He'd "Done Time"

James Sweeney

EIGHT Machine Gun Bandits Slay Driver in $160,000 Elizabeth Mail Holdup." This headline appeared on the front page of the New York Evening Post, and similar headlines were carried by other papers of the New York Metropolitan District on Thursday, October 14, 1926. The columns below told how at nine o'clock that morning in Elizabeth, New Jersey, at the corner of Sixth and Elizabeth Streets, a bandit gang had held up a mail truck carrying $300,000, as registered mail, from the Federal Reserve Bank in New York to the Elizabethport National Bank, some of which was the pay roll of the Singer Sewing Machine Company. The mail truck, driven by John Enz and Patrick S. Quinn, his helper, was proceeding at a normal pace, accompanied by Police Officer Jacob Christman mounted on a motorcycle. Suddenly, a large sedan swung around a corner, headed directly toward the truck, and caused it to veer into a side street and crash into a parked car. Another sedan then swerved to run down the motorcycle policeman before he could get into action. As he lay, dazed, in the street, a shotgun was fired at him. Simultaneously, machine-gun fire was opened on the drivers of the truck from a third sedan parked at the opposite corner of the intersection. Enz toppled from the seat to the ground, shot through the head. Quinn jumped from his seat and fired two shots before machine guns were turned on him, pumping bullets into his left leg, arms, and hands. Charles Decatur, a bystander, was wounded. Persons living near by who attempted to come into the street were greeted by a fusillade of steel. At once four of the gang, with bolt clippers, broke open the lock at the back of the truck. Mail bags containing $151,300 were quickly removed from the truck to one of the sedans, which left the scene at a rapid pace. One of their cars was driven over the dead body of Enz and over the wounded Quinn.

A few pedestrians saw the holdup, and the bandits had a scant lead over an improvised pursuit. In Newark, two cars, [259] later identified as the bandit machines, dashed past a traffic signal set against them. The traffic officer opened fire without effect and then gave chase, but the cars eluded their pursuers and escaped. Their course led to a search of the nearby Orange Mountains. Col. Norman Schwartzkopf and Maj. Mark O. Kimberling of the New Jersey State Police established what practically amounted to martial law in that part of the state, their well-armed troopers being ordered "to shoot on sight and shoot to kill." The Post Office Department detached a score of crack investigators under Chief Inspector Rush D. Simmons to help solve the crime. Orders were issued from Washington for the protection of United States mails by marines.

It was believed that the same gang had been responsible for several recent holdups in the vicinity, some accompanied by killings; and John ("Bum") Rogers and James ("Killer") Cuniffe were mentioned as probable members of the gang.

The first definite clues came from Detroit, where a gangster, Bill Crowley, shot and killed another gangster, Jim Cuniffe, and his companion, Frances Harris, in a hotel room. Police officers killed Crowley while attempting to enter the room to arrest him. Crowley and Cuniffe, together with the girl, Frances Harris, had gone to Detroit with part of the loot from the Elizabeth holdup; and it was a quarrel either over division of the loot or over letting Frances Harris return to New Jersey that precipitated the killing of Cuniffe. By following up these clues the authorities were able to locate a taxi driver in Elizabeth, New Jersey, who stated that during the previous summer he had taken Frances Harris, Crowley, and Cuniffe, together with others, to an apartment house located in a certain section of Newark, although he did not know the exact address. The authorities searched this section of the town and finally located the apartment. The wrappings that had surrounded the bundles of money for the Singer pay roll were found lying on the floor, showing that the bandits had returned to this apartment and divided the loot after the holdup.

The underworld was combed for the characters known to have associated with Crowley, Cuniffe, and Frances Harris, [260] and among others one Benjamin Haas was taken into custody and questioned. On Haas was found a business card of James Sweeney, whose business was "making books on crap games."

Pictures of Sweeney were obtained and presented to the eyewitnesses, who positively identified Sweeney as a member of the gang. Sweeney was extradited from New York and put on trial for the crime by Prosecutor Abe J. David in the Court of Oyer and Terminer of Union County before Supreme Court Justice Samuel Kalisch on April 11, 1927, about six months after the holdup. Sweeney was defended by Col. George T. Vickers of Jersey City.

At the trial, one of the chief witnesses for the prosecution was Thomas Devoy, who testified that five minutes before the holdup took place, he passed the intersection and saw Sweeney standing on one corner. Devoy said that he drove by and, after circling around the block, again passed the fatal intersection and saw Sweeney walk out with a gun in his hand, act as cover man while the rest of the gang were getting into the cars, and jump into one of the cars as they dashed away.

The other chief witness for the state was Samuel Traubman, who passed the scene of the crime in an automobile. He had identified Sweeney both from pictures and in person before the trial, and at the trial he testified that just before the holdup he saw Sweeney standing at the intersection with his hand under his coat in a suspicious manner.

In his defense Sweeney attempted to establish an alibi. He testified that on the morning of the crime he left his home at 1813 Cauldon Street in the Bronx Borough of New York City at 9:00 a.m., and that at 10:00 a.m., by prearrangement, he met a woman named Jean Harrigan and a man named Ray Mulcahey at the entrance to the Dyckman Street subway station. The three then drove to Sing Sing, where Jean Harrigan wanted to visit her husband, Charles Harrigan, alias John McCarthy. Sweeney signed his visitor's slip with the name Michael Branley. The party waited half an hour, and then spent one hour visiting with Charles Harrigan, leaving at 1:00 p.m. [261]

It developed at the trial that Sweeney was a former convict and had served time in Sing Sing. He had been twice convicted of crimes, once for attempted grand larceny. As an ex-convict Sweeney could not have visited Sing Sing under his own name and for that reason he signed the visitor's slip with the name Michael Branley, which was the name of Jean Harrigan's brother. Sweeney's testimony as to his trip to Sing Sing was supported by the testimony of his mother, Anna Sweeney, and by that of Jean Harrigan and Charles Harrigan.

The prosecution was familiar with Sweeney's alibi, as he had presented it in opposition to the extradition proceedings, and took steps to overcome it. This was done by having several citizens of Elizabeth drive in their own cars from the scene of the crime to Sing Sing, keeping exact record of the time required for the trip. These facts were used at the trial to prove that Sweeney could have participated in the holdup and afterward have driven to Sing Sing and arrived at the time alleged by him.

Justice Kalisch, in his charge to the jury, said that he doubted Devoy's story. Nevertheless, Sweeney was convicted and sentenced to life imprisonment.

• • • •

DEFENSE attorney Vickers was positive of Sweeney's innocence and he, as well as others connected with the case, continued to search for additional evidence that would have a bearing on the question of Sweeney's connection with the crime.

By his investigation, Colonel Vickers established that John Yates, a bus driver, heard the shooting as he was stopping his bus to discharge a passenger a block away from the scene of the holdup. Immediately thereafter two big, dark, closed cars, followed by a Ford delivery truck, drove by, traveling at about forty miles an hour. He left his bus and ran to the scene of the holdup, where he saw a policeman lying face down on the street, a motorcycle near him. He also noticed a machine gun lying on the sidewalk at the corner. By this time a crowd was gathering, but it was necessary for Yates to return to his bus and drive tor the end of [262] his route. Arriving there, he entered a lunch wagon and related what he had seen of the holdup to a crowd of men gathered there, including Thomas Devoy. Immediately after hearing Yates tell his story, Devoy got into his Ford and, with Barney Shapiro, drove around to the scene of the crime. It turned out that Devoy had been at the lunch wagon from 7:00 a.m. until after he heard Yates tell about the holdup. These facts were established by the affidavits of Yates and other men who were with Devoy in the lunch wagon and clearly proved that the testimony of Devoy at the trial was false.

Additional facts exonerating Sweeney came to light with the arrest of Frank Kiekart on December 8, 1927, and the rearrest of Benjamin Haas on January 23, 1928. Both of these men confessed, turned state's witnesses, and definitely established the identity of the gang, clearing Sweeney of any connection whatever with the holdup. The actual bandits were James Cuniffe (murdered in Detroit), William Crowley (killed while resisting arrest in Detroit), Frank Kiekart, alias Charles Miller (who confessed), William Fanning, Charles Neary, Daniel Grosso (electrocuted April 10, 1931), and Benjamin Haas (who confessed). There were only seven in the group.

• • • •

WHEN these facts were discovered, those working on the case were impressed by the strong resemblance between James Sweeney and James Cuniffe, who actually participated in the holdup. This resemblance became perfectly apparent from a comparison of photographs of the two men and accounts for the honest though mistaken identification by the witness Traubman.

On the basis of this new evidence, an application was made to the State Board of Pardons on Sweeney's behalf. The application was supported personally by Justice Kalisch and Prosecutor David. Sweeney was set free in November, 1928.

• • • •

THIS error came about through a combination of mistaken identity, circumstantial evidence, and perjury. The fact [263] that Sweeney's card was found on Haas first entangled Sweeney in the case. The facts that he was an ex-convict, that the audacity of the crime had aroused the country, and that he was identified by two people were sufficient in the minds of the jury to overcome his truthful alibi. The mystery was unraveled by the discovery of Devoy's perjury and by the confessions of some of the real bandits. In this respect it is not unlike many cases of cooperative crime, when a single man to whom the finger of suspicion points is exonerated by the confessions of the real participants, all of whom are accounted for. Confessions of that kind can usually be verified and are likely to be reliable. The prosecuting officials and the judge in the Sweeney case, when they realized the error of Sweeney's conviction, took immediate steps to undo the wrong and free Sweeney, one and one-half years after his commitment to the penitentiary. But for the assiduity of his counsel, it is not at all certain that Sweeney might not have served out his life sentence.

• • • •

Acknowledgments: Hon. Abe J. David, Prosecutor of the Pleas, Union County, N.J.; Col. George T. Vickers, Jersey City, N.J. [264]

THE "SYDNEY MEN"

Thomas Berdue

BY the Omnibus Bill of 1850, California was admitted into the Union as a state. Society in this newly organized state was composed of persons coming from all quarters of the globe, drawn there by the gold fever. Many were lawless adventurers who gave no end of trouble to the law-abiding citizens, partly due to the inadequacy of law-enforcement machinery. Among these elements were some escaped convicts from the penal colony in Australia, and they came to be feared as the "Sydney men." In the boom town of San Francisco, the "Sydney men" were the scourge of the city, committing murders and robberies with apparent impunity. Public opinion became enraged at the uninterrupted wave of crime. It broke beyond bounds in February, 1851, when Mr. C. J. Jansen was attacked in his store on the night of the nineteenth, was mercilessly beaten, and was robbed of approximately $2,000.

Mr. Jansen was the senior partner in the much respected firm of C. J. Jansen & Company, dry-goods merchants. As was the custom of many merchants, Mr. Jansen on the evening in question was working upon his books. He was alone in the store and was seated at his desk working by the light of a candle, the sole light in the large room. At about eight o'clock, a bewhiskered man, wearing a gray coat and broad- brimmed hat, entered the store and started looking at various piles of merchandise. He then called Mr. Jansen and said that he desired to purchase some blankets. While these were being shown, another man entered and also desired to see blankets. This man was taller than the first, wore a hat pointed at the crown, and was wrapped up in a coat. As Mr. Jansen was bending over some blankets, one man cried, "Now," whereupon the other struck the merchant, sending him sprawling, and then beat him nearly to death. Thereupon, the desk was opened and the money stolen.

Jansen soon recovered sufficiently to crawl to the door and give the alarm. Theodore Payne, a storekeeper across the street, rushed to the victim's assistance. The authorities were [265] notified and an immediate search instituted. The description given by Jansen of the tall robber corresponded with that of one of the most notorious of the "Sydney men," James Stuart, who had a striking record for knavery throughout the California mining area. He was one of those heroic desperados who delighted in his crimes and in thwarting the law. He was already wanted by the authorities for many crimes, among them being the cold-blooded murder of Charles Moore, near Foster Bar in Yuba County. The attack upon Jansen intensified the search for Stuart.

Within twenty-four hours, the police arrested a suspect, and he was immediately charged with the crime. Another Australian, Robert Windred, was apprehended as the accomplice. Both men denied having had anything to do with the attack on Jansen; and the first man arrested swore that he was Thomas Berdue, an innocent British subject, and that he was not the notorious James Stuart. This was a common trick among the "Sydney men" and he was not believed. Both men were taken before Jansen, who was wavering between life and death, and he identified Berdue as his principal assailant.

When the people heard that James Stuart was in custody, excitement ran high. The legal machinery had slipped so often and had so frequently permitted the criminals to escape, as had Stuart on previous occasions, that there arose a spontaneous insistence that Stuart must not escape punishment.

While the men were being conducted under heavy police guard from Jansen's residence back to the police station, a large crowd of men tried to seize the prisoners to hang them at once, but the attempt failed. On Saturday, February 21, the men were arraigned before Justice Shepherd for examination. They attempted to establish alibis. The crowd outside the courthouse, now numbering nearly seven thousand people, was almost frantic at the further delay and again attempted to seize the prisoners, but the sheriff, assisted by the Washington Guards, saved them. A meeting was then organized which appointed a citizens' committee to stay at the jail to make sure that the prisoners did not [266] escape. Adjournment was then voted until ten o'clock the following day, Sunday. The crowd quietly dispersed.

On the following morning a throng of eight to ten thousand persons congregated. The complete lack of confidence in the courts was manifest. The crowd was determined to see the prisoners punished. Mob violence was feared. Mr. William T. Coleman addressed the throng and suggested the organization of a popular court of citizens to try the prisoners at once before they could escape. This was heartily and boisterously approved. Judge, jury, and counsel were selected and the trial held during the afternoon and evening in the recorder's room of the City Hall—but in the absence of the prisoners. Testimony was heard on both sides. The jury stood nine to three for conviction and reported a disagreement. The three dissenting jurors had doubts as to the prisoners' identities. The congregated people were disposed to lynch the accused just the same, and several attempts to seize them were made, but wiser counsel prevailed and the prisoners were safely secreted and detained for action by the regular courts. On several occasions within a few days, the two accused men had been within a hairbreadth of popular execution. There was no doubt as to their guilt in the popular mind. Windred later escaped.

The man who claimed to be Thomas Berdue was regularly indicted under the name of James Stuart for an assault with intent to kill Mr. Jansen. He was brought to trial on March 14 in the District Court before Judge Parsons. The District Attorney, G. K. Platt, and C. M. Brosman appeared for the prosecution. The prisoner was defended by Messrs. Calhoun Benham and Hall McAllister. The principal witness for the state was Mr. Jansen, who positively identified the prisoner as his assailant. An attempt was made to establish an alibi, but it was not conclusively established. According to the defense witnesses, the prisoner left a group of friends to go to bed at just about eight o'clock on the fatal evening. Eight o'clock was the time of the assault. The jury returned a verdict of guilty, and the prisoner was sentenced to fourteen years' imprisonment in the state prison. The large amount of money which had been found upon the accused when arrested was delivered to Mr. Jansen. [267]

The convicted prisoner was not imprisoned under this sentence, for he was immediately sent to Marysville, in Yuba County, to stand trial in the District Court for the murder of Moore. This trial was held from June 28 to July 4, 1851. There was no question but that the notorious James Stuart had committed this murder. This was not contested by the defendant. The sole issue was whether or not the defendant was James Stuart as contended by the state, or was an entirely distinct and innocent person, Thomas Berdue, as he claimed to be. An interesting account of the testimony as related by one of the attorneys appearing in the case is quoted by Mr. Bancroft in his history of popular tribunals:

> "Witnesses for the prosecution were generally bold and entirely positive; but the witnesses for the prisoner, with the exception of Judge Stidger and B. F. Washington, appeared to feel uneasy, and often hesitated in their testimony. Some three or four witnesses testified that they had worked with Jim Stuart at Foster Bar, and had known him well before he went there. They had eaten with him at the same table often, and had played cards with him; and one or two testified they had slept with him. They testified that Jim Stuart was of the same height as the prisoner; that he had curly hair, like him; that he was slightly bald on the top of the head, like him that his actions were like his the court having made the prisoner stand up several times so that the witnesses could see him better than when sitting; that his voice and accent were the same, being English; that the color of the eyes and hair were the same; and that Jim Stuart had a stiff middle finger on the right hand, and a ring of Indian-ink round one of his fingers, and marks of Indian-ink between each thumb and forefinger; and further, that Jim Stuart had a rather long scar on his right cheek. The jury then examined the hands of the prisoner, and there was found a ring of Indian-ink on one of his fingers, several figures or spots of the same ink between the thumb and forefinger of

each hand; and the right middle finger was not stiff, but had had a felon under the nail of the corresponding finger on the other hand, which had given it a short but stubby appearance, heavier at the end than elsewhere, the nail of the finger being broad and thick, and bending inward over the end of the finger. This was startling to the defence, indeed. It remained now to see if the prisoner had a scar on the right side of the face. His face could not be satisfactorily examined, as it was almost completely covered with a short growth of hair. The court ordered the prisoner to be shaved before being brought into court next morning, and on being examined a scar about the length of the one described by the witnesses was found, commencing on the edge of the jaw on the right side and running down the neck. The witnesses [268] now seemed confident, and said that they had no doubt that the prisoner was Jim Stuart. On a cross-examination they said, in a positive and unhesitating manner, that it was not possible that they could be mistaken in their opinion that the prisoner was Jim Stuart. Colonel Prentiss swore positively that the prisoner was Jim Stuart, and that he could not possibly be mistaken. Some four or five witnesses swore positively as to the identity of the prisoner, and that he was Jim Stuart beyond a question; each giving some one or more new reasons for his belief. No witness on the side of the prosecution would admit a probability that he could be mistaken in the prisoner; that he certainly was Jim Stuart! On the side of the defence, Judge Stidger swore positively that the prisoner at the bar was not Jim Stuart; that there was a strong resemblance between Jim Stuart and this man, but that Jim Stuart was at least two inches taller than the prisoner; that their eyes were different in color; that the expression of the eyes of the two men was different; that Jim Stuart was much quicker in his motions than the prisoner; that Jim Stuart's motions were very uncommon, being as quick as those of a wildcat; that he had always head erect, much more so than the prisoner, and that the real Jim Stuart was straighter in his personal formation, and had a different complexion. This witness testified that Jim Stuart was often arraigned before him as a judge at Foster Bar, and that his recollection of him from this and other facts was clear and distinct. Stidger also testified that Jim Stuart had a stiff middle finger, but not such a one as the prisoner had. B.F. Washington, who was at the time recorder of Sacramento City, testified that he knew Jim Stuart from the fact of his being a notorious character in that city, and from the fact that he had often been brought before him on different charges. Mr. Washington said that the prisoner at the bar was not Jim Stuart; that there was some resemblance, but they were to his eye quite different men; that Jim Stuart was an inch and a half

> or two inches taller than the prisoner. Other witnesses for the defence testified to about the same facts, but they seemed to be uneasy, in some trepidation, and acted in a manner most provoking to the defence. One witness on behalf of the prosecution, a Mr. Thompson, testified that the prisoner, about the date of the alleged murder, came into a camp on Slate Range, in said county of Yuba, on horseback, and seemed to have plenty of money, and was betting with the boys on a string game which he played very skilfully. That he had a conversation with the prisoner in the jail, and that the prisoner admitted that he was at Slate Range at the time mentioned, but denied that he was Jim Stuart."

After deliberating approximately two days, the jury, on July 4, 1851, returned a verdict of guilty. The prisoner was sentenced to be hanged. Resigned to his fate, after attempting to prove throughout the popular trial and the two [269] regular trials that he was not James Stuart, his money exhausted, and deserted by his friends, the prisoner prepared for the end by communicating his wretched fate to his family. All the while he protested his innocence.

• • • •

THE popular discontent with the enforcement of law in San Francisco led, early in June, 1851, to the organization by local business men of a Vigilance Committee. They often took the law into their own hands and proceeded forthwith to try persons and execute those who it was thought merited such punishment. The executions were public and notorious, and were generally supported by public opinion and the press.

On July 1, 1851, a shack in the outskirts of the city had been robbed. A party of men were beating the brush in search of the thief. Unexpectedly they came upon a neatly dressed man who could give no proper account of himself. Although it did not appear that he had robbed the house, he aroused the searchers' suspicions and was taken to the rooms of the Vigilance Committee. The man gave his name as William Stevens and made an excellent impression upon the Committee by his pleasing personality and apparent frankness. They proposed to release him, when one of the citizens on guard duty recognized the prisoner as the much dreaded outlaw, James Stuart. Great was the delight of the Committee. Within a month of the creation of their organization, fortune had placed within their grasp one of the worst desperados of California. Elation did not, however, completely overshadow the recollection of the man who claimed to be Thomas Berdue, who had been convicted as Stuart in San Francisco, and who had been sent to Marysville to be tried for one of Stuart's murders. Letters were at once dispatched to Marysville with the news of the capture of the real Stuart and with the request that the outstanding identification witnesses be sent to San Francisco. The Marysville people were skeptical, but the witnesses were sent as requested. A number of people were found near by who had known James Stuart and they now identified him without any hesitation. Mr. Jansen became convinced of his mistake in identification, [270] though the resemblance between Berdue and Stuart was said to be close. On July 8, 1851, four days after Berdue had been sentenced to death, Stuart signed a written confession of his many crimes, including the assault upon Mr. Jansen. The Vigilance Committee successfully evaded several writs of habeas corpus which were issued to force the delivery of Stuart to the regular authorities, and on July 11, 1851, he was publicly executed in the presence of five hundred members of the Vigilance Committee and thousands of residents. This was done with the approval of public opinion and of the leading newspapers.

Upon full proof that James Stuart, the person executed on July 11, was the true perpetrator of the crimes for which Thomas Berdue had been convicted in the District Courts of San Francisco and Yuba County, Gov. John McDougal pardoned Berdue. The members of the San Francisco Vigilance Committee, learning that the poor fellow was penniless, collected for him a fund which amounted to $302. The money which had been taken from him and given to Mr. Jansen at the time of his arrest, over $1,700, and some gold dust, was returned by Mr. Jansen, with a liberal gift in addition.

On January 21, 1853, Senator Kurtz of San Diego presented to the Senate of California the petition of Thomas Berdue for reimbursement of the $4,000 which it was said he had expended in his fight to prove his innocence. The petition was referred to the Committee on the Judiciary, of which Senator J. W. Ralston was the chairman. The Committee recommended that the petition be refused for the following reasons:

> To grant the prayer of the petitioner, would establish a precedent which, if carried out in all cases of the kind, would more than exhaust the entire revenue of the State. We know of no legislative precedent for such appropriation. The most that has been done, was to refund fines illegally collected from innocent parties, leaving them responsible for their own expenses.

In society it too often happens that the innocent are wrongfully accused of crime. This is their misfortune, and Government has no power to relieve them. It is a part of the price each individual may be called on to pay for the protection which the laws give. He [271] should rejoice that the laws have afforded that protection to him when wrongfully accused, rather than seek remuneration for his expenses from the government whose justice has protected him from ignominious death.

H. H. Bancroft, the historian, comments as follows on this reasoning:

That is to say, stripped of verbiage, to correct the errors of law would cost more than all the expenses of government combined. We have never known a legislature to right a wrong done by the law to a citizen, therefore we will not. Prosecution may be the price of protection; and fortunate is he who is not done to death by laws established to save his life.

• • • •

THE mistaken identity in this case almost resulted, as in the Purvis case (p. 206), in an execution of the wrong man. In three separate trials Berdue was convicted of crimes committed by Stuart. That the popular excitement and demand for revenge, aroused by the frustration of justice on so many occasions, was largely responsible for Berdue's convictions is highly probable. It is not an unusual operative element in similar miscarriages of justice. That Berdue came very close to destruction by mob violence is apparent. That the victim of the crime identified Berdue, naturally operated most strongly against him, and his perfectly sound and truthful alibi was disbelieved. The legislative committee's reason for refusing to reimburse Berdue's expenses is an antiquated one and is destitute of foundation, yet it is on occasion heard now. The Vigilance Committee and Mr. Jansen did what they could to restore the money that was taken from Berdue, but his real injury remained irreparable. His public vindication, which is often denied to less fortunate but equally deserving victims of similar error, lay in the fact that the real culprit proved to be so notorious a criminal as Stuart and in the fact that the case became a landmark in the early history of California as a state. An advance in the conception of public obligation in such matters has taken place, as is manifest in the California law of 1913, which would, had it been in force in 1851, have afforded Berdue a natural opportunity for indemnity and vindication. [272]

BABY RUTH CONFESSES

Lonzo Thornton

LOUIE PARKALAB was walking down one of the less frequented streets of Middletown, Butler County, Ohio, on October 6, 1926, when he was suddenly confronted by two husky young negroes. They demanded that he turn over his money. Parkalab, a recent arrival in the United States from one of the countries of central Europe, was not entirely familiar with this procedure, and started arguing with the colored men about not having any money. Parkalab's remonstrance was stopped almost at once by a blow from one of the men, which dazed him; and before anyone could hurry to the scene of the assault, Parkalab had been relieved of twenty dollars and an insurance policy, which he was carrying with him for safety. When assistance arrived, Parkalab excitedly directed his rescuers by motions, and in his native language, toward two fleeing figures disappearing into the darkness.

A nearby policeman soon received the alarm and, sighting a running figure in the shadows of some buildings, started in pursuit. After many duckings and turnings, threading in and out of dark alleys and vacant lots, the policeman finally caught a negro, and arrested him. The arrested man said that he "hadn't done nothing," but he was told to tell that to the judge. Louie Parkalab definitely identified the suspect as one of the men who had taken his money, whereupon the suspect was placed in the local jail. It turned out that he was a negro well known in the community as "Ivory," his full name, according to official records, being James Ivory. There was no doubt but that he was one of the assailants. All trace of the other negro was lost, but the police were on the lookout for any suspicious characters.

The following morning the jail tender was greatly surprised when a strange negro appeared at the jail and asked, very meekly, to see Ivory. When asked why he wanted to see him, he said that he was after his overcoat, which Ivory had borrowed. In reply to other questions, he said that he had been in Middletown only a few months, and that he had met [273]

Ivory soon after arriving in town. He admitted that he had seen Ivory on the evening before, and that it was then that he had lent his overcoat. When he learned that Ivory was in jail, he came to get the coat back.

The jail attendant told the visitor to wait a few minutes and he would see what could be done for him.

Hurried calls were sent out to the detectives and other officers to come to the jail. When they arrived, new questions were put to this stranger who admitted knowing Ivory. He said that his name was Lonzo Thornton; that, although he was born in Albany, Georgia, he had lived for the past thirteen years in St. Petersburg, Florida; and that he had but recently come to Middletown to be with some of his family. He was questioned closely regarding his whereabouts on the previous evening, and he stated that he had spent most of it with his family at their home at 813 Seventeenth Avenue. When he was accused by detectives of having robbed Louie Parkalab, Thornton was dumbfounded. He denied that he had stolen anything that he had done anything wrong. He was asked how it was that James Ivory, who had committed the robbery with another, had his overcoat. Somewhat confused, Thornton repeated that he had seen Ivory early in the evening and that, as he himself was going home and Ivory was "stepping out," he had loaned the overcoat to him.

The detectives were unconvinced by this story and decided to hold Thornton for further examination. Louie Parkalab was called and, out of a group of suspects, picked Thornton as the one who had helped Ivory attack him. With that, Thornton's fate was sealed. He was bound over with Ivory for investigation by the Grand Jury. On January 13, 1927, they were indicted, and were brought up for joint trial the following month before Judge Clarence Murphy of the Butler County Circuit Court. John P. Rogers prosecuted the case on behalf of the state, presenting the testimony of Louie Parkalab. It was necessary to have a court interpreter in taking his testimony. The identification of both defendants, which was again made in the court room, was positive. Thornton's attorney, Charles F. Higgins, produced five [274] witnesses (Marion Merchant, Mary Morris, James Ware, Boston Brown, and Sam Emery all colored) who corroborated the testimony of Thornton that he was at home at the time of the robbery. In view of the reputations of some of these alibi witnesses, notably Boston Brown, Thornton's position with the jury was not helped. The jury required but a little time to return a verdict of guilty against both men. On February 15, 1927, they were sentenced to the Ohio penitentiary on sentences calling for ten- to twenty-five-year terms. The next day, they were entered at the penitentiary at Columbus under the wardenship of Mr. Thomas.

Like many persons who enter the penitentiary, Thornton sullenly asserted his innocence whenever opportunity presented itself. He was just twenty-three years old, and getting started in life when he was "sent up."

• • • •

IN January, 1928, one Simon Williams, alias Baby Ruth Williams, was arrested on other charges and confessed that he was the one who had helped James Ivory hold up the foreigner in Middletown in October, 1926. Confessions of this kind are always examined very critically by the authorities, for experience has proved that many of them are spurious. Williams' confession, however, was corroborated by collateral evidence on so many points, and the resemblance between Williams and Thornton was so striking, that it convinced the officers. Upon a reexamination of all the evidence, it was concluded that Thornton was really innocent of any connection with the crime. The Ohio Board of Clemency recommended that a pardon be granted to Thornton, and this was done by the Governor of Ohio on February 6, 1928. Williams was charged with the crime and convicted.

• • • •

THORNTON was the victim of unfortunate circumstances. His acquaintance with Ivory, his loan of a coat, the call at the jail at the moment when detectives were looking for Ivory's associate, Parkalab's identification of Thornton, Thornton's resemblance to Williams, the poor character of some of the witnesses who supported Thornton's alibi, the [275] fact that he was tried jointly with Ivory, who was manifestly guilty these constituted a combination of circumstances too strong to be overcome by the simple truth. The jury preferred to believe Parkalab, upon whose identification alone the prosecution had to rely, rather than the five witnesses who supported Thornton's alibi. But for the confession of Williams, which was so amply fortified as to convince the Ohio police officials and the Board of Clemency of the error committed, Thornton might yet be in the Ohio State Penitentiary at Columbus, assuming that he would have been among those who escaped the fate of the three hundred convicts who were trapped in their cells and burned to death in the fire which destroyed the penitentiary in April, 1930.

• • • •

Acknowledgments: Mr. John P. Rogers, Hamilton, Ohio; Mr. Vivian O. Robertson, Columbus, Ohio. [276]

SHERIFF ON THE STAND

Thorvik and Hughes

ON the morning of July 23, 1921, the Farmers State Bank of Almelund, Minnesota, was held up. Five strangers had been seen driving through Almelund in a green Nash touring car. Soon two of them came walking back through town, followed by two more. These four all dressed in dark suits a and straw hats entered the bank. A few minutes afterward, the green touring car pulled up in front of the bank, and the four men ran out. The car dashed off and all escaped. Money and securities had been stolen.

A posse was organized and groups stationed on various roads, especially at the Interstate Bridge between St. Croix Falls, Wisconsin, and Taylors Falls, Minnesota. The robbers got through the posse, however, and disappeared. Rewards were posted for the apprehension and conviction of the criminals.

In October, 1921, one George Hughes was arrested in St. Paul for having a stolen automobile in his possession. The authorities were on the lookout for men answering the description of the Almelund robbers. Hughes attracted their attention. The cashier, Lindquist, and customers, witnesses of the robbery, were called to St. Paul, where they identified Hughes. He was placed on trial the same month in the District Court at Center City before Judge J. N. Searle. Because of a prior criminal record, Hughes preferred not to take the witness stand in his own defense. He was convicted and sentenced to life imprisonment at the Stillwater penitentiary.

In May, 1922, Deputy Sheriff M. L. Hammerstrom appeared before the Chisago County Grand Jury and testified that one Louis Thorvik of St. Paul had confessed to him that he had taken part in the holdup. The Grand Jury thereupon returned an indictment against Thorvik. Thorvik, an uneducated hodcarrier with a Scandinavian accent, heard that he was wanted at the police station upon some charge and went there to find out about it. He was promptly arrested. Witnesses from Almelund went to St. Paul and [277] identified him as one of the robbers. He was taken to Center City and placed on trial before Judge Searle in July, 1922.

At the trial Thorvik was identified by Cashier Lindquist and a bank customer, Bloomquist. Another customer, Carl Wiberg, did not testify for either side. Thorvik was likewise identified by several townspeople who said they had seen the men as they walked through town. The principal remaining testimony against Thorvik was that of the deputy sheriff, Hammerstrom. According to his testimony, Hammerstrom, who had been an itinerant laborer, was made a deputy sheriff of Chisago County in September, 1921, shortly after the holdup of the bank. He said that he had been given Thorvik's name by Hughes when the latter was being taken to the penitentiary after his conviction. He had thereupon gone to St. Paul and frequented the lunchroom and drinking establishment where Thorvik occasionally stopped. There he said he got acquainted with Thorvik, who boasted of the part he had taken in the robbery, related where the gang later went, and stated that the loot had been hidden under a wire screen in a small swamp near the railroad water tank at Bald Eagle. A party went to Bald Eagle in search of the loot, but found nothing save some loose sod. This was ten months after the robbery.

Thorvik in his own defense related his life history from his birth in Norway through his coming to St. Paul, his serving in the army, and his return to civilian life as hodcarrier for the contracting plasterers Nolles & Sapletal. He denied having had anything to do with the Almelund robbery, knowing anything about it, ever having seen Deputy Sheriff Hammerstrom before he was in jail, ever having made any statement in regard to the robbery, or ever having been in Almelund. He testified that on the day of the robbery, July 23, 1921, he was at work for his employers on a house being built for Mr. Strange on Randolph Street in St. Paul, evidence which was corroborated by his employers and others; and that he knew he hadn't left St. Paul that day because it was the birthday of his landlady, Mrs. Martha Johnson, and he joined in the birthday celebration that afternoon [278] with the family. In that he was corroborated by the whole group present.

In rebuttal the state had nothing to contradict the birthday-party testimony. As to the work on the morning of July 23, Mr. Strange was called, and he testified from his private records that the plastering work on his house was done on August 19, 20, 25, 26 and September 1. Furthermore, the state produced one Anderson, who testified to having heard Thorvik's confession to Hammerstrom. This, Thorvik absolutely denied.

The case was submitted to the jury, which returned a verdict of guilty; and Thorvik entered upon his life sentence at Stillwater on August 2, 1922. He doggedly maintained his innocence. He had neither money nor influential friends, however, and could not take an appeal. The very first week he was in Stillwater, Thorvik discovered Hughes, who had been convicted of the same crime, and had also consistently denied his participation in it. Neither had ever seen the other, both stated. For several years no further persons were convicted as participants in the Almelund crime, and Thorvik and Hughes were forgotten.

• • • •

IN the year 1925 a man named James E. Laughlin, also known as Red Stanton, was brought back to Minnesota from North Dakota, where he had been in prison, to stand trial for the robbery of the bank of Almelund, and he was identified by witnesses as the driver of the car used by the bandits. He offered to plead guilty to robbery in the first degree, but the authorities would not agree to it. He went to trial and was convicted and sentenced to life imprisonment in the Minnesota State Prison at Stillwater.

The night Laughlin was sentenced, he told the authorities at Center City that the two men, Hughes and Thorvik, who were serving life sentences for the robbery, had not participated in it. After being taken down to the penitentiary he asked to be taken before the county attorney of Chisago County and Mr. Charles Brown, hea4 of the Minnesota Bankers Protective Association. In a detailed sworn [279] statement, he gave all the particulars of the crime, admitting his connection with it and disclosing that the four other men who were with him were known as Shine Allen, J. B. White, Curley Wheeler, and Bill Bailey. He also told the full story about the bandits' adventures following their escape. It is not known what was done with this confession when it was made.

Early in 1926 Thorvik succeeded in enlisting the help of Mr. M. F. Kinkead, who later became county attorney of Ramsey County. For five years Mr. Kinkead worked upon the case and uncovered convincing evidence which corroborated all the important details of Laughlin's confession. The full narrative of Mr. Kinkead's activities would make a romantic story, were there space to recount it. Each of the men named by Laughlin was accounted for. White was in prison in Walla Walla, Allen in Waupun, Wisconsin. White made a complete confession. Wheeler had been killed in 1922, but his widow helped by showing that Hughes had been mistaken for Wheeler. Only Bailey could not be traced, after an arrest and release in Iowa. Several witnesses testified to the hotels the guilty five had stopped at, the route taken, the place where the loot was divided, and incidental robberies committed on the way to and from Almelund. The witnesses were taken to Stillwater, and all maintained that Thorvik and Hughes were not among the culprits. Unquestionable evidence was found establishing the truth of Thorvik's alibi that he had been working in St. Paul at the time of the robbery, but that he had been mistaken in his testimony as to the house upon which he had worked that day, it being, in fact, a house at 75 Douglas Street. A study of the trial testimony identifying Thorvik as one of the gang brought out clearly that prior to Thorvik's arrest, the bandit who guarded the bank door, supposed to be Thorvik, had been described as tall and dark, whereas Thorvik was clearly of average height and a blond. It was proved beyond question that on July 23, 1921, the day of the robbery, Hughes had registered at the Rogers Hotel, Des Moines, Iowa, six hundred miles from Almelund. All of this evidence was submitted to the Minnesota Board of Pardons, a distinct point being [280] made of the fact that Deputy Sheriff Hammerstrom and the witness Anderson had manufactured the tale concerning Thorvik's alleged confession and all the other incidents supposedly connected therewith.

In July, 1931, after the third hearing on the cases by the Board, pardons were granted to both Thorvik and Hughes on the ground of innocence. Hughes had served approximately ten years, and Thorvik, about nine.

• • • •

THIS is not an unusual case of mistaken identity by the victims of a crime. As already observed in many cases, such evidence is most unreliable. Fortunately for Thorvik and Hughes, Laughlin confessed the entire details and named his confederates. One cannot but admire the efforts of Mr. Kinkead in verifying that confession. But for Laughlin's temporary sojourn of four years in a North Dakota prison, he might have been instrumental in having Thorvik and Hughes released some years earlier. The truth of Laughlin's confession induced a reexamination of Thorvik's alibi, which, though mistaken as to the identity of the house on which he worked, was accurate in .every other respect. Thorvik seems to have had an unfortunate facial resemblance to one of the bandits, but no other physical resemblance at all, so that his identification by the cashier and a customer would be strange were such mistakes not so common. Hughes injured his cause by failing to take the stand; he also bore some resemblance to one of the bandits. According to Mr. Kinkead, Deputy Sheriff Hammerstrom committed rank perjury.

• • • •

Acknowledgments: Hon. M. F. Kinkead, Ramsey County attorney, St. Paul, Minn.; Hon. Wm. H. Lamson, Secretary, Minnesota State Board of Pardons, Minneapolis. [281]

A Polinky Tragedy

Andrew Toth

IN 1885, Andrew Toth, aged thirty-six, came from his home in a small Hungarian village to make his fortune in this land of liberty and promise. He went to Braddock, Pennsylvania, along with many of his countrymen, to work in the Carnegie steel mills. He was a pious man, of cheerful disposition and considerable intelligence, but he found difficulty in learning to speak English. In Hungary, he had left a wife and daughter, both of whom he expected to bring over after he had saved sufficient money; but his four sons came to the United States with him.

In the fall of 1890, there was a great deal of unrest among the laborers of the industrial and mining regions of western Pennsylvania. Large numbers of aliens who were working in steel mills twelve and thirteen hours a day, seven days a week, for very low wages, desired to better their working conditions and were experimenting with the strike as a method of obtaining their demands.

This was the spirit prevailing among the numerous Hungarian workmen in Braddock on New Year's Eve, 1890. The Hungarians celebrated the coming of the New Year with quantities of polinky, a favorite Hungarian beverage. A considerable number were already on strike. As New Year's Day dawned, the Hungarian celebration continued, and it was not long before many of the men were in impassioned moods. They were especially angry because their mill, The Edgar Thompson Steel Works, was operating on New Year's, although it was a holiday, and because a large number of men were working willingly. The indignation around Dugan's Hollow, where most of the Hungarians lived, was seething.

At about two o'clock that afternoon, the working force at the furnaces of the Works was surprised by the sudden assault of a mob of two hundred infuriated Hungarians, armed with clubs, ax handles, shovels, and the like. There were about four hundred men at work, many of them Irish, some Hungarian, and some of other nationalities; but they [282] were scattered about the yard, and were so taken by surprise that many of them were badly beaten before the mob could be stopped. There was fierce, savage fighting for a short time. The working men gradually closed their ranks, and, reinforced from other parts of the plant, soon drove the rioting Hungarians out of the yard on the run. These drifted back to Dugan's Hollow in small groups.

Quite a number of workmen were injured in the pitched battle. Patrick Nyland, the yard boss, was caught between the two fighting crowds and was mercilessly beaten about the head and shoulders. He was taken from the yard on a stretcher, and placed in a quiet place, and forgotten. A couple of hours later he was discovered, where he had been left, unconscious. The physicians despaired of his life. Michael Quinn, a furnace boss, was brutally beaten, and it was necessary to take him to the Mercy Hospital, where he told about his experience. He said:

> I was at work at my furnace when these Hungarians rushed into the mill like a lot of wild animals. Everything had been reasonably quiet all the forenoon, and we were not expecting their visit. I tried to defend myself but it was no use. Four of the Hungarians knocked me down and beat me with clubs. One of them had a shovel with which he struck me three times on the head and twice on the side. They all acted like a lot of brutes. There was no occasion for the trouble except that the Hungarians thought they could force us to support their strike.

The county sheriff arrived in Braddock. Feeling was running high against the Hungarians. He deputized two hundred men, and immediately started making arrests of the leaders of the riot, upon warrants sworn out by Charles M. Schwab, manager of the plant.

In several days fifty-four men had been arrested, and the county officers started their investigations. One paper reported:

> The work of arresting the rioters is still going on with persistent regularity. The apparent object of it is to thoroughly terrorize the semicivilized Slavs about Braddock, and to impress them distinctly with the fact that we have both law and government in America.

When Michael Quinn died five days later as the result of [283] a fractured skull and a broken rib driven into his lung, public opinion became enraged. On January 7, 1891, the *Pittsburgh Press*, in an editorial on the responsibility for Quinn's death, said:

> Had the Hungarian laborers not raised the disturbance Quinn would most likely be alive today. This surely establishes the responsibility for his death, no matter who may have been the individual that struck the fatal blow.

Who had beaten Michael Quinn? The officers discovered several witnesses who said that they had seen it happen. They were given the opportunity to examine the arrested Hungarians as they were marched through a room for identification. Peter Mullen indicated Andy Toth, calling him Steve Toth, and stated that Toth was the man he had seen hitting Quinn over the head with a shovel at Furnace C. Mullen said that Toth had tried to strike him also, but that he had escaped. Two other men said that they had seen Michael Sabol and George Rusnok attack Quinn at Furnace A, Sabol beating him to the ground with a shovel, while Rusnok held him down. Other witnesses were found who said they had seen these three men with shovels or clubs among the rioting Hungarians. The three Hungarians were indicted without delay, and brought to trial in the Court of Oyer and Terminer of Allegheny County before Judge Edwin H. Stowe on February 4, 1891.

The evidence, with a great deal concerning the riot, was submitted to the jury by the District Attorney, D. A. Johnston. Through the testimony of the defendants and other Hungarians, Colonel Blakely and H. L. Goehring, the counsel for the defendants, endeavored to establish an alibi for each of the defendants, especially for Rusnok, who denied being at the works at all on New Year's Day. This left an issue for the jury as to whose testimony was to be believed. A strong plea was made on behalf of the defendants that they should not be made the victims of race prejudice. The District Attorney, on the other hand, demanded a verdict of first-degree murder. With Judge Stowe's instructions indicating clearly the difference between first- and second-degree murder, the case went to the jury. It took the jury a [284] full day and a night to reach its conclusion, which indicated the serious differences later disclosed. Great was the surprise of all concerned, including the District Attorney, when the jury returned a verdict of first-degree murder against all three defendants, a second-degree verdict having been the strongest expected. On February 11, 1891, the defense counsel filed a motion for a new trial, which was denied. On April 8, 1891, the three men were individually sentenced to

> be taken hence to the Jail of Allegheny County whence you came and thence at such time as the Governor of this Commonwealth may by his warrant appoint to the place of Execution, and that you be then and there hanged by the neck until you be dead. And May God in his Infinite Goodness have Mercy on your Soul.

The Supreme Court of Pennsylvania reviewed the case on certiorari and on June 5, 1891, affirmed the judgment of the trial court.

There was a great deal of dissatisfaction with the outcome of this prosecution among the better class of citizens in Braddock. It was felt that the Hungarians, who were able to speak very little English, had not received as impartial a trial as three Americans would have received. Andrew Carnegie and Charles M. Schwab, together with other citizens, took an interest in the case, and the Governor was requested to grant a commutation to life imprisonment. The request was granted on February 25, 1892.

In 1895, applications for the pardons of these men were filed. In March, 1895, Sabol was pardoned, and in September, 1897, Rusnok received his pardon. The Board of Pardons indicated their belief that Rusnok was not in the mills at all on the fatal day, but that he had been mistaken for Martin

Pekar, whom he resembled. However, in view of the direct testimony of Peter Mullen against Toth, the Governor of Pennsylvania refused to grant any further clemency to Toth.

By this time Toth's oldest son had become well established in Braddock, and he took up the fight for his father's freedom. A second application for a pardon was filed in 1902, but it was again denied. The years in prison grew to ten and to fifteen, and it began to appear, as Toth passed beyond his [285] threescore years in 1910, that he would serve out his full life term. He had been a model prisoner, and by reason of his piety, had earned the sobriquet of "Praying Andy." He was taciturn, but on the few occasions when he talked, he affirmed Ms complete faith in his vindication in God's good time.

In 1911 news came from Hungary that one Steve Toth, on his supposed deathbed, had made a confession before a judicial authority that he had been the one to attack Quinn, and that Andy Toth was entirely innocent of the crime. Steve Toth had lived in the same boarding house as Andy, and had left Braddock on the afternoon of the riot, leaving behind his belongings, as well as some money. He was no relative of Andy, but bore some resemblance to him.

So the tide began to turn in Toth's favor, and the fight to prove his innocence was again taken up. Mr. Edward B. Goehring, brother of Toth's first lawyer, succeeded in obtaining from the Pardon Board at Harrisburg a new hearing on the matter. He presented a remarkably clear analysis of the testimony given at the trial, in which he showed that, while Peter Mullen had testified that he had seen Toth beating Quinn at Furnace C, two other witnesses had seen Quinn beaten to the ground at Furnace A, and that when Quinn came to Furnace A, he was uninjured. Mr. Goehring pointed out for the first time in all of the hearings of this case, that Furnace A was over five hundred feet away from Furnace C, and that, therefore, if the testimony of the two witnesses about the severe beating of Quinn at Furnace A, and his sound condition upon arrival there, was true, then Witness Mullen must have been completely mistaken about Toth's beating Quinn at Furnace C. Dr. Stewart, who was in 1891 a timekeeper and one of the witnesses of the brawl at Furnace A, and in 1911 the sole surviving witness, appeared before the Board and repeated in very positive terms his testimony about the events at Furnace A. It was a physical impossibility for Quinn to have been mortally injured at Furnace C, yet to have come five hundred feet to Furnace A, and to have been there attacked as had been described. Presented in this light, Toth's innocence was sufficiently established so that Steve Toth's confession from Hungary was not filed [286] with the Pardon Board. Governor Tener, on the strong recommendation of the Board, granted Toth a full pardon on March 17, 1911. Among the reasons given was that "the trial occurred within about six weeks after the riot and at a time when the public mind was under the influence of the excitement naturally arising from the tumultuous events of the day."

Toth was immediately released from the Western Penitentiary, after having served nearly twenty years for a crime he did not commit. He was met at the prison gate by his four sons and Mr. Goehring. He expressed no hostility toward those who had falsely testified against him and had ruined his life. Toth admitted that he was present at the riot, but that he had gone there only upon the threats of the riot leaders and to save himself from being "licked." On all occasions, he had asserted his innocence and denied having been near Quinn at the time of the riot. The newspapers over the whole country expressed their sympathy for Toth, editorially and otherwise. His case has since become a modern *cause célèbre* of the erroneous punishment of an innocent person.

A movement was immediately started to have the commonwealth of Pennsylvania grant some compensation to Toth for the twenty years of his life which it had taken from him (from the age of forty-three to sixty-two). Delegate A. C. Stein, from Allegheny County, introduced a bill in the House of Delegates providing for the payment of $10,000 "to Andrew Toth as compensation for his detention in the Western Penitentiary of Pennsylvania, through a miscarriage of justice." Clergymen and editors joined in urging this reparation, but it was not voted by the Legislature because it was felt that such a law would be unconstitutional in Pennsylvania. It was said that the commonwealth could pay nothing. Andrew Carnegie, for whom Toth had worked in the steel mills, learned of the situation and arranged for the payment to Toth of $40 a month for the rest of his life. He returned to his wife in his native village in Hungary, now Czechoslovakia, to spend his declining years.

Although considerably broken in health by his long [287] confinement, Toth seems to have come of sound stock. At the present writing (1930) Toth is still living.

• • • •

THE Toth case illustrates the dangers of inadequate investigation by prosecuting authorities and of response to popular demands for vengeance. Mob attacks in addition always carry an opportunity for grave mistakes in identity. It would seem that a little care could have established the fact that Furnace A and Furnace C were over five hundred feet apart and not close together, as the state seemed to assume. It is often hard to tell why such obvious facts are overlooked, even by the defense. The distance between the two furnaces was not established for twenty years, and was overlooked on the occasion of two prior pardon hearings. The disclosure of this important fact would alone have punctured the case against Andy Toth even against Steve Toth, who apparently did strike a blow at Furnace C. In the pardons of

Sabol, Rusnok, and Toth, the Board of Pardons calls attention to the fact that the public excitement incidental to the riots and popular prejudice against Hungarians at the time had much influence upon their convictions. Fortunately, the sentence of hanging was commuted to life imprisonment, when the establishment of the truth could still serve a useful purpose. One explanation of why Andy Toth was identified by Mullen is to the effect that during the "line-up," Mullen stumbled awkwardly and nearly fell, which elicited a laugh from cheerful Andy, whereupon Mullen, vexed, pointed his finger at Toth as the attacker of Quinn "the laugh which cost twenty years," as one writer puts it. Why a bill to indemnify a person whom the state had unjustly convicted and imprisoned should be held unconstitutional, it will be difficult for the layman to understand. Narrowness of outlook occasionally results in attributing peculiar powers to a constitution. When statutes for indemnification become more familiar, as they are throughout Europe, it will perhaps be admitted that the state is but doing simple justice in righting its wrong, and that even an unintentional miscarriage of justice is a public injury which warrants [288] indemnification to the victim. Andrew Carnegie did, as a matter of philanthropy, what the people of Pennsylvania should have done as a matter of duty.

● ● ● ●

Acknowledgments: Edward B. Goehring, attorney at law, Pittsburgh; Francis H. Hoy, Jr., Secretary of the Board of Pardons; William S. Herbster, attorney at law, Pittsburgh. [289]

A Skeleton In The Closet

Vaught, Stiles, and Bates

THE mountainous section of Eastern Choctaw Nation, Indian Territory, in 1907, was covered by great forests of valuable timber, which was manufactured into lumber.

In the fall of 1907, a human skeleton was found in a sparsely settled wood in this section, about three-quarters of a mile from any roadway. The nearest human habitation was the Bates sawmill, four miles away, and not far from Heavener, now in Oklahoma.

At the place where the bones were found there was an old hat, together with remnants of clothing, a pile of burned rock evidencing a camp fire, and some crude cooking utensils and empty vegetable cans.

After the discovery of the skeleton, the bones were preserved by deputy United States marshals, who were the chief law-enforcement officers in the country at that time, and efforts were made, without success, to determine the identity of the dead man.

Not long before, a young man named Bud Terry had mysteriously disappeared. It was learned that Mrs. Knotts, his aunt, with whom he lived, had heard nothing from him since his disappearance. As he had worked at the Bates sawmill, there was a suspicion that Bates (the owner of the sawmill) and his employees, Will Stiles and Millard Vaught, knew more about the case than they were willing to admit. All three of these men, however, were native sons and had good reputations.

Bates was about forty years old, and had married Stiles's sister. Stiles, a farmer's son, about thirty, was of quiet disposition and well liked in the community. Vaught, about twenty-two, of a good family, was high tempered and inclined to belligerency, but was regarded as entirely honest.

J. W. (Bud) Terry, the man who had disappeared, had lived at Caulksville, a small village in Logan County, Arkansas, seventy miles from the Bates sawmill. In 1907, he was in his early twenties, and was well regarded in the [290] community. Having been left an orphan, he was brought up by his aunt, Mrs. Julia Knotts, to whom he was greatly attached. He was a member of the I.O.O.F. Lodge at Caulksville and carried an insurance policy in that lodge for $1,000, with his aunt as beneficiary.

Even after Terry had reached manhood, he never left home for any length of time without fully informing his aunt where he was going; and during his absences it was his custom to keep her advised of his whereabouts.

In April of 1907 Terry went to the Bates sawmill to seek employment. He was given work, as a lumber checker, with Stiles, whom he had known since childhood, and Vaught. One Louis McKibben, about twenty-seven, was the sawyer for Bates, and one Sam Swider, about forty-two, operated a boarding house at the mill and in part time worked as a mill hand. McKibben and Vaught were old acquaintances and neighbors in Arkansas.

Terry stopped working at the mill in August, 1907, when he disappeared without a trace. The Odd Fellows Lodge and Mrs. Knotts made a wide search for him, including extensive advertising. As it all proved fruitless, Mrs. Knotts and the Lodge were satisfied of Terry's death and the insurance was paid.

Terry's disappearance remained unexplained, no further action was taken in the matter, and the case came to be regarded as one of many unsolved mysteries.

Oklahoma was admitted into the Union as a state November 16, 1907, and the area around the Bates sawmill became a part of Le Flore County, Oklahoma.

In November, 1909, Sam Swider was convicted in LeFlore County of the crime of larceny and given a sentence of five years in the Oklahoma State Penitentiary. In the fall of 1911, while Swider was serving his sentence, he made it known to the warden that he wanted to disclose what he knew about the disappearance of Bud Terry. This permission being granted, he related to the warden that he saw Vaught, Bates, and Stiles kill Terry in a fight in August, 1907. McKibben, after having talked with Swider, backed up his story. [291]

The warden immediately imparted this information to the sheriff of Le Flore County, who, on November 18, 1911, swore out complaints for murder against Vaught, Bates, and Stiles, charging them with the murder of Bud Terry in Indian Territory, on August 18, 1907. The three men were at once arrested and placed in jail. On November 27, 1911, they were granted a preliminary hearing before an examining magistrate, Swider and McKibben appearing as witnesses against them.

The magistrate held the defendants without bail to await the action of the Grand Jury. The District Court and the Criminal Court of Appeals of Oklahoma both denied bail, because of the convincing nature of the evidence.

Because the crime had been committed in Indian Territory in 1907, where by Act of Congress the laws of Arkansas prevailed, a Grand Jury had to be organized under Arkansas laws, just as if the state of Oklahoma had not been created. Sam Swider and Louis McKibben appeared before the Grand Jury and testified. On May 7, 1912, an indictment was returned and the defendants were placed on trial before District Judge W. H. Brown at Poteau, Oklahoma, for the murder of Bud Terry.

The trial was long and sensational. Many witnesses were called both for the prosecution and the defendants. The prosecution produced a number of witnesses who testified to facts and circumstances which tended to leave no doubt that the skeleton was that of Bud Terry and that he lost his life at the hands of Vaught, with the assistance and help of Bates and Stiles. The skeleton was produced in court.

Mrs. Julia Knotts, Terry's aunt, positively identified the old hat which was found near the skeleton as the one worn by Terry when she last saw him. She identified the teeth in the skeleton and particularly a gold filling in one of the front teeth, as Terry's, and further testified that when Terry was a boy, some ten or twelve years old, his left leg was broken immediately above the ankle. The leg of the skeleton showed a break at the identical point she described.

Sam Swider, after giving a history of his connection with the Bates sawmill, testified substantially as follows: In the [292] month of August, 1907, he, Bud Terry, Millard Vaught, Will Stiles, and McKibben went to Mena, Arkansas, about forty miles south of Heavener, Indian Territory, and all except McKibben attended for three days the annual fair held at that place. On the last day of the fair they, with the exception of McKibben, returned to Heavener on a train, arriving there about 4:30 p.m. On the same afternoon Bates arrived in Heavener, shortly after five o'clock. He joined the four men who had come from Mena, as did Louis McKibben, who had returned home on the first day of the fair.

The six men then left in wagons for the Bates sawmill. All, including Terry himself, had been drinking, but not heavily. Just before dark, when they had come within two or three miles of the sawmill, they stopped the wagons for some reason and all got out. Bates then said to Vaught, "I understand you have been telling around that you have been going with my wife." Vaught replied: "Whoever says I have been making such talk as that is a liar. I not only never said that, but I have never known or heard anything in my life detrimental to the character of your wife."

Bates answered: "Bud Terry told me that you said that." As soon as Bates gave Vaught the name of his informant, Vaught turned to Bud Terry and accused him of lying. Terry then, so Swider testified, told Vaught that he need not deny making the statement, for he had certainly made it. A heated controversy arose between Vaught and Terry, Bates and Stiles taking sides with Vaught. The discussion became a brawl. Furious with anger, Vaught took from the wagon a standard, about four feet long, and made of a two-by-four piece of lumber, and struck Terry on the head with it a number of times, crushing his skull, from which he immediately died. Bates and Stiles encouraged the fight and were actual participants in it. There was, in fact, a large hole in the skull, extending from about the left ear to the back of the head. The prosecutor explained that after the right-handed Vaught had struck Terry at that point, as the witnesses testified, wild animals could then easily eat away the bones where the skull was broken.

Swider further testified that immediately after Terry was [293] killed, Vaught, Bates, and Stiles picked up his body and placed it on one of the wagons, covering it with a wagon sheet. They warned Swider and McKibben that if they ever told anyone of what they had witnessed they would be killed.

The body was taken to the sawmill camp and placed in the harness-room in the barn, whereupon they all ate supper. Vaught, Bates, and Stiles, accompanied by Swider and McKibben, then took the body and again placed it on the wagon, and after gathering some old buckets and several cans, they hauled the body about four miles from the mill site to the place where the skeleton was later found, and placed it in a sitting posture. They then placed some rocks together and built a fire on them; hung a number of the buckets on the limbs of the trees; and placed some of the cans on and around the fire. Then they left.

Swider further testified that the three men stated that they were doing this so that anyone who might find the body would conclude that the place was a hobo camp and that the dead man was some unknown character who had camped there. He and McKibben were repeatedly threatened with death if they ever told what they knew. Fear made him keep the secret until he first revealed it to the warden of the penitentiary.

On cross-examination, one of the attorneys for the defendants asked Swider why it was, if he was afraid of the defendants, that he decided to tell anyone about the affair. He immediately turned to the jury, looking directly into their faces, and said: "After I saw Terry killed in such a brutal manner, it made my conscience hurt not to tell it and my conscience continued to hurt me to such an extent that I finally made up my mind that I would tell the truth about it if it actually cost me my life, and that is why I am now testifying."

Louis McKibben also testified that he was present and saw Terry killed in the manner described by Swider. He corroborated every detail. Other witnesses testified that in August, 1907, they saw Swider, McKibben, and Terry, with the defendants, in Heavener and saw them all leave together, [294] in wagons, late in the afternoon. They also testified that they never again saw Terry.

The defendants in their defense admitted that Terry, Swider, and McKibben worked with them at the sawmill until the Mena Fair in 1907. Testimony was introduced showing that Stiles, Vaught, Terry, McKibben, and Swider went to the Mena Fair, and that McKibben returned home on the first day. The defendants stated that on the last day of the fair Swider and Stiles returned to Heavener, as related by Swider, but that neither Terry nor Vaught returned.

They testified that Terry's health had not been good for some time; that he had had a lung hemorrhage; that he had said goodbye to Vaught and

McKibben at Mena, stating that he was going south for his health; and that this was the last time any of the defendants had seen him.

Vaught stated that he never did return to the mill after the fair, but that on the evening of the last day he went to the home of his parents, fifteen miles east of Mena, where he remained; that, in going, he rode on a wagon with six or seven persons, one of whom was an elderly lady who had been awarded a rocking-chair at the fair as a prize for having the largest family; and that Vaught, while riding in the wagon, occupied this chair until they arrived at the lady's home, where he ate supper and remained until about 9:30, when he went to the home of his parents, a mile away.

The records of the Mena Fair showed this award to the lady. Moreover, the story of Vaught's having occupied the chair and taken supper at the lady's home was corroborated by the lady herself and by several other occupants of the wagon.

The defendants' alibi was exceptionally strong. They also made proof of good character. But there were insurmountable facts which made it impossible for them to convince the court and jury that they had not killed Terry. One was that Swider and McKibben testified that they saw the defendants kill him. Another was that the skeleton had also been positively identified.

However, the prosecution was handicapped in its effort to [295] secure a conviction, because so much time had elapsed that the statute of limitations made it impossible to convict for manslaughter (unpremeditated killing) or any other crime less than murder (premeditated killing). That compelled Judge Brown to instruct the jury that unless they believed the defendants guilty of murder they would have to acquit them, because prosecution for manslaughter was barred by the statute.

After the jury had deliberated upon the case for forty-eight hours they reported their inability to agree upon a verdict. The court then declared a mistrial and discharged the jury. For the purpose of learning their attitude, Judge Brown interviewed the foreman and other members of the jury and was told that the jury entertained no doubt that the defendants had killed Terry, but that their disagreement was due to the fact that a number of the jurors believed that the defendants were guilty of manslaughter only, which, under the instructions of Judge Brown, prevented their convicting them.

The mistrial was declared May 15, 1912. The defendants had been held in jail since their arrest in November, 1911. Under the Oklahoma law, when there is a mistrial in any capital case, by reason of disagreement of a jury, the court must allow bond. The defendants gave bond and were released from prison May 16, 1912.

When the case was again called for trial, Stiles successfully demanded a severance, and he was alone tried on the charge. Virtually the same testimony was introduced as at the first trial. The same instructions were given, but unlike the first trial, the jury, after deliberating many hours, acquitted Stiles. Judge Brown again interviewed the members of the new jury and was again informed that it was the unanimous opinion of the jury that Vaught, Bates, and Stiles killed Terry, but that as they considered them guilty of manslaughter only, they had, under the instructions of the court, to bring in a verdict of not guilty. Judge Brown unhesitatingly expressed his opinion that the three original defendants had killed Terry, but as the greater part of the testimony indicated manslaughter only and as there was no [296] reasonable probability of ever securing a conviction, of murder, he permitted the county attorney to dismiss the case against Bates and Vaught.

In the public's view, the mysterious disappearance of Terry had been completely explained. All doubt of his fate had been removed.

• • • •

BUT the story was not yet ended. The defendants, particularly Bates, incensed at what they claimed was injustice and at the loss of reputation and fortune, began an unremitting search for Terry. More than five years passed without result. Then fate again intervened. One R. E. McClelland of Los Angeles, California, had two brothers in Le Flore County, Oklahoma, who had informed him years before of the mysterious disappearance of Bud Terry and of the trial of Vaught, Bates, and Stiles for his murder.

About July 1, 1917, McClelland became an inmate of the Los Angeles County Hospital, in California. It was there that he met Bud Terry, also an inmate. He told Terry what had happened in Oklahoma. Terry immediately wrote to McClelland's brothers and to others in Le Flore County, giving an account of his wanderings since his departure from Heavener in August, 1907. Bates learned of some of these letters, located Terry, and immediately arranged for his return to Le Flore County.

In August, 1917, Terry returned and gave his explanation of his ten years' absence. From the Mena Fair he had gone first to Lorain, Louisiana, and then to Galveston, Texas, where he had remained until April, 1917, when he went to California.

Judge Brown still presided over the District Court. Inasmuch as Swider and McKibben had been absent from the state of Oklahoma the major portion of the time after the trials in 1912, the crime of perjury had not yet become barred by the statute of limitations; consequently Judge Brown ordered their immediate arrest.

When Swider and McKibben were confronted by Terry, they promptly confessed that all their testimony was a [297] fabrication. Brought before the court on charges of perjury, Swider and McKibben pleaded guilty and each was given a sentence of twenty-five years in the Oklahoma State Penitentiary.

McKibben died in the penitentiary in 1924, as the result of an accident. Swider, by getting credit for "good time," served out his sentence, but was recently convicted in the Federal court for counterfeiting and sentenced to the penitentiary at Fort Leavenworth, Kansas.

Bates left Le Flore County after his name was cleared and later died in California. Vaught is living in Arkansas, Stiles, in California.

• • • •

WHAT impelled Swider and McKibben to invent their tale was never explained. It has been suggested that Swider, in the penitentiary, sought to curry favor with the authorities by purporting to help solve a baffling mystery, and thus secure release, and that McKibben was willing to help his friend. The perjury was punished, but Vaught, Bates, and Stiles had suffered irretrievably. The circumstantial evidence was played up to fit the preconceived theory of murder. The skeleton and Terry's hat were even identified. An absolutely perfect alibi could not withstand such overwhelming odds. Even Judge Brown was convinced that Terry had been killed. Two juries actually found the innocent victims of the perjury guilty of manslaughter, but owing to the fortunate technicality of the statute of limitations, they were found not guilty of murder.

• • • •

Acknowledgments: Hon. W. H. Brown, Municipal Counselor, 811 City Hall, Oklahoma City, who was Presiding Judge of the District Court of Le Flore County from 1911 to 1919; Hon. Hal L. Norwood, Attorney-General of Arkansas, Little Rock; Hon. R. P. White, Poteau, Okla., one of the attorneys for the defense. [298]

$100 A YEAR!

Moses Walker

THE records of the Circuit Court of Lauderdale County, in Meridian, Mississippi, contain documents evidencing one exciting episode in the monotonous farm life of an elderly negro, Moses Walker. On a small farm east of Meridian, one may find Moses even today and have a friendly talk with him about it, though over twenty years have since elapsed.

Late in the fall of 1906, Moses was arrested by the county authorities and charged with "unlawfully and feloniously shooting at one Harrington with intent to kill and murder him." He was indicted upon the charge by a Grand Jury and on January 9, 1907, was arraigned before Judge R. F. Cochran in the Circuit Court. He entered a plea of not guilty. The case was brought to trial on January 18, 1907. The proof offered by Prosecuting Attorney J. H. Currie was to the effect that Harrington, a white man, who lived in the country some two or three miles from where Moses Walker lived, was sitting in his house between eight and nine o'clock at night, reading by lamplight, when a shot was fired through an open window only a few feet behind him. The proof showed that the load missed Harrington and buried itself in the wall of his room in a line with his head. An examination of the wall showed that the gun was loaded with slugs cut from some soft metal, like babbitt. Some pieces of this metal were cut out of the wall and offered in evidence. The person who fired the shot was not seen, but Harrington stated that he heard him running away from the premises as soon as the shot was fired. The proof further showed that this running was through soft ground, where tracks were plainly made. The tracks were measured and the measurement compared with tracks actually made by Walker. The proof further showed that the tracks led to a dense skirt of woods a short distance from Harrington's house where there were fresh signs that t mule had been hitched to a tree. The proof also showed that there were mule tracks of the same kind leading from the place where [299] this mule was tied, in the direction of Walker's house and running to the house. The proof further demonstrated that a committee of men searched the premises of Walker and found, under the edge of a woodpile near his house, a piece of soft metal, from which parts had been freshly chipped. This piece of metal was introduced in evidence together with pieces taken from the wall of Harrington's house and examined by the jury. Proof was offered that ill feeling existed between Walker and Harrington. This constituted the principal part of the state's evidence.

One other point was made by the state and the testimony of one witness was offered to support it. This witness testified that he passed the place where a mule was said to have been hitched just before dark on the day of the alleged shooting. The road which he was traveling was only a short distance from the place where the mule was said to have been hitched, and tied to a tree on the edge of the woods, he saw a mule which he took to be the mule of the defendant. When pressed on the question of identification of the mule, the witness stated that in his best judgment it was Moses Walker's mule. The court permitted this testimony to go to the jury, over the objection of Walker's counsel, Amis and Dunn, who throughout the trial conducted an able and vigorous defense.

Counsel for the defendant made a motion for the exclusion of all the testimony offered by the state and for a directed verdict on behalf of the defendant. The ground for the motion was that the testimony was not sufficiently strong and certain to sustain a verdict, that the proof was entirely circumstantial, and that to justify a conviction on circumstantial evidence, the proof must be strong and certain enough not only to prove guilt beyond all reasonable doubt, but to exclude every reasonable hypothesis of the defendant's innocence. The trial court overruled the motion, holding that the proof was sufficient to go to the jury, under proper instructions on the question of defendant's guilt or innocence; that the jury was the judge of the weight and worth of the testimony in a case where the evidence, if believed, would be sufficient to convict. [300]

Moses Walker took the stand in his own defense and categorically denied his guilt; denied any knowledge of the facts testified to by the state's witnesses; denied any ill feeling toward Harrington; and denied that he had any connection with the shooting. He further testified that he worked his mule up to a late hour in the afternoon of the day of the alleged shooting and then put him up and fed him; that he did not leave his house that night. He denied placing the piece of soft metal under the woodpile; ever having seen it before it was found by the committee; and any knowledge that it was there. Members of his family also testified that they had no knowledge of the piece of soft metal and they corroborated Walker in his testimony that he worked his mule up to about night, then put him up and fed him and remained at home throughout the night. The defense relied upon this alibi of Walker.

The case was submitted to the jury under proper instructions for both the state and the defendant. After due deliberation by the jury, Walker was found guilty as charged and was sentenced to confinement in the state penitentiary at hard labor for a term of ten years.

Walker prosecuted an appeal to the Supreme Court of Mississippi, but his conviction was affirmed.

• • • •

ABOUT five years after Walker began his sentence, Harrington, the state's chief witness, was killed in a quarrel. Soon thereafter his widow told her father that Moses Walker was not guilty of the crime of shooting at her husband; that her husband loaded his gun with slugs, and shot through his own window, and himself worked out the threads of the testimony introduced in court against Moses Walker, because of Harrington's enmity toward him. Mrs. Harrington's father had taken considerable interest in the prosecution of Moses Walker for shooting at his son-in-law. But when he was convinced of the truth of his daughter's statements, and that she had kept silent these five years only under a threat of death at the hands of her husband if she told the truth, he had a petition for the pardon of Moses [301]

Walker prepared, circulated, and published. He finally procured the pardon from the Governor of Mississippi, April 15, 1912, after Moses Walker had been confined in the state penitentiary five years.

When Moses Walker obtained his freedom, he returned to his family on the farm where he had lived to the farm where he now lives. Walker has never entertained any ill will against the officers of the law or against the court on account of his conviction. He believes that he was honestly prosecuted by the officers of the law and that the court acted in good faith in sentencing him to the penitentiary. His only grievance is against Harrington, who worked up the case against him and had him indicted and convicted on false testimony. It should be stated that Mrs. Harrington was not a witness in the case and knew of the testimony introduced at the trial only as it was told to her by others.

The full facts were presented to the Legislature of Mississippi at its 1930 session. After a lengthy discussion it appropriated $500 "as a donation to Moses Walker of Lauderdale County as a partial recompense for the wrongful imprisonment and detention of the said Moses Walker in the state penitentiary for approximately five years."

• • • •

WALKER was the victim of a malicious "frame-up" conceived and executed by the alleged victim of his offense. The evidence, so far as not perjured, was apparently "planted" by Harrington, and was sufficiently circumstantial to convince the jury. So far as the trial procedure was concerned, it appears to have been regular enough, a fact which may account for the small amount of the indemnity. It is unfortunate that Mrs. Harrington felt obliged to conceal the truth for five years, while an innocent man was suffering for a crime which was never committed; only the strongest duress can justify or explain what would ordinarily be culpable silence. But for Harrington's death, a little delayed, the truth might never have become known. The activity of Mrs. Harrington's father in procuring Walker's pardon is apparently the only redeeming feature of the Harrington connection with [302] the affair. Walker's resignation and forgiving disposition can only increase one's indignation at so calculated a miscarriage of justice.

• • • •

Acknowledgment: Mrs. Lulu Wimberly, Secretary to the Governor of Mississippi. [303]

On The Banks Of The Warrior

Bill Wilson

BILL WILSON was about twenty when in 1900 he married Jenny Wade. He was a farmer in Blount County, Alabama, and soon after he and Jenny were married they began raising a family. In 1907 their third child was born. When the baby was nineteen months old Jenny left her husband and returned to her family. Bill went back to his father's place, taking the two older children with him.

Jenny stayed with her family a short time and then suddenly disappeared. No one knew where she had gone or why. The community was particularly stirred by the disappearance because not long before this Jane McClendon, daughter of another Blount County farmer, had vanished in the same mysterious way.

Foul play was naturally suspected, but after several weeks of gossip and fanciful speculation the community returned to its accustomed calm and the girls were dropped from general conversation.

One fine spring morning in 1912, four years after Jenny disappeared, Dolphus Tidwell and his son were fishing on the banks of the Warrior River, which meanders through the county, and at the point where Tidwell and his son were fishing it passes near the land of Si Wilson, Bill's father.

The Tidwells saw a bone sticking out of the dirt on a bluff near their fishing ground, and young Tidwell climbed up to investigate. He cleared away the soil and found a piece of matting. Under the matting, which was rotted so that it fell apart, were bones. The Tidwells decided that these bones were those of two skeletons an adult and a child. They were in an advanced state of decomposition and were difficult to handle.

The Tidwells examined them carefully and were particularly impressed by the jawbones in both skeletons the larger having a very big, well-worn set of teeth and the smaller showing both a first and second set. Father and son agreed that they had found Indian relics and believed they might find a burial mound near by. [304]

After investigating the immediate vicinity thoroughly, they selected one bone to take home and the rest they covered, pushing the dirt and stones over the skeletons with an old ax handle they found on the bluff.

News of the discovery spread rapidly; and in the following days many persons visited the bluff, some even bringing screening to sift the dirt, in hope of finding Indian ornaments. They found nothing, however, and interest in the relics was about exhausted when Jim House, who worked occasionally for the elder Wilson, took a sudden interest in the skeletons and began spreading an ugly story.

He spread the rumor that the bones were those of Jenny Wilson and her nineteen-month-old baby. The story fairly flew around the county. Repetition began to give it credence. James Embry heard it. He was county solicitor. The tale impressed him, and he became convinced that it had merit. He accepted it officially and obtained Bill's indictment. Five years after Jenny disappeared her husband went to trial charged with her murder.

Embry was the prosecutor. In his opening remarks to the jury he said that Jenny Wilson went to her father-in-law's house to see her two older children late in November or early December, 1908. A quarrel had occurred that night, Embry said, and Bill Wilson murdered his wife and child, took the bodies to the bluff, and burned them.

The elder Tidwell testified to the finding of the bones, and they were offered in evidence as the bones of Jenny Wilson and her baby.

Dr. Marvin Denton, a practicing physician who testified for the state, was somewhat doubtful that the bones could have decayed to such an extent within four or five years. As for the teeth, the doctor said he did not recall ever seeing second teeth in a child under four years of age. The Wilson infant was less than two.

Thus far the state had little support for its theory. But Embry was relying upon Jim House to convince the jury, and presently House was called and told his damaging story.

Late in November or early December, he told the jury, he had met Jenny Wilson near her father-in-law's house, where [305] Bill was living. House said that he was searching for some stray hogs and that he encountered Jenny on a hill near the Wilson farm. She was carrying a basket, he said, and he walked with her to the Wilson gate, trying to dissuade her from going into the house for fear she might find trouble, as Bill was then suing for a divorce.

She was adamant, however, and insisted upon going in, House said. He watched her until she reached the door, where her mother-in-law was standing with Bill's sister. Seeing no sign of hostility, House walked away.

He did not find the hogs that night and continued the search next day. It led to the Wilson farm, he said, and in a field he met Bill. He questioned him about his wife and told the court that Bill denied that Jenny had called at the Wilson home the previous night.

House walked on, he said. Toward the river he ran across some tracks. He found a "child's cloth" and saw some blood on a rock where the tracks crossed the river.

House's story then jumped to the discovery of the bones by the Tidwells. He visited the scene, he said, and while there saw Bill Wilson with several other persons. House said Bill picked up a bone and handed it to him with the remark, "Here's the baby's rib; you'd better take it along." House said he replied, "Yes, Bill, that's the very thing I want."

This was House's story and he stuck to it.

House was followed on the stand by Mack Holcomb, a convict, who had occupied a cell near Wilson's while the latter was awaiting trial. Holcomb told the jury that Wilson's eldest daughter, Ruthie, visited her father in jail one day and that as she was leaving Wilson said to her, "If you tell anything I will tend to you when I get out."

Other testimony quoted Wilson as saying of his wife that he would kill her if she returned. A woman testified that she met Wilson on the train returning from the trial of his divorce suit. He was drunk, she said, and announced the outcome of the trial by saying: "I beat her. Damn her, she didn't appear. She will never appear against me any more because she's over Green River." And another witness said [306] that the defendant had spoken to him voluntarily about the divorce and when asked whether his wife had appeared replied, "Hell, no, she's over the river."

Then the state tried to corroborate House's story and called Forrest Hardin, who testified that he had seen Jenny late in 1908 with her baby and that she carried a basket at the time. He could add no more. Jenny's brother, Velt Wade, testified that he had seen her last in the fall of 1908 and that she was then on her way to visit her brother-in-law, Monroe Graves, who lived near Blount Springs. Since then, he said, he had been told that she was in Ashville. When asked about the ax handle that House said he picked up on the bluff (the one used by the Tidwells to cover the skeletons), he said he had seen it at Wilson's cotton gin.

The defense called a witness whose testimony concerning House cast a great deal of doubt upon the character of the state's star witness. She was Mrs. Lizzie McClendon, mother of Jane McClendon, who had also disappeared.

Mrs. McClendon told the jury that House came to her after her daughter vanished and declared that he would testify that he saw the Wilsons kill Jane if Mrs. McClendon would swear out a warrant for their arrest. In cross-examination, House admitted that there was considerable ill feeling between himself and Bill Wilson, but he denied the statements that Mrs. McClendon attributed to him.

The defense claimed that Jenny was alive after the date on which her husband was alleged to have killed her; that House was prejudiced and unreliable; and that much of the state's testimony was untrue.

Jenny's sister testified that Jenny had come to her home in 1909 and later went to "Mr. Green Merrill's and he carried her to Blount Springs." Merrill corroborated this statement and said that Jenny stayed at his home for two weeks in January, 1909. Then came five witnesses, all of whom swore that they had seen Jenny at various times in 1909, and several of them intimated that she had been living with one John Wilson, no relation of Bill's.

Mrs. Benton Cornelius, a friend of Jenny's, testified that Jenny told her as early as April, 1908, that after her [307] separation from Wilson she intended going to Missouri and that no one in Blount County would ever hear of her again.

The defense scored again when Bill's brother John, his sister Frances, his daughter Ruthie, and John Rice, who worked for the elder Wilson, all denied that Jenny had visited the Wilson home at any time after the separation. Thus, Jim House was the sole source of evidence on the subject of the alleged fatal visit.

Ruthie was asked about the statement attributed to her father in which he told her when she visited him in jail that he would "tend to her" if she told anything. She denied that he had made such a threat, but said that what he did tell her was that if she were not a good girl he would punish her when he got out of jail.

The defense introduced testimony to show that the skeleton of the woman found by the Tidwells indicated that no dental work had ever been done on the teeth, whereas two friends of Jenny's testified that two of her front teeth had been filled. The question of the ax handle was then brought up, and John Wilson, a brother of the defendant, testified that he had worked around his father's cotton gin for twenty years and had never seen it there.

Finally, the defense capped its case with the expert testimony of Dr. J. F. Hancock, who said that he believed it would take at least ten years for bones to decay as those alleged to be Jenny's had done. He also testified that the 'teeth in the large skeleton were those of a very old person and that a nineteen-month-old baby would have no sign of second teeth.

But the jury believed Jim House, for Bill Wilson was convicted of murder in the first degree and sent to the Alabama state prison for life. An appeal was taken but the conviction was affirmed. Petitions for pardon presented from time to time by Bill's friends were denied.

• • • •

DOUBT of his guilt was so strong that even the trial judge, Hon. J. E. Blackwood, urged the Governor and the Attorney General on December 28, 1916 nearly two years after conviction to commute the sentence. [308]

Further doubt of his guilt was aroused in the same year when the incriminating bones were declared by Dr. Ales Hrdlicka, curator of physical anthropology of the Smithsonian Institution at Washington, to be parts of four or five skeletons, both child and adult. Dr. Hrdlicka also said that they apparently came from very old burials, and that there was nothing about them to indicate that they were not the bones, of Indians.

Probate Judge John F. Kelton stated in an affidavit: "Public sentiment convicted Bill, but this has in a great measure changed." It seemed that the only person connected with the case who was still convinced of Wilson's guilt was Embry, the prosecutor, who blocked the attempts of Wilson's friends to obtain a pardon.

Among those working for Wilson's release was Mr. J. T. Johnson of Oneonta, Alabama, who had been Wilson's lawyer on the appeal and was convinced of his client's innocence. Through his patience and persistence Jenny Wilson was finally located in Vincennes, Indiana, where she was living with her second husband.

She was persuaded to return to Blount County and to give in an affidavit a complete account of her movements from the time she disappeared until she was found. The day she returned—July 8, 1918—Bill, as a result of a telephone call from the county sheriff to the Governor, was granted a full pardon which ended an imprisonment of three years, six months, and twenty-one days at hard labor.

On February 15, 1919, the Legislature enacted a statute for the appointment of a commission "whose duty it shall be to ascertain how much and make an award, in writing, to the Governor as to the amount of compensation the said William Wilson should in justice and good conscience receive from the state for his said services" up to the amount of $3,500.

Wilson was broken by his confinement, yet the Legislature sought to pay him "for services rendered the state while in prison," rather than reimburse him for the horrible injury done him by an amazing perversion of justice.

The award was made for the full amount of $3,500 and, [309] ironically, brought Wilson again into the courts. The money was paid to a trustee, described in the record as Probate Judge of Blount County. He made several small payments to Wilson and then fled the state with the balance.

Wilson was forced to sue the judge's bondsman to get the rest of the fund due him. This action cost him $700, and with other expenses it is doubtful if he ever received more than $2,500.

With this money he bought a small farm and tried to begin life over again. But he had lost his courage and the fight was too much for him. He got into debt, had to sacrifice his farm, and when last heard of, was digging coal as a day laborer in an Alabama mine.

• • • •

THUS ends another painful story. It is perhaps more flagrant than many others, because the evidence on which Wilson was convicted was so flimsy, whereas that in his favor was so strong especially the cumulative evidence of five different witnesses to the fact that Jenny was alive after the date of the alleged murder, and that other testimony concerning the pedigree of the bones so utterly discredited the theory of the prosecution. Again we have an illustration of the frailty of juries and of the fact that a prosecuting attorney's persuasion, backed by individual and community emotions of revenge, desire for a victim, and public sentiment, combined with accidents and misfortune, may bring to the penitentiary a perfectly innocent man. Possibly the presiding judge was correct in saying that Wilson's case was not properly conducted, though the record of the cross-examination does not disclose it. It seems quite probable that considerations other than the actual evidence in the case weighed heavily with the jury. Even the Governor and the Board of Pardons, however, were unwilling to parole, commute, or pardon until Jenny Wilson actually appeared in Alabama. It is ironic to find that a probate judge, trustee of a state fund, decamped with Wilson's money. Perhaps we ought to applaud the state of Alabama for its generous contrition in making some amends by a money payment, for [310] that is more than many of our states have done under comparable circumstances of the maladministration of justice.

• • • •

Acknowledgments: Mr. Douglas Arant, Birmingham, Ala.; Mr. Geo. W. Darden, attorney at law, Oneonta, Ala.; Mr. J. T. Johnson, Oneonta, Ala.; Hon. C. A. Moffett, President of the Board of Administration, Montgomery, Ala.; Mr. A. Wetmore, Smithsonian Institution, Washington, D.C. [311]

"SEEN" IN THE ACT

Sidney Wood

THREE masked bandits boarded an interurban electric car between Los Angeles and Pasadena about 8:00 p.m., November 7, 1923. One stayed on the rear platform, a second went to the front of the car, and the third searched passengers after the man at the rear fired three bullets through the roof to show that they meant business.

The looting completed, the bandits forced the motorman to stop the car. They jumped off, ran to an automobile waiting near by with a fourth man at the wheel, and escaped in the darkness.

After a brief investigation the suspicions of the Los Angeles police fell upon two brothers. They were interviewed at their home in Los Angeles. They were entertaining a guest Sidney Wood. The brothers accounted for their activities the night of the holdup satisfactorily, but Wood's story was not believed and he was held for further questioning.

A check-up showed that he had not told an entirely truthful story, though his past record appeared to be spotless. Investigation disclosed that he was a British subject, as he claimed, and that he had spent most of his life in the British navy or on British merchantmen. He had signed off a ship at San Pedro a week before his arrest.

He explained his presence at the brothers' home by saying that he had known one of them at sea and had been invited to visit at their home when he came to Los Angeles. This the brothers confirmed.

At the police station, however, Wood was identified by both the motorman and the conductor of the interurban car as the man who stood on the rear platform and directed the holdup. This identification, together with his unsatisfactory explanation of his whereabouts the night of November 7, convinced the police of his guilt.

An information was filed against him by the district attorney charging robbery, in the first degree, of $35 and jewelry from one of the passengers on the car.

The trial which followed ended in a disagreement of the jury; and the district attorney was about to drop the case, [312] when a witness appeared who had been a passenger on the car and positively identified Wood as one of the bandits, and at the second trial several other passengers confirmed this identification. They based it on a similarity in the eyes, the lower part of the forehead, and the upper part of the nose, these features being all that was visible behind the mask worn by the man on the rear platform. The witnesses also said there was a strong resemblance in the defendant's general physique.

Wood's only defense was an alibi which was not well supported, and his previous good character and excellent record in the British navy and merchant marine. Because of the obvious weakness of the alibi, combined with the positive identifications, the jury returned a verdict of guilty as charged on March 3, 1924.

Two days later, when he was brought before Judge Walton J. Wood for sentence, his counsel, W. J. Laney, told the court that he would make an oral motion at once for a new trial, on the ground that the verdict was not supported by the evidence. He indicated that he would file a formal motion as soon as he could get a transcript of the evidence.

The court replied:

> If that is the ground for your motion, if there ever was a case where the evidence was sufficient to uphold that verdict, it was this case. If the court did not agree with the jury he would set it aside; so far as the evidence is concerned, there is evidence to support the verdict. The witnesses saw him in the act. . . .

The motion was accordingly denied, and Wood was sentenced to San Quentin for five years to life. Mr. Laney requested a stay of execution of five days, saying that the British Consul had called him that day and said he would like to have an opportunity to investigate the case before sentence was passed. Judge Wood granted Mr. Laney two days and told him that further continuance might be granted if necessary after that. A week later, however, Wood was received at San Quentin to begin serving his sentence.

● ● ● ●

THE Los Angeles police and detectives of the Pacific [313] Electric Railway Company continued the search for the other three men known to have been involved in the crime. Among the railway detectives there was some doubt even then that Wood was guilty. Mr. Laney was convinced that his client was innocent and was finally able to impress the detectives with his theory.

Efforts to discover the actual culprits were doubled after one of the railway's agents reported to the vice-president of the company that he seriously doubted Wood's guilt.

Not until January of the next year, 1925, however, was a clue found. At that time police learned that the men they wanted were James Hovermale, Mark Godfrey, a boy of seventeen, Roy Smith, and Russell Smith. They were not found in their usual haunts, and no trace of them was discovered until police were informed that they were hiding in Idaho.

Investigation in Idaho disclosed the whereabouts of Hovermale and Russell Smith. Presently Godfrey was located, when a man and a woman who owned the ranch where he was employed told police that he had confessed his part in the holdup to them when he learned that Hovermale, his brother-in-law, was in custody.

Hovermale, Russell Smith, and Godfrey were extradited to Los Angeles. On April 10, 1925, Godfrey made a complete confession to the police, in which he said he was forced by Hovermale, under threat of death, to take part in the robbery. He said that he was the one who had collected the money and jewelry from the passengers, that Hovermale was the man who stood on the rear platform, that Roy Smith covered the motorman, and that Russell Smith drove the automobile in which they escaped. Asked where Roy Smith was hiding, young Godfrey said he understood that he went to Canada, but he had heard nothing from him or about him since the holdup.

Informations charging robbery in the first degree were filed against all four, and the three in custody were brought to trial. Godfrey was acquitted because of his youth, his assistance in the solution of the crime, and the circumstances of his participation in the robbery. Russell Smith and [314] Hovermale were found guilty and sent to San Quentin. Their motion for a new trial was denied and their appeal to the Supreme Court was dismissed.

On May 5, 1925, about a year and a half after he was arrested, Sidney Wood was pardoned by Gov. F. W. Richardson and was given $100 by the Governor, according to Mr. Laney, who never saw his client after his release.

• • • •

WOOD'S predicament was purely accidental. It became grave because his alibi was not accurate, alone a ground for suspicion. When this was coupled with his identification by the motorman and several passengers, he was beyond help. The identifications of Wood rested on an observance of certain features of a man's face left uncovered by a mask hardly a satisfactory basis for so important a conclusion. The fact that Mr. Laney felt convinced of his innocence and that he ultimately convinced the company's detectives of that fact, supplied the necessary motives to continue the investigation until by chance Godfrey's disclosure in Idaho unraveled the mystery. Governor Richardson's generosity to the extent of $100, while much to be appreciated, should not have been required, for under the California law of 1913 Wood was in a position to claim an indemnity from the state for the injuries he had suffered.

• • • •

Acknowledgments: Mr. George A. Benedict, Los Angeles, Calif.; Mr. Willard J. Laney, Los Angeles, Calif.; Mr. Frank Karr, Los Angeles, Calif.; Mr. Mark E. Noon, San Quentin, Calif. [315]

Sentenced "Against The Law And Evidence"

William Woods and Henry W. Miller

JOHN HANTZ, JR., had been away from home about two months when his father received a letter from the young man's companion, William Woods, saying that John had disappeared and that he was returning to their home in Kinsley, Kansas, without him.

The two youths left home in October, 1877, for a hunting trip into the Indian Territory. The letter from Woods described their travels and said that the last seen of John was at a camp they made near the reservation of the Cherokee Nation on the Verdigris River.

After leaving Kinsley, the two youths, equipped with a two-horse wagon and camping outfit, several dogs, and a riding pony, drove to Troy, Kansas, where they met a stranger, Henry W. Miller, who joined the expedition and shared expenses.

From Troy the three went into the Indian Territory, hunting along the way. Early in November they reached the Verdigris River and made camp in a sheltered hollow near the water.

After a short stay they went on to Fayetteville, where John sold his pony for $30 to raise money to help finance his share of the rest of the trip. From Fayetteville the three continued on to Mulberry Creek hunting grounds before turning north for the return journey.

On the way back, they made for their camp on the Verdigris River and planned to stay there several days. They arrived the day after Thanksgiving. The third day Hantz and Miller, each carrying a gun and a hatchet, went out to lay a trap line.

They had not returned at dusk. Woods began to worry. He built a fire and fired his shotgun at intervals to guide them to camp. Miller came in after dark. He had lost his way. He inquired for Hantz and was told that he had not returned. He said he left him under a pecan tree gathering nuts and that the youth told him to go into camp and he would follow presently. [316]

All night the guns were fired from time to time and the fire was kept burning, but John did not come. They waited until nearly noon next day without any sign of their companion. They then decided to break camp, fearing that John had been attacked by Indians.

They drove to Coffeeville, where they separated to return to their homes. Woods told Miller he would write Hantz's family before starting to Kinsley, and the description of the party's movements outlined above was contained in that letter.

Upon his arrival in Kinsley, Woods turned over to the elder Hantz a number of things that had belonged to John, including a six-shooter, a pair of field glasses, various personal articles, and a trunk full of clothes. He confirmed the story he told in the letter and discussed the disappearance fully and frankly.

The elder Hantz decided to send two of his sons to the place where Woods last saw John on the Verdigris River in the hope that they might find the body. They reached the camp and after thirteen days' searching discovered a body. They sent for their father, and when he arrived a careful examination convinced them that the body was not John's.

The following March the Hantz family received word that another body had been found on the banks of the Verdigris, and for a second time Hantz and his sons set out toward Indian Territory.

The body was lying across a log on the edge of the river, face down in the water, with the feet on the bank. It was decomposed, and part of the nose and upper lip had been eaten away. The left arm was broken and the left jawbone was unhinged. Holes in the back of the head appeared to have been made by buckshot, which apparently passed through the skull from back to front.

It was said by others that the body was in such bad condition that it could not be identified, but John Hantz, Sr., was convinced by the physique and the absence of several teeth on each side of the lower jaw that it was the body of his son. He said the teeth had been extracted before John started on the hunting trip. [317]

A knife found near the body was identified as John's, and Woods said that a cap found on the head was his own. Soon after this identification, various stories began to circulate concerning hunting parties that had seen Woods, Miller, and Hantz passing through the countryside; and as a result of the tenor of these tales, Woods and Miller were arrested.

Woods was taken at his home, and Miller, who lived in Troy, was found to have left in a covered wagon for the Far West a few hours before the sheriff arrived at his home. He was overtaken eighteen miles from Troy, and a search of his clothing disclosed a watch that had belonged to young Hantz.

Further investigation created a dangerous net of circumstantial evidence against the pair, and when they came to trial practically the only thing in their favor seemed to be that they both told exactly the same stories, even to small details, and that new matter with which they were confronted by the authorities from time to time during the examination elicited similar frank replies from both men. In no respect did their stories differ.

After a motion for separate trials was denied on the ground that such a proceeding would waste too much time, the case got under way.

The prosecution contended that the defendants had murdered Hantz to rob him of the little money he had. The murder occurred, the prosecution said, about the time another party, led by Arnold Louther and including T. M. Smith and Len Morrow, was camped near the youths on the Verdigris.

Evidence to support this theory rested upon the testimony of these three men and Louther's son, C. C. Louther, who had a homestead about ten miles from where the men camped in what was known as Commodore Hollow.

The Louthers and their friends were unable to remember the date of their hunting expedition and could only agree that it was after the first of November and before the twentieth. They were sure, however, that it was not after the twentieth, because young Louther's wife gave birth to a [318] child on that date. Young Louther had not gone on the trip, because he wanted to stay at home with his wife.

They said the camp site at Commodore Hollow was occupied by three men the day they arrived, so that they had to go 150 yards to set up their own tents. That night they visited the strangers and talked by the camp fire several hours before going to bed. Louther and Morrow identified two of the men at the camp fire as the two defendants, but Smith said he did not remember them.

During the night, Louther said, he heard shots from the vicinity of the strangers' camp. Morrow and Smith, however, testified that they heard nothing.

Morrow, who had brought the Louthers' camping outfit to the river with his team, started home next morning after his party had set out to hunt. He said he passed the strangers' camp and saw only Woods, who stopped him and gave him a slut hound. On the way home the dog jumped out of the wagon and disappeared. Arnold Louther testified that he found a slut hound near the river next day and that the dog stayed near by several days howling and barking.

Louther and Smith said that, when they returned to their own camp the first day after their arrival, they discovered that the strangers' camp was deserted and there was no sign of the three hunters.

Morrow testified that about a week later he met Woods and Miller on the road near Coffeeville. C. C. Louther was with him, he said, and offered to buy several wolfskins Woods and Miller had with them, but the offer was refused. Again there was disagreement as to the exact date.

When Miller testified in his own defense, he told the same story Woods related on his return to Kinsley. He remembered meeting the other party in the hollow and described the evening discussion around the camp fire. He also confirmed the story of the gift of a dog to Morrow.

He told of the sale of Hantz's horse; and Amos Walter, the man who bought it, testified to the transaction, identifying the defendants as two of the men present at the sale, and he described the third John Hantz, Jr.

Miller then told of the subsequent meeting with Morrow [319] on the road to Coffeeville. He set the date about three weeks later than Morrow and contradicted the latter's statement that C. C. Louther had been present. He recalled no conversation concerning wolfskins, but said he had asked about the dog and Morrow replied that it had run away.

The prosecution made much of the fact that Miller had young Hantz's watch when arrested. He explained, however, that it had been the only watch in the party, and that Hantz had turned it over to him, saying that he often forgot to wind it and it had best be kept going regularly.

Later, Miller testified, he sold John a revolver on credit and was told to keep the watch for security. This revolver was among the articles belonging to young Hantz that Woods returned to the youth's father. Miller testified that Woods and Hantz were short of money and that with the cash raised by selling the pony, young Hantz had bought food, boots, blankets, and whiskey and had between $12 and $15 left. There had been no quarrels, Miller said, and finances were settled every Saturday night. John and Woods each owed him $5.00 at the time of the last settlement.

Miller had returned to his home in December and stayed until April, when he started west in the covered wagon. The county attorney at Troy and a doctor, T. C. Lee, both testified that everyone in Troy knew of Miller's plans to go west and that he was a peaceful and respected member of the community. A number of persons also testified as to Woods's good character.

When all the evidence was finally before the jury, the prosecution declined to make the opening argument; and the defense, under protest, was ordered to present its argument, to which the prosecution replied.

The jury returned a verdict of guilty. Both men were sentenced to be hanged April 19, 1889, and a motion for a new trial was denied.

The condemned men were so insistent in their pleas of innocence that the case finally came to the attention of the Department of Justice in Washington. William H. H. Miller, Attorney-General in the cabinet of President Harrison, made a thorough investigation and recommended a [320] pardon for both men because they had been sentenced "against the law and evidence."

President Harrison pardoned Woods April 8, 1889, but not Miller. The latter's sentence was commuted to life imprisonment without any explanation other than the statement that "there are circumstances in this case which make me unwilling to confirm the death sentence."

Miller stayed in prison fifteen years. Finally, he wrote Attorney-General Philander Knox, again protesting his innocence. Knox began a new investigation and reported that the former Attorney-General, Mr. Miller, had voluntarily brought the matter up, and urged further inquiry. Knox became convinced of Miller's innocence and recommended his pardon to President Roosevelt, saying: "I believe Miller should have been pardoned when Woods was pardoned. After a careful consideration of the entire case, it is my deliberate opinion that both Woods and Miller are absolutely innocent of the murder of Hantz, and that Miller has now suffered for nearly fifteen years for a crime which he did not commit."

Miller was pardoned November 10, 1902, having lost his best years through the credulity of a jury and the unexplained failure of Attorney-General Miller to recommend his pardon when Woods was pardoned.

• • • •

THIS was a conviction on circumstantial evidence alone. On reading the report of the United States Attorney-General, it seems incredible that a jury anywhere could have found these men guilty on the evidence presented. The desire of the Hantz family for vengeance upon someone may have been a contributing factor; again, the verdict may have turned on personal or fortuitous circumstances which the printed record does not disclose. Only by sheer good luck were the men spared hanging. It is strange that so positive a conclusion as that of Attorney-General Knox, to the effect that Miller was "absolutely innocent of the murder of Hantz," should leave the community and the Government unmoved, and that mere pardon, after fifteen years, for an [321] uncommitted crime, should be deemed a sufficient compensation for Miller's sufferings. The records do not show what became of Miller, but that the life of this perfectly respectable young American was seriously impaired, if not ruined, can hardly be doubted. It is not easy to understand why Woods should have been pardoned and not Miller, but there is the record. Possibly, Miller did not have as energetic a group of friends, or was himself less aggressive in asserting his innocence and demanding another investigation. Inertia is often to blame for the failure to right manifest wrongs. Perhaps it ought to be appreciated that he was at least not subjected to the horror of serving out his life sentence in a Federal penitentiary. A jury's verdict is often a difficult, if not insurmountable, obstacle to overcome on the road to justice. [322]

Supplementary Cases

"Aren't You Ashamed Of Yourself?"

J. Anthony Barbera

ON February 5, 1931, the delicatessen store of Anthony Huegler, on Reid Avenue, Brooklyn, was entered by a young man who, with drawn revolver, robbed the place of $70. Mr. Huegler and his wife, Emma, were both present during the robbery. They reported the matter to the police at once, describing the manner in which the robbery had been committed and how the culprit had been dressed. He had worn a cap, pulled down well over his face.

A day or two after the robbery, four young men were observed riding about in an automobile calling on various delicatessen and small stores. The police, knowing two of the men, were suspicious, and followed them. Finally the police questioned them, and finding two guns in the car, arrested all four. Upon learning that the four had at times roomed at a house several doors from Mr. Huegler's shop, the police questioned them about the robbery at that place. One of the group, J. Anthony Barbera, had a general appearance much like that described by the Hueglers. He was taken to the delicatessen store to be examined by them. Not having seen the robber's face, they could not be very certain, so they had Barbera pull his cap down over his face, walk up and down, and speak. Thereupon he was identified by them as the man.

Barbera denied the charge and said that at the time of the holdup he was at a movie theater on Myrtle Avenue with the girl to whom he was engaged to be married. This theater was some distance away from the delicatessen store. After the show he had met a cousin who introduced him to three other young men. All of these persons, when interviewed, corroborated Barbera's story.

The evidence was submitted to a Kings County Grand Jury, and a first-degree robbery indictment returned against Barbera. The case was tried before Judge A. I. Nova in the Kings County Court on March 24 and 25, 1931. [323]

District Attorney William F. X. Geoghan was the prosecutor, and Attorney Vincent O'Connor appeared for the prisoner. The jury chose to believe the Hueglers rather than the alibi witnesses, and returned a verdict of guilty. The minimum sentence for this crime was twenty years in the penitentiary. Barber a had no criminal record.

A few days later, and while Barbera was awaiting sentence, there fell into the hands of the police one Harold Sorenson, nineteen years of age, who was said to have specialized in delicatessen-store robberies. He voluntarily confessed to numbers of them, including the one at the Hueglers' shop. This confession was made to Detective Elliot Holmes, who, incidentally, had handled the Barbera matter and who had doubts of his guilt. Holmes took Sorenson to the District Attorney, who was not inclined to believe the confession. To test him, Sorenson was asked what, if anything, had been said by Mrs. Huegler during the holdup. He replied: "Aren't you ashamed of yourself, robbing poor people?" This was exactly what Mrs. Huegler had said. Mr. Geoghan was convinced.

Without unnecessary delay, the District Attorney brought Sorenson before Judge Nova, on March 30, 1931, where he again repeated his confession. Upon motion of the District Attorney, the verdict of the jury was thereupon set aside and the indictment ordered dismissed. Barbera was freed. Sorenson pleaded guilty to the Huegler and other indictments and was duly convicted.

• • • •

THERE is nothing unusual about this case of mistaken identity except the speed with which the error was undone and righted. But for the willingness of the real culprit to confess his crime the innocent Barbera might well have suffered his twenty-year sentence and his life been blasted. Again the victims of a robbery too readily identified the wrong man, and a jury preferred to accept their identification rather than a strongly corroborated alibi of the accused. When the District Attorney became convinced that a mistake had been made, although the jury's verdict was already in, he moved [324] promptly to set the verdict aside and Barbera was immediately liberated.

• • • •

Acknowledgments: Mr. Burton H. White, New York City; Mr. William F. X. Geoghan, District Attorney, Kings County, N.Y.; Mr. Vincent O'Connor, Brooklyn, N.Y. [324]

FRAUD

Mary Berner

MARY BERNER, aged about thirty, was a resident of Cedar Rapids, Iowa, and at one time was private secretary to former Congressman James Good, who, before his death on November 11, 1929, was Secretary of War in President Coolidge's Cabinet. She worked in Chicago after 1924, and had been employed for some time by a well-known insurance company. At the time of her arrest in December, 1928, she was working for Butler Brothers in Chicago as a stenographer.

For more than a year and a half before that time, some sixty banks in and around Chicago had been defrauded by a woman who fitted Mary Berner's description and who, in each instance, presented a spurious check, presumably a pay check and never for more than $50, which she would cash, withdrawing about 90 per cent of the amount of the check and leaving the rest to start a savings account.

Shortly before the arrest of Mary Berner, the Cicero State Bank was defrauded by this same person; and when the spurious check was returned, it was discovered that it was written on the check blank of a well-known insurance company in Chicago. The cashier of the Cicero State Bank made inquiry and learned that Mary Berner. had quit her job with the insurance company just about the time that many of their checks disappeared and that the insurance company suspected her. An investigation made by the bank disclosed that Mary Berner was then employed by Butler Brothers. The cashier of the bank and an employee who had cashed the check went to Butler Brothers and picked Mary [325] Berner out of a group of about forty girls. She was brought to the Illinois Bankers' Association office, and there the representatives of six department stores positively identified her as the girl who had cashed these several checks. She had a preliminary hearing and was held in jail for the Grand Jury three months until she was tried.

The judge trying her apparently had no doubt of her guilt, because after the jury convicted her, he told her that if she would plead guilty he would put her on probation. This she refused to do in spite of the advice given to her by her father, her uncle, and her lawyer. The judge, however, granted her a new trial and entered for her a plea of guilty. He then placed her on probation.

About April, 1929, a woman who gave the name of Emma Lutz was arrested at the request of the cashier of one of the banks already defrauded. After being held in custody for a day or two, she confessed to the perpetration of all the crimes charged to Mary Berner. All of the persons who identified Mary Berner, except one, positively identified Emma Lutz.

Accordingly Emma Lutz was tried, convicted, and sentenced to one year in the House of Correction at Chicago.

• • • •

THIS case of circumstantial evidence, supported by mistaken identification by the victims of a fraud, does not differ greatly in its general facts from the erroneous convictions in the cases of Andrews (p. 1), Greenwald (p. 79), Lee (p. 132), and Sullivan (p. 253). The fact that Mary Berner happened to leave the employ of the insurance company at the time their blank checks disappeared and the fact that she apparently resembled the real culprit sufficiently to be identified by the victims were enough to fasten the crime upon her. How Emma Lutz got the insurance-company checks does not appear. Nothing was apparently done to compensate or vindicate Mary Berner.

• • • •

Acknowledgment: Mr. Emory J. Smith, Chicago, Ill., for seven and one-half years attorney for the Illinois Bankers' Association, deputized by the Attorney-General as assistant prosecutor of this case. [326]

HOLD-UP

John H. Chance

A MAN, about thirty, wearing a light overcoat and carrying a revolver in his hand, entered the drug store and ordered the lone clerk to put up his hands. The clerk, Charles L. Russell, nervously turned away from the pointed gun, and the bandit fired. Russell fell mortally wounded.

The drug store was on the first floor of the United States Hotel in Boston, and the murder occurred about 8:30 the night of Monday, April 4, 1898. No one saw the shooting, and the robber escaped without any loot.

The shots attracted several persons, who saw a man run from the store, the revolver still in his hand; and from them the police obtained the only description they could find to work on.

The bandit ran through Kneeland Street as far as the old Boston & Albany Station, followed the tracks a short distance, turned off into an alley on Harvard Street, and disappeared.

For three weeks the police were without a clue. Then an overcoat was turned over to them by tenants at 74 Hudson Street, not far from the scene of the killing. The coat had been found in the basement of the Hudson Street house, and it answered the description of the one worn by the bandit.

The police began an inquiry among residents of the neighborhood, and in a house on Indiana Street, near Harrison, they found John Henry Chance. He identified the coat as his own, but said he did not know how it got into the basement.

He told the police, however, that he had loaned it to a friend, Arthur Hagan; but Hagan could not be found. As Chance admitted ownership, was thirty-one years old, and answered the general description of the robber, he was arrested.

The search for Hagan continued, and in October he was [327] finally located in Chicago and brought back to Boston to answer to the indictment for murder in the second degree that had been returned against him and Chance, June 11.

Both men went to trial together February 8, 1899, the prosecution relying upon the theory that one of the men was the murderer and the other an accessory.

Hagan offered an extensive alibi. He did not testify, but instead offered a statement through counsel, made while in jail in December. In it he described his movements in some detail during several days preceding the murder.

He said that he lived for two weeks prior to the crime with one Liz Nagle, a government witness at the trial. He said Chance was living with Mrs.

Chance at this time, and that he saw both of them and a mutual friend, Doc Malley, nearly every day.

The night of April 2 (two days before the killing) Chance and Malley broke into a cutlery store at Broadway and Washington Street, Chance said, and stole eighteen revolvers and about fifty razors. Some of the razors were sold to his brother, a barber in South Boston. Each man kept two revolvers out of the loot and disposed of the rest.

Sunday, the day before the crime, Hagan said, he changed overcoats with Chance because his was shabby and he had an engagement with a girl in Roxbury in the afternoon. He kept the engagement, wearing Chance's coat, and returned to Boston about 6 p.m., went to Chance's home and found him drunk, so he left about 9:30, hired a room, and slept until ten o'clock Monday morning.

He said he spent most of Monday on the water front trying to find a berth on an outgoing ship. He was unsuccessful, and in the evening loitered around Court Square until 7:30, when he walked down Tremont Street to Dover, down Dover to Harrison, and then to Chance's home. He said there was a light in the window and he gave the usual whistle, but got no reply from Chance, who usually answered by coming to the window and moving the curtain. Hagan continued down Harrison Street to Connolley's Corner, where he met Chance talking to one Frank White. -It was then about 8:30, according to Hagan. [328]

After talking with the two men a few minutes he went home, he said, and went to bed. In the morning he called on Chance and read the papers at the latter's home, discussing the murder that had occurred the night before.

He spent Tuesday and Wednesday nights in Roxbury, returning to Chance's Thursday night. He found Mrs. Chance and Malley's wife together. Liz Nagle came in drunk, he said, and was soon followed by Chance, who started an argument with Liz over her condition. Liz got angry and walked out, taking Hagan with her.

They went to a place on Tyler Street, and Hagan set forth in his statement that Liz then told him that Chance was the murderer, basing her conclusion on the fact that she had seen him with a revolver two days before the murder.

Hagan stayed in Boston until the following Monday, when he started for Chicago with a tramp after selling his pistol and other personal articles to Chance for $1.50, so he wouldn't have to carry them with him. He said he arrived in Chicago May 1, and stayed there, working as a barber, until he was arrested in the fall.

Chance's defense was one which could not but impress the jury unfavorably. When arrested he had accounted for his actions the day of the murder and admitted ownership of the coat, saying he had worn it within an hour of the shooting. The day after his arrest he told a different story in which he said he was in bed at the time of the murder, and in a third statement he told another story.

All three stories were admitted in evidence over the protest of Chance's counsel, and the court informed the jury that "the testimony of the woman with whom he lived [Mrs. Chance?] was that he was away from home after eight for a greater or less time" the night of the holdup. Liz Nagle testified that he had returned to his rooms about the hour of the murder.

After the three stories were spread upon the record, Chance introduced another line of defense by offering to prove that one O'Brien was the guilty man. He introduced witnesses to show that Mrs. O'Brien, then deceased, once took two bullets from a closet in her home, exhibited them [329] during a quarrel with her husband, and remarked, "The third one killed Russell." Another witness said O'Brien had worn an overcoat like the one belonging to Chance.

This testimony was excluded by the court, however, and Chance then put forward his strongest argument by claiming that he was a. partial cripple, lame, and, by virtue of such a physical handicap, prevented from running from the store after the shooting as described by witnesses. Even though his infirmity was but partial, he said, he could not have run fast enough to outdistance his pursuers.

It seems, however, that this contention of physical incapacity was not convincing to the jury after experts failed to agree as to just how serious his infirmity actually was, and to what degree it would influence his movements.

Nothing further was produced by the defense, and the case was submitted to the jury February 22. After twenty-one hours of deliberation, a verdict of guilty was returned against Chance, while Hagan was acquitted. Chance's appeal was denied, and he began serving a life sentence in the penitentiary September 11, 1899.

• • • •

HAGAN returned to Chicago, and Chance began a series of appeals for executive clemency on the ground that he was innocent; but he elicited no practical response. On November 20, 1905, he wrote to Governor Douglas repeating his claim of innocence and adding that Hagan was reported to have made a voluntary confession in Chicago in which he admitted that he, and not Chance, was the murderer. He also told Governor Douglas that George R. Swasey, Hagan's lawyer at the trial, knew the truth of the case, and that if he would talk he could state facts that would free him.

This report of the alleged confession was ignored, however, and nearly six years passed before it was finally given serious consideration. Governor Foss, in response to repeated requests from Chance, began an investigation of the Hagan statement and sent Joseph Dugan, chief inspector of the Boston police, and Florence Sullivan, an associate counsel in Hagan's trial, to Chicago. [330]

They found Hagan, who had married and was leading a respectable life, and asked him to repeat the confession. He talked freely about himself and told the two men that the matter had preyed on his mind and that he would tell the truth, which others could corroborate, if promised immunity. His request was granted, and he then admitted that he had shot the drug clerk. He said he ran from the store to Chance's home, discarding the coat in the basement where it was later found.

He said he stopped under Chance's window and called up to his friend, saying: "I just plugged a fellow down the street and had to shake your coat. Let's take a walk down the street and see how things are."

Chance came down, bringing Hagan's own coat, and the two men walked to the corner of Harrison and Harvard Streets, where they met a friend and stopped to talk.

Hagan signed a formal statement of the whole affair, in which he said that three people knew the truth of these matters Sullivan, Swasey, and Liz Nagle.

The confession was taken back to Boston by Sullivan and Dugan. It was submitted to the Governor and his council. Other statements were also presented in behalf of Chance— one from Judge Stevens, who presided at the trial, saying he felt that Chance was completely innocent, and another from Swasey. These documents, supplemented by further investigation, convinced the council that a mistake had been made in the conviction, and a unanimous vote recommended a full pardon for Chance.

The pardon was issued June 7, 1911, and Chance was released the same day. He was about forty-four when he left prison and had served nearly twelve years. Agitation began as soon as he was out to have the Legislature pay him $10,000, but the bill did not pass, despite considerable support.

• • • •

CHANCE'S case arouses no special sympathy. It may even be doubtful whether his compensation should not have failed, because he contributed to his misfortune by telling crucial falsehoods in court. It seems that he was much under the [331] influence of Hagan and tried to shield him, believing that he himself was in no danger of conviction. His several inconsistent stories, his shady record, and the admitted ownership of the incriminating overcoat were sufficient, on the misleading circumstantial evidence before it, to warrant a jury's concluding that Chance was guilty. Luckily he was not given the death penalty. Nevertheless, it seems unfortunate that his repeated pleas for the investigation of Hagan's confession, and those of Swasey, Sullivan, and Liz Nagle, should have been ignored until 1911, when the truth might have been disclosed so many years earlier. The Boston public seems to have been much interested in the case, and the community's belief that Chance had paid too high a price for the miscarriage of justice led to the movement for his indemnification by the state. [331]

Perjury

John Chesterman,, alias Christman

JOHN CHESTERMAN, an immigrant from Poland who also used the name of John Christman, had worked a long time for Charles P. Vokes, who at one time lived in the small town of Hardwick, near Worcester, Massachusetts. John had been the faithful and trusted servant and hired man about Vokes's farm, but Vokes had not paid Chesterman any money for a long time, possibly because Chesterman did not collect it when it was due. Finally, in the fall of 1885, Vokes discharged John on some pretext, without paying the back wages.

One afternoon a short time thereafter, Chesterman came to the Vokes farm, and as related to the police by Mr. Vokes, the following events occurred: While Vokes was working in his barn, which was separated from the house only by a sliding door, he heard the door open. On investigating, he met Chesterman entering the barn from the house. He had under his arm a velvet box which belonged to Vokes's wife. In his hand was a traveling bag. [332]

Upon Vokes asking why he was there and what he was doing, John replied that he was cold and had come in to get warm. Vokes ordered him to drop the velvet box and the traveling bag. Chesterman refused.

This started a heated argument, which almost immediately burst into a violent struggle for the possession of the box and bag. After a severe tussle on the barn floor, during which the contents of the bag were scattered over the barn, Vokes managed to get the box and bag away from Chesterman, and Chesterman ran. Vokes sprinted after him, but abandoned the chase when Chesterman jumped into a wide brook and waded to the other side.

Vokes then returned to the house and called police officers. His complaint was made to Officer Woodward of Hardwick. Vokes showed him the jewelry box, which held his \$60.00 gold watch and his \$10.00 watch chain, two gold bracelets worth about \$5.00 each, and two gold rings worth about \$7.00 each. In the traveling bag he exhibited to Woodward a \$10.00 silk dress belonging to his wife. On the floor were strewn various other clothes, including an overcoat and overalls. He said they were just as they had been left when Chesterman ran away. He told Woodward about meeting Chesterman when he opened the sliding door, and suggested that Chesterman must have gained entry into the house through a window which was found open in a bedroom on the ground floor.

With this story of Vokes and a description of the man, the police began to look for Chesterman. They suspected that he would be found at a certain

Polish boarding house, and so waited until almost midnight, when they would be fairly sure to find him there.

While Officer Woodward was inquiring for Chesterman in the office on the first floor, he heard a man run down the stairs and outdoors. The man was pursued and arrested. He proved to be John Chesterman.

A few days later, on November 16, 1885, Charles P. Vokes appeared before Trial Justice Horace W. Bush and before a Grand Jury at West Brookfield and told his story of the larceny, just as he had told it to Officer Woodward. [333]

With this evidence, an indictment for larceny in a building was returned against John Chesterman, alias Christman, by the Grand Jury sitting at Worcester, Massachusetts, on January 21. Herbert N. Rugg was foreman of the Grand Jury.

On the same day, January 21, 1886, Chesterman was brought before the Superior Court in Worcester, and pleaded not guilty to the charge of larceny. He appeared without counsel, probably because he was penniless.

At the trial Vokes told the same story he had told Officer Woodward and Justice Bush. Officer Woodward testified that he saw the articles scattered about the floor as described by Vokes and that he had arrested Chesterman while he was running away from the Polish boarding house.

The prosecution then waited for Chesterman's story. His story was a flat denial of Vokes's version of the matter. He was the only witness for the defense. His story was told simply, though in very imperfect English.

He said that he had worked for Vokes until he had been discharged. Vokes owed him $42, which he refused to pay him, and had threatened to prosecute him because of some trouble with a girl servant at the Vokes house.

Continuing, Chesterman said that he had gone to the barn that afternoon to ask again for his money, that Vokes had drawn his revolver and threatened to shoot him, and that Vokes had chased him and shot at him once but failed to hit him.

In explanation of why he had run away from the Polish boarding house, he said that he supposed the officer had come to arrest him on the charge on which Vokes had threatened to prosecute him, and that therefore he had tried to escape.

However, in view of the plausibility of Vokes's story (apparently corroborated by Woodward's account) and his standing in the community, and Chesterman's poor presentation of his defense in broken English, the jury believed Vokes's version of the affair, and so, practically on his evidence alone, convicted Chesterman of larceny. The judge gave him a sentence of twelve months in the House of Correction. [334]

• • • •

BEFORE Chesterman had been confined very long, Vokes suffered a change of heart. On the sixth of February following Chesterman's conviction, Vokes appeared before Justice of the Peace Clarence Burgess Roote and made a written confession that his testimony before Justice Bush at West Brookfield was false and pure perjury, as was that given at the Grand Jury hearing and at the trial in January.

This confession was made first before a Mr. Samuel S. Demis, one of the selectmen of Hardwick, and before Deputy Sheriff Sylvester Bothwell, to whom he stated that the whole affair, the basis for the threat of prosecution of Chesterman, as well as the story of the larceny, was a falsehood. Vokes said that he had run Chesterman away with his pistol and had then arranged the clothes and jewelry so that it would appear to the officers that a crime had been committed. His motive was to avoid paying Chesterman the $42 which he owed.

On the basis of this confession, the prosecuting attorney, Hon. W. S. B. Hopkins, asked Gov. George D. Robinson for a pardon for Chesterman. Governor Robinson, being assured that Vokes would be prosecuted for the perjury, granted John Chesterman a conditional pardon on the twelfth day of February, and on the next day he was released from the Worcester County House of Correction.

• • • •

THE Chesterman case is included as typical of many similar cases. It exemplifies a conviction based practically on the testimony of a single prosecuting witness, who proves later to have been a perjurer, but whom the trial jury believes in preference to the accused. This is a common occurrence in rape cases, which have been intentionally omitted from this collection. The prosecuting witness, on whose testimony a conviction was obtained, confesses that the testimony was perjured, and thus the case collapses. These cases teach little except the prevalence of perjury and the dangers of conviction on the testimony of a single witness. [335]

"Husbands Ought To Have Some Protection"

Thomas Gunter

MARLIN DREW and his wife, Pearl, lived, with their three children, at the home of Pearl's elderly parents, Mr. and Mrs. Thomas G. Gunter, in Ashland, Mississippi. Marlin Drew was a railroad section hand and in the summer of 1929 was jobless. Many and bitter were the quarrels between Marlin and Pearl arising out of her complaints about his drinking and philandering, and his insinuations that some other man was the father of her expected child. Pearl's parents usually sided with her.

One hot night early in July, 1929, the neighbors were startled by a pistol shot in the Gunter house. Marlin was found in his bed, dead, with a bullet through his heart. A revolver lay near by. The authorities, after the usual investigation, concluded that it was a case of suicide, resulting from drunken despondency.

Dorothy Louise Drew, seven-year-old daughter of the dead man, was sent north to visit some relatives in Tennessee until things calmed down a bit. There, to the surprise of everyone, Dorothy Louise related how she had been sleeping with her "pop," when her "granddad," Thomas Gunter, came into the room and shot her father. The widow, Pearl, who was nearing confinement in Ashland, confirmed the story of her daughter. Gunter was consequently arrested by Sheriff L. L. Winborn on July 7, 1929. Indictment for the murder of his son-in-law quickly followed, and he was brought to trial on August 16, 1929, before Judge Thomas E. Pegram of the Benton County Circuit Court at Ashland. He was prosecuted by District Attorney Fred M. Belk and County Attorney L. T. McKenzie and defended by J. Marvin Crawford. Gunter pleaded not guilty.

The principal witnesses against Gunter were his daughter, Pearl, and her seven-year-old child, Dorothy Louise. The latter, who said she did not know what a Bible was and had heard of God only one time when she went to Sunday school, [336] made a remarkable witness and convinced the jury and those attending the trial that she was telling the truth about seeing her grandfather commit the murder. Pearl's testimony corroborated that of her daughter. The principal defense witness was the prisoner's wife, who swore that Marlin had been shot by Pearl, in a fit of jealousy, while the prisoner was in a drunken stupor in another part of the house. Gunter had never denied that he was drunk on the night of the murder.

The jury chose to believe the widow and daughter of the murdered man and returned a verdict of guilty. Judge Pegram sentenced the convicted man to five years in the state penitentiary, where he was sent at once. Mrs. Drew and her family moved from Benton County. In October, 1929, she gave birth to her fourth child.

As soon as her strength returned, she sent to Gov. Theodore Bilbo a confession in folk-lore rhyme, a variation of the famous ballad, "A Jealous Lover in Lone Green Valley." The rhyme received wide publicity and created a wave of sympathy for its authoress. The confession was accompanied by a plea that her sixty-three-year-old father be pardoned.

At the request of the Governor, Judge Pegram heard Mrs. Drew's full statement in the presence of the district attorney, the county attorney, and the sheriff. Dorothy Louise also told her story and confessed that she had not told the truth before. Pearl confessed that she shot and killed her husband in a rage after he had made remarks about her expected child. She had coached Dorothy Louise, who had witnessed the shooting, to say that her grandfather had done it. Pearl said that it had always been her intention to tell the truth after the birth of her baby, but that she could not bear the idea of its life beginning in prison. All present were convinced of the truthfulness of this confession, and she was arrested for the murder and bound over for appearance before the Grand Jury of Benton County. Governor Bilbo was advised of this action and at once, on November 19, 1929, granted a ninety-day suspension of sentence to Gunter. On February 13, 1930, the Grand Jury indicted Mrs. Drew for the murder and for perjury. She was [337] arraigned before the court the following day and pleaded guilty. Judge Pegram, under his statutory discretion, suspended sentence.

On February 20, 1930, when the ninety-day suspension expired, Governor Bilbo denied Gunter's application for a pardon, and ordered his return to the state penitentiary. The Governor made the following public statement:

> Somebody ought to be in the penitentiary all the time for the murder of a sleeping man. If Judge Pegram does not believe Mrs. Drew is guilty enough to serve her term, then the man convicted of the murder will have to serve his term.
>
> Husbands ought to have some protection.

Gunter refused to return to the penitentiary. According to the latest news (February, 1931), Gunter and Pearl Drew, both found guilty of the same murder, had fled from the state of Mississippi and the ultimate solution of the legal situation remains in abeyance.

• • • •

THIS case of perjury has curious features. There is Judge Pegram's suspension of sentence of Pearl, and even more amazing is Governor Bilbo's Solomonic judgment that, if the real murderer is not jailed, then the wrongly convicted person must serve time. Gunter and his daughter seem to have decided upon their own method of administering justice in the case.

• • • •

Acknowledgment: Hon. Thomas E. Pegram, Ripley, Miss. [337]

The Jury Believed The Detective

Edward L. Hicks

RAILROAD DETECTIVE FITZGERALD was making his rounds in the yards at St. Louis one night in the spring of 1921, when, according to his report, he discovered a package of shirts apparently hidden in the end of a gondola type of freight car. He recognized them as [338] having been stolen from an interstate shipment of goods which was going through the yards. Fitzgerald concealed himself, and soon a man approached, climbed upon the car, and took the shirts. Fitzgerald drew his revolver and arrested him. He gave his name as Edward L. Hicks, a switchman employed by the Terminal Railroad Association of St. Louis.

This was the report Fitzgerald made when he turned his prisoner over to the authorities, and also when he went before the Federal Grand Jury. The Grand Jury returned an indictment charging the prisoner with having in his possession goods stolen from an interstate shipment of freight.

Hicks was brought to trial before Judge C. B. Faris in the Federal District Court, Eastern District of Missouri, in May, 1921. Fitzgerald, the only witness for the prosecution, repeated the story he had told to the Grand Jury. There was no other evidence against Hicks, who testified in his own defense. He said that his foreman had ordered him from one side of the railroad yard to the other, and that he was taking a short cut between cars, when he was stopped by Fitzgerald at the point of his pistol and ordered to pick up a package, after which Fitzgerald arrested him. Hicks further testified that he and Fitzgerald belonged to the same lodge and that there had been a dispute which culminated in a threat by Fitzgerald to "get" him. The foreman testified that he had ordered Hicks across the yard, corroborating the latter's testimony to that extent. In rebuttal Fitzgerald denied that he and Hicks had ever had any trouble, and denied that he had threatened Hicks.

The jury, having to choose between the stories of Fitzgerald and the defendant, believed the detective and found Hicks guilty. On May 9, 1921, Judge Faris sentenced him to serve two years in the Leavenworth Penitentiary. On May 13, 1921, the court granted a motion to file a writ of error, which was finally dismissed by the Circuit Court of Appeals on March 8, 1924.

In the meantime, however, other events transpired. Fitzgerald's elation over the conviction of Hicks was too great for him not to share it with others. When conferring with [339] Attorney Wayne Ely on other matters, he voluntarily brought up a discussion of the Hicks matter, expressing his satisfaction at the conviction and admitting that he had carried out his threat to get even with Hicks as a result of an earlier antagonism. This boastful admission on the part of the detective was called by Mr. Ely to the attention of the Department of Justice in Washington, which instigated an investigation.

Meanwhile, after further inquiries, Judge Faris and United States Attorney Allan Curry reported to the Department of Justice that they believed Hicks innocent. Shortly thereafter, their pardon recommendation was concurred in by a special agent of the Department of Justice, who made a detailed report of his own independent investigation. On August 11, 1924, President Coolidge granted Hicks a full and unconditional pardon on the ground of his innocence.

• • • •

THIS case, like the Chesterman (p. 331) , McManus (p. 346), and Sands (p. 349) cases, turned on the perjury of the sole prosecuting witness, who, by virtue of his station or official position, would naturally be relied on by a jury to tell the truth. Unfortunately, this confidence is sometimes misplaced and in the dilemma as to where veracity rests, the jury guesses wrong. When an officer of the law or person in authority commits perjury to bring about the conviction of an innocent man, the offense is peculiarly heinous. Whether Fitzgerald was ever prosecuted for perjury is not known.

• • • •

Acknowledgments: Mr. Wayne Ely, St. Louis, Mo.; Mr. W. Blodgett Priest, St. Louis, Mo. [340]

Four Witnesses Said He Was The Man

Elmer P. Jacobs

ON August 16, 1928, taxi driver E. A. Stocks reported to the Los Angeles police that two men, whom he had picked up as passengers, had stolen his cab and $7.00. On August 17, taxi man Newt Troelson made a similar report, with the loss of $12.00. On the eighteenth, E. M. Shaw, and on the twentieth, E. I. McDonald, had the same experience. On each occasion the taxi driver was requested to drive to some place which proved to be a lonely spot, where he was held up. Similar crimes were being committed in and around Los Angeles.

The four victims attended the police-department "showups," where arrested persons in groups of six were marched before victims of all sorts of crimes for identification. Early in September, each of the taxi drivers identified one of the prisoners, Elmer P. Jacobs, as one of the taxi robbers.

Jacobs had been arrested for "borrowing" a parked automobile for a joy ride on August 28, 1928. He pleaded guilty to grand larceny on this charge and was sentenced to Folsom as a second offender, having had a criminal record.

In the meantime, however, he had, as related, been identified as the taxi thief. He was indicted for each of the four taxi robberies just described. He was tried on October 30 and 31, 1928, before Judge Emmet H. Wilson of the Los Angeles County Superior Court. R. S. McLaughlin appeared as Prosecutor for the People, and Deputy Public Defender John J. Hill, for Jacobs. Each victim appeared as a witness and described the holdup, stating that Jacobs was one of the robbers. Jacobs was a man with wavy hair, a crooked nose, tight, thin lips (as viewed from the side) , and almond-shaped eyes a person readily recognizable. Jacobs endeavored to establish alibis that he was elsewhere at the time of each occurrence. The alibi evidence was rather indefinite, and a verdict of guilty was returned by the jury for each robbery. On November 5, 1928, he was sentenced [341] on each count to serve "for the time prescribed by law," which was from fifteen years to life.

• • • •

DURING the first week in November, Harvey Hossafrasse, Fredell Nicholson, John Shelby Hobbs, and William Schmittroth were arrested by the police on various charges. Hossafrasse and Nicholson confessed to robbing Newt Troelson and taking his taxicab. The confessions were corroborated by fingerprints. Confessions followed connecting these two with the Stocks and Shaw robberies, and implicating Hobbs and Schmittroth in the McDonald affair. None of this gang knew Jacobs. Detective Captain McCaleb then had these four men placed in the "show-up" and called in again the victims of the robberies. This time the confessed robbers were all positively identified by the victims. It was clear to every one that their earlier identifications of Jacobs had been erroneous. The court, the prosecutor, and the Deputy Public Defender all cooperated to unravel the legal situation.

On November 16, 1928, the court granted Jacobs a sixty-day stay of sentence so that the cases against the real culprits could be disposed of. They were all convicted and sentenced to the penitentiary for various terms. On December 26, 1928, following a hearing, in which the police officers testified that they were satisfied of Jacobs' innocence, the court vacated the judgment and sentence, set aside the verdicts, and dismissed the robbery charges against Jacobs "in the interest of justice," and for lack of evidence that would justify a conviction.

• • • •

THIS was manifestly a case of mistaken identity. But for the subsequent capture and confession of the real culprits, the mistake might never have been corrected. Fortunately for Jacobs, the error was discovered within a few months. Again we have a demonstration of the fallibility of first impression identifications by the victims of a crime.

• • • •

Acknowledgment: Mr. George A. Benedict, Los Angeles, Calif. [342]

They Looked Alike

Louis Klass

FOUR men succeeded in robbing the First National Bank of Spring Valley, Fillmore County, Minnesota, of $15,000 in cash and bonds. They used the plan quite generally adopted by bandits in attacks upon small banks. One man remained in a car in front of the bank, one kept guard just inside the door, covering all persons present, most of whom were forced to lie down, while the remaining two men collected the loot. They made a clear escape.

This was on the afternoon of May 7, 1928. The following day, Detective La Chapelle of the Burns Detective Agency, representing the American Bankers Association, appeared at the bank and presented to the president (Lyle Hamlin) and the vice-president (C. A. Gilbert) a number of^ photographs for purposes of identification. They selected one of a man who looked like the bandit who had stood guard at the door of the bank. A search was at once started to find him Udka Klashtorni, alias Louis Klass. The picture had come into the possession of the detective agency, due to the fact that Klass had in 1924 been convicted in a Federal court in Iowa for having in his possession 850 gallons of intoxicating liquor and also to the fact that he had endeavored to sell some bonds in Chicago in 1927 which, it was discovered, had been stolen from a bank at Vinton, Iowa, on August 19, 1927. The picture of Klass had been taken in 1924. Upon selecting this picture, both Mr. Hamlin and Mr. Gilbert inquired of the detective whether this man might reasonably be suspected of connection with a bank robbery. The detective replied in, the affirmative and related in. detail Klass's alleged connection with the Vinton bank robbery of the previous year.

Klass, then engaged with his brother in business in Minneapolis, soon heard that he was suspected of participation in the Spring Valley holdup. He went to the county seat at once and surrendered to the authorities. Both Mr. Hamlin and Mr. Gilbert identified him. Klass, however, denied any knowledge of or participation in the robbery. [343]

On June 7, 1928, he was indicted for the crime of first-degree robbery and was brought to trial in the District Court for Fillmore County before Judge Norman E. Peterson. The County Attorney was Mr. A. D. Gray, Jr., and the defense attorneys, John W. Hopp and Henry A. Larson. The two principal witnesses against the defendant were Hamlin and Gilbert. Their identification testimony was positive. In defense, an alibi was offered to the effect that the accused was in the Twin Cities at the time of the robbery. Twelve witnesses friends, relatives, and business associates supported by various documents, testified to that effect. The defendant himself testified.

The prosecuting officer, on cross-examination, brought out the fact that Klass was engaged in the brokerage business, dealing in "sugar, malt, molasses, and yeast," the sugar mostly corn sugar, and that he had an extensive business with customers whom he knew principally by their first names. Furthermore, the prosecutor persistently brought out testimony insinuating that Klass had had some connection with the Vinton bank robbery.

The jury elected to believe the bank witnesses, Hamlin and Gilbert, rather than the alibi witnesses, and returned a verdict of guilty. A motion for a new trial was denied by the court and an appeal was taken to the Supreme Court of Minnesota. The Supreme Court, by a three to two decision, reversed the lower court, saying:

> The constant insinuation that the defendant was connected with the Vinton robbery on August 19, 1927, and that the bonds which he sold a few days later were proceeds of that robbery, was wrong and harmful. The testimony invited the jury to find that the defendant, engaged in the unlawful traffic in intoxicating liquor, was guilty of the Spring Valley robbery, and it was made easier to find so because of the insinuation that he had participated in the robbery of the Vinton bank six months before or was selling stolen bonds with guilty knowledge. This was a distinct and emphasized feature of the. trial. Its tendency to prejudice the jury in the determination of the only issue in the case was such that there should be a new trial.

The new trial started on June 10, 1929, before Judge Albert H. Enersen. At this trial the identification testimony [344] of Hamlin and Gilbert was again stressed, but the prosecution produced a new witness, H. C. Dixon, an itinerant stove supply and repair man. He testified that on the evening of May 8, the day after the robbery, he was in a tourist camp at Albert Lea, about forty miles from Spring Valley, when two men arrived who exhibited a large roll of bills and spoke about Spring Valley as a good place, and how easy it was to rob a bank. Dixon identified Klass as one of the men. Klass denied having been at Albert Lea, and his defense was much the same as at his previous trial. The jury again found him guilty. The court denied a motion for a new trial and an appeal was again taken. Klass was sentenced to the Stillwater Penitentiary for a term not to exceed thirty years.

• • • •

IN the meantime, one Frank Devers, a notorious character known as "Bubbling-over" Devers, had confessed to Mr. Gordon, a Burns Agency chief, that he had participated in the Spring Valley robbery, and that Klass had not. Shortly after, Devers was convicted of a post-office robbery and sent to Leavenworth. Devers later retracted his confession. However, due to this and other circumstances, Mr. Hamlin became less positive of the accuracy of his identification, though he still thought he was correct. Mr. Hamlin conscientiously conveyed his doubt to the state officials and defense counsel. Affidavits by Mr. Hamlin were presented as newly discovered evidence with the motion for a. new trial. The Supreme Court of Minnesota, again by a three to two decision, denied the motion on August 29, 1930. On September 5, 1930, Klass was taken to the penitentiary. The Supreme Court granted a rehearing in the matter, but on November 14, 1930, again by a three to two decision, they refused to reverse the decision of August 29. Judicial appeals were thereby exhausted.

Mr. Hamlin, becoming increasingly disquieted over the matter, finally made a trip to Leavenworth to interview Devers. When he saw him, Hamlin became convinced that Devers was the man who had stood guard at the door and [345] that he had been utterly mistaken in his identification of Klass.

Mr. Hamlin thereupon went before the Minnesota Pardon Board in support of an application for the pardon of Klass, insisting on his mistake in identifying Klass. It was explained that there was a marked resemblance between Devers and Klass. Mr. Gilbert also appeared before the Board and stated that he feared that he, also, had been mistaken in his identification. Several hearings were held by the Board, and on July 16, 1931, Klass was granted a pardon upon the ground of innocence. He was immediately released, after more than three years of litigation and nearly a year in the penitentiary.

• • • •

THE mistake in identification was helped by the suggestive production of photographs by a detective and by the allegation that Klass had been connected with the Vinton bank robbery six months before. Actually, there was nothing to show that Klass had come into possession of the Vinton bonds improperly. The method was provocative. Klass's bootlegging record doubtless did not help him. The jury acted true to form in believing the victims of the crime rather than the alibi witnesses. But another detective was a factor in unraveling the error, so the score for the police is even. Fortunately for Klass, Devers was the very man who stood guard at the door. Whether he named his three confederates the record does not show; but Mr. Hamlin, once suspicion of serious error was aroused, took exceptional pains to establish the truth, and, convinced of his error, helped to secure the pardon. The Supreme Court of Minnesota considered the case three times, and the closeness of the division in the court indicates their doubt of the verdict, notwithstanding the fact that their field of review was limited to questions of law.

• • • •

Acknowledgments: Mr. W. H. Lamson, Secretary, State Board of Pardons, St. Paul, Minn.; Mr. Thomas W. McMeekin, St. Paul, Minn. [346]

Only One Witness

John McManus

JOSEPH M. BALK, a peace officer of the city of Boston, Massachusetts, was standing on the corner of Washington Street and Broadway on the night of February 8, 1911. It was about midnight, and very cold, for a heavy snow had fallen all day long. Suddenly, he saw two men running across Washington Street. They turned into Pine Street. The pursuing man was shooting madly at the other.

Officer Balk immediately gave chase. He followed them into Pine Street before he caught up with them. There he found one of the men, who was later identified as John McManus, on his knees in the street. The other man was brandishing a revolver in his right hand and holding in his left a gold watch and chain.

When Balk asked what the trouble was, he was told by the man who held the revolver that the other had stolen his watch and chain, and that he was protecting himself and his property. Nevertheless, Officer Balk took both men to Station No. 4 and lodged them in jail for the night.

The next morning the man with the pistol was brought into court on charges of carrying a concealed weapon. He gave the name of John Shorey, and claimed that he was a deputy sheriff from the town of Conway, New Hampshire. As he was not privileged to carry a pistol in Massachusetts, he was fined $50 and was released.

The other man, John McManus, was held over for trial in the Superior Court on charges of robbery.

No record of the trial of John McManus was ever made, but his story was probably the same as he related in 1912 to Mr. B. D. Driscoll, Assistant Commissioner of Penal Institutions.

McManus stated that he lived in Boston at 205 Harrison Street, and that at about 11:30 on the night of February 8, 1911, he went out to find work. He had been told by a Mr. Coleman that, as there had been a heavy snowfall that day, the Boston Elevated at Tremont and Washington [347] Streets might be hiring some men to shovel snow. He said that he was badly in need of work and that his wife and three-year-old child were then without food. He failed to obtain any work at the station and left there about twelve o'clock to return home.

On his way home he went up Tremont Street to Warrenton, turned down Warrenton, and crossed the street, as that was the shortest way home. When he reached the other side, he was approached by a man who he thought was an officer, as he could see his badge. The man asked him for a match. He replied that he didn't have one. The man then told him to look and "make sure." McManus replied that he knew he didn't have any, as he had looked for one to light his own pipe.

The man then took him over to look at the number on a house. While they were doing this, a girl appeared in a second-story window and threatened to throw water on them if they didn't leave immediately. From her conversation, McManus thought that she knew the man he was with; and the man then explained to him that he had had dinner with the girl early in the evening, but that she had gotten angry at him. He then went to her door and tried to get in, but couldn't open the door. Neither could he persuade the girl to let him in. Finally he turned on McManus to vent his wrath.

McManus' statement says that Shorey called him foul names, cursed him generally, and then attempted to shove him off the sidewalk into the gutter.

When Shorey shoved at him, McManus shoved back, which infuriated Shorey more than ever. He grabbed his gun and shot it once over the head of McManus, who turned and ran.

Shorey followed, kicking at him and shooting. They ran to Washington Street and down Washington, until they reached Pine, where McManus fell down. Just as he was getting up the policeman came upon them, and he was charged with stealing the man's watch. The policeman, as related, took both to jail for the night.

McManus also gave a short story of his life. He had been [348] in America six years, having landed February 20, 1905, in Boston, where he stayed for five weeks before going to New York to live with his two sisters. He remained in New York for two years, then came back to Boston and got married. He also worked part of one year in New Jersey. He said that his age was twenty-eight, that his child was three, and that he had never before been arrested on any charge.

The only witness to appear against him was the deputy sheriff, John Shorey. He told the story that he had told Officer Balk at the time of the arrest. The jury believed the sheriff, and so on March 15, McManus was sentenced to three years in the House of Correction.

• • • •

WHATEVER his misfortune, luck had not altogether deserted McManus. The next January, Shorey again came to Boston, and got into trouble. This time he got drunk, as he probably had been before, and tried to force liquor on a newsboy near North Station. The story of the arrest of a deputy sheriff for the assault and battery of the boy and for pistol carrying appeared in the papers. (He was given three months for each offense this time.) The account did not carry his name, but Officer Balk read the paper. The story of a sheriff of another state assaulting a newsboy and carrying a pistol excited his curiosity and he investigated. He found that the man was none other than John Shorey, the man whom he had arrested nearly a year before. The whole situation excited his suspicion of Shorey, and he carried his story to the office of the district attorney.

The district attorney assigned an investigator to the case. There seems to be no record of the Investigation, but the conclusion was reached that McManus was innocent. On February 27, 1912, the district attorney made a recommendation that McManus be pardoned, stating that he believed that McManus was entirely innocent of the crime for which he had served nearly a year.

On the twenty-eighth of February the pardon was signed by the Governor, and McManus was again a free man, [349] though still a victim of perjury and of adverse circumstances.

• • • •

MCMANUS was the victim of a not uncommon mistake. As between two inconsistent accounts of a single event, the jury credited the untruthful one. Had Deputy Sheriff Shorey not again indulged in his drunken aberrations, Officer Balk would have found no incentive to unravel the wrong inflicted on McManus.

• • • •

Acknowledgments: Joseph M. Balk, the arresting police officer; John R. Campbell, Clerk, Superior Court, Boston, Mass. [349]

FRAME-UP

Icie Sands

IN April, 1929, Patrolman Sydney D. Tait and Eugene Baccaglini of the Harlem vice squad, New York City, entered the apartment of Miss Icie Sands on West One Hundred Thirty-fifth Street, and arrested her on a vagrancy charge. She was taken before one of the New York City Magistrate's Courts for trial. The testimony of the policemen against her was that a stranger was seen to enter her apartment and that, about ten minutes later, these two officers arrived and discovered them in compromising circumstances the man being "unknown." Icie Sands was given a thirty-day sentence in the workhouse.

• • • •

IN 1930 certain conditions existing in the New York City courts impelled the Appellate Division of the New York Supreme Court to make an investigation. The Hon. Samuel Seabury, former Judge of the Court of Appeals and a distinguished citizen, was appointed as the referee, and the investigation began without delay. Charges had been made in dozens of cases that innocent women were being [350] "railroaded" and fleeced of their money by certain members of the police vice squad, in conjunction with bondsmen, lawyers, and hangers-on about the courts. The investigation spread into the whole system, with startling results. It was learned that frequently policemen or detectives of the vice squad sent stool pigeons out to trap intended victims and then appeared themselves at crucial moments to make arrests. The victims were then fleeced not only by bondsmen, lawyers, and others, but occasionally by the policemen who had arrested them, who, if paid sufficiently, would often suppress the charges. The stool pigeons were paid by the policemen for their services.

One of these stool pigeons, Chile Mapocho Acuña, confessed that he had been making a living by this means, and he disclosed numerous cases in which, at the instigation of police officers, the women were "framed" through him. Sometimes he was the "unknown man" caught with the woman, sometimes not. Acuña named the policemen involved. The case of Icie Sands was only one of many. Acuña said that Officers Tait and Baccaglini took him in an automobile to West One Hundred Thirty-fifth Street, gave him $5.00, and sent him into the Sands apartment to get evidence. The officers were to follow in fifteen minutes. They came in five minutes, however, before Acuña had a chance to arrange a trap. Nevertheless, the officers arrested Miss Sands and a man present in the apartment in addition to Acuña; and, on the testimony of the policemen, the man and Acuña having been permitted to disappear, she was convicted. Tait gave Acuña $10.00, and told him that another informer had not succeeded in the job on an earlier attempt.

Tait denied the truth of Acuña's story. He admitted knowing Acuña and paying him as an informer in some cases, but not in this one. He said that he and Baccaglini had parked their car across the street from the Sands tenement house and had seen a stranger walk in at the door and enter the Sands apartment. Further investigation showed that this was untrue, as there was a turn in the hallway making it impossible to see as far as the apartment of Icie. The Sands woman and the man present corroborated Acuña's version of [351] her arrest and identified Acuña as the man who came into her apartment.

All of the above information was presented to a Grand Jury, which, on January 10, 1931, returned an indictment against Tait for committing perjury at the trial of Icie Sands. He was tried in the Court of General Sessions before Judge Morris Koenig in March, 1931. The prosecution was conducted by Assistant District Attorney James Wallace, and Tait was defended by Caesar Barra. The jury found him guilty, and he was sentenced to Sing Sing for a period of from two and a half to five years. In pronouncing sentence, Judge Koenig is reported to have said that the defendant himself was the victim of a system of "framing" women which had grown up in the police department over a period of many years. The maximum sentence of ten years was not given, because the jury urged clemency.

On December 22, 1930, and prior to Tait's trial, Gov. Franklin D. Roosevelt granted pardons to six women who were then serving sentences under convictions resulting from similarly perjured testimony. No pardon was deemed necessary in the case of Icie Sands, as she had completed her sentence many months before. At the present writing, the courts of New York are struggling with numerous cases of criminal acts of policemen in their enforcement of the law, including cases of innocent persons, convicted on perjured testimony.

• • • •

THE condition of affairs disclosed by these cases is an illustration of the corruption that necessarily follows a wholly erroneous method of dealing with a recognized social problem. Such conditions do not occur in European cities, where the problem is dealt with sanely and without hypocrisy. But it is disconcerting in a high degree to find that certain members of the police, who on the whole are probably efficient, are themselves contaminated by the faulty system of law enforcement, if it may be called law enforcement. The law is as misconceived as the enforcement is inefficient, making criminals out of non-criminals. Judge Koenig's comments [352] were justified. When the investigation is complete and more policemen have paid for their perjury, it would be well to reexamine all the ramifications of prostitution, which few, if any, American cities have yet had the courage and foresight to deal with as a biological, social, medical, and ineradicable problem of municipal administration. [352]

Quick Work

George B. Slyter

DURING the early morning hours of March 18, 1931, while the night man, Aaron Oxendale, was still on duty, two men entered the garage of Nelson Brothers at 500 Eleventh Street South, Minneapolis, Minnesota. At first they ordered Oxendale into an adjoining room, but, when their efforts to open the cash register proved fruitless, they brought him back in and forced him to open it for them, one man keeping a gun trained on him. They secured about $50 and made a successful escape. Oxendale at once telephoned the police and gave a description of the men, whom he claimed to have observed closely.

Several days later, Oxendale saw a man whom he thought he recognized as one of his assailants pass the garage, and he immediately called police headquarters. Detectives Arthur Olson and Charles Wetherville were assigned to watch for the man's return. George B. Slyter was arrested by them shortly after as he again passed the garage. Oxendale identified him with certainty, especially because of the dark circles under his eyes.

Slyter denied knowing anything about the robbery, and said that he had spent the evening in question at a St. Patrick's Day party with his mother and sister. In view of Oxendale's positive identification, Slyter was brought to trial in the District Court in Minneapolis. Slyter made a poor witness, and the sister and another guest at the St. Patrick's Day party gave different versions of the affair and its personnel, though Slyter was described as present. After considering the matter for many hours, the jury, on [353] April 21, 1931, returned a verdict of guilty of first-degree robbery, which is punishable in Minnesota by imprisonment for from five to forty years, with double time for second offenders. Unfortunately, years before, Slyter had been convicted of attempted robbery, and under the Minnesota "Baumes law" his sentence was to be from ten to eighty years. Sentence was deferred for several days.

On Saturday, April 25, 1931, Slyter was brought to the District Court by two deputy sheriffs for sentence. He was taken before Judge E. A. Montgomery. Assistant County Attorney Leo J. Gleason, who had charge of the prosecution, got up to address the court. His statement was unusual. He made a request that, in view of new developments, the verdict of the jury be stricken from the records and that the prisoner be freed. The crowd in the court room was astonished, not least of all the prisoner at the bar. Mr. Oxendale, who was in court, was called on to explain the new developments.

On the night just previous, April 24, Oxendale was in the garage with one of the Nelson brothers, the proprietors, when he was again held up by the same bandit who had taken his money in March. He at once called up Mr. Gleason, told him about the robbery, and said that he had made a mistake about Slyter, who was in jail, because the bandit with the dark circles under his eyes had just been around again. Mr. Gleason at once got in touch with County Attorney Edward J. Goff, and it was arranged, without consulting Slyter's lawyer, that a motion should be made to set the verdict aside. Judge Montgomery granted the motion, and the charge against Slyter was -nolled.

Slyter could hardly comprehend this miraculous turn of events. "You are free," the court is reported to have said. "And I wish to compliment Mr. Oxendale for his courage in admitting his mistake, and to congratulate the County Attorney's office for its prompt action to correct this miscarriage of justice."

"Can I go now?" Slyter asked.

"You may go at once," the judge replied. [354]

• • • •

THE unusual feature of this case is that the error was corrected so quickly. But for the fact that the real culprit continued his depredations as in the cases of Andrews (p. 1), Greenwald (p. 79), Sullivan (p. 253), and others the error might never have been discovered. It was fortuitously considerate to commit the crime again on the very night before Slyter's expected sentence. Oxendale made an honest mistake in identification, but was believed by the jury in preference to Slyter and all his witnesses. Doubtless Slyter's former conviction, with his poor reputation in general, was a material handicap. However, the authorities moved promptly to undo the wrong, when it was disclosed.

• • • •

Acknowledgment: Leo J. Gleason, Assistant County Attorney. [354]

"As Full Compensation"

Cornelius Usher

WHEN the Leonard Shoe Company factory of Lynn, Massachusetts, was opened for business on the morning of March 15, 1902, it was discovered that the shop had been entered during the night and that a quantity of lasting pincers and other tools had been taken. The burglars had left no clues.

A day or so later, as Inspector Wells was leaving Manson's Pawn Shop, he saw a man entering with a bundle. He decided to investigate and, after the man had come out, discovered that he had pawned a pair of Niggerhead last pincers for fifty cents. These pincers were subsequently identified as one of the tools taken from the Leonard Shoe Company; and Cornelius Usher, the man who had pawned them, was arrested and charged with breaking and entering the factory and taking the tools.

Usher protested that he had not participated in any theft, but that all he had done was to dispose of certain tools which had been given him by "Jack" Coughlin. His story was that he had been drinking when he met a man by the name of [355]

Hart, and then Coughlin, and had gone walking with them, that Coughlin had tried to pawn the tools and then had given them to him to pawn. He denied positively that he knew that they had been stolen. He was, however, convicted and sentenced by Judge Sherman to from three to five years in the state prison.

Inspector Wells had, in fact, noticed a man named Coughlin standing near the store, but did not arrest or follow him at the time. When he was finally located and brought before Usher, Usher claimed that he was not the right man and that the real Coughlin was a smaller man, who came from Salem. The police continued the search, using the description given by Usher.

On April 16, 1904, John H. Coughlin was recognized in Salem and arrested. When the news of this arrest was made public, Hart appeared before Chief Burckes and stated that he had been present two years before and had seen Coughlin hand the pincers to Usher and tell him to pawn them. He did not explain why he had not volunteered this information before.

Accordingly, a writ of habeas corpus was issued and Usher was brought from the state prison. Judge John W. Berry, before whom the hearing was conducted, declared that the case was a hard one which ought to be brought to the attention of the Governor and his Council, and assured Usher that he would undertake to do this. He ordered Coughlin to be held for the Grand Jury.

Judge Berry became deeply interested in Usher's case and, when proof of his innocence was completed, visited the Governor and began proceedings to secure a pardon. District Attorney W. Scott Peters, whose approval of the pardon was required by the Governor, refused to take action until after Coughlin's guilt was legally established.

On May 20, 1904, Coughlin was arraigned before Judge W. Gushing Waitt in the Superior Court at Salem. He pleaded guilty to the Leonard robbery and was sentenced to eighteen months in the House of Correction. He said that he was sorry that Usher had been sent to the state prison for the crime. [356]

District Attorney Peters then approved the application for a pardon, which was granted to Usher on May 25, 1904.

In March, 1905, the Legislature of Massachusetts passed a bill to indemnify Usher in the amount of $1,000, "as full compensation for his confinement for a period of 1 year, 11 months, and 26 days . . . for a crime of which he was innocent." The resolve was signed by Governor Douglas on March 27, 1905.

• • • •

THIS mistake, based on circumstantial evidence, was perhaps easy to make. Usher was found pawning some of the stolen tools, and it was not unnatural to assume, in the absence of proof of the full facts, that he had participated in the robbery. His story proved to be true, and was established to the satisfaction of all concerned, when Hart appeared and Coughlin pleaded guilty. The Legislature then made limited amends.

• • • •

Acknowledgment: Miss Opal Slater, attorney, Boston, Mass. [356]

A Bad Reputation

Joseph Ward, alias Winston

On February 19, 1895, May Ivers went shopping in Jordan Marsh's store, Washington Street, Boston, Massachusetts. Just as she was entering the store, a man grabbed at her pocketbook, but she held on and it was taken from her only after a short scuffle. The purse contained only $3.00 and some small change.

The struggle lasted long enough to enable other people to come to the scene; and, before the bag snatcher could get away, he was caught. An accomplice, however, who took a more passive part in the affair, made his escape, but not before he had been seen by several people. The man who was caught gave the name of James Mahoney.

He was taken immediately to the police station. There he was questioned as to the other man, but would give no [357] information. Finally, he procured bail and was given his liberty until the time of trial.

The police then set out to look for the other man. Although Mahoney refused to give the police information, a good description had been obtained from two of the store detectives, Edith and Gertie Thompson, and from a passerby named Ray Ross.

Several weeks later the police picked up Joseph Ward, alias Winston, because he answered the description of the man who had escaped. The eyewitnesses of the affair identified him, and he was held until the Grand Jury met in April. An indictment was then returned against him and his trial set for April 18. Mahoney's trial was probably set for the same date so that they could be tried together; but when the time came for Mahoney's trial, Mahoney was not to be found. He had jumped his bail. The case was therefore prosecuted against Ward alone.

The prosecution, in charge of Assistant District Attorney John D. McLaughlin (later for twenty years Judge of the Superior Court), depended entirely upon the testimony of the several eyewitnesses. May Ivers identified Ward as one of the men, as did Edith and Gertie Thompson and Ray Ross. Police Inspector Joseph H. Knox also identified him. Thomas Barry, L. A. Masury, and Frank Lewis, other officers called as witnesses, appear also to have identified Ward; and, as he refused to testify in his own behalf, the verdict could be none other than guilty. Accordingly, he was sentenced, on April 18, to five years in the state prison.

The reason for Ward's refusal to testify was explained in response to a question by Inspector Knox. He stated to Knox that he was in another state on February 19, but that he was afraid to take the stand in his own defense, for he would then have been open to all questions, and that he was afraid that his former criminal record would be used against him by the prosecution and the jury. He felt sure that if the jury knew that he was a former criminal his punishment would be more severe. [358]

• • • •

THREE months later, in July, Mahoney was rearrested. In the meantime, Jesse M. Gove, Ward's attorney at the trial, had become convinced after some investigation that Ward's story of his presence in another state on February 19 was true. Mr. Gove told Mahoney that Joseph Ward had been convicted as an accomplice in the bag snatching charged against Mahoney. Mahoney then said that Ward was not the man who was with him, that the accomplice was a man named Dooley, from New York, and that Ward had had nothing to do with the affair.

Mr. Gove then took the matter to Inspector Knox, who made his own investigation. Inspector Knox visited the places Ward frequented and he also looked for Dooley. He found from a number of descriptions given of the two men, that Ward and Dooley must have resembled each other closely. After a long investigation, Knox became completely convinced that Dooley really was the man with Mahoney, and not Ward.

Having reached this conclusion, he suggested to Attorney Gove that he apply for a pardon for Ward. He also informed the prosecutor, Mr. McLaughlin, that he was satisfied that Ward was innocent.

On January 16, 1896, Inspector Knox wrote a letter to the Governor suggesting a pardon. District Attorney Oliver Stevens also made a formal recommendation for Ward's release.

On January 30, 1896, Ward was pardoned by the Governor. The Governor gave as his reason Ward's innocence, attested by the prosecuting officers, who had "become satisfied that it was another party, closely resembling Ward, who committed the offense." He further assigned as a reason for the mistake "Ward's bad reputation."

• • • •

WARD'S conviction, like many others, was due to mistaken identity. Ward's reluctance to testify, and his fear that he would lay himself open to all kinds of questions and that his criminal record would bring about a harsher sentence, were not unjustified. The English rule limiting the asking [359] of questions on past record (infra, p. 370) might wisely be adopted in the United States. Inspector Knox, now dead, deserves commendation for his energy in verifying the truth of Ward's statement that he was not in Massachusetts on the day of the crime and of Mahoney's story that Dooley was the guilty man. It does not appear that compensation was ever offered to Ward.

• • • •

Acknowledgment: Hon. J. D. McLaughlin, Superior Court, Salem, Mass. [359]

“GET IT OVER WITH”

James Willis

IN broad daylight, at three o’clock on the afternoon of March 19, 1927, in the streets of Sacramento, California, young Robert Richardson, driving a Buick coach, was approached by a determined-looking man and, at the point of a revolver, was forced to accept the man as a passenger and to drive him about the city for over an hour, the passenger meanwhile imbibing the contents of a whiskey bottle. Finally, Richardson was ejected from his car on the outskirts of the city and the bandit drove off. Shortly thereafter, the bandit held up Paul Winstead, operator of the Union Oil station at Tenth and F Streets, Sacramento, taking about $30. He then proceeded to a service station owned by Oscar G. Jones, whom he shot three times in the arm and once in the back after an argument over money. He then drove off.

Soon after, the Buick was found abandoned near the Sacramento Police Station. It was learned that the shooting of Jones had been done with a .22-caliber pistol. Each of the three victims supplied the police with a description of the fugitive. They arrested as a suspect James S. Willis, twenty-seven-year-old son of a prominent Stockton physician. Willis fitted the description well, and while young [360] Richardson would not identify him, the victims Winstead and Jones did. Furthermore, the police knew that Willis had a police record, having been twice convicted in the state of Washington, was a drug addict, and at that very time was under a charge of having a short time earlier burglarized an office in Stockton from which whiskey and two .22 revolvers had been stolen.

On April 8, 1927, Willis was indicted by a Sacramento County Grand Jury on charges of first-degree robbery and assault with intent to commit murder. Willis repeatedly denied that he was in any way connected with the Sacramento crimes charged.

On April 12, 1927, he was arraigned before Judge J. F. Pullen of the Superior Court of Sacramento County. The defendant was represented by Mr. Coale of Stockton, engaged by the prisoner’s father, who was also present. To both of these men, James stoutly denied his guilt; but when it came time for him to enter his plea, he answered, “Guilty.” He was consequently convicted, and was sentenced and committed to the State Prison at San Quentin for an indeterminate term of from five years to life on the robbery charge; and from one to fourteen years on the other, the sentences to run consecutively.

• • • •

AT about this same time, twenty-three-year-old Vincent Bohac walked into a police station in Detroit, Michigan, and stated that he had shot a man the previous month in Sacramento, California, and that although he didn't know whether his victim had died, he wished to return to California to pay the penalty. The California authorities, on being notified, sent for Bohac; he arrived in Sacramento on May 7, 1927. He at once made a complete confession, going so far as to lead the police to the spot where he had buried the pistol and some of the loot. It was still there. As soon as Richardson saw Bohac he immediately identified him, and so did Winstead and Jones. The latter two freely admitted that their earlier identification of Willis was wrong. Bohac and Willis had the same general appearance. Bohac did not know of [361] the conviction of Willis, and he had surrendered solely to clear his conscience.

In the third week of May, 1927, Bohac pleaded guilty to the crimes of first-degree robbery and assault with intent to murder, and he was accordingly sentenced and sent to San Quentin. Thereupon, the district attorney of Sacramento County brought the facts to the attention of Governor Young, who, because of Willis' prior record, referred the matter to the California Supreme Court for recommendation, which was given forthwith. Accordingly, on August 18, 1927, Governor Young granted Willis a pardon upon the express ground of his innocence.

The Governor's official comment upon Willis' "guilty" plea is interesting:

> Willis, realizing that, in general, he answered the description of the man who committed the offenses charged against him, confronted with his previous criminal record, faced with a burglary charge pending against him in Stockton, and being unable to satisfactorily account for his whereabouts, evidently pleaded guilty in the hope of obtaining some consideration, although maintaining his innocence at all times to his father, his attorney, and the prosecuting and investigating officers.

• • • •

BUT for Bohac's voluntary and completely corroborated confession, Willis might have served out his sentence. The plea of guilty is accounted for by District Attorney McAllister by the suggestion that Willis, confronted with an apparently hopeless case, wanted "to get it over with." The evidence against him consisted solely of identification by the victims, which rested on no better foundation in this case than in many others. Yet the identification would doubtless have sufficed to convict. Probably the voluntary plea of guilty, however it may be explained, would, under the California statute, bar Willis' claim for compensation. Governor Young in his pardon expresses the belief that both young men are capable of rehabilitation. [362]

He Worked All Week

Luigi Zambino

COUNTERFEIT money is a great problem for the secret-service agents of the United States Treasury Department. When one visits the offices of this service, let us say in New York City, the piles of paper and metal money on tables carry one back to the stories of the medieval countinghouses until it is observed that each piece of money has a criminal history attached to it. The agents who operate for the Federal Government from this office are alert to pick up bits of information which lead to persons who are manufacturing counterfeit money or knowingly passing it.

In the latter part of December, 1905, one Frank Manfra was caught in the net of the Secret Service in New York City. On him, at the time of his arrest, were found fifteen counterfeit United States five-dollar silver certificates. Manfra, caught with the evidence, confessed to the authorities. In his confession he implicated Luigi Zambino, whom, he said, he had met in Paterson, New Jersey, in November, 1905. Manfra said that Zambino proposed that they go into the business of "passing money." He said that they did so, spending the counterfeit money quite freely in various saloons in Paterson and Hackensack.

Luigi Zambino, an Italian mill hand, lived in Lawrence, Massachusetts, where he worked in the Pemberton Mills. He was the principal support for his parents, both over seventy-five years old, a wife, and nine children, whose ages ranged from five to twenty. On Manfra's statement, Luigi was taken into custody and transferred to Trenton, New Jersey, where his difficulties increased.

On December 8, 1905, some counterfeit five-dollar silver certificates had been given to Charles L. Wyatt, a wholesale whiskey dealer in Hackensack, New Jersey. Wyatt reported to the authorities that at about six o'clock in the evening, two men entered his store to purchase whiskey. One, whom he identified as Manfra, purchased a quart of whiskey [363] and paid for it with the counterfeit money. Wyatt identified Zambino as Manfra's companion.

Zambino said that he was absolutely innocent of any charge of counterfeiting and that, though he had once known Manfra, he had not been in New Jersey at the time when Wyatt claimed he had visited his shop. With Wyatt's identification and Manfra's implicating confession against him, however, Zambino had very little chance. United States Attorney John B. Vreeland presented the matter to the Federal Grand Jury, at the June Term, 1906, and Zambino was indicted for counterfeiting and uttering United States five-dollar certificates, and in. particular, with intent to defraud Charles L.

Wyatt. He was brought to trial before Judge Joseph Cross, in the United States District Court for New Jersey, on July 11, 1906. He was defended by Mr. Martin Wecksler.

At the time of Zambino's trial, Frank Manfra had already been convicted and was serving his sentence in the Kings County Penitentiary, New York. He was brought to Trenton for the trial and there testified on behalf of the prosecution against Zambino. Wyatt on the stand positively identified Manfra and Zambino. On the question of. Zambino's criminal intent, the prosecutors produced as witnesses Edward F. Quigley of Lawrence, Massachusetts, and Edwin F. Hatch of Lowell, Massachusetts, both of whom testified that the defendant had passed similar counterfeit money on them on August 12, 1905. It appeared that Hatch had picked Zambino's picture from photographs of a group of suspects before seeing him to make the personal identification.

Zambino's defense was an alibi, and he eagerly took the stand in his own defense. He said that he had been working regularly in the Pemberton Mills, and that he was at his job on December 8, 1905. He denied that he had ever made any propositions to Manfra to start passing bad money, and he denied being with Manfra in Hackensack and Paterson as charged. To support the prisoner's alibi that he was at home or at work in Massachusetts throughout the whole day in question, the defense called the prisoner's daughter, [364] Rosina Zambino, a nephew, Domenico Cardegna, and Michael Basco. The testimony showed that the prisoner had no criminal record, but in rebuttal the prosecution was able to pick some minor errors in the defendant's statements. The case went to the jury the same day, and it returned a verdict of guilty. Although Zambino maintained his innocence, no appeal was taken, and on July 16, 1906, Judge Cross sentenced him to six years at hard labor in the New Jersey State Prison, and to pay a fine of $500. In the fall of that same year, Zambino was transferred to the Federal Penitentiary at Atlanta, Georgia still protesting his innocence.

• • • •

THE plight of the family of this prisoner came to the attention of J. C. Sanborn, an attorney of Lawrence, Massachusetts, and he carefully investigated the facts of the case. Much to his surprise he learned that the records of the Pemberton Mills showed conclusively that Zambino had worked the whole week from December 4 to December 9, 1905, and from 6:30 in the morning to 5:00 in the afternoon of each day. William McConville, Zambino's overseer in the dye department, said that he remembered well that Zambino had been at work then, as did Emma L. Gleason, the timekeeper. These two persons had been requested by the defense to appear at the trial, Miss Gleason being sent $15 for her expenses and subpoenaed; but neither one took the trouble to go to Trenton for the trial. Attorney Sanborn, armed with documentary evidence covering these facts, prepared an application for Zambino's pardon, on the ground of his innocence. This was signed by many of the outstanding citizens of Lawrence, who gave Zambino an excellent character for being an honest, hard-working man. At the time of his arrest he had been living in Lawrence over eleven years. It was explained that the Zambino family were poverty-stricken and they could not afford to pay the expenses of an attorney to visit Trenton to check over the trial evidence and possibly to find Manfra's copartner in the affair; it developed that Manfra had a brother who looked a great deal like Zambino, and that Manfra was probably seeking to protect this brother. While [365] Zambino was in Atlanta, Manfra's term expired and he was freed. He was soon rearrested, however, and convicted of uttering exactly the same kind of counterfeit silver certificates which he had formerly said he had received from Zambino. In view of the circumstances, the Attorney-General assigned a special agent to investigate the whole case in Lawrence, in Hackensack, and in Trenton. The contents of this agent's report will probably never be known, as it is kept strictly confidential in the pardon records of the Department of Justice, but apparently the agent learned that all of Attorney Sanborn's statements were true, that the identifications of Zambino by Wyatt, Quigley, and Hatch were erroneous, and that Manfra's testimony was entirely unreliable; for, upon the recommendation of Attorney-General Wickersham, President Taft granted Zambino a full and unconditional pardon on November 4, 1909, after he had served over three years and four months of his sentence. Zambino then returned to his destitute family in Lawrence.

• • • •

THIS case of mistaken identity and perjury is unusual in the fact that a guilty offender, Manfra, chose to name as his accomplice a man whom he knew and who resembled a brother whom he was trying to shield. The resemblance was apparently sufficient to induce three victims of the fraud to identify Zambino as Manfra's accomplice, and, as Manfra claimed, the instigator of the counterfeiting scheme. Zambino's poverty and the failure of his witnesses to appear proved insuperable handicaps, for he was unable to undertake the investigations which could have established his innocence. Good fortune, induced by the poverty of Zambino's family, later brought into the case Mr. Sanborn, who unraveled the mystery and convinced the investigators of the Department of Justice that a mistake had been made. A closer analysis of the facts by a public defender might have established the truth of the alibi at the trial. But to accomplish that, money was necessary and Zambino had none. Where the innocence is conclusively established, as in this [366] case, it would seem proper for the Department of Justice, if only by way of vindication for the unhappy victim of judicial error, to disclose the full facts rather than to keep them confidential. [367]

Conclusion

THE present collection of sixty-five criminal prosecutions and convictions of completely innocent people exemplifies the manner in which these mistakes in the administration of justice occur. The cases fall into certain groups. The particular errors are so typical that it seems permissible to draw certain inferences from them in order that their repetition may be minimized and, if possible, avoided.

Perhaps the major source of these tragic errors is an identification of the accused by the victim of a crime of violence. This mistake was practically alone responsible for twenty-nine of these convictions.[1] Juries seem disposed more readily to credit the veracity and reliability of the victims of an outrage than any amount of contrary evidence by or on behalf of the accused, whether by way of alibi, character witnesses, or other testimony. These cases illustrate the fact that the emotional balance of the victim or eyewitness is so disturbed by his extraordinary experience that his powers of perception become distorted and his identification is frequently most untrustworthy. Into the identification enter other motives, not necessarily stimulated originally by the accused personally—the desire to requite a crime, to exact vengeance upon the person believed guilty, to find a scapegoat, to support, consciously or unconsciously, an identification already made by another. Thus doubts are resolved against the accused. How valueless are these identifications by the victim of a crime is indicated by the fact that in eight of these cases[2] the wrongfully accused person and the really guilty criminal bore not the slightest resemblance to each other, whereas in twelve other cases,[3] the resemblance, while fair, was still not at all close. In only two cases[4] can the resemblance be called striking.

Dean Wigmore has suggested[5] a more scientific method, based on the psychology of recognition, for effecting identifications. He proposes the use of the talking film, by which body, motions, and voice of the subject shall be recorded in numerous poses, the pictures then to be presented to viewers in a series of perhaps twenty-five similar films, selected from [368] a classified stock of one hundred types of men and women on file, the viewers to indicate recognition by the pressure of an electric button. When it is realized how unreliable the haphazard methods of identification have frequently proved to be, it will be apparent that more scientific methods of identification must be devised.

There are a few cases,[6] including cases of alleged rape—a type intentionally omitted from this collection—where the issue of guilt turns mainly upon the veracity of the prosecuting witness and of the accused. But little scientific study has yet been made of the problem of lying witnesses or of defective powers of observation and of the effect of suggestion in criminal cases.

In thirteen of the cases[7] no crime at all was committed, and in three other cases[8] the commission of any crime is doubtful. In the balance of the cases, a crime appears to have been committed, but it was not committed by the accused.

Erroneous convictions on circumstantial evidence exclusively, that is, in the absence of identification and perjury, are not many, yet enough to be disturbing. Of the eleven cases of this type here recorded,[9] eight involve charges of murder in the first degree and convictions of murder in the first or second degree.

No one will suggest that circumstantial evidence should be excluded as a form of evidence. On the contrary, it is often convincing and conclusive. That it is, nevertheless, often misleading and unreliable, the cases here reported attest. Chief Justice Shaw, in his celebrated charge to the jury in Dr. Webster's case, said:

> The advantages [of circumstantial evidence] are that, as the evidence commonly comes from several witnesses and different sources, a chain of circumstances is less likely to be falsely prepared and arranged, and falsehood and perjury are more likely to be detected and fail of their purpose. The disadvantages are, that a jury has not only to weigh the evidence of facts, but to draw just conclusions from them; in doing which, they may be led by prejudice or partiality, or by want of due deliberation and sobriety of judgment, to make hasty and false deductions; a source of error not existing in the consideration of positive evidence.[10] [369]

Cases of circumstantial evidence into which entered a mistaken identification are fifteen in number.[11] Cases of circumstantial evidence in which perjury was an ingredient are eleven in number.[12] Cases in which the perjury of prosecuting or other witnesses, taking advantage of circumstantial evidence, natural or manufactured, was the main factor in the conviction are not inconsiderable fifteen.[13] Among them are four for murder in which the alleged "murdered" person later turned up alive and well.[14] In fourteen cases the victim was "framed" by hostile witnesses.[15]

There is not much that the prosecuting or judicial machinery can do to prevent some of these particular miscarriages of justice. In many of the cases just mentioned, the prosecuting attorney was obliged to take the evidence as presented to him, including the uncontrollable perjury of vengeful witnesses, and lay it before the jury without realization of its worthlessness. Yet in only a few of the cases can it be said that no fault, carelessness, or overzealousness can be charged to the prosecution. In this group we may, by liberality, list sixteen cases.[16] In a very considerable number, the zealousness of the police or private detectives,[17] or the gross negligence of the police in overlooking[18] or even suppressing[19] evidence of innocence, or the prosecution's overzealousness[20] was the operative factor in causing the erroneous conviction. Such lapses from the impartial enforcement of the law are hardly excusable. Yet, without making any claim to generalization, it is common knowledge that the prosecuting technique in the United States is to regard a conviction as a personal victory calculated to enhance the prestige of the prosecutor. Except in the few cases where evidence is consciously suppressed or manufactured, bad faith is not necessarily attributable to the police or prosecution; it is the environment in which they five, with an undiscriminating public clamor for them to stamp out crime and make short shrift of suspects, which often serves to induce them to pin a crime upon a person accused.

Especially is this the case where the accused has been previously convicted or has had unfortunate experiences with the criminal law. Evidence of a prior conviction is often [370] fatal to an accused person,[21] and the prejudice it is calculated to create in the minds of the jury is doubtless one of the main reasons why prosecutors insist upon such evidence. Baffled by crime waves, the result of conditions the public seems unwilling to recognize and face, there has been a growth in public impatience not only with the technicalities of the law, by which so many guilty criminals escape conviction, but also with the normal processes of the law, designed to safeguard the accused against injustice. For example, in connection with the growing prevalence of "Baumes law" statutes, punishing second, third, and fourth offenders with progressively drastic sentences, a trial may open, as in the Nedza case, with the introduction by the prosecution of evidence of the accused's prior conviction. Though this is prohibited in many states, a clever prosecutor often succeeds in evading the law. The accused's case is thereby grievously if not hopelessly prejudiced, and a conviction on the presently charged offense much facilitated. Inasmuch as prior convictions affect the severity of the sentence only and do not constitute proof of guilt of the present crime, such evidence should be reserved exclusively for the judge *after* the jury brings in its verdict.

Even where it is not possible to introduce certificates of prior conviction, many prisoners often refuse to take the witness stand in order to avoid questions by the prosecutor concerning their previous record. To prevent the prejudice which such questions obviously inspire in the minds of the jury, English law permits questions as to a previous conviction under exceptional circumstances only, such as the fact that there is a direct relation between the earlier and the present crime, as in forgery and counterfeiting, or where the accused himself raises the issue of his good character.[22] Justice could be promoted in the United States by similar precautions and restrictions.

For the reason just mentioned, it is not true to say that only guilty persons avail themselves of the constitutional privilege against self-incrimination by refusing to testify. While the subject deserves the fullest consideration before action is taken to repeal the privilege, it seems probable that [371] the privilege is not an essential condition of the impartial administration of justice and that it does not afford to the accused the protection assumed. On the contrary, it is probably responsible for many abuses, not least of all the "third degree," which subjects accused persons to far more brutal and intolerable ordeals than any obligation to tell the truth in open court. Refusal to take the stand—under circumstances where an explanation from the accused is naturally expected—even if it cannot be commented upon by judge or prosecutor, inevitably affects the jury unfavorably; but in addition, the accused's known privilege of refusing to testify influences the police to exact "confessions" which, whether true or not, stigmatize the system of obtaining them as a public disgrace. The Report of the President's Commission on Lawlessness in Law Enforcement should awaken the public to the impropriety of such a system of securing "confessions." Even if the end is sometimes useful, as in eliciting the names of confederates, that does not excuse or justify the means. But even before the constitutional privilege against self-incrimination can be repealed, safeguards protecting the prisoner from duress can be established, by prohibiting the use in evidence of all confessions made to the police, by disciplinary measures, and by insuring that all questioning of the accused shall be carried on only before a magistrate and witnesses, perhaps in the presence of phonographic records, which shall alone be introducible as evidence of the prisoner's statements.[23]

In several of the cases in this collection a species of third degree or undue influence produced "confessions" from the accused confessions which constituted a material factor in their convictions. Notable among these are the cases of Johnson in Wisconsin and Stielow in New York, both men of poor intelligence, influenced by promises of forthcoming advantage to themselves. The confessions in the Boorn and Butler and Yelder cases are explainable only on psychological grounds and have no special interest. The Lyons confession, coming after the conviction, is in the main amusing. While confessions may often seem conclusive, they must be carefully examined. Persons charged with crime are not [372] infrequently of defective or inferior intelligence, and, even without the use of formal third-degree methods, the influence of a stronger mind upon a weaker often produces, by persuasion or suggestion, the desired result. State's Attorney Homer Cummings, in the Connecticut case of Israel, who under pressure confessed the murder of a priest, but whom Mr. Cummings refused to try, said:

It was the opinion of the physicians that any confession made by the accused was totally without value, and they were of the opinion also that if they cared to subject the accused to a continuous and fatiguing line of interrogation, accusation and suggestion, in due course he would be reduced to such a mental state that he would admit practically anything that his interrogators desired. They further stated that this was a common phenomenon with certain types of people, and that where such people are subjected to interrogatories, accusations or suggestions from persons of stronger will, the lesser mind will ultimately succumb and accept the conclusions of the more powerful intellect.[24]

Public opinion is often as much to blame as the prosecutor or other circumstances for miscarriages of justice. Criminal trials take place under conditions with respect to which public interest and passions are easily aroused. In fourteen of the cases in this collection in which the frightful mistake committed might have been avoidable, public opinion was excited by the crime and moved by revenge to demand its sacrifice, a demand to which prosecutors and juries are not impervious.[25] This can by no means be deemed an argument for the abolition of the jury, for judges alone might be equally susceptible to community opinion. But it is a fact not to be overlooked.

In eight of the murder cases[26] recorded here, no crime was committed at all. Nobody was murdered. The convictions rested upon perjury or circumstantial evidence and were later shown to have been without foundation. In six of the cases,[27] the person alleged to have been murdered turned up hale and hearty some time after the supposed murderer had entered upon his sentence in the penitentiary. In several of the cases the convicted prisoner, later proved innocent, was saved from hanging or electrocution by a hairbreadth.[28] [373]

Only by rare good fortune were some of the sentences of hanging and electrocution commuted to life imprisonment or indictments for first-degree murder modified by verdicts of second-degree murder, so that the error could still be corrected.[29] How many wrongfully convicted persons have actually been executed, it is impossible to say. But that these cases offer a convincing argument for the abolition of the death penalty, certainly in cases of convictions on circumstantial evidence, can hardly be gainsaid.[30]

The unreliability of so-called "expert" evidence is disclosed by eight striking[31] cases. It seems clear that there is a necessity for publicly employed impartial experts who have no more interest in the case than the judge. Wisconsin has such a statute providing for experts to be appointed by the court, after notice and hearing.[32]

The errors here recorded were uncovered in various ways:

1. In the case of peculiarly original crimes, by the fact that they continued to be perpetrated after the wrong person was in custody.[33]

2. By the corroborated confessions of guilty third persons or of prosecuting witnesses.[34]

3. By the substantiated confessions of one or more accomplices in a joint crime, by which all the guilty participants were named or identified and thus the wrongfully accused person proved innocent.[35]

4. By sheer good luck, by which the police or the prosecutor or the governor discovered that the wrong man was caught and convicted.[36] How many unfortunate victims of error have no such luck, it is impossible to say, but there are probably many.

After discovery of clear error, police, prosecutor, and court have in many cases shown commendable zeal in undoing the wrong.[37]

Some of the more detailed factors which resulted in the wrongful convictions are mentioned in the comments after each case. Proof that an alibi or collateral testimony offered by the accused was false, though in fact the accused had nothing to do with the crime, was extremely prejudicial, if [374] not fatal, in several cases.[38] Chief Justice Shaw in the Webster case exhibited profound knowledge of human nature when he said:

> … an innocent man, when placed by circumstances in a condition of suspicion and danger, may resort to deception in the hope of avoiding the force of such proofs. Such was the case often mentioned in the books, and cited here yesterday [John Graham], of a man convicted of the murder of his niece, who had suddenly disappeared under circumstances which created a strong suspicion that she was murdered. He attempted to impose on the court by presenting another girl as the niece. The deception was discovered and naturally operated against him, though the actual appearance of the niece alive, afterwards, proved conclusively that he was not guilty of the murder.[39] [Graham was in fact executed, before the child (his daughter, not his niece) reappeared.]

The fact that a person accused of robbery of money was shown to have had no money after the crime should have been a factor in demonstrating the innocence, for example, of Galindo, Nedza, and Stielow, though it seems to have been disregarded by the police and prosecution. The fact that witnesses are often persuaded to make identifications by suggestion of the police is evidenced in the cases of Nedza, Sullivan, and Zambino, where a single photograph was exhibited to a distant witness, and in the cases of Flood, McKinney, and Nedza, where the accused was dressed according to the description of the culprit and forced to perform antics attributed to the guilty man.

In the majority of these cases the accused were poor persons, and in many of the cases their defense was for that reason inadequate. The practice of assigning attorneys or the inability to engage competent attorneys makes it often impossible for the accused to establish his innocence. The establishment of a Public Defender paid by the county or state would do much to remedy this source of injustice.[40]

The Committee on Public Defenders of the New York State Bar Association reported in 1930 as follows:

> In the opinion of your committee, the present system of assigned counsel to represent accused persons is a total failure, it is not fair to the accused person, it creates a public disrespect for the administration of the criminal law, it does not promote justice, and [375] it places an innocent prisoner at a distinct disadvantage in obtaining that fair trial which is guaranteed to all by our laws.
>
> We believe further, that the best interests of such accused persons and of society in general would be promoted by the establishment in the state of New York by law, of elected public defenders, for the present at least, in the more populous counties of the state, and in such other counties from time to time, as may be deemed advisable.[41]

The expense frequently incurred in proving a person's innocence, as is manifest in the Andrews, Kimball, Stielow, and other cases, and the fact that relatively few convicted persons can assume such a burden, makes it seem desirable that, for certain cases in which the suspicion of error is strong, an independent public investigating committee be established, which shall become part of the judicial machinery, and which may be invoked at the request of the trial judge or the governor or the board of pardons, as the case may be. The haphazard investigations now often instigated are hardly adequate or efficient. The expense to the state would not be great and the opportunity of correcting error considerable.

There should be a review by an appellate court on the facts as well as on the law, in cases of felony or at least in capital cases, as there is in New York and New Jersey and in England and Scotland. Appeals for errors of law only often defeat the interests of justice, not only in granting new trials on technicalities where no substantial injustice can be shown, but in refusing to set aside an unjust verdict merely because technical compliance with formal rules is established. The Court of Criminal Appeal in England and Scotland, fittingly enough, came into being through the egregious errors and negligence manifested in the Beck and Slater cases. In nearly all our states the appellate courts can reverse a conviction only for errors of law.[42] They are bound by the jury's finding of fact, however wrong they may consider the conclusion. Many of the convictions recorded in this volume, though utterly mistaken, were affirmed by the highest courts of the state. Contrary to the European practice generally, evidence of miscarried justice or perjury discovered after final judgment is in many American [376] jurisdictions no ground for a new trial, because appellate courts maintain their incompetence to consider it. A petition for executive clemency becomes then the only available remedy. There is no good reason why the courts should not remain open to correct substantial errors in the administration of justice.

The trial judge, though deprived of much discretion by his statutory inability to comment upon the weight or credibility of the evidence,[43] still has much power to pass on motions for new trials. Except for technical legal errors, his discretion in this matter is usually unreviewable. The Massachusetts Judicial Council in its Third Annual Report[44] commented upon this defect in the judicial system as follows:

> A single judge of the Superior Court now presides over murder trials and passes not only on questions of law involved in the trial of the indictment, but upon mixed questions of law and fact arising on motions for a new trial. The Supreme Judicial Court on appeal passes only on questions of law. As the verdict on such an indictment involves the issue of life and death, we think the responsibility too great to be thrown upon one man. If he errs in any matter of discretion as distinguished from law, the result is irreparable. Even if he is right, his decisions may be challenged, especially in a time of public excitement and there is no tribunal to establish the fact that he is right. It is vital that our Courts do justice; it is also vital that people know that they do justice.
>
> While the Supreme Court may determine that, as matter of law, there was no evidence of guilt sufficient to warrant the submission of the case to the jury, yet if there was such evidence it is beyond the power of the Supreme Court to pass upon its weight and to hold that the verdict of the jury was not justified upon the facts.
>
> It is true that the decisions of the trial judge upon matters of discretion, may be reversed if there has been what is called an "abuse" of discretion, that is to say if "no conscientious judge acting intelligently could have honestly taken the view expressed by the trial judge." It is needless to say that such an abuse will so rarely be found by the Supreme Court to have existed that there is no real appeal from that judicial fact.
>
> It follows that the final decision of many of the most important questions which arise in connection with a murder trial, as in other cases, is committed so far as the courts are concerned to a single judge of the Superior Court. An unjust decision by him upon such a question can be redressed by the governor and council alone, upon

[377] an application for a pardon or commutation of the sentence. The power of the executive to intervene in an appropriate case is highly important and should by no means be curtailed. The attempt to evoke its exercise is sure to be made, not infrequently, so long as it can be rightfully urged that important questions in the case have been passed upon only by a single judge. When the appeal to the governor is made, as matters now stand, there are bound to be cases where he will feel it necessary to make a thorough and painstaking investigation, either personally or through selected agents. In England, before the creation of the Court of Criminal Appeal, the Home Secretary, in whom is vested the executive power of clemency, occasionally found it advisable to have murder cases thoroughly investigated and reviewed, in his behalf, by one or more competent persons selected by him.

Such investigations by the executive, involving, as they are apt to do, something in the nature of a retrial of the case, are extremely burdensome, and in many ways objectionable. The occasion for them can be reduced to a minimum if we alter the system by which murder trials are presided over by a single judge and the appellate court passes only on questions of law.

The New York statute might well be adopted in other states. It reads:

> When the judgment is of death, the court of appeals may order a new trial, if it be satisfied that the verdict was against the weight of evidence or against law, or that justice requires a new trial, whether any exception shall have been taken or not in the court below. [45]

The English Court of Criminal Appeal Act of 1907 provides that any person convicted on indictment may appeal to the Court of Criminal Appeal, as of right, on a legal question and with the leave of the appellate court or upon the certificate of the trial judge, on any question of fact or on any other ground which appears to the court to be sufficient. The statute further provides:

> The Court of Criminal Appeal on any such appeal against conviction shall allow the appeal if they think that the verdict of the jury should be set aside on the ground that it is unreasonable or cannot be supported having regard to the evidence, or that the judgment of the court before whom the appellant was convicted should be set aside on the ground of a wrong decision of any question of law or that on any ground there was a miscarriage of justice, and in any other case shall dismiss the appeal.[46] [378]

Thus, the English Court of Criminal Appeal may quash the conviction without ordering a new trial, if they think the conviction constitutes a miscarriage of justice.[47]

Finally, if, in spite of these practical precautions against error, an innocent man is convicted of crime, and it is later established that he had no connection with it, the least that the State can do to vindicate itself and make restitution to the innocent victim is to grant him an indemnity, not as a matter of grace and favor but as a matter of right. On a few occasions Parliament in England has by special act made such grants, as, for example, in the cases of Slater (£6,000), Beck (£5,000), and Habron (£500);[48] and several states of the United States have taken similar action, as in the cases of Purvis ($5,000, Mississippi), Philion ($5,000, Utah),[49] Evans and Ledbetter ($4,533.36 and $3,313.39, respectively, California), Wilson ($3,500, Alabama), Brown ($2,492, Florida), Rohan ($1,692, California), Usher ($1,000, Massachusetts), Murchison ($750, Alabama), Walker ($500, Mississippi), and Henry ($431.81, Florida).[50] But such action is spasmodic only, and not all persons have the necessary influence to bring about legislation in their behalf. Although California, North Dakota, and Wisconsin provide for such relief by general statute,[51] the statutes, probably by reason of their apparent novelty, have been narrowly construed and but little has been accomplished by them.[52] The present volume has for one of its main objects the introduction of such statutes in all American jurisdictions, state and Federal. [379]

NOTES

1. *Mistaken identity.* The number of victims or witnesses who identified the accused as the guilty man is indicated after the names of the cases as follows: Andrews, 17 witnesses (p. 1); Beck, 14 (p. 7); Boyd, 8 (p. 22); Broughton, 3 (handwriting) (p. 28); Collins, 7 (p. 45); Flood, 3 (p. 62); Galindo, Hernandez, and Mendival, 4 (p. 73); Greenwald, 5 (p. 79); Everett Howell, 5 (p. 99); Frank Howell, 1 (p. 104); Lee, 4 (p. 132); Nedza, 5 (p. 166); Pezzulich and Sgelirrach, 3 (p. 177); Preston, 1 (p. 190); Purvis, 1 (p. 206); Shannon and Clements, 3 (p. 214); Stain and Cromwell, 10 (p. 232); Sullivan, 7 (p. 253); The "Sydney Men" Berdue, 3 (p. 264); Thorvik and Hughes, 4 (p. 276); Toth, 1 (p. 281); Wood, 5 (p. 311); Barbera, 2 (p. 322); Berner, 5 (p. 324); Klass, 3 (p. 342); Slyter, 1 (p. 352); Ward, 8 (p. 356); Willis, 4 (p. 359); Zambino, 3 (p. 362).

2. Andrews (p. 1); Greenwald (p. 79); Hess and Craig (p. 93); Nedza (p. 166); Purvis (p. 206); Sullivan (p. 253); Thorvik and Hughes (p. 276); Jacobs (p. 340).

3. Beck (p. 7); Boyd (p. 22); Collins (p. 45); Frank Howell (p. 104); Kimball (p. 120); McKinney (p. 154); Powell (p. 182); The "Sydney Men" Berdue (p. 264); Barbera (p. 322); Berner (p. 324); Willis (p. 359); Zambino (p. 362).

4. Lee (p. 132); Thornton (p. 272).

5. Note in 25 *Illinois Law Review* 550 (January, 1931).

6. Chesterman (p. 331); Hicks (p. 337); McManus (p. 346); Sands (p. 349).

7. *No crime committed.* Boorn (p. 14); Butler and Yelder (p. 39); Dabney (p. 50); Evans and Ledbetter (p. 58); Johnson (p. 110); Lyons (p. 144); Vaught, Stiles, and Bates (p. 289); Walker (p. 298); Wilson (p. 303); Chesterman (p. 331); Hicks (p. 337); McManus (p. 346); Sands (p. 349).

8. *Commission of crime doubtful* MacGregor (p. 149); Stain and Cromwell (p. 232); Woods and Miller (p. 315).

9. *Circumstantial evidence.* Boorn (p. 14); "Frenchy" (p. 66); Habron (p. 85); Hess and Craig (p. 93); Johnson (p. 110); Krueger (p. 128); Lyons (p. 144); MacGregor (p. 149); Woods and Miller (p. 315); Chance (p. 326); Usher (p. 354).

10. *Commonwealth v. Webster*, 5 Cush. (59 Mass.) 295, 312 (1850).

11. *Circumstantial evidence and mistaken identity.* Andrews (p. 1); Galindo, Hernandez, and Mendival (p. 73); Hess and Craig (p. 93); Frank Howell (p. 104); Kimball (p. 120); Krueger (p. 128); McKinney (p. 154); Nedza (p. 166); Powell (p. 182); Shannon and Clements (p. 214); Slater (p. 224); Stain and Cromwell (p. 232); Sweeney (p. 258); Thornton (p. 272); Berner (p. 324).

12. *Circumstantial evidence and perjury.* Brown (p. 32); Butler and Yelder (p. 39); Dabney (p. 50); Evans and Ledbetter (p. 58); Murchison (p. 161); Prevost (p. 197); Stain and Cromwell (p. 232); Sweeney (p. 258); Walker (p. 298); Wilson (p. 303); McManus (p. 346).

13. *Perjury, circumstantial evidence contributing.* Brown (p. 32); Butler and Yelder (p. 39); Dabney (p. 50); Evans and Ledbetter (p. 58); Lesher, Garvey, and Rohan (p. 137); Thorvik and Hughes (p. 276); Vaught, Stiles, and Bates (p. 289); Walker (p. 298); Wilson (p. 303); Chesterman (p. 331); Gunter (p. 335); Hicks (p. 337); McManus (p. 346); Sands (p. 349); Zambino (p. 362). [380].

14. Butler and Yelder (p. 39); Dabney (p. 50); Vaught, Stiles, and Bates (p. 289); Wilson (p. 303).

15. *"Frame-ups."* Brown (p. 32); Butler and Yelder (p. 39); Dabney (p. 50); Evans and Ledbetter (p. 58); Lesher, Garvey, and Rohan (p. 137); Prevost (p. 197); Vaught, Stiles, and Bates (p. 289); Walker (p. 298); Wilson (p. 303); Chesterman (p. 331); Gunter (p. 335); Hicks (p. 337); McManus (p. 346); Zambino (p. 362).

16. *Prosecution not at fault.* Boorn (p. 14); Evans and Ledbetter (p. 58); Kimball (p. 120); McKinney (p. 154); Nedza (p. 166); Olson (p. 172); Pezzulich and Sgelirrach (p. 177); Powell (p. 182); Shannon and Clements (p. 214); Sisson and Sullivan (p. 220); Thornton (p. 272); Barbera (p. 322); Chance (p. 326); Hicks (p. 337); Slyter (p. 352); Usher (p. 354).

17. *Overzealousness of police.* Andrews (p. 1); Beck (p. 7); Boyd (p. 22); Flood (p. 62); "Frenchy" (p. 66); Galindo, Hernandez, and Mendival (p. 73); Habron (p. 85); McKinney (p. 154); Preston (p. 190); Slater (p. 224); Thorvik and Hughes (perjury by sheriff) (p. 276); Toth (p. 281); Sands (frame-up) (p. 349). *Detectives.* Johnson (p. 110); Stielow and Green (p. 241); Hicks (frame-up) (p. 337); Klass (p. 342). See also E. J. Hopkins, *Our Lawless Police* (New York: Viking Press, 1931).

18. *Gross negligence of police.* Andrews (p. 1); Boyd (p. 22); Broughton (p. 28); "Frenchy" (p. 66); Galindo, Hernandez, and Mendival (p. 73); Greenwald (p. 79); Habron (p. 85); Johnson (p. 110); Slater (p. 224); Sullivan (p. 253).

19. Beck (p. 7); Preston (p. 190).

20. *Overzealousness of prosecution.* Beck (p. 7); Boyd (p. 22); Broughton (p. 28); "Frenchy" (p. 66); Galindo, Hernandez, and Mendival (p. 73); Habron (p. 85); Lyons (p. 144); MacGregor (p. 149); Preston (p. 190); Prevost (p. 197); Slater (p. 224); The "Sydney Men" Berdue (p. 264); Wilson (p. 303).

21. *Prior convictions or unsavory record.* Broughton (p. 28); "Frenchy" (p. 66); Galindo, Hernandez, and Mendival (p. 73); Hess and Craig (p. 93); Everett Howell (p. 99); Johnson (p. 110); Lee (p. 132); Lesher, Garvey, and Rohan (p. 137); McKinney (p. 154); Nedza (p. 166); Olson (p. 172); Powell (p. 182); Preston (p. 190); Slater (p. 224); Stain and Cromwell (p. 232); Sweeney (p. 258); Chance (p. 326); Klass (p. 342); Slyter (p. 352); Usher (p. 354); Ward (p. 356); Willis (p. 359).

22. Four exceptions are listed in Criminal Evidence Act, 1898 (61 & 62 Viet., c. 36), 1 (e); Halsbury, *The Laws of England* (London, 1909), IX, 404.

23. See, however, the critical article of Bates Booth, "Confessions, and Methods Employed in Procuring Them," 4 *Southern California Law Review* 83 (December, 1930).

24. 15 *Journal of Criminal Law and Criminology* 406, at 416 (November, 1924). Of special interest is Mr. Cummings' analysis of the evidence adduced against Israel.

25. *Community opinion demanding a conviction.* Such a factor was conspicuous in the convictions of Boorn (p. 14); Boyd (p. 22); Brown (p. 32); Butler and Yelder (p. 39); Dabney (p. 50); Galindo, Hernandez, and Mendival (p. 73); Johnson (p. 110); MacGregor (p. 149); Purvis (p. 206); Stain and Cromwell (p. 232); Stielow (p. 241); The "Sydney Men" Berdue (p. 264); Toth (p. 281); Wilson (p. 303).

26. *No murder committed.* Boorn (p. 14); Butler and Yelder (p. 39); [381] Dabney (p. 50); Lyons (p. 144); MacGregor (p. 149); Vaught, Stiles, and Bates (p. 289); Walker (attempted murder) (p. 298); Wilson (p. 303). Probably Woods and Miller (p. 315) could be added.

27. *"Murdered" person reappears.* Boorn (p. 14); Butler and Yelder (p. 39); Dabney (p. 50); Lyons (p. 144); Vaught, Stiles, and Bates (p. 289); Wilson (p. 303).

28. *Hairbreadth escapes from execution.* Brown (p. 32); Dabney (p. 50); Hess and Craig (p. 93); Purvis (p. 206); Slater (p. 224); Stielow and Green (p. 241); The "Sydney Men" Berdue (p. 264); Wilson (p. 303).

29. *Commutations prevented execution.* Brown (p. 32); Hess and Craig (p. 93); Lyons (p. 144); McKinney (p. 154); Purvis (p. 206); Stielow and Green (p. 241); Toth (p. 281); Woods and Miller (p. 315).

30. See the cases of Brown (p. 32); Hess and Craig (p. 93); Lyons (p. 144); Purvis (p. 206); Stielow and Green (p. 241); Toth (p. 281).

31. *Unreliability of "expert" evidence.* Andrews (p. 1); Broughton (p. 28); "Frenchy" (p. 66); Krueger (p. 128); Prevost (p. 197); Stielow and Green (p. 241). See Mr. Cummings' analysis in the Israel case, 15 *Journal of Criminal Law and Criminology* 406 (November, 1924), and Mildred Gilman's account of the Hoffman case, *New Republic*, June 12, 1929, p. 90.

32. The constitutionality of this statute was upheld in the case of *Jessner v. State*, 202 Wis. 184, 231 N.W. 634 (1930), commented on in 26 *Illinois Law Review* 82 (May, 1931). See also Wigmore, *Evidence*, 563.

33. *Same crimes continue after conviction.* Andrews (p. 1); Beck (p. 7); Broughton (p. 28); Collins (p. 45); Greenwald (p. 79); Lee (p. 132); Sullivan (p. 253); Berner (p. 324).

34. *Corroborated confessions of others.* Brown (p. 32); Galindo (p. 73); Hess and Craig (p. 93); Frank Howell (p. 104); McKinney (p. 154); Murchison (p. 161); Purvis (p. 206); The "Sydney Men" Berdue (p. 264); Walker (p. 298); Barbera (p. 322); Chance (p. 326); Chesterman (p. 331); Hicks (p. 337); Klass (p. 342); Willis (p. 359).

35. *All participants in joint crime accounted for.* Flood (p. 62); Everett Howell (p. 99); Sisson and Sullivan (p. 220); Sweeney (p. 258); Thorvik and Hughes (p. 276); Wood (p. 311).

36. *Sheer luck discloses error.* Lesher (p. 137); Nedza (p. 166); Jacobs (p. 340); Klass (p. 342); Slyter (p. 352); Usher (p. 354).

37. *Prosecution aids in disclosing error.* Andrews (p. 1); Evans (p. 58); Greenwald (p. 79); Frank Howell (p. 104); Lesher (p. 137); Nedza (p. 166); Pezzulich (p. 177); Sweeney (p. 258); Barbera (p. 322); Jacobs (p. 340); Klass (p. 342); Slyter (p. 352); Usher (p. 354).

38. *False alibi though innocent.* McKinney (p. 154); Preston (p. 190); Thorvik and Hughes (p. 276). See also Anderson case, *United States Attorney General's Report*, 1914, p. 349; Hoffman case, *New Republic*, June 12, 1929, p. 90.

39. *Commonwealth v. Webster*, 5 Cush. (59 Mass.) 295, 317 (1850).

40. M. C. Goldman, *The Public Defender* (2d ed.; New York, 1919); Samuel Rubin, "The Public Defender an Aid to Criminal Justice," 18 *American Journal of Criminal Law* 346 (November, 1927).

41. 14 *Journal of the American Judicature Society* 195 (April, 1931). The system of Public Defenders is now in force in Connecticut, Minnesota, Nebraska, Tennessee, Virginia, and in certain California cities. The Connecticut system provides for the appointment of a Public Defender by the superior court of each county, the Public Defender submitting at the end of each term a bill for reasonable compensation, which

the court is [382] authorized to allow. In Los Angeles, the Public Defender is appointed after competitive civil-service examination under a salary fixed by the Board of Supervisors. The Los Angeles Public Defender, the first such office in the country, has a skilful staff which has established an excellent reputation. A voluntary Defenders Committee was organized in New York in 1917 as a branch of the New York Legal Aid Society. Its usefulness is limited by lack of funds and staff. In Illinois and other states, no provision is made for paying assigned counsel. In Chicago a system of voluntary Defenders is aided by the Northwestern University Law School under a small endowment. The work is now reinforced by a professional Defender paid by the county commissioners. In other states, such as Michigan, appointed counsel are paid by the public, but the system has proved extremely expensive.

42. The rules for appeal in criminal cases in American states are summarized in the *Proposed Code of Criminal Procedure* (American Law Institute, 1930), pp. 597, *et seq.* Only in a few states, such as Louisiana, Michigan, Pennsylvania, Rhode Island, and Wisconsin, can a new trial be granted on the ground that an accused was prejudiced in his defense and a failure of justice has occurred. *Ibid.*, pp. 348-349. See also *Report on Criminal Procedure*, No. 8, National Commission on Law Observance, June 9, 1931, p. 44.

43. This defect in our system of criminal trials, which often leaves the jury without appropriate guidance from the judge, has been the subject of much comment in proposals for reform. Professor Morgan, in his report to the committee of the Commonwealth Fund, on "The Laws of Evidence, Some Proposals for Its Reform," says:

> "At present in some forty-two states the trial judge is prohibited by constitution, statute, or controlling decision from commenting upon the weight or credibility of the testimony. ... In some states he may review the evidence, but he must not indicate his opinion about it; and in none of them can he say a word as to the credibility of a particular witness. In some half dozen states the court has the privilege of comment. ... In the federal courts the privilege is unimpaired. . . . The prevailing practice is unwise and it should be provided by statute:
>
> "The trial judge may express to the jury, after the close of the evidence and arguments, his opinion as to the weight and credibility of the evidence or any part thereof." See also "Province of the Judge in Jury Trials," 12 *Journal of the American Judicature Society* 76 (October, 1928).

44. Public Document No. 144, November, 1927, p. 40.

45. New York Code of Criminal Procedure, § 528.

46. Pendleton Howard, "The English Court of Criminal Appeal," 17 *American Bar Association Journal* 149 (March, 1931); Lord Hewart, address before the Canadian Bar Association, August 24, 1927, *London Times*, August 25, 1927; Third Report of the Judicial Council of Massachusetts, *op. cit.*, p. 131.

47. See the recent case of William Herbert Wallace, 23 *Crim. App. Rep.* 32 (May, 1931), in which the conviction of a husband for the murder of his wife was quashed because guilt, in the view of the court, was "not proved with that certainty which is necessary in order to justify a verdict of guilty."

48. Other English cases of miscarriage of justice in which indemnities were granted are: Barber, 1858, £5,000; Galley, 1881, £1,000; two men in Brooks case, 1882,

£500 each (Best, *Evidence* [11th ed., 1911], p. 584). [383] Sibley, *Criminal Appeal and Evidence* (London, 1908), p. 266, reports that between 1880 and 1883 twelve persons were released by the Home Secretary on the ground of their innocence. The Home Secretary, Gladstone, reported that there had been twelve cases within a period of twenty years in which indemnities varying from £1 to £5,000 had been paid. London *Times*, June 7, 1907, noted in Sibley, *op. cit.*, p. 267. The Barber, Galley, and Habron cases are described by Sibley, *op. cit.*, pp. 268, *et seq.*

49. Utah—Laws 1931, c. 64, p. 271. The $5,000 was granted for the ordeal of having been mistakenly extradited and tried for murder, though in fact Philion was acquitted.

50. Florida—Laws 1911, p. 62.

51. California—Stats. 1913, p. 245; North Dakota—Laws 1917, c. 172, § 1; Wisconsin—Stats. 1913, c. 189.

52. California did not apply the statute until 1930, and has granted indemnity in two cases only: Evans and Ledbetter (p. 58) and Rohan (p. 137). The Rohan case was first dismissed on the ground that the conviction was not erroneous, because it was the result of a jury's verdict. This curious interpretation of the word "erroneous" was on rehearing changed.

Wisconsin has had approximately twelve applications for indemnity under the statute. Miss Alice Kelly of the Wisconsin Legislative Reference Library advises that in only one case, the Hammond case (1926), an erroneous conviction for abduction, was compensation awarded $888.30 plus $78.00 for expenses. In another case, Eli J. Long (1921), the court discharged a life prisoner for murder on newly discovered evidence, but because the court and not the Governor's pardon had cut short his term, compensation was denied. The Wisconsin Legislature in 1927 passed a bill allowing Long $2,750, but it was vetoed by the Governor on the ground that the statute extends only to persons who serve their imposed term of imprisonment and not to those who merely serve time pending appeal. On both grounds, this construction seems unduly narrow and the possibility of its repetition should be removed by amendment of the statute. In three other cases, also, the claim was denied because the convicted person did not serve his entire sentence but was released on reversal of the conviction upon retrial, or by a higher court. Compensation in such cases, if the convicted person is completely innocent and without fault, should be provided for, as it is in Europe generally. In four other cases, the claim was based upon the fact that prisoners undoubtedly guilty were held in prison, after the expiration of their sentences, to serve the unexpired portions of former sentences for which they were on parole at the time when their offenses were committed; but compensation was denied, the Compensation Board taking the view that the law was not applicable to such cases, even when the Supreme Court held that the former sentences had expired and that the further imprisonment was illegal. In that view, the Board seems to have been correct. In the Johnson case (p. 110), compensation was denied because Johnson was said to have contributed to his imprisonment by a plea of guilty, a plea induced, however, by third-degree methods, which might well have served to excuse the prisoner, for the State's injury is only increased by forcing him into a false confession and plea of guilty. In another case, the prisoner's claim of innocence was not believed by the Board; and in another case, the matter was not carried to a hearing.

North Dakota does not appear to have had any applications under its statute.

Made in United States
Orlando, FL
11 November 2026

90609409R00197